WALTER BRUEGGEMANN

GIFT
and TASK

A Year of Daily Readings
and Reflections

WJK WESTMINSTER
JOHN KNOX PRESS
LOUISVILLE · KENTUCKY

for Tia

© 2017 Walter Brueggemann

First edition
Published by Westminster John Knox Press
Louisville, Kentucky

17 18 19 20 21 22 23 24 25 26—10 9 8 7 6 5 4 3 2 1

Book design by Drew Stevens
Cover design by Marc Whitaker, MTWdesign.net

Library of Congress Cataloging-in-Publication Data

Names: Brueggemann, Walter, author.
Title: Gift and task : a year of daily readings and reflections / Walter
  Brueggemann.
Description: Louisville, KY : Westminster John Knox Press, 2017. | Includes
  bibliographical references. |
Identifiers: LCCN 2017005496 (print) | LCCN 2017028531 (ebook) | ISBN
  9781611648157 (ebk.) | ISBN 9780664263218 (hbk. : alk. paper)
Subjects: LCSH: Church year meditations. | Devotional calendars.
Classification: LCC BV4812 (ebook) | LCC BV4812 .B78 2017 (print) | DDC
  242/.3--dc23
LC record available at https://lccn.loc.gov/2017005496

CONTENTS

PREFACE

The title I have given this book, "Gift and Task," is a translation of the more felicitous German, *Gabe und Aufgabe*. The
God whom we meet in Scripture is one who gives generous
gifts in the wonder of creation, in the miracle of emancipation and reconciliation, and in the surprise of transformation.
Human persons, along with all other creatures, are recipients
of those abundant gifts of God that are to be taken in awed
gratitude, for which our best word from Greek is "Eucharist."
This gift-giving God whom we meet in Scripture is also the one
who assigns a worthy task, who from the first act of creation
and the first utterance at Sinai has issued commandments, who
has summoned to discipleship, and who empowers to glad,
trustful obedience.

What follows in this book is a daily reflection on the Scrip-
tures prescribed in the Daily Office for Year 2 in the Episcopal
Book of Common Prayer, the Daily Readings in the Presbyterian
Church (U.S.A.) *Book of Common Worship*, and perhaps other
traditions as well. Of course the exact dates of the church year
change because Easter is a movable feast and Advent changes
with the calendar, so in this book I have ordered the readings
according to the church year that begins in Advent of 2017.
I have judged that the specificity of that one particular year
was worth the requirement of agility among readers for use
in subsequent years, and I am counting on purists to pardon
the inevitable variations from prescribed readings that result.

Suggestions for adapting this resource for use in subsequent years can be found in appendix A.

In many of these study reflections, it will be most beneficial to read the biblical text before reading the study material. It is preferable, when possible, to read the text out loud, as biblical texts are meant for hearing. I have exercised freedom in selecting which text or texts from among the designated readings I would comment on each day. Readers of my work will not be surprised that my tilt and inclination are toward Old Testament texts. With only a few exceptions, I have not commented on the psalm for each day, as I have had ample opportunity elsewhere to exposit the Psalms. I have taken the liberty of selecting texts from Sirach (Ecclesiasticus), because it is quite fresh material for me and because Ben Sira is an uncompromisingly practical theologian and moral teacher. Mindful that these texts are not included in many Protestant Bibles, I have provided the text to those passages from Sirach in appendix B.

What I have written is intentionally distinguished in two ways. First, I have written reflections that are intended for serious church members who are willing to consider in critical ways the cost and joy of discipleship. This means that I have resisted any temptation toward a more generic "devotional," because most materials offered in that genre are, in my judgment, quite romantic. Second, while I have not imposed much critical scholarship on the texts, I intend that my exposition should be critically responsible and not excessively accommodating to popular itches.

While I follow the daily readings designated by certain church bodies, I, of course, hope that my commentary will reach a larger reading community that is genuinely ecumenical, as no tradition has a monopoly on serious attention to Scripture. Thus I hope my exposition makes room across the theological, ecclesial spectrum for "progressives" and "evangelicals," for we commonly share as recipients of the wondrous gifts of God, and we are commonly addressed by the summons of the God of the gospel. It is my conviction—and hope—that serious Scripture reading is and can be a source of missional renewal in the church.

I am glad again as always to voice my thanks to David Dobson, Julie Tonini, Jessica Miller Kelley, and their colleagues at Westminster John Knox Press for the faithful and attentive way in which they have transposed my words into a book.

I am pleased to dedicate this book to the well-beloved Tia Brueggemann. She has been engaged with this writing project all the way from its inception (her idea) to final authorial editing (her work), with sustaining energy in between. I am grateful to a host of persons who have made it possible for me to undertake this reading. That includes many pastors, teachers, and nourishing traditions; as indicated in my commentary for the last day of the church year, it most especially includes the tradition of German evangelical pietism that is my true home.

Walter Brueggemann
Columbia Theological Seminary
July 2016

ADVENT

First Sunday of Advent

Psalm 146; Amos 1:1–5, 13–2:8; 1 Thessalonians 5:1–11; Luke 21:5–19

God of all our beginnings, we thank you for this new beginning in Advent. Give us the freedom and courage to enter into your newness that exposes the inadequacy of where we have been and what we have done in time past. Be the God of all truth in our midst. Through Christ. Amen.

We rightly expect that Christmas will go "out like a lamb." What comes from Christmas is indeed the Lamb that is slaughtered on Friday who is worthy of praise on Sunday, who takes away the sin of the world (John 1:29; Rev. 5:12). Before that, however, Advent is "in like a lion," a roaring truthfulness that disrupts our every illusion.

The text from Amos begins, "The LORD roars from Zion." The image is of a lion (from the temple in Jerusalem) who is seeking prey, thus a threat to the status quo. What follows in the poetry of Amos is an exposé of the sociopolitical failures of Israel's neighbors and of Israel. The offenses of Damascus (Syria) and Moab and Ammon (Jordan) bespeak violation of human rights and savage military assault. The affront of Israel is economic: "trampling the head of the poor."

Such texts assure that our preparation for Christmas is not a safe, private, or even familial enterprise but is preoccupied with great public issues of war and peace and issues of economic justice that concern the worth and bodily well-being of human persons. Our Advent preparation may invite us to consider the ways in which we ourselves are complicit in the deep inhumanity of our current world. All these texts attest a coming upheaval because the roaring lion can wait no longer. The lion opens space for the Lamb, who will arrive soon.

Monday after Advent 1

Psalm 1; Amos 2:6–16; 2 Peter 1:1–11; Matthew 21:1–11

Your coming, O God, evokes in us joy as we ponder your new rule of mercy and justice. Your coming at the same time confronts us with a deep shattering of the way we have arranged our common life. Grant that we may not default on joy or flinch from the shattering that your coming portends. In Christ. Amen.

The Gospel reading voices a vigorous welcome for the new king. The crowd is eager for his arrival. The juxtaposition of the Amos text and the Epistle reading, however, suggests that not everyone gathered to cheer his arrival. The epistle expresses an ethic that is congruent with his new rule: virtue, knowledge, self-control, steadfastness, godliness, and "brotherly affection with love." The conduct of those who sign on with the coming Messiah concerns discipline that serves the common good, brotherly affection, that is, social solidarity.

That ethic, to be performed by Jesus and embraced by his faithful community, contradicts what the prophetic tradition found in ancient Israel. Amos indicts the economy for uncaring exploitation of the poor, for self-indulgent sexuality, and for cynical abuse of holy things for self-service. As a contrast to such demonstrative self-indulgence, Amos cites the Nazirites, a company of the young under strict discipline.

The prophetic text and the Epistle reading together articulate a powerful either-or that might preoccupy us in Advent. On the one hand, we live in a predatory economy that operates without restraint or compassion. On the other hand, the epistle anticipates that Jesus' company of followers will refuse such a way in the world that can result only in failure and jeopardy. The way in which we may "confirm our call and election" is by alternative ethic that refuses the ordinary practices of our consumer economy that endlessly negates the poor.

Tuesday after Advent 1

Psalm 5; Amos 3:1–11; 2 Peter 1:12–21; Matthew 21:12–22

God of the prophets, who interrupts and makes new beginnings, we thank you for prophetic words that continue to sound among us. Give us attentive minds and hearts, that we may heed when addressed and obey when summoned, in the name of the living Word. Amen.

Jesus is in the temple, the citadel of entitlement and certitude. He himself is here located in the prophetic tradition. He deftly combines two prophetic utterances, a hope-filled word from Isaiah, "My house shall be called a house of prayer for all peoples" (56:7), and a word of judgment from Jeremiah (7:11), "Has this house, which is called by my name, become a den of robbers." He does more, however, than quote the prophets. He effectively performs their words that judge the temple as a venue of exploitation and that anticipate a revised temple of embracive faith. His performance of prophetic reality is compelling enough that he evokes a confrontation with the "chief priests and scribes," managers of the citadel. They sense, quite rightly, that something dangerous and subversive is stirring around Jesus, specified by the messianic affirmation on the lips of the "children in the temple."

Prophetic speech breaks open our settled opinions, our treasured ideologies, and our uncritical social practice. Thus Amos condemned the "violence and robbery" of a systemic kind. And the Epistle reading presents prophetic words as "a lamp shining in a dark place."

Our world is "a dark place" of fear, anxiety, greed, and violence. The prophetic light exposes such destructive practices and requires us to consider both the ideological rootage of our practices and their concrete outcomes from which we often benefit. Advent is a time for being addressed from "elsewhere" and being unsettled. It is a time to ponder exposés that we do not welcome. Sometimes we are like priests and scribes resisting the raw word of God's intrusion that shatters our citadels.

Wednesday after Advent 1

Psalm 119:1–14; Amos 3:12–4:5; 2 Peter 3:1–10; Matthew 21:23–32

Lord of eons and immediacy, we wait with some impatience for Christ-mas celebration while our commercial world is already at its fake celebration. Grant us patience to be geared to your time that is both slow and sure. In his name. Amen.

These readings seek to find a proper place for trust amid two temptations. On the one hand, there is the seduction of phony piety. Jesus warns against an eager ostensive obedience without follow-through. The prophet Amos ups the rhetoric to mock the busy routines of piety that his contemporaries love to enact. He sees, moreover, that such exhibitionist piety is readily linked to economic exploitation. The Epistle reading, on the other hand, identifies an alternative temptation, namely, skepticism. The writer points to "scoffers" who mock faith by pointing out that the promises of God are never kept and that things go on and on as they were without interruption or change.

Both of these temptations have to be faced with Christmas coming. Among us, phony piety may take the form of excessive generosity, of giving gifts without any real passion, both gifts to those who need no gifts (whom we may not love too much) and gifts to the needy that are less than serious engagement. It is likely, however, that the temptation to skepticism about a real coming of newness is more poignant among us. The result may be just going through the motions of tired celebration.

The Gospel reading uses the term "believe" three times, describing an act of trust that leads to repentance. Christmas is properly not about phony piety or about skepticism; it is about change of heart and change of life that are rooted in trust in the promises of God that are as sure as they are slow.

Thursday after Advent 1

Psalm 18:1–20; Amos 4:6–13; 2 Peter 3:11–18; Matthew 21:33–46

Grant, good Lord, that we may receive you in your hidden majestic power that runs beyond our imagining. Forgive us that we domesticate you in order to accommodate the worlds we prefer. Give to us your new world of well-being. In his name. Amen.

These readings invite us to be at the pivot point in the life of the world, poised between what is old and passing and what is new and emerging. The hard words of prophetic speech concern the undoing and dismantling of a world that is failed. Thus Amos can chronicle the undoing by environmental crises that leave us as desolate as Sodom and Gomorrah. In his parable Jesus imagines that status as God's people with blessings of chosenness will be taken away, forfeited in disobedience.

This same moment, however, is one of radical newness. The newness consists in new heaven and new earth, a cosmic emergence of well-being that the creator has always intended. That new world of well-being will not be according to common expectation. The "stone rejected," judged inadequate by conventional norms, will be Jesus, the Messiah, who fits none of our expectations.

To stand in that vortex of divine resolve requires some intentional preparation. The epistle urges specific disciplines of "holiness and godliness," being "without spot or blemish," being "at peace," growing in "grace and knowledge." This means to be focused in a way very different from our careless society that does not think anything will be undone and does not anticipate any deep newness. It is the peculiar invitation of the gospel that we may be witnesses and recipients of a turn of the ages. Only the disciplined can perceive and receive. Homework is required.

Friday after Advent 1

Psalm 16; Amos 5:1–17; Jude 1–16; Matthew 22:1–14

Lord of justice, give us courage to face the costs that belong to faith; give us readiness to be "properly dressed" for your great festival. In his name. Amen.

The parable of Jesus is rightly familiar to us: A feast is offered by the king to specifically qualified guests. When they decline the invitation, others are invited at random from the streets, those who are less clearly "qualified" for such an invitation. The parable (also told, somewhat differently, in Luke 14:15–24) suggests inclusiveness in the company of God, even for those who are not qualified. Matthew, more stringently, adds a surprising conclusion to the story. When the king comes to look at the more recently invited guests, he is appalled that some are not appropriately dressed for the occasion; they are roughly eliminated from the party. Even those "unqualified" who are belatedly invited are held to certain standards in order to join the feast.

This twist in the parable voiced by Matthew prepares us for heavy words of judgment in all these readings. Amos grieves over failed Israel; but then he issues a series of imperatives commending altered conduct: "Seek me, seek the LORD, seek good, hate evil, love good, establish justice." The sequence of commands culminates with the specificity of "establish justice," that is, economic equity and compassion, a practice skewed in the Israel of his time. The words of judgment are even more severe in the Epistle of Jude concerning those who distorted faith and skewed the community in its practice.

All these readings together attest that entry into the community of God is no free lunch or cheap ride. Advent is a time for coming to terms with the uncompromising requirements of gospel faith that are too often treated as though they do not matter for the coming celebration.

Saturday after Advent 1

Psalm 20; Amos 5:18–27; Jude 17–25; Matthew 22:15–22

God of all mercy, give us the capacity to situate ourselves in your good-
ness, that we may resist every temptation to trade your goodness for
other ways of security and well-being. In his name. Amen.

The detractors from and distorters of faith are everywhere in
these readings:
- In the Amos text, they are those too comfortable in Zion,
  with their eagerness for the coming day of reckoning
  when they think they will be affirmed.
- In the Gospel reading, they are the Pharisees and Hero-
  dians who have no interest in serious interpretation of
  the tradition but only want to trick and trap Jesus.
- In the epistle, they are "scoffers" who are propelled by
  interests and passions alien to faith. They are indicted on
  three counts: (1) They set up divisions, causing splits in
  the community. (2) They are worldly, reasoning in prag-
  matic ways without allowing for the gracious slippage of
  grace that makes forgiveness and reconciliation possible.
  (3) They are devoid of the spirit, unwilling and unable to
  be led beyond their own settled opinion.

The epistle is eager that the "beloved," those seriously
embedded in the gospel, should distinguish themselves from
these troublemakers and practice disciplines that will sustain
their distinctiveness. Four disciplines are commended:
- "Build yourselves up" in a holy faith. This includes attentiveness to apostolic teaching.
- "Pray in the Holy Spirit," a habit of yielding and a readiness to be led.
- "Keep yourselves in the love of God," not seduced by
  quarrel or calculation.
- Wait for "the mercy of our Lord Jesus Christ," a bid for
  uncommon patience.

These disciplines will sustain with enough authority to con-
vince and save others.

Second Sunday of Advent

Psalm 148; Amos 6:1–14; 2 Thessalonians 1:5–12; Luke 1:57–68

God of faithfulness, before whom we stand exposed in our complacency and complicity, we thank you for this season in which we may make amendment of life. Give us resolve that we may not waste the season. In his name. Amen.

We do well to ponder this newly arrived character, John, who creates a pause in the narrative before the birth of Jesus. The work of interpretation is to be sure that John is not elided into Jesus so that the sharp and stern word of John is not overwhelmed by the graciousness embodied in Jesus. John's work is very different; it is to "make ready a people prepared for the Lord" (Luke 1:17). That preparatory work requires hard truth-telling that exhibits the ways in which the world, as presently practiced, is completely out of sync with the purposes of God.

We are led to ponder how it is that the world is out of sync in concrete ways with God's will for justice, righteousness, mercy, and compassion that are continually thwarted by policy and by practice. That thwarting of God's intent is evident in the systemic practice of greed, the readiness for violence against the vulnerable, and the complacent acceptance of economic injustice. This out-of-sync quality is voiced by Amos with his double utterance of "woe" that anticipates trouble to come. The sharp rhetoric of the epistle, moreover, shares the urgency of facing up to the deep failure of present practice. Unlike the trivia of commercial Christmas, serious Advent is a time to consider how being out of sync with God has become conventional and "normal" among us. It is also a time to consider the (inevitable?) outcomes of such a way of life. Christmas comes abruptly in the wake of Advent; we cannot slide from one to the other.

Monday after Advent 2

Psalm 25; Amos 7:1–9; Revelation 1:1–8; Matthew 22:23–33

God beyond our explanations, give us imaginative freedom, that we may rest before the splendor of your power for life that relativizes both our accomplishments and our anxieties. In his name. Amen.

The Sadducees are exemplars of "the arithmetic of this age." They think they can figure it all out, explain everything, and so control and manage their life in the world. Jesus counters their domesticated reasoning by witnessing to the alternative reality, known in Scripture, of the power of God that is not controlled or domesticated by our calculation. The defining reality is the God attested by our Genesis ancestors who is the God of the living. Thus God has the singular capacity and resolve to bring life out of death, to call into existence things that do not exist.

The soaring rhetoric of our reading in Revelation situates the power of God, fleshed in Jesus, outside the scope of our capacity. It does so by appeal to the old tradition of "coming with the clouds," that is, outside our explanatory systems. The ultimate claim is that this Holy One, embodied in Jesus, is "the Alpha and the Omega," the beginning before our explanations, the completion after our management. The rhetoric shows how impotent and irrelevant is the closed reality of people like the Sadducees who think they can manage the mystery and gift of life.

It is a sobering admission of Advent to recognize that we are not the alpha. We are not the beginning point, not self-made, not self-sufficient; before us and behind us is the power for life that is pure gift to be received in trusting gratitude. It is an equally sobering admission of Advent to recognize that we are not the omega. We are not the point of it all. We are not the best imaginable outcome, the completion of creation. It is no wonder that the crowd was astonished by Jesus' testimony to the resurrection!

Tuesday after Advent 2

Psalm 26; Amos 7:10–17; Revelation 1:9–16; Matthew 22:34–46

God of liberating disruptions, grant us wisdom to identify the certitudes by which we live, and the courage to notice your governance even beyond our treasured certitudes. In his name. Amen.

It is comforting to have an explanatory system that accounts for everything; and we all have them. Such a system may be a theological orthodoxy that delivers unfailing assurance. Or such a system may be a moral code that confidently reduces everything to simple right and wrong with appropriate rewards and punishments. Or such a system may be an economic orthodoxy, like free-market capitalism, that can reduce everything to production and consumption. Any such system comforts us and keeps us safe.

In the purview of Advent thinking, however, any such system — theological, moral, or economic — is an illusion. It is sure to be interrupted and exposed as inadequate and placed in jeopardy. In Christian life, Advent is the big interruption of all of our explanatory illusions.

— In the Amos reading, the liturgic certitude of Bethel is interrupted by the prophet who speaks of justice. The priest banishes the prophet, but his words do not go away.
— In the book of Revelation, the interruption takes the form of "a loud voice." In what follows after our text, the voice will confront the several churches with gospel truth.
— In the Gospel reading, one of the Pharisees put a trick question to Jesus, trying to contain him in their brand of Torah interpretation. He, however, outflanks them with his enigma statement that eludes their decipherment.

In Advent it is useful to identify the explanatory systems on which we rely and then to consider how they are being disrupted in disconcerting ways. We would mostly like to stop such interruption; but, of course, we cannot.

Wednesday after Advent 2

Psalm 38; Amos 8:1–14; Revelation 1:17–2:7; Matthew 23:1–12

God of summoning words, in your presence we are yet again aware of your calling that we be different in the world. Grant us enough resolve to resist being narcotized by our society of indifference. In his name. Amen.

Going through the motions in a mindless way is a durable temptation. In a society of too many consumer goods, too many TV options, too much wearisome news, and the endless pursuit of commodities, it is easy to give up on intentionality and simply go through the motions of what is expected . . . at home, at work, in church. In the oracle of Amos, the merchants, busy at exploitation, wait impatiently through the motions of Sabbath keeping. In the Gospel reading, the opponents of Jesus are indicted for going through the motions of religious performance. And in the address to the church at Ephesus in Revelation, the cooling of "first love" perhaps causes church life to be less than zealously engaged.

In each case the readings warn against such indifferent living. Amos raises hard questions about economic exploitation. Jesus calls his followers away from empty performance to serious, attentive obedience that takes the form of servanthood. And Ephesus is called to "repent, and do the works you did at first."

Commercial Christmas is much going through the demanding motions of office parties, shopping, decorating, sending and receiving cards, wrapping gifts . . . enough to create deep fatigue. Advent is a wake-up call away from such careless participation in the restless "festival of stuff." An awakened "season of giving" may be marked by a new passion for economic justice, for sustained servanthood grounded in humbleness, and for listening to what the Spirit is saying to the churches.

Thursday after Advent 2

Psalm 37; Amos 9:1–10; Revelation 2:8–17; Matthew 23:13–26

*God of uncompromising purposes, forgive our indifference to the claims
you make upon us; give us fresh awareness of the way in which obedience
to your purpose is our true freedom. In his name. Amen.*

We may find entry into these difficult and severe texts by
appealing to the categories of Psalm 37, the "wicked" and the
"righteous." We must give up any simplistic, moralistic notion
of these terms. Rather, "wicked" refers to those out of sync
with the purposes of God who live with indifference about the
common good. Conversely, the "righteous" are those who give
themselves to social solidarity with neighbors in obedience to
God's purpose. The psalm probes the destiny and outcome for
these two contrasting ways of life.

Amos sees that the wicked are at risk before the judgment
of God and cannot finally escape the long reach of God's governance. He allows, however, that in the final "sifting," some
will not be judged. In Revelation, the address to the church
in Smyrna recognizes that the church—like ancient Israel for
Amos—is an ambiguous community. Jesus' tirade against the
religious leadership of his time concerns a series of practices
that distort and misrepresent authentic faith. The rhetoric of
"woe" allows that trouble will inescapably come on such failed
leadership.

Advent reflection may consider the ways in which we,
in church and in society, have lost our way concerning the
requirements of faith that are very different from common popular values. While the judgment of God is an awkward theme
for many of us, it is worth considering the extent to which our
current failed common life is itself a judgment on long-held
conventional commitments against the common good.

Friday after Advent 2

Psalm 31; Haggai 1:1–15; Revelation 2:18–29; Matthew 23:27–39

God of inexorable purposes, help us to hold more closely to your good-will, that our lives, our practices, and our policies may more fully reflect our love for you. In his name. Amen.

The severe rhetoric of these readings surely reflects various times when the community was in danger and profoundly at risk. The readings reflect a stern theology of quid pro quo in which disobedience results in negative outcomes from God, while obedience yields well-being. The same calculus pertains in each reading.

In Haggai, severe drought has come on the community because it has been preoccupied with its own well-being to the neglect of the things of God. In Revelation, the church in Thyatira is under judgment because it has "tolerated that woman Jezebel," that is, the church has made "compromises with a popular culture that results from idolatry and thereby compromises the distinctiveness of life and outlook" that concern the writer.* The result is "great distress." In Matthew, Jesus indicts religious leadership that "kills the prophets" with the result that "your house is left to you, desolate."

In each case, the reading urges repentance and renewed faith: (a) In Haggai, this is expressed as temple building. (b) People in Thyatira are urged to "hold fast" because "your last works are greater than the first." (c) From Jesus, the charge is to live in hope until the messiah comes.

This quid pro quo theology of stern sanctions is not in vogue among us. But the summons and warnings of Advent largely operate in the sphere of that theology. We may reflect on the ways in which it is true that our actions produce our futures in direct ways. Then it follows that different actions—of generous, hope-filled obedience—may indeed yield different futures among us.

---

*Christopher C. Rowland, "Revelation," in *New Interpreter's Bible*, vol. 12, *Hebrews–Revelation* (Nashville: Abingdon Press, 1998), 581.

Saturday after Advent 2

Psalm 30; Haggai 2:1–9; Revelation 3:1–6; Matthew 24:1–14

God of our futures, give us wisdom to receive your future by living in the present differently. Move us beyond our excessive commitment to present norms. In his name. Amen.

These readings are deeply committed to a good future from God that will not be extrapolated from the present. They invite the faithful to relinquish the grip that the present has on our lives and imagination and to shift energy toward that good future from God. This summons a deep challenge to the ideology that affirms that the future will be only an extension of the present, as though we cannot imagine otherwise. It is an ideology preferred by those among us who enjoy disproportionate well-being in the present.

Thus Matthew has Jesus speak of "birth pangs," an image that suggests that entry into God's future is not an easy slide but a genuine newness that comes with struggle. Haggai can anticipate that in "a little while" the present-tense earth will be "shaken up"; and the church in Sardis is called to be worthy of "the book of life," an image of the roster of the blessed in time to come. Advent is preparation for newness that evokes a very different participation in the present world, a participation that is not marked by fear, anxiety, or greed.

Psalm 30 dramatically voices the wondrous turn from present to future. It honestly recognizes that weeping (pain, suffering, distress) lingers all through the night, a very long night. And surely we are in for a long night of weeping over poverty, violence, child abuse, sex trafficking, and a predatory economy that requires such practices. But the weeping, it is promised, will end. It will end in the morning of God's rule that will be marked by justice, mercy, and compassion. We have much preparation to make that includes disengagement from sorry practices that have become much too "normal."

Third Sunday of Advent

Psalm 63:1–8 (9–11); Amos 9:11–15;
2 Thessalonians 2:1–3, 13–17; John 5:30–47

*God, Father of our Lord Jesus Christ, we await his coming, that we
might receive you. In his name. Amen.*

The Jesus presented in the Gospel reading of John 5 is not
a cute baby who permits romantic sentimentality. This rather
is the Jesus who stands at the pivot point of judgment of the
world. The issue of this difficult reading is the identity of Jesus
to whom there is important testimony. Thus we are confronted
by the most elemental claim of faith, namely, the identity of
the Son with the Father. In the life of Jesus, we are given the
fullness of God's own life. The challenge of the text is to see
that this Jesus (who comes at Christmas) who is crucified and
risen is indeed the elemental truth of all reality.

Psalm 63 overflows with testimony about the character of
the Father, who is variously presented as water in a dry land,
as steadfast love, and as help, that is, as the full satisfaction of
the deepest needs of the world. In Christian confession, it is
Jesus who fully embodies that deep holy satisfaction of the
world's deepest hungers and thirsts.

Both the Gospel reading and the Epistle suggest that this
elemental claim is under assault; the church is tempted to
compromise or renege on its confession. The antidote to such
seduction is to reengage the trusted tradition of the church,
to "hold fast to the traditions" of the church, attentive to the
"writings" of Moses, that is, to the Old Testament. For sure,
we live in a culture that gives in too readily to safer, easier
religious claims that cost little and that deliver little. In a world
of slobbering consumerism, that may require disciplined study
so that we may recognize afresh the radical claim of the Father
of all truth who comes as the crucified and risen Son. These
readings pose the question of the carol: "How shall we receive
him?"

Monday after Advent 3

Psalm 41; Zechariah 1:7–17; Revelation 3:7–13; Matthew 24:15–31

Creator God, who transforms chaos, give us the wits to trust you amid the growing disorder of our world. In his name. Amen.

These readings utilize extreme rhetoric to portray a world that is in big trouble. This apocalyptic rhetoric imagines that the present "world," that is, the present sociopolitical economy, can no longer be sustained. It is not possible or responsible to take this biblical imagery (or any part of the Bible) and apply it directly to our own circumstance or context. We may, however, permit this wild imagery to give us access to the reality that our own present sociopolitical economy cannot be sustained much longer in its present form. This is evident in the environmental crisis, the economic displacement of great numbers of people, and the violence of war that produces displaced persons beyond count. This imagery offers us a way to see our context fully and honestly, without any false assurance from comfortable ideology.

It is precisely in such a context, however, that these readings assert that the coming rule of God will bring a new order of well-being. The news is that the present acute disorder has not outflanked or superseded the rule of God. God will rule in and through and beyond the chaos.

Given that assurance, these readings are a summons to the faithful to endure the chaos patiently, not to give in to it, not to deny it, but to practice God's word, a word of fidelity that issues in obedience that takes the form of mercy and justice. The deep anxiety of our disordered world eventuates, much too often, in selfishness, fear, and violence toward others. These readings urge that such a time is not time to compromise the radical ethic of faith. It is rather time for mercy and justice as active forms of patience that match the mercy and justice and compassion of God.

Tuesday after Advent 3

Psalm 47; Zechariah 2:1–13; Revelation 3:14–22; Matthew 24:32–44

God of newness, give us honesty about our present illusions. Give us readiness for your newness that eludes all our categories. In his name. Amen.

The present world of modern morality, advanced technology, and uncompromising ideology feels like (and claims to be) a closed system in which all possibilities for the future are well in hand. It is an arrangement of power and resources that benefits some at the cruel expense of others.

Advent is the awareness that this seemingly closed, guaranteed system is rendered penultimate by the holy power of God. We can see in the Gospel reading how the rhetoric strains to give voice to possibility of newness in a world that seems close to perpetuity. The Matthew tradition has Jesus appeal to the old imagery of a rescuer sent by God on the wings of a cloud, an agent of such awesome power that his entry will not be resisted.

According to Zechariah, a "man" will, in that opening for newness, make possible a new Jerusalem where God will dwell. That new city of justice and righteousness, in Israel's imagination, will be the epicenter of a new heaven of presence and a new earth of justice. It will not be like the old, current, fractious Jerusalem of lethal political quarrels, but a metaphor for and embodiment of all things new.

The church in Laodicea is chided for being "lukewarm," refusing to decide. So it is with many of us, lukewarm about a choice between *an old impenetrable system* or *a newness that centers in God's own presence*. Advent is a time to break out of lukewarm indifference, to opt for the coming newness of God. Faithful witness is to recognize the illusions of well-being in present tense, to walk through the door into God's new world.

Wednesday after Advent 3

Psalm 119:49–72; Zechariah 3:1–10;
Revelation 4:1–8; Matthew 24:45–51

Good God who comes soon, hear our pledge that we will be about the good work you expect of us at your coming. In his name. Amen.

The reading in Revelation gives us a peek into the throne room of God. The one seated on the throne is beyond description in power, awe, majesty, and dominion. That awesomeness is acknowledged in the never-ending doxology, "Holy, holy, holy."

The wonder of that holiness is that from it is offered a derivative holiness for human creatures in the world. Thus Zechariah can contemplate Joshua, the high priest in the exilic period of ancient Israel. As representative of Israel in that difficult moment, the priest is unworthy and unclean and unqualified. That is, Israel cannot be in the presence of the holy God. But the promise is that the holy God will make Joshua (and so Israel) holy and qualified to be before God. This is divine holiness "making holy."

But notice that this overwhelming act of transformation comes with rigorous expectation: "if you walk in my ways and keep my requirements." Being made holy depends on obedience to the requirements of God, without which there will be no "holy making." That same requirement is voiced in the Gospel reading. When the master (the holy God in the form of the crucified and risen one) comes (as he surely will), the master will look for servants who are "faithful and wise " The measure of "faithful and wise" is to provide "food at the proper time" for the household. That is, the way to be ready for the coming of God is to be at work managing the life resources of creation in a wise way that will sustain all creatures. This requirement thus pertains to the political economy, the care of the neighbor, and protection of the environment. Such readiness is our work in Advent.

Thursday after Advent 3

Psalm 50; Zechariah 4:1–14; Revelation 4:9–5:5; Matthew 25:1–13

*God of our future, forgive our foolish lack of preparation for your new-
ness. Let us be prepared for your future that undoes all our present tense.
In his name. Amen.*

In these readings, God's future is hidden and unavailable. The
oracle in Zechariah reflects a particular moment in the history of ancient Israel in the midst of exile. With the collapse
of royal governance in Jerusalem, the small colony of Judah
was jointly administered by a governor (Zerubbabel) and a
priest (Joshua). It was "the day of small things," when historical possibility was modest indeed for God's people. But the two
anointed (governor and priest) were nonetheless the carriers
of God's possibility. The governor, moreover, was linked to the
house of David, thus keeping royal expectations alive.

That royal expectation, in Christian tradition, was assigned
to Jesus, said to be of "the house of David." The reading in
Revelation offers another vision of the divine throne room that
is permeated with doxology. The Holy One, in this particular
rhetoric, holds a scroll that is the clue to God's future in the
world. And the scroll can be opened only by "the Lion of the
tribe of Judah," that is, an heir to David, that is, Jesus. Only
Jesus knows the clue to the future that God will surely enact.
It is implicit in Christian confession that Jesus, as clue to our
future, finds that future in obedience to crucifixion and in surprise in resurrection. That is the access point to the future that
only the Lion (become the Lamb) knows.

The Gospel reading concerns readiness for the future that
the "bridegroom" (Jesus) will disclose and perform. These
lessons remind us that God's future is not a future of wealth,
power, or security. It is rather a future of *costly obedience* and
inexplicable surprise. Without attentiveness to the "bridegroom,"
we are likely to be foolish and unprepared.

Friday after Advent 3

Psalm 40; Zechariah 7:8–8:8; Revelation 5:6–14; Matthew 25:14–30

Lord Jesus who risked all for the future of the world, let us be your good disciples. In your name. Amen.

The oracle of Zechariah recites the "normative" history of ancient Israel in two familiar stages. First, Israel failed to obey the prophetic ethic of justice for the vulnerable. The result was a scattering in exile and displacement. But second, because of God's passionate love for Israel and for Jerusalem, there will be wondrous, joyous restoration of well-being in Jerusalem.

In the reading from Revelation, this "normative" narrative of ancient Israel is seen to be reperformed in the life of Jesus. It is Jesus who was slain, by whose death every "tribe and language and people and nation" is saved. That "slaughtered" Lamb is now "worthy" to receive power, wealth, wisdom, might, honor, glory, and blessing; the words pile up in a doxological surplus of well-being and joy. This rhetoric of "slain" and "worthy" bespeaks crucifixion and resurrection that is a reperformance of Israel's exile and restoration. It is no wonder that all the saints praise the one who opens the scroll and enacts the future.

So what about our future? Shall we play it safe and hunker down in the status quo? The parable of Jesus is a celebration of risk in obedience to the master who risked his life for the future of the world. The parable is not about managing money or calculation of income or interest. It is about life risks that reperform the risk of his own life that Jesus has willingly undertaken. If risk is the order of the day, then Advent consists in breaking out of business as usual in order to receive God's future. The prophetic norm of mercy for the vulnerable (widows, orphans, immigrants, the poor) continues to be a starting point for the risk of glad obedience.

Saturday after Advent 3

Psalm 55; Zechariah 8:9–17; Revelation 6:1–17; Matthew 25:31–46

God of our future, forgive our yearning for cheap grace. Let us recognize your mighty promise and your stark expectation. In his name. Amen.

We have largely been narcotized in the church to expect that Jesus is unconditional love for us all. That shallow assurance is reinforced at Christmastime with an easy, casual disregard of the hard realities of the world and the hard realities of the gospel that meet the world. We should know better, because it is right there in front of us in one of the most familiar of Jesus' parables. We readily appeal to this parable when we want to champion social justice and compassion toward the needy. In doing so, however, we do not often recognize that the list of ministries to the "least" in the parable is not an imperative that commands action. Rather it is an occasion for judgment that reviews past actions. The judgment is severe toward those who have not practiced a neighborly ethic. The hard part is that the coming one, the Son of Man, conducts a trial and implements a judicial sentence.

The teaching is, of course, only a parable, not to be heard literally. It is a declaration by Jesus that the rule of God operates with stark expectations that are uncompromising and come with severe sanctions. The disregard of this expectation issues in ominous prospects for the future, ominous even if and when we are protected by our narcotized illusions.

The parable has behind it a thick prophetic tradition. Zechariah anticipates a new well-being, a "sowing of peace," a "blessing," "good to Jerusalem." That good promise, however, requires truth speaking and judgments that make for peace. These are not heroic actions for an emergency. They are rather the new norm for which the Lamb was slain. They are, in the parable, the price of "eternal life."

Fourth Sunday of Advent

Psalm 24; Genesis 3:8–15; Revelation 12:1–10; John 3:16–21

God of light and love and generosity, we are drawn to your light; yet we love the darkness. Give us freedom to redecide. In his name. Amen.

The reading from Revelation narrates the great drama of Christmas and the life of Jesus in highly imaginative language. At the outset there is a woman who is about to give birth. This vulnerable woman brings forth a male child.

The drama is escalated when opposition to the male child is reported. We know that Jesus encountered determined opposition at every turn. King Herod, in his fearfulness, tried to kill him. The religious leadership (Pharisees and scribes) early on conspired against him. In this text the opposition is said to be cosmic: the "great dragon," "that ancient serpent, who is called the Devil and Satan"; rich imagery is utilized to characterize the violent opposition of the empire of Rome in its defense of the kingdom of Caesar. But the male child is kept safe. The child is "taken to God"; the angels join the unequal cosmic struggle to protect the vulnerable child who embodies "the salvation and the power and the kingdom of our God."

The enemy of the gospel is not named explicitly, but in context it is the empire of Rome. Let us imagine that we now live in an empire of violent greed that practices fearful predation against every child and every vulnerable person. That empire takes the form of an unjust political economy backed by a scarcely restrained military. In the face of it comes this vulnerable child who performs mercy and compassion and justice. We are left to find our location in the midst of the drama that is quite local and at the same time of cosmic scale. It is the mystery of faith that this child is well protected beyond all the hostility that can be mounted to defeat him.

CHRISTMAS

Christmas Day

Psalm 2; 1 John 4:7–16

God who gives all of self to us, hear our pledge of our all back to you. As you hold nothing back from us of yourself, so we would, as we are able, hold nothing back from you. In his name. Amen.

Christmas Day is an occasion for wonder, awe, praise . . . and gift giving. Gift giving done rightly is an imitation of the self-giving of God. Too much of our gift giving, however, is a pitiful distortion. We give too much to those who do not need. We overwhelm our children with too much stuff. We give in calculation. Or in spasms of compassion we give to those in need, but only for a day, without attention to the socioeconomic structures that produce and sustain need.

There is no distortion in the self-giving love of God. The great God of heaven finds a way, we confess, to enter into the life of the earth and to do so in the form of a vulnerable human person, greatly at risk. In the mystery of the Trinity, the "eternal Son" of God was "made man," made human, made subject to the vagaries of earthly existence. And in him the Father whom we do not see is as vulnerable as the Son whom we see.

We may stand in amazement at this primordial self-giving of God. But there is more to it than amazement. There is also a mandate: Because God so loved . . . we ought to love one another. God's love summons and evokes our love. We are summoned to "love one another." We are summoned to love our neighbors as ourselves. Eventually, we are summoned to love our enemies. Such responding love is the way we act out our amazement. This love scarcely participates in the romantic familial love of conventional Christmas. It is rather love that calls us into the dark places, there to abide with transformative power. For that reason, we sing, "Love so amazing, so divine, demands my soul, my life, my all."*

*Isaac Watts, "When I Survey the Wondrous Cross" (1707).

Second Day of Christmas

Micah 4:1–5; 5:2–4

Welcome, Prince of Peace! Come and dwell among us; come and empower us as peacemakers. Come that we may walk in the ways of justice and peace. In his name. Amen.

The wonder of Christmas is that in this inexplicable birth God has kept the great promises made to ancient Israel; the earliest testimony in the New Testament finds these ancient promises indispensable for understanding what it is that God has done in the coming of Jesus.

The oracles in today's reading in Micah do two things. First, in 4:1–5 it is promised that a time will come when adherence to Israel's Torah will lead to a new peaceableness that will permit disarmament. Second, in the face of the mighty empire of Assyria, Micah anticipates a new "ruler in Israel" who will bring peace, well-being, and security. The new ruler will emerge, moreover, from a very small clan in the tribe of Judah.

Jesus is confessed, in our use of these oracles, as the bringer of peaceableness through adherence to the Torah; he is, moreover, from the little town of Bethlehem. It was a huge act of imagination to connect Jesus to these ancient oracles. We may see the ground for such a connection when we consider Jesus' teaching in the Sermon on the Mount. He asserts in Matthew 5:17 that he came to fulfill the law (Torah). In 5:9 he says, "Blessed are the peacemakers." The linkage of *peace* and *Torah* reiterates the accents of ancient Micah in the life of Jesus. Our Christmas opportunity may be to reflect on the way in which this Prince of Peace, grounded by Israel's Torah, summons to peacemaking. A great gift of Christmas is peace in our families, churches, and communities, and among the nations. The vicious cycle of hate, fear, violence, and war is broken by his presence. We need only engage that new possibility. The final verse of Micah 4:5 affirms that peacemaking is done with those who think and believe otherwise.

Third Day of Christmas

Psalm 85

Lord of heaven and God of earth, we are dazzled by the power of your reconciling energy. Give us sufficient grace to live in your reconciliation, appearances to the contrary notwithstanding. In his name. Amen.

This psalm is a glad reflection what God has done and the difference God's presence makes in the world. The psalm begins with a sixfold affirmation of God's good past action (vv. 1–3). Then it issues to God a strong imperative petition: *Restore* (v. 4)!

This extended lament is answered with a dramatic affirmation: *Surely* (v. 9)! God has acted; "salvation is at hand." Then follow the lovely images of God's qualities of fidelity portrayed as lively personages. The cast of good characters includes steadfast love, faithfulness, righteousness, and peace. They all meet; they all embrace. Everything is in harmony. More specifically, faithfulness is from the ground; righteousness is from the sky. Heaven and earth are fully reconciled. The world is one under God's generous governance.

Thus the need of verses 1–7 is answered by the creator God with faithful reconciliation in verses 9–11. Read at Christmas, this psalm voices the gladness that into a world of need God has come with reconciling power. In the birth of Jesus, the goodness of heaven (sky) and the possibility of earth meet: word become flesh! The outcome is that the good earth is generative and productive (v. 12). Christmas has implications for the environment!

It is to be noted that there are no imperatives for us in the psalm. We are not mandated to do anything! We are invited to notice, to wonder, to be amazed, to be in awe. Christmas is a time to consider that the world is in God's good hands. In the life of Jesus, newness is "at hand." We are invited to dwell in that new alternative reality.

Fourth Day of Christmas

John 3:31–36

God of all truth, free us from our several false loyalties, that we may single-mindedly accept Jesus, crucified and risen, as your certification. In his name. Amen.

This difficult reading reflects struggles in the early church, struggles that continue even now in various forms. The first struggle is to adjudicate the difference and distinction between John (see vv. 25–30) and Jesus. While the two are connected, they are very different. John is "of the earth"; Jesus is "from above" and is therefore superior. The text is at pains to affirm Jesus' heavenly origin that set him above John and above the world as its ruler.

The second struggle faced by the early church is that the witness of Jesus (and to Jesus) is not widely accepted; many are not persuaded by the claims that the church made concerning Jesus. The contrast in verse 36 between "believe" and "disobey" is much clearer in the Greek, where the two words are more symmetrical as "trust" and "not trust."

These church struggles continue, both because alternative claims from elsewhere (from the ground) compete with the gospel claim of the lordship of Christ and because the claim of Jesus violates our reason and compels to radical obedience. The gospel is not "popular," a circumstance that tempts the church to compromise the claims of the gospel.

The accent of this text is that Jesus "verifies" God: God is true! From that everything follows. It follows that the world is God's creation. It follows that obedience is our true freedom. It follows that God's spirit blows away all our certitudes. It follows that Jesus' attentiveness to the vulnerable and undeserving is the clue to a viable life in a sustainable community.

The truthfulness of God gives the lie to many of our preferences, but it is the way to "eternal life."

Fifth Day of Christmas

Psalm 18:1–20; 2 Samuel 23:13–17b; 2 John 1:1–13; John 2:1–11

God of self-giving love, grant that in response to your deep love for us, we may in turn be self-giving. Grant this day that we may notice our neighbor with positive regard. In his name. Amen.

The "lady," the church, has received only one commandment from its Lord: Love one another! It is not a new commandment. It is as old as Sinai, but it is as urgent as today. It means to get our minds off ourselves and to have primal regard for "the other." In Paul's words, "look . . . to the interests of others" (Phil. 2:4).

As always, but now acutely, the church faces "deceivers" who want to talk us out of that commandment that is at the core of Christ's teaching (doctrine). Among us now, the deceiver is most likely to be the voice of consumerism or the urging of individualism that regards the self as the goal and culmination of all well-being. That is the big lie that the church, with its voice and its body, must contradict.

The Old Testament narrative offers a wondrous small anecdote from the life of David. In the midst of battle he wistfully wishes for the taste of hometown water. His comrades, who adore him, at great risk secure that water and gladly present it to David; they know how pleased and grateful he will be. But David surprises them and refuses the water (that he so wanted) that his men had gotten at great risk. David, in his gesture, thinks of his comrades and their risky venture. He renounces his own thirst in his regard for them. When this is read in the presence of the epistle, David does indeed engage in an act of love for his men in response to their bold act of love for him. Both parties have looked to the interest of the other.

In a culture of greedy self-preoccupation and self-regard, notice of the other at the expense of our own hungers and thirsts is a core obligation of faith.

Sixth Day of Christmas

Psalm 23; 1 Kings 17:17–24; 3 John 1–15; John 4:46–54

God of life, free us for your wonder, that we should not be contained in the debilitating power of death that holds us in fear and despair. In his name. Amen.

We have two resurrection stories that narrate mighty contradictions to the power of death. In the case of Elijah, he brings a boy back to life by prayer and by what seems to be artificial respiration. The verdict is that "the life of the child came into him again, and he revived." His *nephesh* (self) returned. In the narrative of Jesus (which is surely a reiteration of the act of Elijah), the restoration of a boy is accomplished by only an assuring word from Jesus.

Both stories witness to God's power for life. Both stories witness, moreover, to the power of the human agent who carries God's power for life. The gospel of life is the news that the power of God is not contained in our conventional categories that assume a closed world no longer open to God's rule. Along with and prior to the Easter resurrection of Jesus, the tradition attests to other resurrections that are local, that refuse the despairing power of death. There are no explanations, only testimony.

The phrase "life [*nephesh*] returned" is the same idea we familiarly recite in Psalm 23: "He restores my soul." It is not a "soul" that the God of the gospel restores. Rather it is a fully functioning, bodily, historical existence. We find comfort and assurance in Psalm 23 because it affirms the truth about God. The psalm, moreover, is more than comfort and assurance. It is a summons to us to find freedom and hope beyond the closed world given us by conventional reasoning. In the life of the church, there are indeed many restorations of life that happen beyond explanation. We indeed, like Elijah, may be agents of such restorations.

Seventh Day of Christmas

Psalm 93; 1 Samuel 1:1–2, 7b–28; Colossians 1:9–20; Luke 2:22–40

Jesus, Son of the Father, give us courage to see you in your exposed vulnerable vocation that led to your execution. Give us courage to follow your cruciform destiny, if not closely, then at least at a distance. In your name. Amen.

In these readings we are confronted with the scandal and wonder of gospel faith. Second Samuel offers an account of a baby given wondrously to a couple who was unable to bear a child and had no ground to anticipate one. The circumcised baby in the Gospel story is on the way to wisdom as a growing person in the world. In the lyric of Colossians, we have soaring poetry that voices the son in grand royal rhetoric that eventuates in Trinitarian thought. The lyric dares to present this baby as participant in the very mystery of God, as the clue to all reality.

The narrative of the baby attests to his humanness. The doxological lyric affirms his identity as an inexplicable divine force in the world with transformative capacity. The two claims together are a scandal to our reason; we are tempted to choose one or the other. This strange claim is the core truth of our faith, but it is a claim that requires us to give up our explanatory capacity. As a result we try to escape the claim. We escape it to credit only the humanity of the baby, and even with a dose of sentimentality. He is like us, only more so! Or we choose to accent his identity with the Father. But we may not choose. We are given the truth that *God's own life* is fully among us, so that his solidarity with vulnerable "rejects" of the world led finally to his execution. All of our explanations turn out to be inadequate. We are left with an invitation to trust and to follow. The Christmas baby comes soon to adulthood; the scandal of his birth eventuates in the scandal of his ministry among us, embodied grace and truth.

Eighth Day of Christmas (Holy Name)

Psalm 103; Isaiah 62:1–5, 10–12;
Revelation 19:11–16; Matthew 1:18–25

God of all newness, we celebrate your new naming. In gratitude we receive and accept our new identities you give us in love. Grant that we may give new names and new futures to our neighbors who have been lost in the shuffle. In his name. Amen.

New Year's Day marks a dramatic fresh beginning. New realities and possibilities are acknowledged and realized by the issuing of new names and the practice of new historical relations. In these readings, we may notice three new names for three new realities.

In the reading from Revelation, we are offered a glimpse into the throne room of God adorned in awesome splendor. The one who occupies the throne is called "The Word of God." The name of Jesus is not uttered, but clearly it is Jesus who sits enthroned. Here he is capable of fierce power that calls the nations to account. In the Gospel narrative we anticipate the birth of Jesus. The angel quotes Scripture (Isa. 7:14) to Mary and announces a new name for the coming child: Immanuel, God with us! He is so named because in his body (his person, his life, his ministry) he overcomes the gap of alienation between God and God's world. In concrete ways he overcomes that alienation by his presence.

Just as Jesus is called by new names (The Word of God, Immanuel), Israel is given a new name in Isaiah 62. This people who had been abandoned are now called Married, capable of fruitfulness and new possibility. The new name of Israel is possible because of the new names and new emergence of God. As Israel in exile is given a new name and new future, we see that Jesus went about giving new names, new identities, and new futures to those who had lost their identity and their future in the rough and tumble of cruel history.

Ninth Day of Christmas

Psalm 34; 1 Kings 19:1–8; Ephesians 4:1–16; John 6:1–14

Giver of all good things, scarcity tastes bitter. Give us heart enough to refuse a diet of bitterness, that we might gladly receive your abundance and generously share your abundance with others who, like us, are weary of bitterness. In his name. Amen.

Scarcity does strange things to us. It makes us anxious, greedy, and quarrelsome.

We live in a political economy that is propelled by a sense of scarcity that eventuates in mean-spirited fearfulness. These readings contradict notions of scarcity and witness to the wonder of God's abundance. Two of our readings articulate God's abundance in terms of ample food. Elijah despairs of his life; he is astonishingly awoken by one of God's angels with ample food and admonished to "get up and eat." Jesus, in ways that are not explained, feeds a multitude of hungry people, and there is a surplus of twelve baskets of bread; loaves abound!

The imagery is different in the Epistle reading. But the issue is not different. This early church community is beset by cunning, "craftiness," and deceit, a tug-of-war for truth, power, and authority. The apostle resists such conflict by summoning the church to "grow up" in love, to refuse such in-house combat, and to be "knit together" in love.

The beginning of the year is a good time to reflect on the anxiety, greed, and quarrelsomeness that besets us in church and in society because we subscribe to the claim of scarcity. These readings attest that such a scenario, so powerful among us, is not true. It is not true because the God of the gospel gives more than enough, more than enough for Elijah, more than enough for the multitude, more than enough for the church. We may ponder how we have been recruited by claims of scarcity and how we may reverse course by receiving the abundance of love and sustenance given by God. There is more than enough!

Tenth Day of Christmas

Psalm 72; 1 Kings 19:9–18; Ephesians 4:17–32; John 6:15–27

God of faithful power and abiding presence, draw us away from easy addictions that distort our lives and skew our futures. Draw us toward your new emancipated reality. In his name. Amen.

In a pathological society, we are regularly tempted into addictions that betray our faith and compromise our full humanness. It is useful to consider these readings as narratives of addiction and recovery:

— Elijah comes close to falling into despair because he senses his abandonment.
— The church in the epistle is addicted to Gentile practices of licentiousness, greed, lust, bitterness, slander, and malice, all the practices of a rootless society.
— In the Gospel reading the disciples are "terrified," a predictable state for those who have no sure reference point and so are readily driven to anxiety.

In the face of such seductions, these readings urge resistance and offer alternative:

— The counter to Elijah's despair is a summons back to risky work with an assurance that he is not alone but belongs to a great company of faithful risk takers.
— The epistle invites to a new obedience in "righteousness and holiness."
— The Gospel reading responds to the anxiety of the disciples with an assurance of Jesus' transformative presence.

The addictions among us are now so powerful because they are made to seem normal in an unthinking society. In fact, given the rule of Christ, such addictions are abnormalities that kill. The new year is a time to embrace the gospel's "new normal" of engagement in faithful risk, life characterized by holiness, and trust in the presence of gospel power. Addictions are so easy. The new normal requires sustained intentionality.

Eleventh Day of Christmas

Psalm 85; Joshua 3:14–4:7; Ephesians 5:1–20 John 9:1–12, 35–38

God of the generations, we are glad to belong to your family and to live in hope of receiving your legacy to us. Help us to pay attention to those who surprisingly show up as joint heirs along with us. In his name. Amen.

Planning for the future is an important and long-term enterprise. It requires forethought and discipline and intentionality. It provides for the transfer of wealth, identifies heirs, and focuses on a durable legacy. The phrase "inheritance in the kingdom" in the Epistle reading draws my attention to such a focus. The Bible, since the ancient promise to Abraham and Sarah, has been preoccupied with inheritance and provision for heirs. The Joshua reading about entry into the land of promise looks back to the land promise to Abraham (Gen. 12:1–3). All of Israel is understood to inherit the land.

In Christian rhetoric the notion of heir and inheritance has been transposed from actual earthly territory to a relationship of fidelity and well-being. Thus the phrase "kingdom of God," or in the epistle, "kingdom of Christ and of God," refers to a life of well-being assured by faithful communion with the living God. The point of the epistle is that such a good and durable future is not a free lunch but is offered to those who live under the disciplines of the "fruit of the light." In the Gospel reading, the blind man receives a future from Christ because he "believes in" (trusts) Christ and worships him. He is indeed an heir to the rule of Christ.

We do well to think of our inheritance for time to come and the disciplines that pertain to it. We may think carefully about what we may receive from God in the future because of our faithful, attentive obedience. Or we may ask, "Who are the legitimate heirs of God's future?" They are perhaps not to be equated with those who inherit the things of this age.

Twelfth Day of Christmas

Psalm 2; Jonah 2:2–9; Ephesians 6:10–20; John 11:17–27, 38–44

Creator God who manages the forces of chaos, we know about the reality of chaos in our world. We also know about your lordly governance, and so we give you thanks. In his name. Amen.

The truth is that we are not self-sufficient. It is a lesson we keep learning and keep forgetting. The temptation to self-sufficiency is very powerful in a society that affirms the autonomous individual and that celebrates the "self-made" successful.

These readings are reflections on the inadequacy of self-sufficiency. Jonah had fled from the prophetic assignment he had received from God. But he finds he is helpless in "the heart of the seas." The church in Ephesus must contend "against the rulers, against the authorities, against the cosmic powers of this present darkness, against the spiritual forces of evil." It cannot manage to resist these forces. And in the Lazarus narrative, he and his sisters are helpless before the power of death. In all three texts, there is inescapable confrontation with the mighty powers of negation that are beyond human coping.

The good news is that in each case provision is made by the faithfulness of God to counter the power of negation that we cannot overcome on our own. Jonah is rescued by the big fish, a rescue that evokes his thanks to God. In the epistle, the church is provided by Christ with tools of resistance to withstand the power of evil. And in the Gospel narrative, it is the magisterial command of Jesus, "Lazarus, come out," that lets the gospel power of life overcome the force of death.

It is a great illusion in our society that if we have enough money, enough technology, enough pharmaceuticals, or enough weapons we can secure our own future. These texts invite a move beyond illusion to trust in the gracious God who in love acts on our behalf.

EPIPHANY

Epiphany

Psalm 46; Isaiah 49:1–7; Revelation 21:22–27; Matthew 12:14–21

Lordly ruler of all tongues, tribes, peoples, and nations, your large-heartedness overwhelms our small-mindedness, and we are grateful. In his name. Amen.

Our faith traditions have most often focused on the particulars of a specific community. Thus ancient Israel was largely preoccupied with its own covenant with God. The early Jesus movement was a Jewish enterprise. And the church much too often has claimed a monopoly on God's graciousness, sometimes even to denominational exclusiveness.

Epiphany is the dramatic moment when the reach of God's gracious governance extends beyond the confines of our self-preoccupation. In the poem of Isaiah, God's servant is dispatched beyond Israel to the well-being of the nations. In the vision of Revelation, the anticipated temple in Jerusalem provides guidance and well-being for the kings of the earth. In the Gospel narrative, in the face of dangerous opposition, the first verses of Isaiah 42 are quoted to describe the mission of Jesus to give justice and hope to Gentiles. Epiphany is about Gentiles whom we should not romanticize. They are people unlike us who nonetheless belong in the goodness of God.

The fearful recurring accent on self-protection is everywhere among us. There is a new tribalism in the United States that seeks to "take back our country." There is a parallel move to accent the monopoly that the church has on the gospel, to the exclusion of others. These texts—and the season of Epiphany—are urgent counters to such parochialism. The traditional claim of whites, Westerners, or Americans to be chosen for "manifest destiny" is vetoed by the reach of the gospel. The news is that those unlike us are subjects of God's governance and God's graciousness. No nation or race or class can claim to be privileged. Retrograde parochialism, whether grounded in fear or in price, is inimical to the will of God.

First Sunday after Epiphany

Psalm 146; Genesis 1:1–2:3; Ephesians 1:3–14; John 1:29–34

Majestic Creator who inhabits the life of Jesus and the body of the church, forgive our small, cramped sense of life. Draw us into your large mystery that we might participate in it with gladness. In his name. Amen.

The lyrical texts for this Sunday are breathtaking in their scope and claim. The lyrical poem of creation is a wondrous imagination of the way in which the world is given by God and infused with God's blessing for life. The human couple, alongside all the other creatures, are welcome denizens of this healthy habitat, made livable by the "spirit of God" that pushed back chaos.

That same Spirit presides over the baptism of Jesus. As the Spirit made life possible in creation in the face of chaos, so the Spirit now in the person of Jesus performs a new creation that will be enacted in the ministry of Jesus. His baptism is a beginning as dramatic as the beginning of creation.

The imaginative witness to the Spirit in both creation and new creation in baptism continues in the Epistle reading. Paul dares to say that the further wonder is that creation set in motion a divine resolve that has eventuated in the community gathered around Jesus.

This vision of the faithful has little to do with most of our preoccupations in the institutional church. It has to do with recognizing, embracing, and participating in an immense purpose that pivots on Jesus, a purpose that culminates in a life of glad praise to God. Such a vision calls us well beyond our small anxieties, beyond our petty quarrels, beyond doctrinal niceties, beyond our pious scruples, to be carried away in wonder that is performed as forgiveness.

Monday after Epiphany 1

Psalm 117; Exodus 17:1–7; Colossians 1:15–23; John 7:37–52

*God of life, we are urged by consumerism to "Stay thirsty, my friend."
You now gladly sate our deepest thirst. Help us to drink deeply and to be
grateful for your free gift of life. In his name. Amen.*

We are just at the beginning of the water wars. We are running short of good drinkable water, and we cannot live without
water. As a result, we will, in time to come, have great conflicts
about who gets water, who pays for it, and who decides who
remains thirsty. By way of the imagery of water, thirst, and
drink, the Gospel reading plunges us into the water wars about
who gives life, who receives life, and how the water of life is
administered.

Appeal to the Exodus narrative concerning water from rock
is a way in which Christians have attested that in Jesus the
water of life is free, inexplicable, and beyond our administration. It just flows out, and we have life. Jesus is the source of
life and the giver of ample water for life!

The Epistle reading gives us the wondrous phrase "the
fullness of God." This breathtaking formula asserts that all
of God—nothing held back—is present and visible in Jesus.
What we see in Jesus as God's presence is graciousness, generosity, and life-giving abundance.

Two responses to this wonder are suggested. On the one
hand, the authorities are unnerved by him; they would like to
arrest him because he is a threat to their control of the water
supply. They have been rationing the water of life as though
they had to manage its scarcity. Jesus threatens their authority with his abundance for all. On the other hand, those who
embrace Jesus are empowered for a different kind of life,
grounded in abundance and marked by being holy, blameless,
and irreproachable. Jesus, as God's water for life, changes
everything!

Tuesday after Epiphany 1

Psalm 121; Isaiah 45:14–19; Colossians 1:24–2:7; John 8:12–19

God of inscrutable purposes, forgive us for imagining that we already know where you will show up next. In his name. Amen.

These readings invite reflection on the purposes of God that are deeply at work in the life of the world but are not easily and readily visible. The purposes of God are "hidden" and are marked by "mystery" and become known to us in surprising and shocking ways.

In the poetry of Isaiah, the hidden purpose of God is that Israel should be saved, even though Israel is a tiny, vulnerable community in the world of the great powers. In the lyric of Colossians the hidden mystery of God reaches even further. The text uses the word "chose," which recalls to us the recognition of Isaiah that God chose Israel for rescue. But now God's choosing is that the riches of God's glory are situated among the Gentiles, thus beyond the ancient choosing of Israel.

And in the Gospel reading, the Pharisees, representatives of old chosenness, are shown up by the claim that in Jesus, God's governance shines in all the dark, failed places of the world.

In all three readings, we are invited beyond the normal expectations of the world. First, the rescue of Israel is beyond all conventional power politics. Second, the choice of Gentiles is beyond all comfortable notions of a chosen people. Third, the identification of Jesus with God the Father is a scandal to ordinary religious leaders.

Epiphany is a season in which to be surprised by the mystery of God. God's purposes do not conform to our expectation or our comfort zone. We may expect to be stunned as God does new things among us.

Wednesday after Epiphany 1

Psalm 138; Jeremiah 23:1–8; Colossians 2:8–23; John 10:7–17

Good God of freedom, forgive our enslavements that we cherish and our imagined autonomy that distorts our true life. Give us readiness to accept your generous rule. In his name. Amen.

In the ancient world, "shepherd" is an image that often refers to a ruler or king. Jeremiah identifies bad shepherds (failed kings) as the cause of the destruction of Jerusalem. He anticipates, in time to come, a new good shepherd of the dynasty of David who will enact a new rescue of God's people (from Babylon) that will surpass in wonder even the ancient exodus.

That same imagery is used in the Gospel reading, where the failed shepherds (bad leaders) are labeled as "thieves and bandits" because they only wanted to fleece the sheep. Jesus is contrasted with them: he will finally give us life for the well-being of the flock, the beloved of God. Jesus is the only real leader who shows that real power is exercised through willing and risky vulnerability.

The Epistle reading, in a different rhetoric, identifies Jesus as the "head of every ruler and authority" who has completely defeated all other failed authority. Jesus' new rule consists in forgiveness and a new regime of freedom for those who live in Christ's community and who trust his governance. In his rule of forgiveness and freedom, Jesus enacts the "fullness of deity." That is what God is about!

The practical result of this new governance marked by freedom is that the old disciplines of fear, whether of being self-abasing and so *too little* or puffed up and so *too big*, are completely nullified. We are invited to a long meditation on the freedom given in the rule of Christ. It is freedom that is grounded in God's self-giving that overcomes both phony piety and phony self-actualization.

Thursday after Epiphany 1

Psalm 148; Isaiah 55:3–9; Colossians 3:1–17; John 14:6–14

We give you thanks, living Lord, for your works of transformation among us. Give us energy and freedom that we might be about such works that echo your truthfulness and exhibit your alternative path to life. In your name. Amen.

Given the passion, depth, and vigor of our various convictions and ideologies, it is mind-boggling to recognize that God has a will for the world other than our own will. In the reading from Isaiah, the exiled Jews in Babylon assume that the best way to live is to "get along and go along" in the empire of Babylon. But the poet calls them to their senses as the people of God summoned to a different future than the one they are choosing for themselves.

The same claim is voiced more singularly in the Gospel. Jesus—none other—is the way (a path of life in a hazardous world), the truth (the reality of God against all idols), and the life (not the existence anticipated in our several passions and ideologies). Jesus contradicts much of the way we are prone to choose and live!

As always in the Bible, these deep claims have practical consequences. Jesus ends his testimony to himself, "Do the works that I do." We know from the ancient story what his works are: He healed the sick; empowered the lame, blind, and deaf; cured lepers; and welcomed the poor. His work is practical bodily transformations for well-being, most especially among those left behind. The practical implications of the reality of Christ are fully voiced in the epistle. The new way, the new truth, the new life is a way of compassion, kindness, lowliness, meekness, and patience, and above all love. Self-giving love is the hallmark of gospel life. The radical call of baptism into Jesus is a continuing process of putting off old behavior and putting on new conduct. No more business as usual!

Friday after Epiphany 1

Psalm 98; Genesis 49:1–2, 8–12; Colossians 3:18–4:6; John 15:1–16

*Self-giving God, we are grateful for your generous self-giving to us. We
are aware of your mandate to us. Give us the courage to have our usual
ways profoundly contradicted by your way of the cross. In his name.
Amen.*

The image of vine branch assures that when we are organically
connected to Jesus, the outcome of our life will be self-giving
love. That self-giving love contradicts everything we know and
believe and practice about wise ways to be in the world.

Our readings witness to two ways in which the gospel contradicts perfectly good texts. The Genesis text anticipates that
the Israelite tribe of Judah (in the form of the Davidic dynasty)
will have great power to impose its will, to command obedience, and to put a hand on the neck of enemies. But Jesus, as
the heir to David, contradicts such a way of power, even if the
church has been sometimes seduced into such power.

In the epistle, conventional social relationships between
husbands and wives, between masters and slaves, are top-
down relationships of power and control and are readily open
to abuse. But the gospel contradicts those old patterns and
imagines that every relationship can be reordered according to
the self-giving love commanded by Jesus.

We are, for the most part, inured to a conventional, domesticated faith that very often simply echoes social custom. For
that reason we have a long history of power relationships of
men over women, whites over blacks, Western colonial power
over colonized people, and rich over poor. Such ways of domination and exploitation are exposed by the gospel as modes
of death for all parties. They result from "fruit" that is discon-
nected from Jesus. These texts, in quite concrete ways, imagine relationships altered by the command of Jesus.

Saturday after Epiphany 1

Psalm 20; Genesis 6:9–22; Hebrews 4:1–13; John 2:13–22

God of life, we praise you for your power for new life. Open our eyes to see the wonder of your life-giving rule. In his name. Amen.

The characteristic move of God in the world is a two-step arrangement. It consists in God's *negation* of all that is out of sync with God's purpose and then God's *restoration* of well-being that resonates with God's intention. This movement of *negation and restoration* is reiterated often in Scripture and in the world.

In the flood narrative in Genesis, we read today of God's negation of corruption and violence in the earth. God's strategy for restoration is through the ark for Noah's family, out of which will come a restored humanity grounded in covenant. In the Gospel reading, the negation concerns the Jerusalem temple that had been reduced to exploitative commoditization. Jesus utters a profound subversion as he anticipates the destruction of the temple, then central shrine of Judaism. His promise of a rebuilt temple confounds his adversaries, because they do not understand that the "three days" utterance is an allusion to his own resurrection.

Given an ordinary commonsense perspective, it is easier to believe that there is no divine judgment on worldly arrangements that we treasure. And surely it is easier to conclude that resurrection is not possible. Or as a skeptic said to me recently, "I don't do resurrection."

By contrast, gospel faith that trusts in the uncompromising will of God and in God's relentless resolve for the world breaks with ordinary commonsense. We are able to see, with different eyes, that in truth the world that betrays God is indeed coming unraveled and is unsustainable. Conversely, God is at work raising up new historical possibilities that the world thinks are impossible. Blessed are the eyes that see these God-powered turns in the world.

Second Sunday after Epiphany

Psalm 148; Genesis 7:1–10, 17–23; Ephesians 4:1–16; Mark 3:7–19

God of all our divisions and distinctions, by your transformative power free us of fear that causes us to sort out people as acceptable or unacceptable. In his name. Amen.

In our reading from Genesis one can see the agenda of the priests in ancient Israel who prescribed that on the ark of rescue there would be "clean animals" and "unclean animals." The priestly rules of the book of Leviticus had concluded that eating certain animals would render one "unclean," unfit for worship of the holy God, and unsafe in society. It is astonishing that provision is made for including the unclean animals on the ark.

In the Gospel narrative, Jesus is amid many people who have diseases and disorders that were judged to make them "unclean," unacceptable in the community and dangerous to contact. Remarkably these "unclean spirits" fall down before Jesus and acknowledge his status as Son of God. He is Lord over unclean spirits. Beyond that, he commands his disciples to go and "cast out demons" and overcome unclean spirits. For ordinary people it was thought (and still is thought!) that contact with an unclean spirit would render one unclean. But Jesus reverses that process! He touches the unclean and thereby makes them clean, that is, socially acceptable. He thereby obliterates the category of "unclean."

Every society, including ours, has tacit rules of what is clean and unclean, safe and dangerous, acceptable and unacceptable. This concerns those with whom we readily have contact, who are granted access to good schools and good jobs, those who are eliminated from full membership in the political economy. The assignment of the disciples is to overcome such distinctions by the touch of recognition and transformation. One could imagine that the Lord of the ark intended that all the animals, by the end of the flood, would be seen as clean.

Monday after Epiphany 2

Psalm 25; Genesis 8:6–22; Hebrews 4:14–5:6; John 2:23–3:15

God of all our births, give us in this season a fresh capacity to see your hope for your world and resolve to live according to that vision. In his name. Amen.

It is remarkable that when the flood narrative ends, nothing has changed about the human condition. Human imagination is evil at the end of the story, as it was at the beginning. If anything new is to happen, it must come from God's side. And it does! God is no longer angry at the end of the story but instead gives assurance of a sustainable life in God's creation.

The matter of the "inclination of the human heart" as evil, however, is worth pondering. The Christian tradition takes an honest, dim view of human capacity, quite in contrast to the optimism of modernist ideology. We have a propensity to evil grounded in our fear or pride. So in the Gospel reading, Jesus knows "what was in everyone," and it is not good.

Jesus affirms to Nicodemus that it could be different. It could be different enough to enable one to see the kingdom of God. But it will be different only when one is "born anew," that is, if one is restarted in a new life by the transformative power of God's spirit.

On this day when we remember Martin Luther King, we recall especially his "dream speech" in which he articulated a version of the kingdom of God when there would be reconciliation and solidarity across all our distinctions. King spoke out of a renovated imagination. He no longer imagined the world according to the corrupt imagination of fear and hate. He summoned his listeners into that renovated imagination through which God's future could be seen differently. Nicodemus is invited by Jesus to a different world, the same world restored. We are invited by Dr. King to engage in the new creation, apart from old ways of wounding and division.

Tuesday after Epiphany 2

Psalm 26; Genesis 9:1–17; Hebrews 5:7–14; John 3:16–21

God of generous covenant making, grant us mercy enough to receive your self-giving and resolve enough to enact your covenant with all our neighbors. In his name. Amen.

The Epistle reading celebrates the priestly work of Jesus, who, by "prayers and supplications" and by the offer of his life as a sacrifice, has wrought reconciliation between God and the world. This is, in the purview of priestly imagery, the "first principle of God's word." Reconciliation has been accomplished!

The culmination of the flood narrative in Genesis arrives at a like conclusion. After the anger and regret of God that evoked the chaotic waters of the flood, God has changed disposition enough now to initiate peaceable abiding covenant with all creation and all creatures in it. The alienation and animosity between God and world has been decisively overcome by the resolve of God, which, in Christian confession, has been enacted in Jesus.

Christians who are "born anew" are on the far side of the drama of alienation and reconciliation. We have peace with God. That assurance is the first principle of the gospel. It is the foundation for a new and different life.

But that affirmation leaves everything from our side still to be done in response to God's reconciling capacity. It leaves for us the chance to reimagine the world—and our place in it—outside of the tired categories of fear and inadequacy. It leaves for us the glad task of becoming specific about the implications of peace with God that pertain to all the old alienations of race, class, gender, and ethnic origin. It leaves for us the challenge of actual bodily engagement in the performance of God's reconciliation. The assurance is of God's readiness to be a gracious covenant partner to all flesh. And now to act our part in that covenant from our side!

Wednesday after Epiphany 2

Psalm 38; Genesis 9:18–29; Hebrews 6:1–12; John 3:22–36

God of generous life, send your blessing for life on those who most need it; free us from craving a false sense of our own destiny. In his name. Amen.

The theme of blessing and curse recurs in the readings from the Old Testament and the epistle. In the epistle, the text is concerned with those who were faithful but who then compromised faith through apostasy. Those who had believed and then compromised are beyond restoration. The writer uses land as an image for the argument. Land that "produces a crop" is blessed by God, but land that produces weeds is cursed. The blessing or curse of land is a way of speaking about the blessing or curse of those who do the work of faith or who do not.

In the narrative of Noah and his sons, Canaan, son of Ham, is cursed for the sin of his father seeing drunken Noah naked, whereas Shem, who covered Noah without looking at him, is blessed. Clearly Shem, Ham, and Canaan, personal names in this story, are in fact peoples in the ancient world. Thus blessing and curse in the mouth of Noah declares destinies of ongoing historical communities. In the case of Canaan, such a destiny is based on a single narrative act, a huge leap of imagination; Shem by contrast becomes a carrier of the blessing to chosen Israel.

Blessing and curse are real. Some are indeed given the go-ahead for flourishing, while it is withheld from others. No argument there. But since the "curse of Canaan" has played such a pernicious role in racial attitudes in Western culture, with Canaan taken as a stand-in for dark-skinned peoples, we should be suspicious of such verdicts as Noah announces. We must distinguish carefully between actual blessings and curses and those used as a self-serving ideology, as in this case. Most such uses turn out not to be innocent.

Thursday after Epiphany 2

Psalm 37; Genesis 11:1–9; Hebrews 6:13–20; John 4:1–15

God of all nations, deliver us from assertion of national or ethnic pride and the hunger for domination. Open us to your free gifts offered to us all. In his name. Amen.

The story of the tower of Babel is an early account of globalization, a strategy of universal control by powerful people who aim to control all the money and to impose uniformity on all parts of the world population. It is clear in the story that the impetus for such a strategy is insecurity (fear of being scattered), and the aim is to become powerful in all the earth.

The threat of such a strategy of globalization is that it will evoke a prideful authority that need not and will not stop at anything in trying to achieve the impossible. This is reported in the text as a threat to the rule of God. Not stated in the text but clearly an outcome of such a strategy is that "lesser people" get lost in the shuffle as the powerful assert control. The "scattering" and "confusion" wrought by God is to assure that no assertive power can gain ultimate control and emerge as the single superpower.

The Gospel reading takes place, by contrast, in very small scale, a Jewish teacher and a Samaritan supplicant. The interaction between the two is a negotiation about national and ethnic difference and the shared agenda of water and "living water." Jesus, the Jew, reaches across ethnic lines, that is, he mobilizes and transcends his Jewishness to minister to one from an "enemy" people. The narrative attests the singularity of Jesus in his ministry beyond ethnic boundaries. By contrast to the practice of globalization, his "living water" is free. Globalization characteristically commodifies everything, and so water must be bought and sold. This water for life, however, has no price. We might ponder the life of Jesus as alternative to the stridency of globalization.

Friday after Epiphany 2

Psalm 31; Genesis 11:27–12:8; Hebrews 7:1–17; John 4:16–26

God of all peoples, let your Spirit teach us about our racist inclinations; let that same Spirit energize us to an alternative identity congruent with your generous governance. In his name. Amen.

The Epistle reading presents Jesus as "a priest forever, according to the order of Melchizedek." This identification trades on the peculiar narrative in Genesis 14 wherein Abraham deals with the priest-king of Salem (Jerusalem). For the writer of the epistle, what counts is that this priest-king comes from nowhere and has no genealogy but is an inexplicable gift from God. The claim made here for Jesus is that he is an heir to this "no-genealogy" priestly order and so works freely and effectively beyond the conventional cultic practices and claims of Judaism. Our Genesis reading attests that Abraham and Sarah have no heir; Sarah is barren! The heir (Isaac) who will be given to them is a gift from God beyond all usual family arrangements.

The Gospel reading has Jesus engage the ethnic contest between Samaritans and Jews. He rejects a future grounded in either ethnic community. Jesus moves deeply beyond racial-ethnic categories in his articulation of God.

This series of texts on genealogy and lack of genealogy invites us to reflect on the role that racial ethnic identity plays in public life in our society. There can be no doubt that the socioeconomic political cards have long been stacked in favor of whites and that our primary assumptions about public life are deeply racist in terms of white supremacy, white superiority, and white privilege. This sequence of texts speaks powerfully against such assumptions and invites us to see that the rule of God, embodied in the life of Jesus, is life beyond such potentially violent identification.

Saturday after Epiphany 2

Psalm 30; Genesis 12:9–13:1; Hebrews 7:18–28; John 4:27–42

Giver of good gifts, give us honesty to acknowledge our profound fear-fulness and then to accept your goodness beyond fear in glad, unencumbered freedom. In his name. Amen.

So much of our lives are grounded in fear; fear causes us to do crazy and ignoble things. In the Genesis reading, Abraham must go to Egypt amid the famine to get food from Pharaoh, who is notorious for his acquisitive inclination. In this narrative Pharaoh desires Sarah because she is "very beautiful." In order to save his own skin in the face of Pharaoh's desire for Sarah, Abraham lies about his status as Sarah's husband. He escapes the risk of hindering Pharaoh's desire, but he exposes Sarah to Pharaoh's sexual aggressiveness. This ignoble report on Abraham is honestly kept in the tradition.

Let us take from the narrative the fact that our life in the world is permeated with self-protective fear that distorts our conduct. We might imagine, even, that our worship is ordered by fear and our sacrifices are offered to God in order to appease God. Or we may consider that even our food is saturated with fear that we will run out or not have enough.

These readings propose that the life offered by Jesus is a life free from distorting fear. On the one hand, the epistle attests worship conducted by Jesus, "a priest forever," who is not defined by usual liturgic protocols. That worship is pure and effective, unlike more familiar liturgic practices. On the other hand, the Gospel reading presents Jesus' offer of food of another kind that is untouched by the usual commercial markings of production and distribution. This narrative may indeed refer to spiritual food of a sacramental order. It nonetheless invites us to ponder gospel food given to us so that we may be unafraid. What a wonder is Jesus who invites us to worship that is not calculated in fear and to food that exposes our assumed scarcity!

Third Sunday of Epiphany

Psalm 63:1–8; Genesis 13:2–18; Galatians 2:1–10; Mark 7:31–37

*God of wonders, break us out of fearful parsimony, that in generosity
we may enact transformations in our daily living. In his name. Amen.*

These texts concern recurring defiance of the ordinary that is
made possible by the power of God. In the Genesis narrative it
would be ordinary for father Abraham to choose the best land
for himself and bequeath to Lot the leftovers. But Abraham
does not do that. Instead he generously permits his nephew
to choose first. One consequence of his generosity is that the
wondrous promise of land and heirs is reiterated to Abraham.

In the epistle, it would be ordinary for the earliest Jewish
Christian community to require circumcision of its Gentile
recruits. But Paul champions a "gospel for the uncircumcised"
because God shows no partiality. In the Gospel narrative, it
would be quite ordinary for the deaf to remain deaf and the
mute never to speak. But Jesus, with his inexplicable authority, refuses that ordinary and gives a deaf man hearing and a
tongue that works properly.

The gospel is inherently subversive of all the ordinary protocols that we assume as tried and true. The oft-reiterated
truth of the gospel is that the power of God is not contained
within the claims of business as usual. In all these cases, the
wonder is an act of generosity that refuses the usual parsimony
of the world. It would have been self-protective parsimony for
Abraham to choose first and best. It would have been parsimonious to limit the gifts of the gospel to the circumcised, to
those who have "qualified." It would have been parsimonious
to deny transformative care to the man with disabilities. We
may ponder how God's extraordinary power may yet unsettle
our settled ordinary.

Monday after Epiphany 3

Psalm 41; Genesis 14:8–24; Hebrews 8:1–13; John 4:43–54

Creator God who brings life out of death and hope out of despair, we pray for the disruption of your restart power in the midst of our own lives. In his name. Amen.

In a score-keeping calculus of quid pro quo, there is no free lunch, no second chance, and no gracious forgiveness. There is no starting over. Much of the world is organized in that way, a way that produces fear, despair, and violence. The news is that by the power of God, there is a second chance, a restart.

The Epistle lesson concerns the restart of covenant wherein the old covenant of Judaism, says the writer, had a "fault." This is a tricky text, because it is not credible to say or think that the Christian movement has superseded Judaism because it had failed. The making of "new covenant" is reiterated enough in the tradition that we may understand it as a renewal of an extant covenant; not a displacement, but a reinvigoration of what had become less than vital. Thus the early followers of Jesus found in the person of Jesus the reinvigoration of the faith of Judaism and its covenant with God. Thus the Christian movement of new covenant can be taken as a movement within Judaism for its reinvigoration.

In the Gospel reading, the son of an official is given a restart, a mending from illness. The narrative is terse and offers testimony about Jesus without explanation. It is enough to see that the power of Jesus brought new life to the son.

These texts offer a chance to consider a restart of life when it has failed or been diminished. The restart requires the freedom of grace, a move beyond scorekeeping, and an interruption of quid pro quo. We may also consider the graceless forces in our world that preclude such restarts.

Tuesday after Epiphany 3

Psalm 47; Genesis 15:1–11, 17–21; Hebrews 9:1–14; John 5:1–18

Well-beloved Son of God, we give you thanks for your transformative presence in the world. Forgive us for too often joining the opposition to your powerful promise-keeping life. In your name. Amen.

The covenant God made with Abraham assures that God's people (first Israel and then the church as well) will live under God's good promise. The promise made to Abraham keeps the future open for possibilities that in human perspective are impossible.

It is the confession of the church that just as the promise of God came to fruition for Israel in Abraham's heirs (see Josh. 21:43–45), so the promise of God came to bodily expression in the person of Jesus. Three things strike one about the Gospel reading. First, the presence of Jesus comes with immense transformative power. In the narrative, Jesus, by his imperative utterance ("Stand up, . . . walk"), restores the man to health. The act is inexplicable. It is a wonder of God's power. Second, Jesus refers to God as "my Father," an address that suggests an inchoate beginning of what became the Trinitarian formulation of the church. To say "my Father" identifies Jesus as the Son or, as his critics here say, "equal to God." It is not abstract thinking but the performance of transformation that pressed the church to confess Jesus as Son of God.

But third, Jesus' action evokes hostility from official leaders who "were seeking all the more to kill him." The reasons they give for their resistance are weak. The real reason for their opposition is that transformative power unsettles the status quo. Jesus did not die because of any theoretical necessity but because he opened the world to the fulfillment of God's initial promises. How odd that transformative power evokes fearful opposition! Who knew?

Wednesday after Epiphany 3

Psalm 119:49–72; Genesis 16:1–14; Hebrews 9:15–28; John 5:19–29

God of life, extend your resurrection power to the failed places of our world; forgive our efforts to ration your will for new life. In his name. Amen.

The barrenness of Sarah causes Sarah to give to Abraham a handmaiden, Hagar. When Hagar bears a son (Ishmael), the unbearable complexity of the triangle arranged by Sarah takes on emotional extremity. Nonetheless this son of Hagar, who is outside the family of promise, receives an immense blessing from God: I will greatly multiply your descendants. The promise operates outside the horizon of the family of covenant. God's future is kept open for outsiders.

The complex statement of the Gospel reading is in response to the healing act of Jesus that evoked mean-spirited hostility. Jesus' action is justified by the affirmation that Jesus bears the power, authority, and freedom of God. As a result, Jesus "gives life to whomever he wishes." In this case, he gives life to a sick man and, speaking of expansive authority, he does so on the Sabbath. God gives life to whom God will, even to the outsider Hagar and her son, Ishmael, the forerunner of Arabs, competitors with Jews.

The claim is that anybody can be a recipient of God's power for life. The negative counterpoint is to recognize that the *administration of life* by human arrangement is not foolproof. Life from God may arise beyond conventional life-giving social arrangements. Every society seeks to control the supply of life. We do it in the church by the administration of the sacraments. We do it politically by voter repression and limiting access. We do it economically by redlining and payday loans. We do it in every way we can. In the end, however, Ishmael is still blessed beyond Sarah's inclination. The man healed on the Sabbath is still healed. Life abounds!

Thursday after Epiphany 3

Psalm 50; Genesis 16:15–17:14; Hebrews 10:1–10; John 5:30–47

God of lively presence, we would not have you trapped in our precious symbolic acts. Show yourself anew to us in emancipated ways that make all things new. In his name. Amen.

The covenant with Abraham, already enacted in Genesis 15, is now given formal ratification. Abraham's family is marked to perpetuity as God's peculiar partner in the world. Circumcision is identified as the sacramental marker of that defining relationship.

The Epistle to the Hebrews accents the novelty and efficaciousness of the life and ministry of Jesus and contrasts his life and ministry with the old saving apparatus of Judaism. The text is unfortunately open to a reading whereby Christian claims have superseded Jewish religious claims that have been rendered obsolete. That, however, is not a necessary reading; one can also see that the several practices of Jewish cultic life—circumcision, Torah reading, the sacrificial system—were all lively and generative sacramental acts. They may, however, like all such symbolic acts, lose their vitality and generative capacity, and become either empty pro forma acts or marks of exclusiveness. While most of Judaism surely experienced better than that, this biblical writer so experienced them. But this is not a peculiarly Christian take on the matter. Clearly the prophets of Israel declared that God had no interest in sacrifice, and our psalm for today affirms that God has no need for our sacrifices.

These readings invite us to consider the ways in which our own cultic practices have grown cold and pro forma or become empty marks of exclusiveness without vitality. As God has provided new ministry in the life of Jesus, we may pray that God's Spirit may provide fresh enlivening modes of covenantal interaction.

Friday after Epiphany 3

Psalm 40; Genesis 17:15–27; Hebrews 10:11–25; John 6:1–15

God of overflowing abundance, give us innocence enough to trust your
abundance, even when we are tempted to fearful scarcity. In his name.
Amen.

God made an outrageous promise to Abraham and Sarah: an
heir and a son in their old age. Abraham is incredulous. But
God raises the ante. Not only will a son be given to Abraham
and Sarah, namely Isaac, but God will also bless Abraham's
other son, Ishmael, the one who belongs only awkwardly in
the scope of promise. God will do future-creating acts that are
beyond the horizon of Abraham. God is not tamed by Abraham's limited, feeble expectation.

The Gospel reading, in very different categories, reiterates
the nature of God's capacity beyond conventional expectation.
How could Jesus have fed five thousand people with a surplus,
when he started with so little? We are not told how. We are
only told that he did.

Both narratives attest the generous capacity of God, who
can readily enact abundance. In the Abraham narrative, God
has the capacity to bless twice, once by providing an heir in
old age and again by promising that the other son will become
"the father of twelve princes." In the Gospel narrative, God
has the capacity of abundance so that loaves may abound. In
both cases, God breaks decisively and wondrously beyond the
scale of scarcity that governs conventional expectation. That
scale of scarcity caused Abraham to doubt. That scale of scarcity caused Andrew to doubt. It is that same scale of scarcity
that has caused biblical interpreters to try to explain away the
wonder performed by Jesus. That same notion of scarcity,
moreover, governs so much of our life in which we greedily,
anxiously assume that there is not enough to go around. Thus
we organize our economy to be sure that some, the vulnerable,
do not have access to limited resources. To such notions, these
texts make a clear, firm response: scarcity is not true!

Saturday after Epiphany 3

Psalm 55; Genesis 18:1–16; Hebrews 10:26–39; John 6:16–27

God, given to us in signs that elude explanation, give us emancipated imagination that we may receive your signs in their full transformative power. In his name. Amen.

The Old Testament and Gospel readings feature two decisive and inexplicable miracles performed by the power of God. In the Old Testament reading, three strangers approach Abraham and Sarah but soon morph into "the LORD" who promises that they, in their old age, will have a son and an heir. Sarah is highly skeptical of such a promise, upon which hang the future of her family . . . and eventually the future of the biblical narrative. In response to Sarah's skeptical laugh, the Lord asks: "Is anything too wonderful [impossible] for the LORD?" The implied certain answer is, No, nothing is impossible for God, not even an heir in old age.

In the Gospel reading, the power of God is performed by Jesus. He walks on water. The narrative is terse. The disciples are frightened, not by the storm but by his abrupt appearance. The appearance of Jesus in his lordly power is beyond explanation. Thus they take him into the boat, but he had not entered the boat. This is no ordinary narrative event but rather testimony to the lordly hidden power of Jesus, who masters the storm. The whole is to be taken as a sign, as an assurance that more and other are operative here than meets the eye. The Jesus narrative is not to be contained within conventional experience, any more than Sarah's old age is an impediment to God's new future.

The Fourth Gospel is making a case that Jesus is indeed the full disclosure of the truth and the power of the Father God, the one who shatters all preconceptions. In both narratives, the wonder of God is mobilized not simply to exhibit God but to transform needful human reality. God's power is in the service of God's generative compassion.

Fourth Sunday of Epiphany

Psalm 24; Genesis 18:16–33; Galatians 5:13–25; Mark 8:22–30

Lord of freedom, grant that we may relish the freedom you give us and that we may use it as you have intended it for us. In his name. Amen.

Paul's great affirmation is that in Christ we are given freedom from all kinds of enslavements, all the way from religious scruples to more ignoble addictions. But Paul immediately provides a specific nuance to the freedom given in Christ. That freedom is given in order to "love your neighbor." That is a very different freedom from narcissistic individualism or from Enlightenment rationality that has morphed into self-indulgent consumerism.

In what follows Paul contrasts the freedom of the gospel and the freedom of unrestrained, self-indulgent individualism. The former enacts the "fruit of the Spirit: love, joy, peace. . . ." The latter type of freedom, so evident in our predatory economy, yields the "works of the flesh . . . : fornication, impurity, licentiousness. . . ." The freedom of Christ must not be confused with the antineighborly ethic that is operative in a self-indulgent culture.

We may judge that Abraham, in this Genesis text, is a daring practitioner of gospel freedom. He has freedom to stand boldly before the Lord, boldly enough to challenge God and to summon God to enact justice. Abraham uses that daring freedom as God's friend on behalf of his nephew Lot, whom we may take here as a stand-in for "neighbor." The demanding negotiation between Abraham and God suggests the readiness of God to be persuaded.

We may well ponder the freedom given us in Christ. It is not freedom to do as we please. Nor is it freedom to be a bystander to the vexed human drama before our eyes. It is rather a freedom to be engaged in daring, demanding ways for the good of the neighborhood. That, of course, is what Jesus did for the blind man. No wonder Peter could see him as "the Christ."

Monday after Epiphany 4

Psalm 56; Genesis 19:1–29; Hebrews 11:1–12; John 6:27–40

God, you always stand before us with a summons to choose differently with our lives. Give us courage and freedom to walk by faith beyond sight. In his name. Amen.

These texts present a series of either-or decisions in which there is no safe middle ground. In the wondrous roll call of the faithful in the Epistle reading, Abraham receives the most expansive coverage. He is championed as a practitioner of trusting faith who moved out on the basis of God's promise; he becomes, along with Sarah, a way to the future, because he did not settle for the circumstance of his old age or the safety of his old dwelling place.

The Old Testament narrative concerning Lot and Sodom is not included in the recital of Hebrews. But Lot made a choice to assure the hospitality of his guests rather than to hand them over to violence.

A decisive either-or is stated in the Gospel reading concerning food that nourishes or food that fails. In the discourse Jesus is that good food, and signing on with Jesus is the decision that is to be made. Thus the either-or in these readings consists in (a) faith or sight, (b) hospitality or accommodation to violence, and (c) food that gives life . . . or not.

The easy choices are always before us to attract us. In our case, such a choice might be to engage in the economic rat race, or to put confidence in the accumulation of commodities, or to participate in fear that is debilitating. The counterchoice might be to resist the rat race of production and consumption, to refuse the security of more things, or to disengage from the fear that so governs our society. The psalmist is clear enough: "In God I trust; I am not afraid."

Tuesday after Epiphany 4

Psalm 61; Genesis 21:1–21; Hebrews 11:13–22; John 6:41–51

*God of our fathers and our mothers, give us grace to tell our true story
and to evade none of its awkward complexities. In his name. Amen.*

The recital of the faithful in Hebrews gives us the normative
canonical list of ancestors from the book of Genesis: Abraham, Isaac, Jacob (and Esau), and Joseph. It is all simple and
straightforward, just the way we might want it. But, of course,
almost every family is more complex and complicated than the
public recital of its canonical narrative. In the case of the family of Abraham, the Genesis account tells us more.

It would have been enough that Isaac was born, a generous
gift of the promise of God. But the story goes on to the complex triangle in which Abraham is enmeshed with Sarah and
Hagar. Sarah, mother of the canonical line, expels Hagar and
her (here unnamed) son. The two are abandoned in the wilderness, and Hagar assumes her child will die. But God hears his
weeping and wills otherwise. The expelled son, unwelcome in
the canonical recital, has a future from God. Hagar is addressed
by God: Fear not. And then follows a promise for Ishmael to
become a great nation. The official recital belongs to Jews, but
the Bible (and the God of the Bible) is never finished with the
Arab counterpoint in the family of promise.

The Gospel reading is clear enough that Jesus is the only
bread that nourishes to eternal life. We may, however, notice
what may be a playful complexity in the text. Jesus is recognized as the son of Joseph. But in his comment, Jesus refers
to God as his father. He does not refute father Joseph, but he
looks elsewhere for his identity. These uses of "father" suggest
that actual lived reality is not simple, direct, and unilateral for
any of us. Allowance must be made for the complex narrative
that is closer to reality than the story we may prefer to tell.

Wednesday after Epiphany 4

Psalm 72; Genesis 22:1–18; Hebrews 11:23–31; John 6:52–59

*Giver of futures beyond our present tense, free us from excessive commit-
ment to the way things are now. In his name. Amen.*

We are given three instances of faith that summons beyond the
world that is immediately in front of us. In the Abraham narrative, the father risks everything in absolute trust in God. He
assures his bewildered son, "God will provide." In the Moses
narrative, Moses trusts beyond the exploitative regime of
Pharaoh and knows that the world does not need to remain as
it was.

Such faith requires imagination that looks beyond the evident. Thus Abraham could anticipate a lamb for an offering.
Moses could imagine a freed people. In the Gospel narrative,
the public whom Jesus addresses has no imagination at all.
They could not recognize that Jesus' speech utilizes bread as a
metaphor for his life, his body. The Gospel reading is surely an
allusion to the sacrament of Communion. As we pray in thanks
after the meal:

> You have fed us with spiritual food
> in the Sacrament of his Body and Blood.°

The language is very careful not to claim too much. And
clearly the reception of bread as "body" is an act of faith. Or as
the tradition of Calvin has it, "Be it according to your faith."†
Faith, in this context, is the capacity to receive bread as body
with all of its salvific, emancipatory force.

But think what it means not to recognize a metaphor! Think
what is lost by being glued to and imprisoned by visible in-hand
reality. Without imagination, everything present is taken as
given, or even as perpetually given. Faith knows otherwise.
Faith knows other kinds of *provision*. Faith knows something of
emancipation. Faith knows another kind of *nourishment*.

°*The Book of Common Prayer* (New York: Seabury Press, n.d.), 365.
†John Calvin, *Institutes of the Christian Religion* 4.17 (Philadelphia: Presbyterian Board
of Christian Education, n.d.), 651.

Thursday after Epiphany 4

Psalm 70; Genesis 23:1–20; Hebrews 11:32–12:2; John 6:60–71

God of all futures, give us courage to trust your good future and so live now toward it. In his name. Amen.

Faith is living forward into the future. The recital of the faithful in the Epistle lesson concerns those who risked everything "in order to obtain a better resurrection." It is a conviction that God has something better in store than the way the world is now organized. The concluding words of the recital contain an imperative that summons the present generation of readers (whenever it is read) to valorize by obedience the risks taken by those brave folk named in the recital. The present will valorize past risks.

The rhetoric of the New Testament and the expectation of the early church easily become otherworldly. But the Old Testament draws us back to the promises of God that will be kept in present life, albeit with a wholly new governance and a new power arrangement.

In the Old Testament reading, Abraham and Ephron the Hittite engage in long, shrewd negotiation over a plot of land. The initial intent is to find a burial place for Sarah. But in subsequent use by exiles, the purchase of land meant that Abraham had already acquired a "possession" in the land of promise with a full deed of title. The exiles have a "purchase" on God's promised future. The story functions as an assurance that God has already begun to keep the land promise to the exiles who had lost their land. This may be an assurance that God is at work now in the world, keeping promises to those who have been excluded from a safe place.

These three readings are an assurance, in this age and the next, that God has good things in store. And we on the receiving end of the promise, are to live in hope and act toward that good future that is as sure as God's own promise.

Friday after Epiphany 4

Psalm 69; Genesis 24:1–27; Hebrews 12:3–11; John 7:1–13

Lord Jesus, who contradicted the empire at great cost, bless us with stamina, courage, and durability, that we may not be easily talked out of our faith. In your name. Amen.

It was dangerous business for the Jesus movement to live in the Roman Empire. It was dangerous because the person and life of Jesus contradicted the empire at every turn. The Gospel reading makes clear that Jesus himself was quite aware of the danger. "The Jews" who opposed him were the Jerusalem leadership that had colluded with Rome, a collusion that is on exhibit during Jesus' final days of trial and execution. Thus he remained in Galilee, his home turf, out of reach of such Jewish authorities. When he did risk going to the city, he did so in private, not in the public way of his later triumphal entry.

The Epistle reading makes clear that the danger about which Jesus knew was a danger faced as well by the early church. The pressure of the empire must have caused many early Christians to compromise in fear. Thus the accent here is on endurance that requires great discipline and intentionality. The text does not urge martyrdom, but it knows that durability in faith is on a collision course with the empire.

These texts invite us to consider the ways in which the gospel contradicts the empire in our own time, perhaps the empire of the national security state in the United States that trades on fear and is committed to a strong military in defense of an unsustainable standard of living. Christians are here not urged to seek trouble. But they are urged to be aware of the ways in which gospel living is at odds with dominant values and of the ways in which those dominant values, by seduction and intimidation, erode the durability of faith. Christians are pressured to give in or to sell out in the face of the contradiction. Suffering, not to say inconvenience, belongs to discipleship.

Saturday after Epiphany 4

Psalm 75; Genesis 24:28–38, 49–51; Hebrews 12:12–29; John 7:14–36

God of upheaval, God of unshakable reliability, give us the wits to see things clearly and to trust you in the face of fear and threat. In his name. Amen.

The epistle employs the old language of "shaking" that refers to a cosmic upheaval and the collapse of cosmic order. The writer anticipates, in apocalyptic rhetoric, that a time of shaking is at hand that will jeopardize established order. It is affirmed that it is God, none other, who shakes up the earth when it has become unbearably disobedient. In the dispute in the Gospel reading, Jesus is identified as the shaker who will bring deep judgment on a corrupt and failed cosmic arrangement.

But the epistle also affirms that there is a "kingdom that cannot be shaken," that is, the rule of God that is not subject to the rhetoric of shaking. The contrast between shaken and unshakable is that one opposes the will of God and the other is the rule of God. The bid is to transfer loyalty and trust from one to the other.

This rhetoric strikes me as pertinent to our own time and place, as we are experiencing a shaking of what was once taken to be reliable. The old order of male domination, white privilege, and Western entitlement is now deeply at risk. This shaking, quite predictably, evokes great hostility from those who are losing their long-standing advantage. It is credible nonetheless to assume that this shaking in our time is authorized by God.

We are invited by these texts to face up to the shaking and then to seek a regime that cannot be shaken, that is, to sign on with the Jesus movement. It is, as we know, his prayer that God's kingdom will come "on earth as it is in heaven" (Matt. 6:10). That is a regime very different from old arrangements.

Fifth Sunday of Epiphany

Psalm 93; Genesis 24:50–67; 2 Timothy 2:14–21; Mark 10:13–22

God of the poor, forgive our endless effort to be in control. Give us mercy that we may travel light in your company. In his name. Amen.

The man in the Gospel narrative asks the right question: eternal life . . . true human destiny? The first answer of Jesus is reassuring: keep the Commandments. The second answer Jesus gives ups the ante: travel light and follow. Locate your treasure. What do you value? What do you value too much? Possessions bespeak security, control, and success, all the things we most prize. The children who are on stage just before the man are likely not possessors of much. Maybe they came to Jesus in innocent expectation. The contrast between the two—a possessive adult and trusting children—sets before us the choice to which the gospel always calls us.

The epistle focuses on speech. Likely the admonition is addressed first of all to preachers and teachers in the church. It expresses, however, a more general concern about chatter that works against us like gangrene; it eats away at our life and our faith. We live in a culture of endless chatter, of relentless loud advertising, of mendacious political rhetoric, of religious talk that is shot through with ideology, and of electronic connections—tweets and cell phones—all of which trivialize reality and create an illusory world. Discipleship requires a reticence that makes an opening for silence in which the goodness of God may be hosted.

The man is summoned to follow Jesus, away from his possessions. The epistle urges readiness for "every good work." Dominant values in our society do not esteem the good work of neighborly practice and policy. Our calling, however, is away from dominant values, by following and by purification, for the sake of another way in the world.

Monday after Epiphany 5

Psalm 80; Genesis 25:19–34; Hebrews 13:1–16; John 7:37–52

God of unchanging fidelity and unfailing reliability, give us courage and energy to do your transformative, emancipatory work in the world. In his name. Amen.

The Epistle reading consists in a series of admonitions for a life that is congruent with the gospel. The list seems to be *ad seriatim* without a governing theme. We may consider the logic of the opening verses in three parts.

First, the ground of this appeal is the reliability of the God known in Jesus. God has promised never to forsake or fail us. Jesus Christ, moreover, is unchanging in fidelity.

Second, in the opening verses we have identified three groups of people that merit generous attention because they are outsiders without protective resources. (a) Strangers are those who are outsiders to the community who are for that reason at risk. Christian love extends hospitality and thereby treats outsiders as insiders. The matter is acute in our time because of our widespread xenophobia. (b) Prisoners were, in the ancient world as in our world, without resources, without good lawyers, and likely to be in debt. The admonition is for intense solidarity with prisoners, "as though you were in prison with them." (c) The ill-treated are those who are dismissed as subhuman and without worth. Among them are those tortured ("in the national interest") and those subject to sexual violence and sex trafficking. All these groups are profoundly at risk and are to receive special attention from the church.

Third, warning is given against "the love of money." It is precisely the love of money, the craving for commodities, that tempts us to neglect and demean those without adequate resources or credentials. When we pursue money, we may regard them as throwaway persons. The hard gospel either-or of God or capital is right in front of us (see Matt. 6:24; Luke 16:13).

Tuesday after Epiphany 5

Psalm 78; Genesis 26:1–6, 12–33; Hebrews 13:17–25; John 7:53–8:11

God of water and food and all life's resources, grant that we may live responsibly and generously, wise in restraint and risking for public neighborliness. In his name. Amen.

The water wars are very old among us and very urgent. On the one hand, the Old Testament text is permeated with the promise of God that had been made to Abraham and Sarah, now reiterated to Isaac. In the midst of famine, Isaac will remain in the land and find water because God has blessed the land; even the Philistines can eventually see that "the LORD has been with you."

The other theme is human competition for scarce water. Isaac is presented as a peaceable man. He does not quarrel with his neighbors who harass him, but he moves on. He does that several times; his land of promise is filled with adequate water.

The upshot of that reality is that he is a peacemaker. He lives in God's abundance and so draws his would-be adversaries to him. Isaac responds to them generously with a peacemaking feast. All ends in peace with the glad affirmation, "We have found water."

We now approach great water wars in which water will be scarcer than oil. The seductions of bottled water only for those who can pay or the lavish use of water for commercial and military purposes turns God's gift into a tradable commodity. There are two issues that concern water and that pertain to responsible faith. First, use of such a gift is best done with great restraint, a restraint that may require a cutback on excessive consumer usage. Second, such resources belong to the entire community and may not be monopolized by the elite who can pay more. Discipleship might focus on such restraint and generous sharing with the vulnerable.

Wednesday after Epiphany 5

Psalm 119:97–120; Genesis 27:1–29; Romans 12:1–8; John 8 12–20

God of durable promises, we thank you for the long company of compro-
mised carriers of the gospel, among whom we are glad to count ourselves.
In his name. Amen.

There is something highly ironic about the juxtaposition of
these readings from the epistle and the Old Testament. The
Epistle reading features Paul's most impressive catalog of
practices for Christian conduct as a consequence of the grace
of God. He urges a life that is genuinely enacted for the well-
being of the neighbor beyond self-interest. By contrast the Old
Testament reading features a particular family that is beset by
manipulative intrigue, perhaps not unlike many family systems
that have unresolved tension and competing expectations for
the future of the family. In this case mother Rebekah conspires
to deceive father Isaac and so to gain the blessing for her favorite younger son. But Paul and his bold faith are only possible
because he is an heir to that family of intrigue and conspiracy,
without whom there would be no continuing tale of gospel.

The learning we may gain is that the promises of God, the
very ones to which Paul appeals in Romans 4, are carried in the
memory of Genesis by the family of Abraham that is a mixed
lot of deception, manipulation, and ignoble cunning.

The upshot may be to recognize the wonder that the truth
of the gospel is kept alive by compromised carriers like us. Out
of that compromised company has come a vision of a differently ordered humanity, one with renewed minds committed
to generosity and hospitality. Paul well understood that the
power and energy of the gospel are not carried by only good
people but may be carried by the seemingly disqualified who
do not measure up to noble norms. This may give us generosity
toward other carriers and patience even with ourselves.

Thursday after Epiphany 5

Psalm 83; Genesis 27:30–45; Romans 12:9–21; John 8:21–32

God of both younger and older, both blessed and betrayed, give us largeness of spirit to violate the usual norms of retaliation. In his name. Amen.

The manipulative intrigue of mother Rebekah works effectively to the great advantage of Jacob, her favorite younger son. Only belatedly does Isaac discover, to his great anguish, that his younger son has betrayed the family and his older brother, Esau.

The pathos of the betrayed father is echoed by his bewildered firstborn, Esau, who has been robbed of his future by his brother. In his shocked awareness and forlornness, he wonders to his father if there is only one blessing. But father Isaac has yet another blessing. It is less than the first blessing, but it is nonetheless significant. Insofar as the Esau-Jacob narrative is read as an anticipatory parable of the future of Arabs and Jews, the work of the narrative is that the blessing is not monopolized by Jacob, a stand-in for Jews. There is a second blessing from God for Esau, surrogate for Arabs. The promise of God given by Isaac is a double promise. While Jacob receives a promise of the fatness of the land with ample grain and wine, Esau is blessed with freedom, without need to be subservient to Jacob.

By the end of the narrative Jacob flees for his life at the behest of his mother because she anticipates that Esau will seek lethal vengeance. The mother, however, underestimates her older son. He is not a killer. He does not go after Jacob. He does not seek revenge. To our great surprise, he violates the law of vengeance, perhaps in anticipation of Paul's final imperative, "Never avenge yourselves." Esau breaks the cycle of vengeance and eventually will generously offer Jacob a covenant of peace. This story is bigger than Jacob's cunning theft. The larger vista is a move beyond the provincial dimension of chosenness.

Friday after Epiphany 5

Psalm 88; Genesis 27:46–28:4, 10–22; Romans 13:1–14; John 8:33–47

God of urgent wake-up calls, awaken us from our comfortable, indiffer-
ent slumber. Let us be alert for living in ways that honor you and that
valorize every neighbor we meet. In his name. Amen.

Jesus' opponents are very proud of their pedigree. They keep
reiterating that they belong to the family of Abraham. Jesus,
however, disputes their claim, because the authentic children
of Abraham will adhere to truth, and he is the embodiment of
truth. The truth to which he summons his opponents to live is
beyond the enslavements of sin, for his way of discipleship is
a way of generous freedom that leads one to live in sync with
God's will.

The epistle details what it is like to live in sync with the
truth of God. Paul enumerates the Commandments, a list that
implies other commandments that are not enumerated. That
list of commandments, however, is bracketed by the most
important accent:

> Before the list: "love one another."
> After the list: "love your neighbor as yourself." Love
> does no wrong to another.

The truth is all about neighborly love, which is the accent that
a boastful pedigree seems to omit.

Paul regards that core commandment as a wake-up call. It is
time now to awaken from sleep. Paul addresses those in Rome
who have been narcotized. And the opponents of Jesus in the
Gospel reading have likewise been narcotized. As perhaps
we also have been narcotized by social practices and assumptions that have normalized ways of living that do not love the
neighbor. Paul calls such living the "works of darkness." Even
a glance at our society, with its predatory economy, its exclusionary politics, and its disregard of the vulnerable, will make
clear that such works of darkness are deeply antithetical to the
freedom of the gospel. When we awaken, we are empowered
to clothe ourselves in the light of neighborliness.

Saturday after Epiphany 5

Psalm 87; Genesis 29:1–20; Romans 14:1–23; John 8:47–59

*Living Lord of the church, give us grace to recognize that you (and not
we) are arbiter of the great ends of the church and of the small issues
that arise among us. Let us fall back, in the midst of our passionate
quarrels, into your bottomless generosity. In your name. Amen.*

In the epistle, Paul faces the concrete reality of the church
that persists in pettiness in, with, and under all its theological
claims and its missionary passion. The result is that the church
is beset with endless conflict and quarrels about which folk
feel very strongly. Paul offers his wisdom concerning how the
church lives faithfully amid such tensions.

The challenge is that in the church we tend to escalate and
absolutize every quarrel as though the whole truth of the gospel depended on our being right. Paul is aware of the immense
diversity in the church (and in local congregations) and the
depth of religious scruple. He particularly singles out for attention the traditional matter of ritually clean and unclean food,
but the question could have been on any specific matter. In our
own time such powerful scruples have concerned matters of
sexuality. Paul urges respect for such scruples but also insists
that such respect for those with scruples does not concede any
real authority to such claims, only a neighborliness that permits shared well-being.

The particulars of the argument are framed by Paul in a
larger vision. With reference to God, all members of the church
belong to Christ, obey him, and trust him. With reference to
fellow members of the body, the goal is not about being right
or winning or having one's own way. It is rather about mutual
up-building, a matter that requires valorizing the other and
yielding on such points of scruple. The invitation is to large-
hearted generosity rooted in gratitude in recognition that the
point of most quarrels is not definitional for faith.

Sixth Sunday of Epiphany

Psalm 66; Genesis 29:20–35; 1 Timothy 3:14–4:10; Mark 10:23–31

Good God of impossibilities, forgive our timorous notions of what is possible; grant us to trust the generativity of your impossibilities even in our own lives. In his name. Amen.

The narrative of Leah in the Genesis reading concerns the gift of sons when she had been "unloved." In naming these unexpected sons, Leah refers their births to the power of God:

Reuben: "The LORD has looked on my affliction."
Simeon: "The LORD has heard that I am hated."
Judah: "I will praise the LORD."

The births are reckoned in the narrative as impossible, but the impossible has happened by the power of God. Another "impossibility" is at the center of the Gospel narrative: the rich will be welcomed into the kingdom. Either way, it is the power of God that makes difference for those who cannot otherwise enter the kingdom.

That transformative power of God is the truth of God embodied in the life of Jesus and entrusted to the church. The church is the "pillar and bulwark of the truth." The utterance and performance of that truth contradicts the pretend truth of the world. For the world readily assumes that what is *apparently* impossible—like unexpected births, like entry of the rich into the kingdom of God—is in fact impossible. But now we know: such "impossibilities" are possible because God is good. Everything created by God is good. And that goodness can be received in thanksgiving. That triad of *truth, goodness, thanksgiving* marks the life of the church and makes it peculiar in a society that specializes in falseness, that dismisses many of God's creatures as dispensable because they are not good, and that is incapable of gratitude. We do well to consider the impossibilities of which God is capable.

Monday after Epiphany 6

Psalm 89:1–18; Genesis 30:1–24; 1 John 1:1–10; John 9:1–17

It is an immense joy when we sing to you, gracious God, "I was blind, but now I see." As we see more clearly, give us courage to follow more nearly. In his name. Amen.

Stumbling around in the dark can be dangerous business. Turning on the light eliminates the risk and permits us to see. The Epistle reading plays with the image of God as light.

"Walking in the light" is glad obedience to Jesus and fellowship with the church community. The Gospel narrative takes the instance of the blind man to make a decisive point: Jesus, the light, lets us see!

Jesus the light lets us see God as God is, for Jesus has embodied and disclosed the reality of God. When we see God in Jesus, we know that God is faithful and just, that God makes and keeps promises, that God embraces the world in love and wills its well-being. When we do not see God as shown in Jesus, we are likely to misperceive God, perhaps as a cream-puff imitation of ourselves writ large or perhaps as a demanding tyrant who operates on the basis of fear. Seeing God as God is permits us to trust daily in the goodness of God.

Jesus the light lets us see the world as it is, for Jesus has disclosed to us the reality of the world. That world is loved by the Creator, given generative power for a sustainable life. The world is seen to be an arena for the practice of justice, mercy, and faithfulness. When we do not see the world as shown to us by Jesus, we are likely to misperceive the world, perhaps as a hostile place of fear and danger or perhaps as our private domain to use and abuse as we think best. Distorted vision concerning God and the world is a ready temptation to us, a temptation propelled by distorting propaganda and self-serving ideologies that preclude joyous life in creation, generosity toward the neighbor, and attentiveness to the well-being of creation.

Tuesday after Epiphany 6

Psalm 97; Genesis 31:1–24; 1 John 2:1–11; John 9:18–41

Giver of new vision, overcome our resistant blindness. Give us fresh vision that we may discern worldly reality through the lens of suffering love. In his name. Amen.

The Gospel reading is thick with playful meaning. The up-front plot concerns giving sight to a blind man. This wonder attests to the authority of Jesus. We are given two affirmations concerning that authority. First, "If this man were not from God, he could do nothing." The clear evidence is that he is indeed from God. Second, Jesus' purpose is "that those who do not see may see." He is a giver of new sight.

But the simple plot of restoration is transposed into a disruptive narrative in which Jesus is engaged in conversation with his opponents who are here called "the Jews." In fact they are the leadership that is completely committed to the status quo who found Jesus' transformative work a threat to their status as leaders.

These opponents of Jesus do their best to discredit him: he has no pedigree and we do not know where he came from. He healed on the Sabbath. In the end, it dawns on some of the Pharisees that they have been trapped in the dispute and finally must face themselves. They begin to recognize that they are involved in an interaction that is not merely a debate about the status of the blind man. They begin finally to wonder about themselves and their role in the drama: "Are we also blind?" And the answer is, "No, you are not blind. If blind, you would have an excuse for not seeing the evidence of Jesus' power. You are guilty because you have seen and should have known better than to refuse the power of God." The story is an invitation to move beyond our treasured status quo in order to engage the transformative power that is in our midst in the person of Jesus. They should have known better. We also should know better.

LENT

Ash Wednesday

Psalm 95; Amos 5:6–15; Hebrews 12:1–14; Luke 18:9–14

Lord of neighborly justice, give us honesty in this season of Lent to be more fully engaged in the public good. In his name. Amen.

We live in a culture that caters to its privileged children in every way thinkable. That often means that children lack the discipline necessary to grow into responsible adulthood. Lack of discipline leads to narcissistic selfishness and indulgence. But Lent, against such a cultural propensity, is a call to discipline. This Epistle reading uses the word "discipline" no fewer than nine times. The writer appeals to the image of a parent disciplining a child. It was, in that ancient society, the work of a parent to discipline the child so that the child could grow up to be a responsible and trustworthy member of the family.

The question of discipline surfaces in the prophetic poem of Amos. The undisciplined in ancient Israel, says the poet, "trample on the poor." They did so by sharp market dealings, by bribery, and by skewed judicial procedures "in the gate." All these exploitative practices were in the service of self-indulgence, to satiate one's appetite at the expense of the vulnerable.

In the face of such exploitation, Amos utters a series of imperatives that are in sum a summons to discipline. Thus he says, in terse sequence, "Seek the Lord," "seek good," "hate evil," "love good," "establish justice." These are the principal neighborly disciplines that connect the purpose of God to the urgency of neighborly well-being.

Lent, which begins today, is a season of discipline that calls us away from indifferent self-indulgence that takes place through antineighborly practice. The issue for Amos is greed in the marketplace. These calls to discipline move beyond private piety to public practice. We are, in Lent, not unlike the tax collector in Jesus' parable, cognizant of our sin in public practice.

First Thursday of Lent

Psalm 37:1–18; Habakkuk 3:1–10, 16–18;
Philippians 3:12–21; John 17:1–8

God of all futures, give us the tenacity to hope, that we may not give in to fear, despair, or cynicism. In his name. Amen.

In the Epistle reading, Paul sets up a sharp either-or that contrasts "they" with "we." "They" are "enemies of the cross." The cross of Jesus expresses the self-giving love that is willing to suffer for the sake of the neighbor. The enemies of the cross are those who refuse such self-giving love and sign on with the empire of Rome that will finally execute Jesus in order to silence criticism and maintain a system of greed and exploitation. Thus the cross becomes a contestation between self-giving love and the empire of greedy oppression.

Paul imagines that we, all of us, are on one side or the other. "They" (enemies of the cross) take their "belly" (insatiable appetite) as god, are unashamed of their boastful living, and pursue worldly possessiveness. By contrast "we" (advocates of the cross and its performance of self-giving love) live in hope of the new governance of God. Paul's rhetoric assumes that a decisive choice has been made by the faithful.

In the poem of Habakkuk, the vivid poetic rhetoric anticipates the powerful coming of God that works cataclysmic disaster on the enemies of God. But the faithful are commended to hope in God, even in the face of shattering trouble that is sure to come. The final verses of the Old Testament poem witness to the tenacity of hope in the coming rule of God that does not flinch in the face of big trouble. The threefold "though" of the poem faces into reality of immense loss: *though* fig trees fail, *though* olives fail, *though* sheep fail, that is, though the entire agricultural economy fails . . . *nevertheless* (yet!) those who hope count on God and rejoice. The "we" of the community of hope is unflappable in the face of big trouble. The last act is joy!

First Friday of Lent

Psalm 95; Ezekiel 18:1–4, 25–32; Philippians 4:1–9; John 17:9–19

God of righteous expectation and generous self-giving, grant that we may change our conduct in order to dwell in your generous peaceableness. In his name. Amen.

It was then, as it is now, a time of profound anxiety. It was then, as it is now, a time of ominous violence and unreliable economics in which the social fabric was so frayed that all were at risk. In the face of such social reality, Paul commends having no anxiety "about anything." In the place of anxiety, Paul commends peace with God. Paul knows that being right with God is more urgent than all our strategies of self-maintenance and self-security. Paul knows, moreover, that peace with God is beyond all our categories of explanation; it surpasses all understanding.

For many of us the question is, how do we arrive at peace with God? The answer, already given in the testimony of Ezekiel, is to turn away from transgression. In the Ezekiel text, in verses we have skipped over, the prophet details three dimensions of the turn to God: first, reject idolatry, the worship of phony ultimates. Second, reject exploitative sexuality that treats others as objects rather than persons. Third, reject economic exploitation that regards neighbors as usable commodities. In all three instances, live in the risky world of persons rather than in the controlled world of things. Behind these three instances is the awareness that such commoditization of sexuality and economics leads to the commoditization of God as an object to be controlled. The relentless insistence of the Bible is that peace with God depends on right neighborly conduct. It is for that reason that Paul commends "whatever is true," "honorable," "just," "pure," lovely, and gracious. The news is that God delights in life that flourishes: "turn . . . and live!"

First Saturday of Lent

Psalm 30; Ezekiel 39:21–29; Philippians 4:10–20; John 17:20–26

God of all our pluses and minuses, give us freedom to submit our lives to your goodness. In his name. Amen.

Lent is a time to sort out what we know. It strikes me that these readings pivot on what can be known and what we know in the gospel. In the Ezekiel passage, the "nations shall know." They will learn of God by observing the life of Israel. They shall know, by the exile of Israel, that God is not mocked. Moreover, they shall know, by the restoration and gathering of Israel, that God is faithful.

In the prayer of Jesus, the glory of Christ, given in his crucifixion and resurrection, is given in order that the world may know that Jesus is the full self-giving of God. That crucifixion and resurrection are together the reperformance of the old wonder of the scattering and gathering of Israel. The nations will know God as they have not known God, when the life story of Jesus is seen as a narrative of profound divine love.

Out of knowledge of God, who scatters and gathers, and knowledge of Jesus, who is crucified and risen, Paul knows the pastoral secret of living in the world. He knows that in a world governed and ordered by God, who supplies every need, the external circumstance of more or less is not definitional for well-being. What is definitional is the assurance that God's gracious governance pertains to every circumstance of our life. The consequence of this secret is the awareness (that Paul surely shared) that practical differentiations of plenty and want are only provisional and not definitive for us. The assurance of all these modes of knowledge is that the generous self-giving graciousness of God outstrips our categories. It is enough to be in God's hands!

First Sunday of Lent

Psalm 63:1–8; Daniel 9:3–10; Hebrews 2:10–18; John 12:44–50

We praise you, God of history, that you overturn our failed reality by your self-giving that makes us new. In his name. Amen.

These readings articulate the enormous differential between God and all of us. God is attested in the prayer of Daniel as one "keeping covenant and steadfast love," as God of "mercy and forgiveness." In the Epistle reading, Jesus is the high priest who is "merciful and faithful." This rhetoric of fidelity is deeply rooted in our oldest covenant memory.

By contrast, Israel suffers from "open shame" in its recalcitrant disobedience and treachery; more broadly, in the epistle, human persons in fear of death live in bondage. The bondage of fear is all around us. It is that fear and open shame that governs so much of our interaction and that shapes so much of our public policy.

Lent is a time to overcome the romanticism of human self-actualization to recognize the unflinching honesty of the theological tradition that sees how we are deeply alienated from God. These readings, however, do not linger over the human condition. Rather they focus on the wonder of God's ready capacity to bridge the gap of alienation by self-giving suffering in Christ. Given this huge contrast of Creator and creation, the news is that from God's side, God in Jesus becomes like us "in every respect" so that we are drawn into the faithfulness of God, moved from the darkness of futility and drawn into the abiding well-being of his light.

It is appropriate in Lent to think through the deep alienation of creatureliness from the Creator. Such reflection is not a guilt trip but an act of self-awareness. These readings, however, move forcefully to the greater reality that God in Christ has overcome that alienation and ended the bondage of fear. A new life beyond alienation is made possible. But it must be lived!

Monday after Lent 1

Psalm 41; Genesis 37:1–11; 1 Corinthians 1:1–19; Mark 1:1–13

God of generous sustenance, we thank you for good angels who sustain us beyond our own fearful control. In his name. Amen.

The narrative rendering of the temptation of Jesus has a curious and wondrous ending. It is reported on the one hand that Jesus is tempted by Satan. The offer of the devil has a certain attractiveness for him. But alternatively, angels minister to him. Jesus is situated between satanic temptation and angelic sustenance. He finds the sustenance dispatched by God via angels to be more than adequate. It is a wonder that in the face of temptation, there is alternative sustenance.

These readings may move us promptly from the narrative of Jesus to the concrete reality of heavy contestation about which we know in both tradition and experience. In the Genesis narrative, Joseph yields to the temptation to dream himself superior to his older brothers. In the epistle, it is clear that dissension in the church arose when one party in the Christian community imagined itself superior to other brothers and sisters in faith. It is possible to think that for Joseph and for early church partisans, the temptation to be first and know best is indeed the work of Satan, who seeks to disrupt the family of Jacob and to disrupt the fellowship of the church. Clearly in the long tradition of the church, that same temptation has been destructively effective.

But imagine that in the midst of every such temptation to be first and know best, there are ministering angels. These angels of nourishment remind us that we are dependent on someone other than ourselves and that we live by inexplicable gifts that show up in our several wildernesses. Lent may be a time to notice and cherish ministering angels.

Tuesday after Lent 1

Psalm 47; Genesis 37:12–24; 1 Corinthians 1:20–31; Mark 1:14–28

God of weak foolish governance, we thank you for your transformative power that makes a way out of no way. We thank you that you have entrusted that inexplicable power even to us. In his name. Amen.

The presence of Jesus poses the question, What counts for real and effective power in the world? What figures as genuine authority? In the Gospel narrative, Jesus teaches and heals with an inexplicable authority. His capacity is unlike that of the "scribes" who are the learned authorities but who in fact have no capacity for transformative power. They are custodians of the status quo.

Paul takes up the same issue of authority. He writes of the conventional authority of the scribes who are credentialed with social authority based on "wisdom." But then he contradicts such conventional authority by the self-giving authority of Jesus, who seemed foolish and weak but who was in truth laden with uncommon authority to effect positive change.

In the Gospel narrative, Jesus calls four fishermen to be his followers and to participate in his peculiar authority. Paul also carries the case for alternative power from Jesus to the Christian community. The church, when it is faithful, does not specialize in worldly wisdom or worldly power. It is a community of the foolish, the weak, and the uncredentialed. It turns out, however, that in Jesus' own life and in the life of the faithful church, real power to transform is not administered by learning or by leverage but by self-giving presence. That self-giving presence from time to time has brought to naught the exploitative power and too-certain knowledge. These texts invite us to consider our own exercise of this peculiar transformative power for the sake of our part of the world.

Wednesday after Lent 1

Psalm 119:49–72; Genesis 37:25–36;
1 Corinthians 2:1–13; Mark 1:29–45

Lord Jesus, who came among us making all things new, come again among us in your inscrutable ways and make new in our world of need. In your name. Amen.

It is a suggestive exercise to read the Old Testament lesson through the lens of Paul's eloquent testimony in the epistle. Paul juxtaposes the wisdom of men with the power of God. In the Joseph narrative, the older brothers of the brother-baiting Joseph exercise such "wisdom of men." By stealth the brothers conspire to sell Joseph to slave traders, thereby maintaining their preeminence in the family and eliminating the threat of Joseph, with his dangerous dream. But they have not reckoned with the power of God, who will take this "crucified" younger brother and inexplicably raise him to new life in the kingdom of Egypt. The hidden, inscrutable power of God can outflank the best human calculation.

It is, of course, not different in the Gospel narrative. Conventional human wisdom anticipated the permanent disability of all kinds of people and counted on the social differentiation between the clean and the unclean. They did not think that social arrangement could be altered; they did not want change. But the testimony to Jesus is that he is a carrier of the power of God. He moves into contexts of disability and uncleanness, and by his presence, his word, and his touch, he makes all things new. The power of God is a wild card amid the social schemes we devise, suggesting that newness can come in unexpected ways.

We live in a society that has confidence in technological fixes and economic leverage that have sorted out futures for winner and losers. But God has a purpose other than our arrangements and an inexplicable capacity to change what cannot be changed. We may find ourselves recruited for the power of God. Vigilance is required!

Thursday after Lent 1

Psalm 50; Genesis 39:1–23; 1 Corinthians 2:14–3:15; Mark 2:1–12

God in whose hand are all our times, give us a proper sense of your speed so that we know when it is wise to hurry and when prudent to wait. In his name. Amen.

The gospel has more than one speed in its effective impact. "Immediately" is a favorite term of the Gospel of Mark. In this episode we are told that Jesus counters his critics; "immediately" he heals the paralyzed man. The man "immediately" went out, healed. There is an instantaneous effect of Jesus' ministry, according to Mark. No waiting, no delay, no indecision!

By contrast, the imagery Paul employs to counsel the church amid dissension and dispute suggests longtime careful planning and execution that can take place only over extended time. He uses the image of planting that takes a long season of growth and maturation. He uses the image of a building that must be constructed step-by-step from the ground up. Neither process can be hurried. Paul is willing to let the church community develop over time without rush. The Joseph narrative is framed at the beginning and at the end with the affirmation that "the LORD was with him." For that reason the narrative between can take its time.

The great German pastor Johann Christoph Blumhardt famously counseled his companions in faith to "hasten and wait." The phrase catches both the urgency of the Gospel lesson and the slow processes of the imagery of Paul. There is a time of urgency for faith when action must be taken, and there is a time for watching and waiting until the time is right. Lent is a time to reflect on our several inclinations about hurrying and waiting. Some of us are impatient all the time. Others of us are inclined to watch and wait all the time. Faith requires us to have more than one speed and to know when context and circumstance require speeding up or slowing down.

Friday after Lent 1

Psalm 95; Genesis 40:1–23; 1 Corinthians 3:16–23; Mark 2:13–22

God of all our futures, give us openness to your dreams, to prefer your newness and to resist the nightmares of coercion, exclusion, and injustice all around us. In his name. Amen.

Joseph, the proto-Israelite, specializes in dreams. Here he interprets two dreams; later on he will interpret two dreams for Pharaoh when his own intelligence community cannot read the dreams. These dreams are looking forward. They are not, in Freudian fashion, looking back to repression. They rather anticipate what is to come from the providence of God. Such dreaming is the capacity to receive newness from God when there is no firm evidence in hand. It is that newness to which Jesus calls Levi, a newness radically beyond his old life of exploitation.

We live in an ideological frame of reference that assumes it can contain, in scientific technological horizon, all possible futures, and that wants to limit any dreaming beyond. Thus dreaming forward is a highly subversive enterprise amid such an ideology of control. Two thoughts occur to me about such dreaming. On the one hand, the well-remembered "dream speech" of Martin Luther King is an instance of high anticipation of God's future. King hoped for and lived toward the new historical reality that God intends. On the other hand, Ta-Nehisi Coates has reminded us that the "American Dream" in common parlance is a white dream of uncommon comfort and well-being that depends on the cheap labor of others. We exclude others from access. That mode of dream, he shows, is indeed a nightmare for many others.

Lent is a time when we may probe our capacity to dream, our readiness to embrace new worldly possibilities that are congruent with the purposes of God. We may, moreover, reflect on the killers of the dream who employ many strategies to prevent newness and maintain the status quo.

Saturday after Lent 1

Psalm 95; Genesis 41:1–13; 1 Corinthians 4:1–7; Mark 2:23–3:6

How strange and how wondrous that your mighty governance has come to us in the form of a servant! Give us imagination to see how ruling power can be exercised in generative ways. In his name. Amen.

Here are three texts concerning issues of leadership and the making of a viable social life. Paul's defense of his ministry is articulated under the rubric of steward, one who manages the property of another. Paul champions his own modesty and humility in contrast to his detractors who are "puffed up" in self-importance. Paul challenges them by declaring that everything we have is a gift from God, not a ground for self-importance.

Behind Paul's dispute about leadership is the dispute Jesus has with the Pharisees. In contrast to their adherence to religious scruple, Jesus asserts that his work is for "humankind," that is, for human well-being. His test case here is his readiness to violate Sabbath scruple for the sake of well-being.

Further behind Paul is the case of Joseph. In his transposition from slave to Pharaoh's steward, Joseph is abruptly "restored to office." In the narrative that follows, Joseph is an administrator of food to sustain Pharaoh and his subjects. In light of his monopolistic food policies, we may wonder about his kind of leadership.

We may consider from these texts what constitutes the common good, and what kind of leadership is essential for it? The question pertains to both the church and civil society. Issues of the common good are much contested among us, as they were in the cases of Joseph, Jesus, and Paul. Lent is a time to consider Jesus as servant-Lord. Followers of this servant-Lord have a crucial role to play in support of the common good.

Second Sunday of Lent

Psalm 2; Genesis 41:14–45; Romans 6:3–14; John 5:19–24

You are the God who presides over our deaths and who gives us new life.
Our hope is in no other, save in you alone. In his name. Amen.

There is a strange, disquieting tension between the Epistle reading and the Old Testament lesson. Paul's lyrical testimony concerns the way in which the crucifixion and resurrection of Jesus are reperformed in the life of a baptized person. As Jesus was crucified, so the old self is made dead to sin. As Jesus was raised from the dead, so the baptized are raised to new selves.

In a parallel way, Joseph is indeed raised to new life. The narrative is careful to credit his transformation from slave to steward to the power of God. Given that attribution of new life to the power of God, it is evident that much of his elevation to power is the work of Pharaoh. In the end, moreover, Joseph is given the insignia of office by Pharaoh and he rules on behalf of Pharaoh.

Perhaps all of that is nonetheless divine providence. But I am suspicious. I suggest that Joseph's narrative of old self in slavery to new life in power is accomplished at the behest of Pharaoh. Pharaoh is in fact credited with the change, and so he can rightly expect Joseph to look after his interests. If his transformation is in fact the work of Pharaoh, without attentiveness to YHWH, we may suggest that it is a fake transformation that is accomplished by the ruler of this age. We may consider that such fake transformation is a poor substitute for gospel transformation. Such fake transformations are all around us: political advancement, economic enrichment, academic credentialing, or transformation by a technological advance or a new consumer product, any one of which may feature a "new self." A genuinely new self, however, is a result of fresh grace; there is no substitute for that.

Monday after Lent 2

Psalm 56; Genesis 41:46–57; 1 Corinthians 4:8–20; Mark 3:7–19a

Lord Jesus, who calls to discipleship, give us freedom to follow you, to live into the contradiction that you pose in the world. In your name. Amen.

It may be that Paul is engaged in a bit of self-pity, attesting how much his ministry has cost him: "As though sentenced to death, . . . fools for the sake of Christ. . . . We are weak, . . . in disrepute. . . . We are hungry and thirsty, we are poorly clothed and beaten and homeless."

But it is this stance of weakness and foolishness that has permitted him to practice an extraordinary life: "We bless; . . . we endure; . . . we speak kindly." In doing this work, Paul is, like the disciples called in the Gospel reading, endowed with great authority to cast out demons and restore the world to its good sense. It is amazing that Paul—and those disciples—are taxed with a ministry that has immense public significance. They are all to *follow* Jesus, just as Paul asks his partners to *imitate* him in a way of life that contradicts the world of coercive power.

It may be too much to hang on one word, but I am struck by the report that Joseph, as Pharaoh's food czar, *sold* food during a severe famine. Pharaoh, we know, will have a monopoly on food. It was, however, no state policy that there should be a grant of free food to desperately hungry people. Food was regarded as a commodity for buying and selling, a form of social power.

We are in a society now engaged in a mighty contest between the *practice of social life as a commodity* in which there is no free lunch and the *practice of social life as a mode of giving.* The gospel is a summons, as with Paul, to an alternative way.

Tuesday after Lent 2

Psalm 61; Genesis 42:1–17; 1 Corinthians 5:1–8; Mark 3:19b–35

God of good gifts, give us courage to trade off the old habits of self-centeredness, to yield ourselves to your call to devout and holy life. In his name. Amen.

Paul is confronted by a case of sexual misconduct about which the perpetrator brags. Paul has a vision of the gospel community as a fellowship that has purged from its midst such exploitative practices. Such misconduct is never an isolated act; it comes with a cluster of self-indulgent practices that are rooted in anxious greed that characteristically culminates in violence. These are the "desires of the flesh" to which Paul contrasts "the fruit of the Spirit" (Gal. 5:16–26). The arrogance about the affront makes clear that the community has compromised the norm that Paul champions and has arrived at a capacity for shamelessness in imitation of a larger society that traffics in shamelessness.

For the nature of the community, Paul utilizes the image of leaven. By this usage he recalls that it was unleavened bread that ancient Israel ate in its hasty departure from Egyptian slavery. The mention of the "paschal lamb" and the "festival" attest that the early church has departed the shameless habits of greed and exploitation that mark the empire of Egypt and belatedly the empire of Rome. The imagery is a reminder that the community gathered around Jesus is indeed an alternative community in which the conduct of its members matters for its testimony to the world. Clearly compromised conduct, when visible in the church, undermines the claim and the news that the church intends to perform for the world to see.

Given this exodus allusion, we may note the somewhat remote connection that the sons of Jacob must return and submit to Egyptian authority for the sake of food. Such bread, with old leaven, is seductive and may talk the community out of its vocation of holiness.

Wednesday after Lent 2

Psalm 72; Genesis 42:18–28; 1 Corinthians 5:9–6:8; Mark 4:1–20

Lord of the church and governor of the nations, we pray for wisdom that might include the shrewdness of Joseph and the compassion of gospel truth. In your name. Amen.

Joseph is practicing the rough art of statecraft, testing the suppliants who have come to him for food. But he is also toying with his brothers, secretly working revenge on them by keeping them in suspense and letting them experience the danger of being before him.

By contrast, Paul continues his rigorous instruction to the Corinthian Christian community. He makes a sharp contrast between those inside the church community who are held to a higher moral expectation and those outside the church. He urges that because of a more radical ethic, the church will do well to maintain its own discipline.

The juxtaposition of these texts poses the difficult question of the relationship between a public ethic that governs both the state and the corporate world, and a more intense ethic that guides the church. On the one hand, Reinhold Niebuhr has famously allowed that much more latitude is to be recognized in the public domain, as public affairs require greater "realism" about issues of justice, unlike the church, with its more insistent requirement of mercy and compassion. On the other hand, Stanley Hauerwas more recently, in a sustained appeal to the "peace church" tradition, refuses such a sharp distinction and expects more in the public sphere.

This is an issue with which Christians must be engaged, especially since our public economy has largely been taken over by an oligarchy of wealth that skews all social relationships and that readily leaves behind those it judges to be dispensable. Paul seems to want an exclusive focus on the church. In our time we might do well to require more of the state and the world of corporations.

Thursday after Lent 2

Psalm 70; Genesis 42:29–38; 1 Corinthians 6:12–20; Mark 4:21–34

Creator of our bodily reality, give us gratitude for our bodily life together, and generosity toward the bodily life of others. In his name. Amen.

These readings invite reflection on our bodies, on the bodily, material reality of our lives, on the body politic, and on the church as the body of Christ. The convergence of these points witnesses against every seduction of the excessive romanticism or spirituality of our faith.

Paul summons to reflection on the body by three questions, "Do you not know," that have a tone of reprimand about them:

> "Do you not know that your bodies are members of Christ?"
> "Do you not know that whoever is united to a prostitute becomes one body with her?"
> "Do you not know that your body is a temple of the Holy Spirit?"

All these questions and their implied answers attest that bodily participation in the life of Christ — by purity and by discipline — is a way to glorify God.

The Genesis reading is a negotiation about the body of Jacob's well-beloved son Benjamin. It matters who has control over the body of the boy. Joseph, the unrecognized son, and Jacob, the sad father, negotiate over the body of the boy.

In Jesus' parables, Jesus speaks of the coming kingdom by way of creaturely reality, first seed to scatter and then mustard seed to grow. The kingdom of God is not an idea; it is a visible, palpable, bodily reality.

These readings invite us to attend to our bodies, how we care for them, where we invest them, how we share them. They also invite us to consider the neighbors' bodies in ways that lead to socioeconomic, political issues, how to assure bodily well-being for all.

Friday after Lent 2

Psalm 95; Genesis 43:1–15; 1 Corinthians 7:1–9; Mark 4:35–41

God of generous mercy, surround our best, wisest efforts with your gracious care. Give us freedom to run risks. Give us wisdom to run knowing risks. Give us, above all, your good mercy. In his name. Amen.

Father Jacob is torn. He cherishes his young son, Benjamin. His love for him is intensified by the earlier loss of Joseph. But he is also lord and father of a great clan, and he must provide food. For that reason, he must appeal to the empire of Egypt, which has a food monopoly. He seeks to manage the risk by careful planning and preparation. He supplies his sons with delicacies that will function as persuaders, if not bribes. He doubles the funding for the trip. Money is no object; he must run the risk.

But then, as he dispatches his sons, he gives them a blessing: "May God Almighty grant you mercy before the man [Joseph]." He invokes the name of the high God and utters the defining word, "mercy." It is God who will oversee the venture. And Jacob, for all his careful preparation, must trust himself and his sons to the benevolent will of God.

Our lives are like that. They are operations of wisdom, cunning, planning, and preparation. But then, at the limit of human capacity, there are also risks that appeal, beyond our management, to the goodness of God. Our lives are an endless, tricky mix of managing and trusting. If we plan without acknowledging the rule of God, we are likely to end in hubris (if successful) or in despair (if not successful). If we trust in God without our best wisdom, we are likely to end in destructive foolishness. God is the ruler yet! Such submission to God's providence is not in vogue in a society of technological fixes that let us imagine full control of our lives. But mercy is at the heart of God's life; it is the final truth of our lives as well.

Saturday after Lent 2

Psalm 75; Genesis 43:16–34; 1 Corinthians 7:10–24; Mark 5:1–20

God of our baptismal identity, who has called us to a different obedience, give us courage and freedom to live differently, to redefine our social reality according to your good truth. In his name. Amen.

Paul takes up a triad of social relationships, between women and men in marriage, slaves and free people in the economy, and circumcised and uncircumcised in the orbit of faith. The triad recalls and reiterates the baptismal formula of Galatians 3:28: In Christ (that is, in baptism), "there is no longer Jew or Greek, there is no longer slave or free, there is no longer male and female; for all of you are one in Christ."

In all these relationships, Paul counsels: "Let each of you lead the life that the Lord assigned, to which God called you."

Taken at face value, Paul seems to approve status quo relationships, an argument that is, of course, problematic with reference to "slave or free." Such a reading, however, disregards Paul's main point, which is baptism. To be "in Christ" changes everything. In Paul's horizon it redefines all other distinctions as of secondary importance. For that very reason, Paul's counsel is not to quietism or to the status quo. It is rather a manifesto of freedom to live out a completely different identity that is marked by baptism.

Lent may be a time to reconsider baptismal identity that is inimical to conventional conformity, whether to religious tradition or to the coercion of the empire. The hallmark of baptism is gospel freedom to live differently in the world. There is no circumstance in which being "in Christ" is not emancipatory and authorizing of difference.

Third Sunday of Lent

Psalm 93; Genesis 44:1–17; Romans 8:1–10; John 5:25–29

*God of our bodily selves, who has called us into a community of restor-
ative justice, free us from the seductions of self-preoccupation that are
propelled by our fear and anxiety. In his name. Amen.*

Paul witnesses to the freedom given in the gospel of Jesus
Christ. In this text Paul speaks of the life according to the
Spirit, in contrast to life in the flesh. It is unfortunate that
the word pair "spirit-flesh" has been so badly misunderstood
among us. That misunderstanding has led to much world-
escaping spirituality and a bad rap for bodily existence. The
church has been endlessly preoccupied with things sexual that
have reduced "flesh" to sexuality in a way that my friend Daniel Maguire calls the church's "pelvic theology."

That, of course, is not what Paul intends, as we can see from
his indexes of "desires of the flesh" and "fruit of the Spirit"
(Gal. 5:16–26). It turns out that "desires of the flesh" refers to
all self-centered, self-seeking, self-indulgent appetites. I have
been reading *The Impulse Society* by Paul Roberts, which details
the contagious practice of "instant gratification" that in our
society is focused on consumer goods and the accumulation in
overabundance of whatever is sought, whether food or money
or adulation. Such "works of the flesh" lead to an individual-
istic society of toxic competition that in turn leads to isolation,
the disregard of the common good, and the collapse of a viable
social infrastructure.

The alternative, "the fruit of the Spirit," does not result in
conventional spirituality but in a full engagement in the neighborly community. Such a life is to be in sync with the will of
the Creator for the good of all creation. Once we have Paul's
categories clarified, we can see how the issue of spirit-flesh is
an urgent one in the community of Christ that has deep commitments to the common good.

Monday after Lent 3

Psalm 80; Genesis 44:18–34; 1 Corinthians 7:25–31; Mark 5:21–43

God of all truth, we love to tell your story. Give us emancipated tongues that this old, old story may become our new, new song. In his name. Amen.

In the Gospel reading, we are at the most elemental level of evangelical witness. Before anything else, the earliest followers of Jesus had stories to tell. These stories contradict all the usual categories of reality. This extended reading offers two stories of transformation, one of which interrupts the other. The "container" story in verses 21–24, 35–43 features a girl restored to life. The watching crowd first mocks his intervention and then is amazed.

The story that interrupts in verses 25–34 features an intense woman. She and Jesus have an exchange about touch: She touches him. She says, "If I but touch his clothes, I will be made well." He says, "Who touched my clothes?" The disciples say, "You say, 'Who touched my clothes?'" It is all about touch. It is about his bodily engagement that has a capacity for life that overrides the inclination to death.

That is all. There Jesus is in these stories, without pedigree, with no credentials, with no medical learning. And there the church is with this memory, no orthodoxy yet, no theological explanation, no learned conclusion. Only a story inside another story. These stories do not yield any certitude or any sustained philosophy of life. They are much more modest. And our faith is grounded in no more than these modest tales that happened to unnamed people that were remembered by other unnamed people. It is all flimsy!

We may reflect on the grounding of our conviction. We have been taught so much. We have breathed in all kinds of truth; we have inhaled many urgent ideologies. And now we have these two stories. He touched death-bound bodies! It was a moment in Easter . . . with new life!

Tuesday after Lent 3

Psalm 78:1–39; Genesis 45:1–15; 1 Corinthians 7:32–40; Mark 6:1–13

Lord Jesus, who summons to radical economics and who invites to restoration, grant that we may be fully engaged in your work, unhindered by resistance or doubt. In your name. Amen

The Gospel narrative presents Jesus coming back home to Nazareth. His return causes a considerable upheaval in his village. On the one hand, he teaches in the synagogue in ways that offend. We know from Luke that his offense was that extended the Jubilee to include those beyond conventional norms and thereby proposed a radical form of economics that would favor the disadvantaged. His teaching, it turns out, was quite unwelcome and did not fit with the uncritical practices of his own people.

On the other hand, there must have been great expectations because of his reputation as a healer. Remarkably, it is reported that while he does a few healings there, he does not do as many wonders as he might have done. He finds his own people unresponsive and without trust in him. Mark is more specific and says that a lack of faith resulted in a lack of healing. While our translations have the term "unbelief," it is better to speak of lack of trust, for what was operative was not a cognitive resistance but a relational resistance to his presence and his offer of restoration. This suggests that Jesus' restorative work in some measure depended on the readiness of those in need to trust and hope for healing. Who knew, then or now in our technological culture, that lack of faith would prevent restoration?

Undeterred by their lack of trust and hope, Jesus nonetheless dispatches his disciples to do his restorative work. He commands them first to travel light, a proper Lenten discipline. And second, he urges them not to invest their time in unresponsive people. We can imagine ourselves on either end of such transactions, as the healer who travels light or as one in need of healing who must commit an act of trust and hope.

Wednesday after Lent 3

Psalm 119:97–120; Genesis 45:16–28;
1 Corinthians 8:1–13; Mark 6:13–29

Ruler of nations, maker of royalty, authorizer of governors, give us honesty, wisdom, and innocence for life given only by you. In his name. Amen.

These readings invite us to reflect on the risky ambiguity of worldly power. In the Old Testament and Gospel readings, the central characters are Pharaoh and Herod. The two are often seen as parallel figures of great power and great danger. Pharaoh is featured as uncommonly generous to Israel and as welcoming to the family of Jacob in extravagant ways. Worldly power is capable of great generosity. But we know how the story goes later on with a new pharaoh who does not know Joseph and who is a fierce adversary of Israel.

Herod is featured as patron of John the Baptist. He has enough perceptiveness to recognize the holy authority of John and to keep him safe, even while he fears him. But the story witnesses to the unreliability of Herod; in the revelry of dance and drink, Herod commits, perhaps unwittingly, to the death of John.

Both Jacob and John receive protective attention and rely on it. But such generous hospitality is fragile and unreliable. In the end, both Pharaoh and Herod violate the well-being of the faithful in violent ways.

Gospel faith does not happen in a sociopolitical vacuum. There are a variety of postures for that relationship with worldly power that run from sectarian disengagement to glad accommodation. In our more common practice in the US church, we tilt mostly toward glad and easy accommodation. We are on notice, however, about the riskiness of such engagement. We are driven to ask, in Lenten time, whom shall we trust? What shall we risk? In the end, we are turned back to the power of God that lies beyond worldly embodiment.

Thursday after Lent 3

Psalm 83; Genesis 46:1–7, 28–34; 1 Corinthians 9:1–15; Mark 6:30–46

Giver of good gifts, we are stunned and staggered by your generosity.
Give us readiness to trust your abundance and to depart our parsimony.
In his name. Amen.

The Jesus story is all about abundance. It is as though in the wilderness Jesus has jump-started creation so as to generate ample bread for the hungry multitude he finds there. He feeds "five thousand men" and has twelve baskets of bread and fish left over. All are welcome at the meal. All are fed.

In some ways Pharaoh's welcome of Jacob to Egypt is also an act of generous abundance. At the end of our reading, however, there is a curious note that merits attention. The family of Jacob were shepherds, preoccupied with flocks and herds. But Joseph warns his family. He advises them to lie to Pharaoh when Pharaoh asks about their occupation. Pharaoh would welcome "keepers of livestock." But he does not like shepherds, so "don't tell Pharaoh you are shepherds." Shepherds are an abomination to Pharaoh. They disgust him! That leads me to suspect that Pharaoh, in his bestowal of goodies, could be discriminatory, generous to cattle keepers but parsimonious to shepherds. The text indicates ambiguity in the report to Pharaoh, suggesting unease at Pharaoh's arbitrariness. We are not told the basis of Pharaoh's disgust, but it is an indication that Pharaoh is not openhandedly generous with abundance. One has to qualify; one has to meet certain norms. And that discrimination is surely grounded in scarcity; there is not enough for all. Some will not qualify; the goodies will be kept for the ones who are approved.

Pharaoh's practice is quite ordinary. We are always sorting out people to see who qualifies for abundance, whether by race, class, gender, character, education, performance, or production. This is standard practice in every society. But Jesus is extraordinary. No norms of qualification. No questions asked. All are welcome! All are fed! Jesus' extraordinary generosity contrasts with the ordinary parsimony of Pharaoh!

Friday after Lent 3

Psalm 95; Genesis 47:1–26; 1 Corinthians 9:16–27; Mark 6:47–56

Lord Jesus, who brings order into our chaos, restore us to our true iden-tity, that we may trust you in confidence and freedom from fear. In your name. Amen.

Joseph is presented here as fully in the service of Pharaoh. In that service, he is required to confiscate all food and money to add to Pharaoh's exploitative monopoly. As a result, when the famine comes and the peasants have no food, they are required to deal with Pharaoh's food monopoly by coming to terms with Joseph's uncompromising demands.

The outcome is that when the peasants do not have money to buy food, they must forfeit their cattle and eventually their land and their bodies; they are helpless before the economic monopoly of Pharaoh and are forced into debt slavery. Thus Joseph, son of the covenant, became an agent of the slave-making economy of Pharaoh that reduced poor people to bondage. In the process, Joseph had lost his covenantal iden-tity and did not any longer know who he was.

In the Gospel reading, the disciples are frightened by the storm. They do not trust Jesus; they do not understand about his abundance. They do not understand, we are told, because they have "hard hearts," that is, they think in the fearful cate-gories of Pharaoh, who was frightened by the thought of scar-city. The disciples had forgotten who they were as followers of Jesus!

It is easy enough in an exploitative economy to forget who we are as followers of Christ and to participate in the deep anxiety about scarcity. Lent is a good time to reflect on who we are and what it means to be disciples of Christ. In the narrative he says to them, "Do not be afraid." The story attests that the authority of Jesus is more powerful than the threat or chaos. But it requires recovery of our identity in Christ. The alter-native to such a gospel identity that yields freedom and well-being is greedy fear. But we may choose otherwise!

Saturday after Lent 3

Psalm 87; Genesis 47:27–48:7; 1 Corinthians 10:1–13; Mark 7:1–23

God of fidelity who calls us to trust, free us from excessive scruple; deliver us from excessive self-preoccupation. Grant that we may respond to your fidelity with the faithfulness of our lives. In his name. Amen.

These two New Testament readings together suggest two modes of idolatry. In the Epistle reading, Paul addresses the self-indulgence of the Corinthians by allusion to the narrative of the golden calf (Exod. 32), wherein Israel engaged in idolatry by manufacturing a god who sanctioned their indulgence. That kind of idolatry is evident enough.

But the Gospel reading suggests a different kind of idolatry, namely, an excessive commitment to tradition that contradicts the claim of God in the world. In this particular case, the tradition that is excessively honored concerns rules of purity that govern food, on the assumption that what one takes in (eats) will contaminate. To the contrary, Jesus insists, it is what "comes out" in speech and action that may defile. Thus the tradition is said by Jesus to contradict the command of Sinai in the service of a particular religious scruple.

But the point is a broader one. There are all sorts of traditions that maintain the status quo, that protect privilege and entitlement, that keep people in the proper place under the aegis of religious or political scruple.

Mature faith is to live without either idolatry. The ground for such an alternative way of life is the assurance that God is faithful. The fidelity of God precludes narcissistic notions that we are the center of the universe. Conversely, the faithfulness of God assures that well-being does not depend on our scrupulous carefulness but on the goodness of God. We are invited to a freedom that trusts itself to goodness that is beyond our summons or manipulation.

Fourth Sunday in Lent

Psalm 66; Genesis 48:8–22; Romans 8:11–25; John 6:27–40

Spirit of God, who stirs beyond our safe categories and our usual assumptions, give us attentiveness to your surging newness, that we may receive your stunning emancipation that moves in and through our practiced futility. In his name. Amen.

The aged Jacob transmits the blessing to his grandsons Manasseh and Ephraim. He does so by laying on hands. At the last moment, however, he inexplicably crosses his hands so that his right hand (of power) is laid on the head of his younger grandson. The crossing of his hands to reverse the blessing is unexplained. We do not know if it was luck or providence or the puckish way of the old man. When Joseph protests this reversal, father Jacob only affirms the outcome of the blessing for the future. Jacob's act was revolutionary. It violated all the old habits that protected the privilege of the firstborn. This overthrow of conventional privilege by a puckish act offers a harbinger of the acts of freedom that are characteristic of the gospel.

In Paul's wondrous lyric, it is as though the creation is hemmed in in futile ways, but the glorious liberty given by God will permit an emancipation of all creation, including our bodies. In the Gospel narrative, Jesus, in elusive wording, breaks free of all old "bread routines" to assert that he himself is "the true bread from heaven" that violates all conventional categories.

In the church's run-up to Easter, it is worthwhile to ponder how it is that the creation—and our daily experience of it—is so much an enterprise of futility in which we regularly make all the conventional moves of coercion, fear, frustration, anxiety, and alienation. This is the daily truth of our lives that is abruptly and deeply interrupted by the power of God. Jacob did more than he knew. He exemplified the opening of the world to new possibility that in the Gospel is termed "eternal life."

Monday after Lent 4

Psalm 89:1–18; Genesis 49:1–28;
1 Corinthians 10:14–11:1; Mark 7:24–37

Good God of generosity, forgive our provincial insistence on our own way. Give us largeness of heart to make room for those unlike us who belong, like us, to your good governance. In his name. Amen.

In the church there is a durable temptation to adhere to party or clique or sect. Such zealous advocacy for one's own opinion or one's own kind or one's own group makes coherent unity exceedingly difficult. Paul struggles with the issue of unity in the face of Greek-Jewish differences that ran very deeply. In the Epistle reading, the issue turns on who can eat what, given religious scruples and gospel freedom. Paul enunciates guidelines for living well together.

1. What is acceptable ("lawful") is not always helpful ("builds up"), so do not do it just because it is lawful.
2. The first test is one's neighbor. The matter concerns a relationship, not a rule.
3. The proper stance in all such matters is one of thanks. Gratitude yields a disposition that is very different from one of entitlement or autonomy.
4. The final test is the glory of God, that is, what celebrates and enhances the wonder of God.

These wise pastoral guidelines call away from hairsplitting distinctions or power plays or insistence on one's own way. They call rather for a largeness of spirit that yields to the other for the sake of the community.

It may give great comfort to notice that in the Gospel reading even Jesus is summoned away from his parochialism by an outsider woman on behalf of non-Jews, whom he calls "dogs," who also merit a share in God's goodness. We ourselves might be a hindrance to unity . . . or not!

Tuesday after Lent 4

Psalm 97; Genesis 49:29–50:14; 1 Corinthians 11:17–34; Mark 8:1–10

Giver of enough for all, let us rest our lives in your abundance. Give us a capacity to wait for our neighbors who also share in your abundance. In his name. Amen.

Eating is a most elemental activity in which all the great human questions are operative, questions of production, questions of distribution, and questions of consumption. Food poses questions of scarcity and abundance and creates an environment in which we may act out fearful competitiveness or generous sharing.

In the early church, all the questions of food were evident, setting Christians against each other in greed and selfishness. The horizon of the Epistle reading, moreover, should not be confined to church behavior, because the same issues are at work in the larger economy. In an economy of acute individualism, the strong and powerful can, in greedy ways, monopolize food and other resources and take them from the table of the vulnerable; or conversely, policies and practices of the community may generate an equitable distribution of food and other essential life resources so that all may participate together in well-being. There is no doubt that it is the (most often quite unrealistic) fear of scarcity that propels greed and generates undue surplus at the expense of the other.

Paul counsels: "Wait for one another." The ground for such waiting is the assurance that there is enough for all to eat. That assurance of enough for all is dramatized in the Gospel narrative wherein Jesus feeds four thousand folk and has a surplus of seven baskets of bread. The narrative attests that where Jesus governs, there is an abundance for all, more than enough. This gospel claim contradicts the greedy anxiety of economic policies that imagine that we will soon run out and we must get and eat all we can now. The church may be a practice of alternative eating.

Wednesday after Lent 4

Psalm 101; Genesis 50:15–26; 1 Corinthians 12:1–11; Mark 8:11–26

God who breaks the cycles of fearful scarcity, break those cycles in our lives. Give us enough gracefulness to receive your abundance and to accept it as the new norm for our daily existence. In his name. Amen.

The disciples of Jesus, like almost all of us, were habituated into scarcity. They assumed there was not enough. They feared running out. As a result, they had no interpretive categories by which to compute the overflow of abundance of bread that Jesus made possible. His wondrous act of feeding the hungry crowd attests to his capacity for abundance. But they missed the point, even when they could count the surplus baskets of bread as twelve and seven. They had abundance in their hands, but they missed the point.

In the same way the brothers of Joseph lived in fearful parsimony. They assumed that Joseph would act in kind toward them and retaliate against them for their hateful action earlier in their lives. They did not anticipate that his largeness of spirit would break the vicious cycle of parsimonious interaction. Or more properly, they did not reckon on the providential goodness of God who stood behind the generosity of Joseph.

These two narratives explicate the habit of fearful scarcity that is so powerful among us. That fearful scarcity dictates so much of our neighborly life and so much of our grudging policy toward needy neighbors. But these two stories also bear witness to the breaking of the cycles of parsimony that we assume will continue to perpetuity. In both cases, the new unexpected abundance is given by human agency that is propelled by the generosity of God. It is more than possible that we ourselves might be such agents of abundance propelled by the same God of generosity.

Thursday after Lent 4

Psalm 69:1–23; Exodus 1:6–22; 1 Corinthians 12:12–26; Mark 8:27–9:1

We give you thanks, God of liberated futures, for the life of Jesus, who came without pedigree, and for all those like him who have acted your vision for the well-being of the world. Slow us down to notice the unnoticed. In his name. Amen.

If we make a list of the great emancipators in human history, that list may run from Moses to Nelson Mandela, Mahatma Gandhi, and Martin Luther King in our own time. It is highly unlikely that these two midwives in the Exodus story would be on the list. But there they are! They are included in Israel's memory with their names—Shiphrah and Puah—because they feared God, engaged in risky civil disobedience, and advanced the cause of liberation of the slaves.

A gospel reading of human history has a way of noticing important agents of emancipation who often fail to make the official list that is given formal public approval. Such an inclination to notice the unnoticed is congruent with Paul's imagery of a body of many parts. Paul gets down to the specifics of anatomy in his recognition that the unpresentable parts of the body are indispensable, even the parts of the body not acknowledged in polite society.

The gospel tradition, however, knows that the emancipatory work of the God of the gospel is most often performed by the unnoticed, less presentable parts of society who do the grunt work of solidarity and risk. Shiphrah and Puah merit only one paragraph in our memory. But they are surely among those who willingly "lose their lives for my [Jesus'] sake." They were willing to risk their lives—a real risk!—for the sake of emancipation. We might in these Lenten days consider how our vision is skewed by official lists and reflect on those whom we do not notice who do the risky work of the gospel.

Friday after Lent 4

Psalm 95; Exodus 2:1–22; 1 Corinthians 12:17–13:3; Mark 9:2–13

Lord of justice, performer of love, grant that we may live responsibly in the real world, not yielding to romanticism, not imaging that might makes right, not shirking from our proper work. In his name. Amen.

The interface of the Old Testament narrative and the Epistle reading invites us to consider how it is that history is turned toward well-being. Paul's familiar language in 1 Corinthians 13 is preoccupied with the unity of the Christian congregation. The variety of gifts essential to the life of the church are held together by agape love that does not seek its own way. The Exodus narrative is concerned with the transformation of power arrangements in the public order. Moses is portrayed as a "freedom fighter" (terrorist?), an unrestrained advocate for his exploited people, who readily performs indignant violence against their brutal taskmasters.

Thus we are confronted with *fierce violence* in public performance and *agape love* in the assembly of faith. There is a long practice of political realism in Christian tradition that affirms that public processes require such ferociousness as Moses embodied, because no exploitative power is ever ceded willingly. There is also a countertradition in Christian thought that the gospel way in public affairs refuses such violence and trusts that real transformation of public power can come otherwise, beyond violence. But, of course, the alternative to violence is not abdicating passivity. It is rather a summons to a different kind of force that exposes the claims of exploitation as fraudulent. We might in these days reflect on how public change comes about in the interest of emancipatory justice that is willed by the God of the exodus. Further we may ask how we ourselves may participate faithfully in the life-or-death struggle for emancipation in our own time.

Saturday after Lent 4

Psalm 107:33–43; Exodus 2:23–3:15;
1 Corinthians 13:1–13; Mark 9:14–29

God of emancipation, who stands against bondage and exploitation, give us sensitivity to the cries of the exploited, attentiveness to your resolve, and notice of human agents whom you may have authorized in the struggle. In his name. Amen.

The urgency of the Exodus narrative continues in the face of the agape love of 1 Corinthians 13. The Exodus narrative is a paradigmatic story of emancipation that is endlessly lived out in the real world. Here we notice three elements in that model story. First, new history begins with the exploited groan under their bondage, bringing their pain to public notice. This component of the story is often reiterated in protests and vigorous resistance to exploitation.

Second, God is called into the narrative of emancipation by the cries of the slaves. God hears, sees, remembers, notices, and speaks a new resolve. The emergence of God in the story of justice is perforce and hidden and is given only mysteriously in the burning bush. God is presented as a passionate partisan, ally, and legitimator of those who stand vigorously against slavery.

Third, while God speaks a vigorous resolve to bring out of Egypt and bring in to a new land, in fact God turns over to Moses the actual performance of the confrontation. Thus divine resolve morphs immediately into authorized human agency. The divine resolve remains hidden; what we see is human agency.

This sequence of pain brought to speech, hidden divine resolve, and authorized human agency is a pattern that is reiterated in many liberation struggles. While many such struggles seem frightening to us and threaten what we treasure, we may recognize that the Exodus narrative is an old memory that is waiting to be reperformed in many contemporary venues. We may entertain the thought that we often find ourselves on the wrong side of such reperformances.

Fifth Sunday of Lent

Psalm 118; Exodus 3:16–4:12; Romans 12:1–21; John 8:46–59

*God of transformative power and transformed vision, release us from
our timid conformity to this world. Grant that we may see and live differently according to your goodness. In his name. Amen.*

Paul's singular instruction in gospel conduct in the Epistle
reading pivots on the introductory contrast between *conformity
to this world* and *transformation by the renewal of your mind*. Paul
describes the radically different way of life that emerges from
transformation in the gospel. That new behavior, of course,
requires a deep break with old patterns of conformity that
eschew such gospel practices as generosity, hospitality, and a
refusal of vengeance.

The same issue is put before Moses in a different idiom.
Moses is reluctant to perform God's vision for a different way
in the world. Confrontation with Pharaoh and all that he represents is a dangerous mission, and Moses for good reason is
reluctant to go. Here he offers two resistances: (a) They will
not believe me. (b) I am not eloquent. (In the total narrative,
Moses offers three other resistances as well). But God will not
be put off. God offers assurances to Moses. At the end, however, God is uncompromising: "Now go!" Moses is summoned
to break conformity to the regime of Pharaoh and to enact the
transformed world of God. In this process he himself is transformed from a reluctant man to a vigorous, bold leader.

The issue of conformity or transformation is a central
theme for Lent. For the most part our conformity is unnoticed
because it seems so normal. We conform to a society that is
shot through with race and gender bias. We conform to an
economy that preys on the vulnerable. We conform to the endless demand for new technology that often distracts from real
life. The news of transformation persists. Paul's summons is
still urgent today.

Monday after Lent 5

Psalm 31; Exodus 4:10–31; 1 Corinthians 14:1–19; Mark 9:30–41

God of generative speech, forgive our timid silence and our failure to speak. Send your spirit of boldness on us for the sake of new historical possibility. In his name. Amen.

The Bible is a talking tradition. Its many voices attest that utterance spoken out loud is an effective force that actually does something in the world. In the case of Moses, being able to talk well matters on two counts. Moses must effectively bear witness to his fellow slaves that God can be relied on to see them to liberty. Moses also must witness effectively to Pharaoh that the power of God in the service of emancipation is real power that Pharaoh dare not dismiss. On both counts Moses' speech is effective, eventuating in Miriam's dance of freedom.

The matter is very different in the church in Corinth. The capacity to "speak in tongues" was an exhibit of enormous freedom for speech addressed directly to God and propelled by God's own Spirit. Paul, moreover, boasts that he, "more than all of you," speaks in tongues.

Such speech, however much it witnesses to unfettered freedom, by itself does not build up the body of the church. For that, interpretation is essential. Thus Paul prefers to speak "five words with my mind," that is, five words of meaningful interpretation.

These two texts invite us to reflect on the practice of speech in our social context, about the power of speech and the restraint of speech, about who is permitted to speak and who is regularly reduced to silence, about how dangerous speech may become if it is left uninterpreted, and about who has the authority to interpret. Or more personally, we may reflect on the chances we have to bear witness to God's freedom outside the socioeconomic pharaonic restraints of our society or the chances we have to speak in the presence of pharaonic forces that enslave the vulnerable. Five words that make sense might be, "Let my people go free."

Tuesday after Lent 5

Psalm 10; Exodus 5:1–6:1;
1 Corinthians 14:20–33a, 39–40; Mark 9:42–50

God of restful freedom, we give thanks for your disruption of our overly busy, overly demanding lives. Give us freedom enough to choose against our habitual busyness. In his name. Amen.

The imperative of Moses to Pharaoh is, "Let my people go." That imperative issued to Pharaoh evokes from Pharaoh a rash of new imperatives for greater production of bricks through the hard labor of the slaves. In the face of the God of emancipation, Pharaoh doubles down on the harshness of bondage. I have concluded that with a little finesse it is possible, in this long tirade of Pharaoh, to identify ten urgent commands of Pharaoh, ten commands of production that are alternative to the ten commands of Mount Sinai. All ten of Pharaoh's commands are concerned with greater production under unbearably harsh circumstance.

It is clear that this encounter between the God of emancipation and the lord of endless production is not merely a historical memory. It is rather a script that helps us to read our own socioeconomic circumstance alertly. Much like these ancient slaves, we are caught, in our society, in an endless process of acquisitive greed with an insatiable appetite for more: more power, more energy, more technology, more security, more well-being, even more drugs.

That urgency for more depends on harder work until we are exhausted with an overextended schedule in which all of life is reduced to an exhausting rat race that can never be won.

In the midst of that rat race that reduces everything to commodity, there is this alternative summons to break off such coercive servitude for the sake of God's freedom. It is an alternative that requires bold intentionality in the face of Pharaoh's ever-expanding quotas of production and performance.

Wednesday after Lent 5

Psalm 119:145–176; Exodus 7:8–24;
2 Corinthians 2:14–3:6; Mark 10:1–16

*Holy Spirit who convenes the church, we give you thanks for the church
and for our particular congregation. Give us steadfastness to trust and
act beyond the easy expectations of our wishful thinking. In his name.
Amen.*

"Peddlers of God's word!" What a phrase from Paul! The
old-fashioned image of a peddler was a door-to door salesman
(always a man) who offered a variety of practical goods for
the household. More recently, peddlers are smooth operators
who seek to convert our wants into needs, so as to create false
appetites. The notion of apostle as peddler suggests catering
to people's wants or needs in ways that may flatter, seduce, or
falsely assure. That ancient image may describe the church in
which the local congregation and the pastor are required to
pander to peoples' wants, to offer a gospel of reassurance that
demands nothing substantive and that conforms to dominant
social expectations and ideology.

Against such an image of church, Paul insists that his apostolic authority and responsibility have other, deeper roots in
the reality of God. "Our competence is from God." Paul, moreover, sees his faithful congregation as witnesses ("letters of rec-
ommendation") to the truth of God from whom his ministry
derives. Against pandering peddlers in a comfortable church,
Paul champions serious members of the body who embrace
the deep claims of the gospel. Those deep claims of the gospel, for Paul, concern the self-giving grace of God that outruns
our moralistic bargaining and God's uncompromising requirements that are more demanding than our easy accommodating
ideologies. This text invites us to reflect on what it means to be
a faithful member of the congregation who embraces the gospel without flinching, both its uncommon gift and its uncommon task.

Thursday after Lent 5

Psalm 131; Exodus 7:25–8:19; 2 Corinthians 3:7–18; Mark 10:17–31

*God of wondrous gifts and inscrutable power, draw us into the orbit of
your fidelity and away from false loyalties that cannot give good gifts or
make our lives whole. In his name. Amen.*

In the contest between God, the emancipator, and Pharaoh,
the lord of bondage, the first two episodes have ended in a
draw. Matters are different in the third episode, concerning
gnats. The Egyptian technicians, in the service of Pharaoh,
"could not" match the performance of Moses and Aaron in the
production of gnats. Pharaoh could not match the power of
God. The predatory empire of Pharaoh, with all its technology,
had reached the limit of its capacity.

The news of that limit, whenever it is recognized, is a stunning declaration, because it signifies that Pharaoh, symbol of
every predatory power, does not need to be feared, does not
need to be trusted, and so does not need to be obeyed.

In a very different mode, Jesus' encounter with the man
with "many possessions" makes a like point. The man presents
a winning combination of qualities to Jesus. He is both obedient to the commandments and successful in the real world
of economics, a most compelling dossier! Jesus' word to him,
however, is that the combination of obedience and success
is no passport to abiding well-being, because these points of
merit have only limited currency.

We live in a world that pays endless tribute to the impressive combination of money, power, technical competence, and
worldly wisdom . . . all important qualities. In both of these
narratives, however, there is the uncompromising recognition
that such capacities are limited. They cannot deliver well-
being. They cannot prevent emancipation. We have a chance,
with these stories, to sort out our proper commitments from
our illusions about what or whom to trust.

Friday after Lent 5

Psalm 95; Exodus 9:13–35; 2 Corinthians 4:1–12; Mark 10:32–45

God who governs the earth for good, we thank you for the fertile generativity of the earth. Give us courage to protect it from mistaken exploitation that violates your hope for the world. In his name. Amen.

Paul's imagery of "treasure in clay jars" makes a definitive difference between the treasure of the gospel and the clay pot of the church and its ministry. The endless seduction of the church is to confuse itself with the gospel, to assume that the clay pot is itself the treasure. Paul's lyrical rhetoric asserts, against any such confusion, that "this extraordinary power belongs to God." Then he adds, Not to us!

In the Exodus narrative, Pharaoh thrives on such confusion between his form of power and the real source of life. Pharaoh and his loyal subjects assumed that Pharaoh was an embodiment of divine power that was therefore entitled to absolute authority. This episode in the narrative suggests that God is determined to show that Pharaoh has made a huge mistake. While the exodus is enacted to liberate the slaves, it is also performed in order to exhibit the power of God against all would-be competitors. Thus God sends the plagues "to show you my power, and to make my name resound through all the earth." Later on God sends hail that "you may know that the earth is the LORD's." The land does not belong to Pharaoh!

This show of God's power has the effect of declaring all other power, including that of Pharaoh, penultimate and accountable to the rule of God. Pharaoh's great pretense is to imagine that he is ultimate and can therefore do whatever he wants. We now live in a time when great economic power imagines its ultimacy to the detriment of the earth. The Exodus narrative exposes that phony assumption that is as contemporary as it is old.

Saturday after Lent 5

Psalm 137; Exodus 10:21–11:8; 2 Corinthians 4:13–18; Mark 10:46–52

God of all, you dazzle us by taking sides in history against our usual assumptions. Give us courage to stand alongside your way in the world. In his name. Amen.

It is a wonder that the great sovereign God would act in solidarity with a particular people, namely, the Hebrew slaves. The divine administration of the ultimate plague made "a distinction between Egypt and Israel." That same sense of being chosen continues to be a wonder (and, I suggest, a vexation) for the New Testament church. Thus Paul can say of the resurrection of Jesus and God's exhibit of grace that it is all "for your sake," that is, for the cluster of people gathered in faith around Jesus. Paul does allow that that company "extends to more and more people," but it is still a distinct community as the chosen of God.

When we come to the Gospel narrative, we can conclude that it is the blind beggar, Bartimaeus, who is the object of God's special healing attention enacted by Jesus. For that reason we may judge Bartimaeus to be chosen, so that the gift of healing is "for his sake." It is a scandal of the ministry of Jesus that the socially disadvantaged are the chosen of God. Indeed, his entire ministry was among social rejects, including dining with "sinners and tax collectors" (Mark 2:16). It is no wonder that his adversaries resisted his reach beyond the pale.

We may well reflect on the freedom of God in this series of choices, that God may take sides on behalf of the slaves in Egypt, for the earliest followers of Jesus, and with disadvantaged Bartimaeus. We may further wonder how that capacity of God to focus in such a way is now operative. In each case, God's chosen consists in those whom the world does not value. God's grace is extended exactly in a direction that contradicts the way the world allots privilege and entitlement. There is indeed a contrariness to God's choosing!

Palm Sunday

Psalm 24; Zechariah 9:9–12; 1 Timothy 6:12–16; Luke 19:41–48

God of ancient prophets, we thank you for your ancient utterance of truthfulness. Give us good ears to hear the reverberation of those old words in contemporary cadence. In his name. Amen.

Passion Sunday is a time for pondering the suffering of Jesus. We must consider the city of Jerusalem to which he came. He had conducted his ministry until this time in Galilee, his home territory that was more removed from Roman imperial control, remote as well from the mechanisms of the Jewish elite who administered the capital city. But now he comes to that city, and there he must confront a massive concentration of socio-political power consisting in Jewish leaders who had colluded with Roman power. Like every such concentration of power, this one was inimical to critical exposés of its exploitative ways.

In the Gospel narrative, Jesus lets the ancient prophets speak. He quotes Isaiah 56:7 and its large vision of the Jerusalem temple as a "house of prayer for all peoples." The poetry of Isaiah had especially welcomed eunuchs and foreigners. But then Jesus reverses field by quoting Jeremiah 7:11: "You have made it a den of robbers." Jeremiah means that the leadership had practiced predatory economics in the city and then piously hid out in the liturgy of the temple. Jeremiah goes on to say that such a city is unsustainable.

What Jesus does in this text is to let the ancient prophets speak, because it turns out that their old words are powerfully contemporary to the time of Jesus. They are, moreover, powerfully contemporary to our own circumstance as well. Today and in the Holy Week that follows, we might consider how these prophets still speak, how they continue to host a large vision of inclusiveness, and how they continue to sound a sharp critique of socioeconomic practices of oppression . . . surely the reason they sought to silence him.

Monday of Holy Week

Psalm 51:1–20; Lamentations 1:1–2, 6–12;
2 Corinthians 1:1–7; Mark 11:12–25

*God of ancient fidelity, we live in a season of loss, absence, and sadness.
Be, as you have promised, the God of all comfort, that in our loss your
hope may well up in powerful ways. In his name. Amen.*

All this Holy Week we will be reading the book of Lamentations. That much-neglected book consists in five poems, all of which grieve the destruction and loss of the ancient city of Jerusalem. In the contemporary practice of Judaism, these poems continue to be read in commemoration of that destruction. The city embodies the core memory and core hope of Judaism, the epicenter of theological identity that hosts the unconditional promise of God to David and the unconditional presence of God in the temple.

In Christian usage, these poems spill over into Passion Week and the death of Jesus. In Christian imagination Jesus has displaced Jerusalem as the epicenter of memory and hope. Thus the poetry invites us to grieve that as God's presence in the city has been forfeited, so now the person of Jesus, as the presence of God, is lost by the execution of a hostile empire. There is so much to grieve in both traditions!

In contemporary usage in US society, there is yet a third wave of grief for many people, namely, for the collapse and disappearance of an old world of security and well-being. The social reality of white male privilege, political domination, and economic entitlement provided assurance and buoyancy for many US people. And now it is gone—like Jerusalem, like Jesus, because of the enemy. But it is gone as well—like Jerusalem, like Jesus—because God's purposes are worked out in hidden and unwelcome ways. These losses require of us honest embrace and recognition.

Tuesday of Holy Week

Psalm 6; Lamentations 1:17–22; 2 Corinthians 1:8–22; Mark 11:27–33

God of comfort who presides over our deepest losses, give us honesty to embrace our losses; give us hope to live faithfully amid our grief. In his name. Amen.

The acute sadness of the poetry of Lamentations is voiced in the repeated phrase "no one to comfort," twice voiced in our reading. It is a mood not unlike that of father Jacob in Genesis when he had lost his son Joseph: he "refused to be comforted" (Gen. 37:35). The grief in this poetry vacillates between two explanations for loss, either sin ("I have been very rebellious") or enemies ("All my enemies heard of my trouble"). Israel in its loss nonetheless keeps wondering how to understand what has happened to the city.

But, of course, there is a gospel response, even to such loss. That response is voiced in the Old Testament in the familiar words of Isaiah 40:1: "Comfort, O comfort my people." God does answer and offers assurance. In the New Testament, the rhetoric of comfort abounds in 2 Corinthians 1:1–7, our reading yesterday. Those verses attest to "the God of all consolation." In today's Epistle reading, Paul asserts that even in the face of such loss and grief, "God is faithful." Indeed, there is no maybe with God. "In him it is always 'Yes.'" In Christian tradition the yes of God is the resurrection of Jesus. In Judaism the yes of God may take the form of restoration to the land of Israel and to the city of Jerusalem.

These readings push one to emotional extremity that is commensurate with the extremity of historical experience. We are situated between loss that is beyond comfort and comfort that answers such loss. On the one hand, the offer of comfort precludes abiding despair. On the other hand, comfort taken too quickly may shortchange the loss and end in denial. Grief and comfort as voiced here require agility, a refusal to settle for easy or quick resolution.

Wednesday of Holy Week

Psalm 55; Lamentations 2:1–9; 2 Corinthians 1:23–2:11; Mark 12:1–11

God of high expectation and keen disappointment, we give you thanks that even in the face of our unproductive ways, you have begun again, making fresh use of the rejected stone. In his name. Amen.

The poetry of Lamentations is not reasoned doctrinal explanation. It is, to be sure, poetry that is crafted according to skillful artistry. That artistry, however, is a vehicle for raw anguish. This raw anguish does not hesitate to assign to God the most powerful and violent verbs of destruction: cast down, destroy, break down, cut down, burn, slay, bring to ruin. This vivid rhetoric is closely linked to the poetry of Isaiah 5:1–7 that characterizes God as the vineyard owner who loses patience with the vineyard (Israel) that has not produced fruit.

That imagery is furthered in the Gospel reading. As in Isaiah 5, the vineyard, Israel, is intended to produce fruit, and it has not. The expected fruit is justice and righteousness, that is, a neighborly inclusive ethic. The parable of Jesus has upped the ante to include the son of the vineyard owner who is killed by the unproductive folk at the vineyard.

The teaching of Jesus does more, however, than extend the imagery and up the ante. In the last verse Jesus adds a remarkable twist. After the son of the owner is killed in the parable, Jesus turns abruptly from the imagery to quote a psalm in which the rejected stone (that is, the slain son) is the "cornerstone" of the new edifice. His teaching has a salvific edge to it. In Christian rhetoric the sound of lament does not end in despair or defeat, because God has something more in mind. That more is the future of Jesus, who is not defeated by the failure of God's people. The rhetoric of reject and reuse is reference to his crucifixion and resurrection, a beginning beyond failed violence.

Maundy Thursday

Psalm 102; Lamentations 2:10–18;
1 Corinthians 10:14–17; 11:27–32; Mark 14:12–25

*God known through grand seasons of transformative presence, grant us
to be with you in your absence, obeying you even in the deep moment of
your apparent defeat. In his name. Amen.*

The use of this poem from Lamentations on Maundy Thursday operates with a double focus. In original context, the poem
grieves the destruction of Jerusalem at the hands of Babylon.
In Christian liturgical usage, however, the poem grieves the
death by execution of Jesus, the Messiah. We are not, however, required (or, I think, permitted) to choose between those
two endings. We cannot compartmentalize; we engage in both
acute sadnesses at once. The destruction of Jerusalem and the
death of Jesus both signify an end of what is most treasured;
both result in a collapse of a world of meaning.

While we engage in such a double reading in a refusal to
compartmentalize, we may add a third reference of loss and
grief, namely, our contemporary loss of familiar order, the forfeiture of stable social reliabilities, and the reality of disorder
that borders on chaos. We know about the collapse of old certitudes and the risk of impending violence.

Focus on our own circumstance does not detract from
attentiveness to the coming death of Jesus. If, however, we
give attention to our own moment of acute social loss, we may
thereby enter more deeply and honestly into the loss bespoken
in the poem of Lamentations and into what the death of Jesus
signifies in the memory and practice of the church, a loss of
hope and of historical possibility.

A quite remarkable feature of this loss is that Jesus invited
his disciples to walk into that loss with him. The Last Supper
is an invitation to solidarity with him in loss. He promises to
those in solidarity the coming of a new regime.

Good Friday

Psalm 95; Lamentations 3:1–9, 19–33; 1 Peter 1:10–20;
John 13:36–38; John 19:38–42

*God who knows the depth of death, forgive our too-eager rush to joy. Give
us resolute honesty to resist the easy assumption of our culture that
refuses this long Friday and craves easy well-being. In his name. Amen.*

This reading from Lamentations articulates one of the greatest disruptions in all of the Bible. The first part of the reading goes deeply and at length into suffering, loss, and grief. The one who speaks knows about physical suffering, helplessness, and isolation. The culmination of such loss, voiced in verse 18 (which our reading skips over), is the pathos-filled confession, "Gone is . . . all that I had hoped for from the LORD." The poem might well come to an end here, for what else can be said?

But the poem continues! The adversative "but" in verse 21 is a refusal to permit the poem to end in hopelessness. The speaker goes back behind the loss and so hopes. Thus in quick rhetoric we go from "hope is gone" to "therefore I have hope." What permits hope in a context of hopelessness is Israel's memory of God given in a great triad of covenantal terms: steadfast love, mercy (plural here), faithfulness. Israel recalls old divine fidelity and so anticipates new divine fidelity.

The observance of Good Friday is a readiness to go deeply into the loss known in ancient Israel and in the life of the church. We will, of course, move liturgically to the joy of Sunday. It is, however, important not to rush that move too quickly or too easily. Indeed, the Gospel narrative about the recovery of the body of Jesus and the preparation of his body for burial is about the reality of his death. There is not in the narrative any inkling of further possibility. We linger there, not rushed yet to hope.

Holy Saturday

Psalm 95; Lamentations 3:37–58; Hebrews 4:1–16; Romans 8:1–11

Lord Jesus, subject to the violence of the world, we give thanks that in the midst of your death we may pray to the Father and receive an answering assurance; give us heart to continue that dialogue with the Father. In your name. Amen.

Like the destruction of Jerusalem, the execution of Jesus was a plunge into despair. Nobody knew what came next, or even if anything came next. The earliest disciples found the grieving of Israel an appropriate script. In Lamentations, Israel could say, "I am lost."

Such an acknowledgment, however, is not the whole truth of Saturday. Faith operates beyond rational explanation and without the constraint of linear reasoning. Even in its deep despair, Israel had no recourse except petition to God. Thus at the same time Israel could dwell in loss and still address God in anticipation. In the voice of Lamentations, we get, "I called on your name, O LORD." This faith is both honest and not quite defeated. Faith is the capacity to host both honest reality and open possibility, thus shunning both despair and illusion.

Beyond the bid of petition, Israel in Lamentations can declare: "You heard my plea." You, God, answered. "You said, 'Do not fear!'" This declaration is the most elemental assertion of divine presence and attentiveness. It is the work of the faith of Israel that Israel, in its depth of helplessness, continues in dialogic engagement with God, both to petition and to have assurance of response.

Faith of this sort, just right for Saturday, defies the reasoning of the world. The world concludes that in defeat, there can be no prayer. If there is hope-filled prayer, there can be no defeat. But faith knows better. Both parts give us Saturday truth: "I am lost. . . . Do not fear." We do not choose one or the other!

EASTER

Easter Day

Psalm 148; Exodus 12:1–14; Isaiah 51:9–11; John 1:1–18; 20:19–23

*God of life and new life and resurrected life, give us courage to receive
your gift of life and to perform that gift in ways that give new life to the
world. In his name. Amen.*

The liturgical sequence of the church year and the liturgical
calendar of Judaism are parallel enough that Easter and Passover always are close together. The convergence of the two
festivals makes it compelling that on Easter Day our reading
should concern the detailed instructions for the observance of
Passover. Beyond the particularities of liturgical practice, the
central theological point is that God has acted decisively to
save God's people. In the Exodus narrative, it is rescue from
Egyptian bondage. In Christian parlance, it is rescue from the
power of death and sin. In these festivals, Jews and Christians
are on the glad receiving end of the power of God that transforms both the history of God's people and the world in which
they live.

It is quite remarkable that in the Gospel reading from John
20 the encounter of the disciples with the risen Christ does
more than assure them of his presence and his rescue. More
than that happens in this account. First, Jesus greets his disciples in peace (shalom) . . . twice. Second, he breathes on them;
he extends to them a second breath not unlike the breath of
the Creator for the first human couple. But third, he authorizes this inchoate church to be an agent of forgiveness of sins,
to break the vicious cycles of deathly alienation and bondage.
Since only God can forgive, it is clear that the church is given
authority to do the work of God. Easter is a fresh intrusion
of God's power for life into the world. The gift of power for
life, however, is not simply a gift to and for the church. It is
a gift through the church and beyond the church. As we will
see in the Easter season that follows, the resurrection of Jesus
is a missional event in which the followers of Jesus are given
transformative work to do in the world.

Monday after Easter 1

Psalm 93; Exodus 12:14–27; 1 Corinthians 15:1–11; Mark 16:1–8

God who gives and occupies our deepest stories, give us faithful imagination to see how the story of the world is retold according to your singular saving actions. In his name. Amen.

The wonder and vexation of the Bible is that it is rooted, for both Jews and Christians, in a quite particular event, for Jews and Christians *the exodus* and for Christians *the Easter resurrection*. In both cases the truth of our faith pivots on particular happenings that occurred in actual historical time.

The wonder of that claim, for both Jews and Christians, is that the mystery of God is fully invested in the particularity of world history so that world history is the venue for the enactment of God's will and purpose. A consequence of that amazing claim is that the primal mode of faith is narrative particularity. That is, "We love to tell the story," and the story itself is the grit of gospel faith. The events (exodus, Easter) evoke storytelling witnesses. These stories, moreover, fly in the face of all established authority, whether of Pharaoh or of Rome.

The vexation of this way of faith is that such specificity is an intellectual embarrassment in the modern world that takes as the norm of truth either provable scientific data or logically compelling universal truths. Storytelling truth meets neither scientific nor logical norms, and so the faithful are often tempted to transpose narrative particularity into either logical or scientific modes, a temptation faced by both fundamentalists and progressives.

The beginning of the Easter season is a time to consider how much we, in faith, are shaped by these two strange narratives, how much we are tempted to find a better truth, and what it means to be entrusted with these narratives that are to be told in the face of all established authority and all settled truth.

Tuesday after Easter 1

Psalm 103; Exodus 12:28–39; 1 Corinthians 15:12–28; Mark 16:9–20

God of good blessings, we are dazzled by the way your power to bless emerges through unexpected sources. Grant that we may receive such blessings and share them in a world where your blessing is so urgently required. In his name. Amen.

The Exodus narrative is preoccupied with Moses' attempt to depart with the slaves from Pharaoh's domain and Pharaoh's resolve to prevent such a departure of his supply of cheap labor. In this reading, the pressure on Pharaoh to release the slaves becomes unbearably great. Pharaoh must reverse field and now is eager to have the slaves depart. He issues a series of imperatives to Moses, still imagining that he is in charge: "Go, take, be gone!" Good riddance!

But Pharaoh utters one more remarkable imperative to Moses: "Bless me also." Pharaoh had finally come to recognize that the power of blessing, that is, the infusion of life, is now in the hands of Moses. This is an ominous recognition for Pharaoh, because he had long assumed that he and his priests administered the power of blessing. This belated recognition by Pharaoh amounts to a complete undoing of Pharaoh's authority and an awareness that the power to bless lies with the mixed multitude of nobodies with whom the creator God is now allied. The same learning came later to the Roman Empire when it recognized in Jesus the power to bless. It is, moreover, the same learning we have when we see that the assumed sources of life — money, learning, technology — have no power to bless and save. We keep relearning that such a capacity to bless arises from below and not from forces we have made into idols that cannot bless or save. And now, in the wake of Easter, the disciples are sent with this truth to "the whole creation." The gospel news is that the power of blessing does not reside where we imagine. We keep relearning that it wells up elsewhere in ways that shatter our preferences.

Wednesday after Easter 1

Psalm 97; Exodus 12:40–51; 1 Corinthians 15:29–41; Matthew 28:1–16

God of new possibility, reshuffle our old tribal distinctions and release us from the fears that make such distinctions necessary. Give us freedom to join fully in your evangelical subversion. In his name. Amen.

We do well to keep these two stories—exodus and Easter—together in our purview. Such a double reading permits us to move readily between these two texts. The Exodus reading reflects a discussion—which was always recurring—about who gets to celebrate Passover. We can see that the community is preoccupied with proper regulations; at the end, however, is the quite remarkable conclusion, "one law [*torah*]" for natives and strangers. This is remarkable because communities of faith—Jewish and Christian—are always tempted to tribalism that wants to exclude all but "our kind." But here such tribalism is explicitly rejected. The Passover celebration of emancipation pertains to all; none is excluded from the God-evoked celebration.

It is suggestive to juxtapose this affirmation with the caution voiced in the Gospel narrative in which the authorities engage in a cover-up so that the Roman governor does not find out that the body is missing, that is, does not learn of the resurrection. The reason this new reality must be concealed from the governor is that the governor is the one who must maintain social order and therefore must maintain social distinctions and social stratifications that keep everyone in his or her place. Thus we may see that the truth of resurrection is powerfully subversive because it places in jeopardy all those distinctions on which imperial power is based. This recurring subversion of exodus and Easter is urgent in our society, with its anxiety, its xenophobia, and its hostility to those who do not belong. In Easter we become participants in an immense subversion.

Thursday after Easter 1

Psalm 146; Exodus 13:3–10;
1 Corinthians 15:41–50; Matthew 28:16–20

*We worship you, Lord Jesus. We worship you in your lowly human
solidarity and in your majestic divine hiddenness. We believe; help our
unbelief. In your name. Amen.*

At the conclusion of Matthew, just prior to the familiar,
grand Great Commission to the disciples, we are told, "They
worshiped him; but some doubted." We may judge that the
ones who worshiped and the ones who doubted are the same
people, worshiping but doubting, doubting but nonetheless
worshiping.

They worshiped Jesus, gladly acknowledging him in his
risen life as the ultimate truth of their existence. Some were
open to doubt, perhaps because his resurrection is intellectu-
ally implausible. More likely because adherence to Jesus was
risky business in the empire of Rome.

We may imagine that the Passover community in the land
of promise worshiped YHWH, the God of the exodus. This
commitment to and reliance on the God of the exodus set Israel
against the other peoples in the land with their several gods.
But surely some who celebrated Passover doubted. Indeed
later prophets inveigh against those who compromised and
worshiped the gods of the land who gave rain and who were
not so insistent on social justice.

Surely we are like that in consumerist America. We do worship the Christ. But doubt about this scandal of particularity
makes it easy to embrace easier, more palatable, less demanding religious options. We face the seductive temptations of
nationalism and racism and sexism as viable ultimate claims.
We also face options of religion in which there is an easier way;
nor are we so committed to un-American ideas of suffering for
the neighbor or sharing our abundance. These texts invite us
to consider both our doubts and our gladness in worship of
Christ. No alternative has such news about new life.

Friday after Easter 1

Psalm 136; Exodus 13:1–2, 11–16;
1 Corinthians 15:51–58; Luke 24:1–12

*God of new life, heal us from our fear of death, that we may no longer
participate in the deathly swirl of greed and violence. Give us liberty to
do your good work in the world. In his name. Amen.*

The lyrical words in the Epistle reading reiterate the most
characteristic pattern of covenantal faith, a *declaration* from
which issues an *imperative*. The declaration has been the subject of Paul's extended testimony in this chapter concerning
the resurrection of Jesus. Paul declares God's victory over the
power and the sting of death. Paul's claim does not announce
that we will not die. It announces, rather, that we do not need
to live our lives in response to the power and sting of death that
wants to negate our life, because death has been disarmed of
its power to hurt us. This is defining news for us because we
live in a society that is largely propelled by the fear of death.
The outcome of that fear is anxiety, greed, and violence, all
grounded in an elemental fear of scarcity; death specializes in
scarcity and parsimony.

All of that, however, is now obsolete and irrelevant to our
life because such a negative force has lost all its authority
among us. As a consequence, Paul issues an imperative introduced by "therefore": As a result, be steady and constant without anxiety; above all, overflow with the performance of God's
work. That work is justice and peace, security and freedom.
It is work that intends to restore the well-being of God's good
creation and to bring joy to all creatures—human and nonhuman—who inhabit God's creation. Restorative work means to
overcome the wounds inflicted by the impact of fear, greed,
and violence. That good work is the continuing response to
the news of Easter. It is to wrench the world from the power
of death by the enhancement of life that is God's good and
continuing gift.

Saturday after Easter 1

Psalm 145; Exodus 13:17–14:4;
2 Corinthians 4:16–5:10; Mark 12:18–27

God of deep resolve and hidden work, forgive our readiness to trust in
what we can see, to obey what we see, to be intimidated by what we see.
Give us faith to take a step and then another step. In his name. Amen.

Walking by sight is an endless temptation for the church. It
means to go by what we can see. What we can see is that pro-
death, anti-gospel power prevails everywhere in our world. In
the time of Jesus, that power was embodied by Rome, which
specialized not only in military domination but also in economic exploitation. And the chance for the church countering
that power was nil. In the Exodus reading, the Hebrews can
see the immense power of Pharaoh that had first enslaved and
then pursued to kill them. Their chance against Pharaoh was
remote.

Against such a futile exercise as walking by sight, Paul urges
gospel folk to "walk by faith," that is, to trust what we cannot
see. To trust the gospel is to bet on the hidden will and purpose
of God that persists and that will come to a good outcome, an
outcome vouched for by the resurrection of Jesus. Walking
(living) by such confidence permits us to run great risks, to
hope great hopes, and to commit acts that are judged, by what
we can see, as foolish.

In our own time the decision to depend on sight or faith is
an immediate challenge to the church. When we walk by sight,
we focus on members, dollars, measurable programs, and visible successes. Such a practice surely leads us to discourage-
ment. Gospel faith, however, does not order its life by such
sightings. Rather gospel faith proceeds in confidence, knowing
that the power of God is at work for life. This is a time, then,
in the face of tough sightings, to lift up our hearts to the Lord
in confidence. As a result, we may run risks and not lose heart.

Second Sunday of Easter

Psalm 146; Exodus 14:5–22; 1 John 1:1–7; John 14:1–7

We give thanks, saving God of truth, that your life is so fully engaged in the life of the world. Help us to know that our own transformative actions in the world are acts of praise that magnify you. In his name. Amen.

Two allied purposes are served by the exodus liberation. On the one hand, the purpose of which we are immediately aware is that the slaves are emancipated from Pharaoh's predatory economy. Moses could assert, "The LORD will fight for you." The news is that the emancipatory God takes sides in history on behalf of the vulnerable who cannot fight for their own well-being. On the other hand, less noticed is the claim that in the exodus deliverance, the Lord "gains glory" over Pharaoh. That is, God's reputation is enhanced by defeating Pharaoh; God is shown to be powerful and sovereign, even in the face of Pharaoh.

It is a wonder of gospel faith that God's glory is connected to the emancipation of the vulnerable. God's "godness" is deeply linked to transformative work in the world. This linkage tells us something decisive about the character of this God whose rule is effective in the deep contestations of history.

For that reason the gospel is always calling us to decide our deepest loyalty, because our trust in God is linked to our life in the world. Thus in the Epistle reading, the great cosmic contest of light and darkness is acted out in concrete fellowship with the community of Christ. That alliance of *divine glory* and *worldly well-being* is a core truth of gospel faith. For that reason, we give thanks that Jesus is indeed *the truth of God* that is performed as *the truth of the world* for the sake of the world. The truth that Jesus embodies links God and world in deep fidelity.

Monday after Easter 2

Psalm 1; Exodus 14:21–31; 1 Peter 1:1–12; John 14:8–17

God visible in Jesus and in his trail of many transformations and in many healings and emancipations in the world, give us courage to hope for the unseen through what we have seen. In his name. Amen.

In these readings we are invited to reflect on *what we see* and how we extrapolate to *what we do not see yet trust*. The Exodus narrative is presented in almost childlike innocence: "The LORD is fighting for them against Egypt." At the end of the reading, however, it is reported that "Israel saw the great work that the LORD did." They did not see the Lord. They saw the outcome of escape and emancipation. And they "believed" (trusted) in the God who had done this.

In the Epistle reading, "Although you have not seen him, you love him." You love the Lord whom you have not seen! In the Gospel reading: *We see Jesus.* In seeing Jesus, *we see the Father.* But we do not see the Father who remains unseen. It is faith of the church from the beginning that in Jesus the mystery of God the Father is fully present among us.

We may in the Easter season reflect on what we have seen. What we have seen is the exodus emancipation and many emancipations since then. What we have seen (and tell stories about) are the wonders of Jesus who transformed the life of many vulnerable people. What we continue to see are transformative actions in the world that are not subject to explanation (and many that we can explain!). They are subject only to confession and testimony. And from that testimony and confession we are able (sometimes) to trust that the holy sovereign faithful God is deeply present in these transformative, emancipatory actions that are visible in the world. Such seeing does not yield certitude; it yields, as Peter asserts, a living hope that keeps the world open for more gifts that are in sum "imperishable."

Tuesday after Easter 2

Psalm 5; Exodus 15:1–21; 1 Peter 1:13–25; John 14:18–31

God of new futures, give us freedom to relinquish old modes of life. Give us energy to receive the new life you give, and discipline enough to embrace it. In his name. Amen.

The God of the gospel is a future-generating God. In the Exodus text, the songs of Moses and Miriam celebrate God's victory over Pharaoh that led to the liberation of the slaves from the unbearable conditions of Pharaoh's labor policy. This doxology to God celebrates the conviction that there is none like YHWH, none like YHWH with the capacity to defeat Pharaoh, no other who is filled with loyal love toward the slaves. It is no wonder that the women danced and sang over their new futures of well-being outside the reach of Pharaoh.

The epistle characterizes the former life of the addressees as one "conformed to desires." Now, because of the saving work of Christ, those in the Jesus movement are called to a new life. That is a life of holiness, of utter, uncompromising loyalty and devotion to God. That holiness is expressed as a "genuine mutual love" for the other members of the movement. Holiness that issues in love is a life of well-being that is contrasted with the old life of conformity to passions.

Easter is a season in which to explore alternative futures that are given in God's victory over the powers of death. That future is a contrast to the anxiety of greed, to the rat race of competition, and to an endless fear of being left behind or not having enough. This is a season to consider a gospel future that is marked by singing and dancing, by holiness and love, by a life unencumbered by the pressures, demands, and expectations of an overly busy 24/7 world preoccupied with getting and having and achieving. That new life requires a disciplined insistent disengagement from the old life that is not easy. The pressure to old conformities is immense. Nonetheless the gift of a life of peace governed by God's Holy Spirit is on offer, even to us.

Wednesday after Easter 2

Psalm 119:1–24; Exodus 15:22–16:10; 1 Peter 2:1–10; John 15:1–11

God of mercy, we are left in wonderment by your capacity to transform nobodies (like us) into your people. We are glad to receive your mercy. Grant that we, in turn, may be agents of your mercy toward the "left behind" among us. In his name. Amen.

A major theme of the Bible is the wonder that the nobodies of the world receive mercy from God. The juxtaposition of *nobodies* and *mercy* is a way of thinking and acting that contradicts the way of the world. In the Epistle reading, the writer marvels how a nondescript collection of unnoticed people could be formed into the people of God. He applies wondrous labels from the Sinai tradition—"a chosen race, a royal priesthood, a holy nation, God's own people"—to this community newly formed around the gospel and then declares: "You have received mercy." God's restorative attention has made a new people!

So it is in the Exodus reading. The mixed multitude that departed Egypt was likewise nondescript. In a venue of extreme jeopardy (wilderness), they lacked food and water. But the God who brought them out had mercy on them, mercy to give water, bread, and meat.

The contemporaneity of these acts of mercy is evident. All we need to do is identify the nobodies in our society who are "no people." The inventory of nobodies consists of all those who fall behind in the rat race of the predatory economy. That might variously include racial or ethnic minorities, the aging, the disabled, and, most simply, the poor. These are the ones who are the most likely candidates for God's mercy, for God's free, unearned good gifts of sustenance. If we move from the free gift of the epistle to the urgency of the Gospel reading, we might imagine that "bearing fruit" is participation in enacting God's good mercy. Such mercy, given by God, acted by the faithful, makes new community possible in the face of community-denying forces.

Thursday after Easter 2

Psalm 18:1–20; Exodus 16:10–21; 1 Peter 2:11–25; John 15:12–27

God of fresh water and ample loaves, give us the courage to trust our good memory of abundance and so to refuse the fearfulness of the world that draws us away from your commandment to love. In his name. Amen.

These readings situate the community of Christ responsibly in the world. The Gospel reading has Jesus affirm: "You do not belong to the world." You are not defined by the world and do not need to meet the expectations of the world. But the Epistle reading is a counsel about living in the world by getting along with the authorities. But live there as free persons! The two texts together suggest a peaceable posture, but with an acute awareness that such accommodation to sociopolitical reality does not compromise one's peculiar evangelical identity.

We may consider that the manna narrative in Exodus provides a clue about how to live as one free in the world, but not of the world. The manna narrative affirms that there is an abundance given by God beyond the administration of Pharaoh; rooted in God's glory, that abundance is beyond the measure or control or even awareness of Pharaoh and any other ruling authority. This suggests that the assurance of abundance is something of a secret kept in the memory of God's people; it is a secret that may make one immune to the demands of dominant society.

The epistle warns against "the desires of the flesh" that include greed, anxiety, fear of scarcity and inadequacy, and self-preoccupation, all of which may eventuate in violence. To be "of the flesh" is to assume that such "desires of the flesh" are normal and acceptable. But the community of the gospel knows better. Its secret assurance of God's abundance means that we do not need to practice greed, do not need to be anxious, and do not need to fear scarcity. That is genuine freedom. It is a kind of freedom that the world little suspects; it is the truth of our faith.

Friday after Easter 2

Psalm 16; Exodus 16:22–36; 1 Peter 3:13–4:6; John 16:1–15

God of truth who contradicts the way of the world, give us access to your truthfulness, that we may discern more fully the falseness of our society and that we may choose differently in ways congruent with our baptism. In his name. Amen.

Nobody said that living in the gospel would be easy. Indeed, if our practice of the gospel is easy, it may be that we have not quite understood the obedience to which we are called. Jesus warns about falling away or going astray from our calling. The reason for going astray is that obedience to the gospel contradicts the world and evokes hostility. Gospel obedience in our culture, as in the ancient world, is indeed profoundly subversive of dominant culture, now as it was then.

The people of God have been going astray for a very long time. In the ancient manna story, Moses is explicit that bread is given for the day; it is not to be stored up. But the Israelites, in their deep anxiety, store it up anyway. Moses reprimands them for their distrust of daily bread and rebukes them for disobedience to the commandment.

The commandment that he has most immediately in mind is the commandment to keep the seventh day holy as a Sabbath. Who knew that Sabbath violation, wrought in anxiety about having enough bread, constituted such a serious affront? But perhaps Sabbath is exactly the antidote to going astray in the practice of anxiety and greed and worry about scarcity that beset our culture. Sabbath, to be sure, is a pause in our work; more than that, it is also a pause in anxiety that keeps us fearful, preoccupied, and overly busy in a way that is inimical to God's commandment to trust and to love. Sabbath in Christian tradition, may be an opportunity to consider our baptismal identity in which we renounce many of the seductions of our culture.

Saturday after Easter 2

Psalm 20; Exodus 17:1–16; 1 Peter 4:7–19; John 16:16–33

God of inexplicable fidelity, give us wits to identfy our places of obedient
risk; give us fidelity that we do not miss "the hour." In his name. Amen.

In our covenant with God, the relationship is not quite symmetrical. On the one hand, God calls God's people to account.
In both New Testament readings, the tone of the text is one of
imminent showdown. It is called "the hour" when a decision
must be made for the future. Jesus summons his follower to
face into this hour and to decide to run risks for the gospel.
That hour is like the delivery time for the mother of a child.
It is an occasion for stress that yields the happy result of the
newborn. But the hour cannot be avoided.

On the other hand, the Old Testament text is an instance in
which God's people call God to account. In a moment of great
anxiety when they are without water in the wilderness, the
faultfinders take the initiative. They escalate their insistence
with a question to God: "Is the LORD among us or not?" Are
you to be trusted? Put up or shut up! That act of enormous
chutzpah is much practiced in Israel and is the basis for urgent
petitionary prayer.

The outcome of Israel's challenge to God is that God hears
and responds. God gives water. The water is an inexplicable
wonder, for it comes when Moses strikes the rock. The rock is
an unlikely source of water. God's powerful fidelity is substan-
tiated. But conversely, the summons of Jesus to face that hour
of the ordeal when faith is tested is not a historical memory. It
is a contemporary summons. Our proper Easter wonderment
is, how and in what way are we still summoned to face the
hour? God's response to the plea for water is one of great fidelity; our response awaits.

Third Sunday of Easter

Psalm 148; Exodus 18:1–12; 1 John 2:7–17; Mark 16:9–20

God of freedom and enemy of enslavement,
God of love and adversary of hate,
God of light and comprehender of darkness,
Give us the foolish freedom to choose wisely. In his name. Amen.

The gospel always puts before us an either-or that requires a decision:

— In the Old Testament text, Jethro gets from Moses the news of the God of the exodus who is "greater than all gods," including the gods of Pharaoh. The exodus required a daring decision.

— In the Epistle lesson, the trusting community is invited to choose light rather than darkness. These open-ended metaphysical categories are given moral dimension with a concern for relating to other members of the community.

— The ultimate either-or voiced here is love or hate for the brother and sister. By the end of the reading the text works back to God the Father or the world.

These four forms of either-or—exodus God or Egyptian gods, light or darkness, love or hate, God or world—are all of a piece. The evangelical choice is to opt for emancipated transformative relationality wherein life is lived from and for and in response to God.

That choice is most often voiced in the Bible in grandly dramatic ways. The truth is, however, that the most elemental choices of love or hate are the small daily choices in which everything is at stake. That either-or operates in face-to-face relationships of an intimate or casual kind and in acts of policy formation. There are deep choices for the gospel to be made everywhere always.

Monday after Easter 3

Psalm 25; Exodus 18:13–27; 1 Peter 5:1–14; Matthew 3:1–6

God of good order, we give you thanks for the leadership authorized for our well-being. Give us stamina and attentiveness to care about the mundane, that your purposes may be served by programs, procedures, regulations, budgets, and meetings. In his name. Amen.

These texts invite reflection on the body politic and the leadership required for its well-being. Consideration of leadership in both church and civil society tells powerfully against any imagined individualism that dismisses institutional life and institutional responsibility as of little interest or importance.

The Epistle reading focuses on "the elders," the leaders of the early Christian congregations. The letter commends leaders who work by persuasion; it warns, moreover, against self-serving leaders who seek "gain." The purpose of such persuasive leadership together with such trusting followership is that the congregation may maintain its integrity and mission, and not be talked out of them. The Old Testament reading features Moses, at the behest of Jethro, attending to organizational matters. The leaders who will assist Moses are those who have integrity and take no bribes. In both of these readings there is concern about the seduction of money!

These readings invite us to consider the mundane matters of practical leadership, institutional order and procedures, and the way in which authority is exercised in the church. US Supreme Court decisions and nominations in recent years invite reflection as well on the role of judicial leadership in society, especially when court appointments and court rulings are so distorted by political and ideological interest. Such matters belong centrally to wise and responsible faith. We are invited to a fresh awareness of the large scope of responsible piety and spirituality.

Tuesday after Easter 3

Psalm 26; Exodus 19:1–16; Colossians 1:1–14; Matthew 3:7–12

We give thanks, ruler of our life and giver of new creation, that we belong, body and soul, to your new regime. Grant that we may live in responsible fidelity to our new sphere of belonging to you. In his name. Amen.

In faith we have been "transferred" to a new membership. The Epistle reading declares a "transfer" into "the kingdom of his beloved Son," where new conduct is appropriate. Now it belongs to us to draw strength from Christ's authority, to endure everything, to give thanks, and to share a different future. This inventory of gains and gifts — strength, patience, thanks, hope — marks the Christian community in contrast to its social environment.

The same transfer is enacted in the Exodus reading. Israel is transferred from the exploitative regime of Pharaoh to covenant with YHWH, a new people devoted to an obedient life with YHWH.

We notice in this declaration at Sinai the qualifying "if" of covenant with YHWH: "If you obey my voice and keep my covenant. . . . " The offer of this new relationship depends on glad obedience to YHWH's purpose. In Colossians 3:10, the church is also called to a new obedience, to put on "the new self." In the Gospel reading, moreover, John warns against presumption on the part of those who live in covenant. There is no guaranteed pedigree on offer. Everything turns on a readiness to "bear good fruit," that is, a life congruent with God's intent for the world.

We may consider what it means to join the church. This is more than a clerical act or a liturgic form. This transfer is a momentous redefinition of one's life. We are welcomed into a new sphere governed by forgiveness. Think what it means to live a forgiven life!

Wednesday after Easter 3

Psalm 38; Exodus 19:16–25; Colossians 1:15–23; Matthew 3:13–17

God of fierce holiness, give us courage to receive your intrusion. Give us openness beyond our comfort zone for your coming that makes all things new and different. In his name. Amen.

Today we have readings that defy our usual explanatory categories. The narratives have adopted a *mode of presentation* that escapes our reason because the *substance of the message* is beyond our understanding. Thus there is a match between mode of presentation and substance.

In the narrative of the baptism of Jesus, the heavens break open and a voice speaks to identify and acknowledge Jesus. His verification requires endorsement from elsewhere, that is, from God's own mouth. Likewise in the Sinai narrative, the spectacular phenomena of smoke, quake, trumpet, and thunder constitute a narrative strategy for letting the voice of God break in on the community of Israel. The entire narrative suggests that such an intrusion from heaven is a very risky encounter, and the community is properly fearful of such and on notice. The holiness of God is a fierce interruption into the life of the world.

These two strange intrusions of holiness yield parallel claims concerning the awesome holiness of God.

At Sinai: God's own self has come to communicate with Israel.
At the Jordan: God's own self authorizes Jesus.

The intrusions of God at Sinai and at the Jordan attest that God is present in fullness to the community. The spin-off of this event at the Jordan is the claim (made in the epistle) that Jesus is the new God-authorized presence in whom "all things hold together." In a world that is indeed falling apart, we are invited to his authority, his truth, and his presence. The world is not on its own. It has been decisively interrupted from holy elsewhere.

Thursday after Easter 3

Psalm 37:1–18; Exodus 20:1–21; Colossians 1:24–2:7; Matthew 4:1–11

God of costly, wondrous love, we give you thanks for your riches shared with us. Give us wise steadfastness that we may not yield the wonder of your good news. In his name. Amen.

The Epistle reading warns that we should not be deceived by "plausible arguments." The reference is to ways of reasoning that are inimical to the covenantal claims of the gospel: (a) In the Gospel narrative the tempter makes plausible arguments to try to talk Jesus out of his peculiar vocation as messiah. (b) Amid the covenantal claims of Sinai, the soon-to-follow golden calf is a plausible argument for a god who does not demand and who is palpably available. (c) In the epistle, the Christian congregation is confronted with the plausible alternative of a whole-life philosophy that explains the whole of reality.

These three plausible arguments all have in common a more reasonable way to live. Thus the golden calf is more reassuring than the God who makes uncompromising demands. The offer of the devil is more compelling than the hard way of the gospel. And the philosophy on offer in Colossae is without the embarrassment of the cross that contradicts all easy truth.

Plausible arguments to the contrary are alive among us: the self-security of capitalism, the rationality of scientism, the self-sufficiency of technology, all without the acute neighborly demands of Sinai that are at the center of the gospel.

In the face of such alternatives, the epistle speaks of the "riches" of the "mystery" of Christ. The mystery is that the grace and truth of the holy God has become bodied in human form in Jesus. The riches are not a head trip in the Christian congregation. They are rather the practical experience of a fellowship of love, a community of forgiveness, and an ethic of social justice. These riches expose the poverty of the alternatives.

Friday after Easter 3

Psalm 105:1–22; Exodus 24:1–18; Colossians 2:8–23; Matthew 4:12–17

God of light . . . and life and joy, grant us the wisdom to stand in fresh ways for your good regime, that we may turn away from the crippling powers that deny our full humanness. In his name. Amen.

Matthew imagines that the geographical movement of Jesus signifies the advance of his rule. Matthew employs archaic geographical terms in order to quote the familiar poetry of Isaiah 9 and reread it with reference to Jesus. The Isaiah text anticipates the rise of a new Davidic ruler who will counter the "darkness" of the Assyrian threat. Now Matthew suggests that the assertion of Jesus' kingdom will be a displacement of the darkness, whether the political darkness of Rome or the theological darkness of sin. The rule of Jesus will overcome and displace the failed rule of powers that have prevented well-being. Jesus calls people to "repent," that is, to renounce old loyalties in order to embrace the new emancipatory governance of Jesus.

The Epistle reading ups the rhetorical ante by asserting, in lyrical fashion, that the "whole fullness of deity" is present in Jesus. Jesus comes with immense authority and power to put an end to governance that has restricted and precluded well-being. Thus like the old conflict between David and the Assyrians, the epistle presents a conflict between Jesus and the "rulers and authorities" who might be political powers. The letter also sees that a compelling philosophy also operates that wants to curb conduct in a way that "disqualifies" members of the congregation. But the authority of Christ overrides all such enemies of human well-being.

Various forms of darkness beset us, including the orthodoxies of economics, the scruples of frightened religion, and the distortions of compelling ideologies that keep score and impair full humanness. Against all of that comes the light of joy, liberty, and well-being. Imagine our special darknesses defeated and robbed of power.

Saturday after Easter 3

Psalm 30; Exodus 25:1–22; Colossians 3:1–17; Matthew 4:18–25

Lord Jesus, voice of summons and carrier of healing, grant that we may leave behind enough to follow you more closely. Free us enough to participate in your healing vocation. In your name. Amen.

The imperative Jesus issues to Peter and Andrew, and to James and John, is terse and unqualified. They respond without qualification. The Gospel narrative juxtaposes "immediately they . . . followed" and "he cured." They leave the boat, which means they give up their livelihood and their financial resources. They leave their father; they move beyond their tribal world that is familiar to them. They leave all that gave them security. No doubt Jesus had done the same. He had no moneymaking capacity; he moved beyond his tribal horizon. "Moving beyond" was surely a factor in his healing capacity; he was, in an unencumbered way, open to the healing forces of the Creator that are lively and available in the creation. He was free to mobilize those forces.

The following undertaken by the apostles was geographical and economic. The epistle readily suggests that following the way of Christ is also behavioral. Paul can admonish believers to "put to death" old patterns of conduct that perhaps are sanctioned by our tribal locations. Paul names modes of behavior that are not unusual in a dog-eat-dog competitive world: "fornication, impurity, passion, evil desire, and greed." The baptized are called to leave all of that behind, along with our "boat" and our "father," our finances and our tribal security.

The alternative is a new unencumbered self, situated in a new community. The new norms of conduct are not unfamiliar to us: "compassion, kindness, humility, meekness, and patience," and above all, forgiveness. No doubt from such life practices comes the transformative capacity to heal. It is no wonder that "great crowds followed him."

Fourth Sunday of Easter

Psalm 63:1–8; Exodus 28:1–4, 30–38; 1 John 2:18–29; Mark 6:30–44

God, creator of abundance, give us awe and wonder to trust your good abundance, and sufficient freedom to renounce the deep lie of scarcity that is all around us. In his name. Amen.

The Epistle reading utilizes very harsh terms for those who oppose the teaching of the apostles. They are labeled the "antichrist" and accused of lying. Whatever that alien teaching was in the midst of the early church, we may consider such pejorative terms for the lies told among us that have become accepted as conventional wisdom. Among such lies, propelled by anxiety and an ideology of greed, is the assumption that we live in a world of scarcity. There is not enough to share with all, not enough water, oil, food, money, health care, or housing. And because of such undoubted scarcity, we conjure practices and devise policies that assure that the strong get a disproportionate share of creation's goods at the expense of the vulnerable.

This Gospel story, however, witnesses against such a lie of scarcity. The setting is a "deserted place" without life resources. There is a hungry crowd, and Jesus is moved with compassion. His compassion has material consequences. In an inexplicable act, he takes a small supply of food and feeds a crowd of five thousand men. Nothing is explained; we are told only that he performed abundance by a verbal sequence: he took, he blessed, he broke, he gave. It requires no imagination to see that these four verbs are the verbs of the Eucharist, the church's great meal of abundance.

This meal of Jesus, when he enacted it and each time we enact it, exposes the lie of scarcity. Almost all of us have been recruited into the lie of scarcity. And now, in this Easter season, we are invited into the truth of God's abundance, a truth that permits different relationships and that evokes different policies. Loaves abound!

Monday after Easter 4

Psalm 41; Exodus 32:1–20; Colossians 3:18–4:6; Matthew 5:1–10

God of transformative capacity, we give thanks that you have recruited and empowered us to make a difference by the way we live. Give us freedom to be as vulnerable as you have shown yourself to be. In his name. Amen.

The story of the golden calf invites us to consider the ways in which we, in our anxiety, manufacture gods that reassure us. This particular manufactured god is a combination of gold (the commodity with which the haves leverage the have-nots) and virility (because the "calf" is in reality a bull) wherein we perform our self-sufficiency. The combination of gold plus bullish virility is a compelling icon for our society, dramatized by the liturgy of professional football that is all about money and virility!

We might miss the crucial role of Moses in this story. Moses is a check on God's anger. By his intervention, Moses evokes a change on God's part. Moses' effective intervention is an exercise of human agency that makes a decisive difference in worldly affairs.

The Beatitudes of Jesus place a great bet on human agency. Those who perform these particular social possibilities are carriers of blessing whereby the world may be blessed. Jesus clearly intends that his followers should be active and vulnerable, not resigned to the way the world is.

The dominant ideology of gold-plus-virility does not want or prize such dangerous human agency. That ideology would prefer that we be passive couch potatoes who settle for entertainment, medical fixes through pharmaceutical drugs, and consumer satiation. Idols (of money and virility) do not evoke human agency. Our story, however, consists in daring human agents who act differently and so transform the world.

Tuesday after Easter 4

Psalm 45; Exodus 32:21–34; 1 Thessalonians 1:1–10; Matthew 5:11–16

God of covenantal freedom, faithfulness, and risk, grant that we may imitate you in the way that we witnessed in Jesus. Give us courage to resist the idols that summon us. In his name. Amen.

Idolatry is serious business for the God of the gospel. Idols popularly take the form of lifeless icons. Most elementally an idol is an investment of ultimacy in something other than God, thus a distortion of truth. In the Exodus narrative, Aaron's idol making is treated with harshness, because God will not be mocked. In the face of such a distortion, God's holiness is ferocious, perhaps because God is very proud, perhaps because such a distortion will lead to the death of Israel.

The celebrative message of Paul to the Christian community of Thessalonica culminates with the affirmation, "You turned to God from idols, to serve a living and true God." The consequence of such a turn is that the church community is affirmed for its work of faith, its labor of love, and its steadfastness of hope, thus the great Pauline triad of faith, love, and hope. All these practices, the most defining practices of the church, concern risky, open-ended relationships. It is useful to recognize that when such open-ended relationships are found to be more risky than we can bear, the fallback is to create idols of certitude that entail no risk. Such closed-off certitude precludes the work of faith, the labor of love, and the steadfastness of hope. In a commodity-propelled economy such as ours, the idols of certitude are powerful and compelling.

The summons of Jesus is to risky relationships grounded in faith, hope, and love. Jesus clearly anticipates that his disciple community will have freedom to be transformative (light, salt) in the world. Such relationships are always less popular than certitude.

Wednesday after Easter 4

Psalm 119:49–72; Exodus 33:1–23;
1 Thessalonians 2:1–12; Matthew 5:17–20

*God of dialogic faithfulness whose name we know, we thank you for your
commitment to us and to our future. Give us the chutzpah to live well in
response to you. In his name. Amen.*

There is a powerful drift in US religion and spirituality to
dissolve the God of the gospel into a force or an idea or an
experience. That dissolution is done in order to avoid the
embarrassing "primitive" notion of the tradition that God is a
character who exercises agency and participates actively in the
narrative, memory, and hope of Israel and the church. There
are no doubt gains in such an interpretive maneuver; but there
are also costs.

In contrast to that powerful drift, the imagery and rhetoric
of the Bible is insistent on the character and agency of God.
This presentation of God permits a genuinely dialogical faith
with the risks, gifts, and demands that inescapably belong to a
serious relationship.

In the Exodus narrative, that dialogic mode of life is on
exhibit. In the wake of the episode of the golden calf, Moses
must renegotiate the covenant with YHWH, the Lord of the
covenant. In the culmination of that negotiation, YHWH
declares mercy and graciousness, but given in full sovereign
freedom: "I will be gracious to whom I will be gracious, and
will show mercy on whom I will show mercy." But there is a
limit to God's self-giving and self-disclosure: You cannot see
God's face! You cannot dissolve the mystery of God. You cannot curb God's freedom. It is on that basis that Israel's life with
God will continue.

As a postscript, notice the counsel of the epistle. The church
is urged to "lead a life worthy of God." God has expectations.
Indeed, God tests hearts to see about the seriousness of covenantal fidelity. Life in dialogic engagement is indeed demanding . . . and generative of possibility beyond our horizon.

Thursday after Easter 4

Psalm 50; Exodus 34:1–17; 1 Thessalonians 2:13–20; Matthew 5:21–26

God of covenants broken and remade, we live by your faithfulness toward us. In your good mercy, grant that this day may be among us a day of restoration and renewal. In his name. Amen.

After the breaking of the covenant via the golden calf and after the strenuous negotiation between YHWH and Moses, in our reading today YHWH takes a big breath and then utters this most remarkable formulation of divine self-disclosure. In these verses, all of Israel's vocabulary for covenantal fidelity is reiterated: God is merciful, gracious, slow to anger, filled with steadfast love and faithfulness, and capable of forgiveness.

That recital culminates, however, with a strong adversative "but," after which God enunciates demanding self-regard that does not go easy on those who violate covenant. This formula in two parts gives us both the wondrous fidelity of God and the edginess of divine holiness that will not be taken lightly. This formula is repeated in subsequent Scripture in many variations, sometimes without the adversative second part. This means that the tradition was and is capable of interpretive freedom. It also means that we, as interpretive heirs, exercise that same freedom. We are left, every day, adjudicating the unsettled tension between generous fidelity and stern accountability.

In our reading today, Moses responds to this divine self-disclosure with a petition on behalf of Israel for pardon. And YHWH in turn responds with (a) readiness to remake the covenant that had been broken and (b) a promise of divine marvels to be enacted for Israel. We are heirs of this unsettled tradition. We live, as did the generation of Moses, always in the midst of covenant broken, with the prospect of covenant remade. Because this is a serious relationship, everything depends on divine readiness.

Friday after Easter 4

Psalm 40; Exodus 34:18–35; 1 Thessalonians 3:1–13; Matthew 5:27–37

Lord Jesus, Lord of the church, we give you thanks for your place in the church. Let us be led by your spirit to more engaged giving and receiving with our sisters and brothers elsewhere in the church. In your name. Amen.

Paul figures here as a church administrator as well as a pastor. He is honest and aware of "persecutions" (in the familiar translation, "afflictions"). More important than trouble, however, is his affection for the congregation that he founded at Thessalonica. Paul makes a remarkable statement: "We now live, if you continue to stand firm in the Lord." The fidelity of that congregation becomes a source of support and sustenance for Paul in the midst of the troubles that he faces elsewhere. Paul understands, from his own experience, that one part of the church can be sustained and supported by the faithfulness of other parts of the church. Paul's horizon for the church was the entire sweep of the Mediterranean coastline that he worked, his whole known world. He understood that what one part of the church does matters to other parts of the church.

Unfortunately we are mostly divided into denominations or national churches, or even closer, with a horizon that is too much limited to the local congregation. Paul's letter invites us to think about the worldwide church and its connectedness, a connection not primarily by way of structure or administration but in solidarity in missional obedience. We may have in purview the church in places of persecution, seduction, or lethal compromise. We in our fidelity and courageous missional obedience, including our prayers, may be sources of support for other parts of the church. Conversely we in our accommodated US churches may draw strength and staying power from an awareness of other parts of the church that are steadfast in hard places. We all belong to Christ; we also belong to each other.

Saturday after Easter 4

Psalm 55; Exodus 40:18–38; 1 Thessalonians 4:1–12; Matthew 5:38–48

God of glory, God of grace, give us sufficient trust to yield the ultimacy of our lives into your good hands; let us be peacemakers who break the cycles of violence in which we are enmeshed. In his name. Amen.

As I considered these readings, I recalled the song of the angels at Bethlehem: "Glory to God. . . . Peace on earth." The angels placed in juxtaposition *divine glory* and *human peace.*

The Exodus reading concerns the glory of God dramatically situated in the tabernacle, Israel's traveling sanctuary. The glory is the unapproachable, holy, dangerous *mystery of God* that refuses all mundane domestication. The reason for the tedious punctilious specificity of the tabernacle is that the glory of God evokes awe before holiness that is like nothing we know.

The Matthew text concerns peace on earth. Jesus understood that violence will never make for peace, because the goal of peace must be congruent with means that are peaceable. One way of enforcing order is by brute retaliation of an eye for an eye. Jesus proposes breaking the vicious spiral of violence by an interruptive act. He offers examples of such action: a turned cheek, a given coat, an extra mile. He knows the Torah mandate to love neighbor; but he disrupts by putting "enemy" in the place of "neighbor." And the ground for turning enemy into neighbor is that we are all children of the same Father.

The angels understood that *human peace* is related to *divine glory,* because God's majestic glory reduces all of our place holding to the penultimate. In the presence of such glory, our little agenda of winning, controlling, and being right fades away. We are in fact displaced from our place holding by such stunning ultimacy. We may be peacemakers when we fall back into God's awesome glory.

Fifth Sunday of Easter

Psalm 24; Leviticus 8:1–13, 30–36; Hebrews 12:1–14; Luke 4:16–30

God who presides over the economy with a special eye toward the poor, give us courage and discernment that we may find our place in the ministry of Jesus, that by our lives of obedience the poor may indeed rejoice. In his name. Amen.

The dramatic entry of Jesus into the synagogue at Nazareth focuses on the kingdom of God as an alternative economy. His quote from Isaiah 61 about "the year of the LORD's favor" is a reference to the jubilee year in the Torah of Leviticus 25. That Torah provision concerns the cancellation of debt and the restoration of the poor to viable participation in the economy. It is no wonder that this is good news for the poor!

His citation of the "widow at Zarephath" and the Syrian general Naaman (allusions to stories in the narratives of Elijah and Elisha) is an indication that the gospel reaches out beyond the entitled and privileged with a passionate concern for the vulnerable who have been left behind. There is no surer way to be left behind than to fall into hopeless, unpayable debt.

His reading of the text from Isaiah evokes wonder and admiration among his hometown folk. That wonder and admiration, however, comes to an abrupt end when he spells out in detail the implications of his own intent for Jubilee. The work of Jesus specified here is the cancellation of economic debt and the restoration of the poor to full participation in the economy.

This text reminds us that Easter concerns a renewal and restoration of the earth and its economy. We will do well in this Easter season to run our imagination toward the public, material matters to which Jesus addresses himself. Since we have signed on with the Jesus movement, part of our continuing work concerns debt cancellation and empowerment of the vulnerable poor.

Monday after Easter 5

Psalm 56; Leviticus 16:1–19;
1 Thessalonians 4:13–18; Matthew 6:1–6, 16–18

God of all comfort, we thank you for the truthful news of Easter. May we, in response to the new life you give, extend comfort to those among us who urgently need a hope-filled sister or brother. In his name. Amen.

Paul has made use of mythic language about a new world that displaces the old in order to express his pastoral agenda. But that pastoral agenda is not to be "caught up in the clouds." It is in fact that members of the congregation may "encourage one another." Comfort for those in the Christian community is important because faithful communities are living a demanding life of obedience that runs upstream to dominant culture. Paul does not say any abstract, generic "be comforted," but rather he commends an active, engaged neighborly act of comfort.

The ground of that comfort is that Christ "rose again" and so has overcome the dread of death. From that Paul derives hope that pertains to both those who have died (fallen asleep) and those alive to whom he writes. Both populations will be "caught up together" in the powerful rule of Christ. The common hope for those who have died and those who will die is that they, all of them, will be "with the Lord forever."

As members of the Christian congregation, it is worth considering the peculiar gift of hope that belongs to our faith. Those needs and hungers do not draw us to despair, because our despair is outflanked by the truth of Easter, even if that truth is uttered in the picturesque rhetoric of myth. As the hymn says, "We share our mutual woes; our mutual burdens bear. And often for each other flows the sympathizing tear."* For all of its warts and flaws, the Christian congregation is a community of caring grounded in Easter. That hope in God's future is actually practiced, attentive to reaching all in the community, that none may be neglected or disregarded.

---

*John Fawcett, "Blest Be the Tie that Binds" (1782).

Tuesday after Easter 5

Psalm 61; Leviticus 16:20–34; 1 Thessalonians 5:1–11; Matthew 6:7–15

God of long-term patience and sudden surprise, give us patience in our waiting and impatience in our alertness, that we may welcome every sign of the coming of your day. In his name. Amen.

God's time pivots around "the day of the Lord," that elusive moment when God's good purpose will overwhelm and out-flank all human designs for ordering the world. That day represents, in the elusiveness of poetry, a threat to all our pet projects; it is, however, good news for those who live in sync with God's will and who hope for the full arrival of that will.

The community gathered around Jesus belongs to the day. To "belong to the day" means to live in alert hope and eager expectation so that we do not miss the signs of the coming of that day and the enactment of God's purpose. To be "children of light" means to live in alert hope and eager expectation, under discipline and in attentiveness to what God is doing in the world. The alternative is to be drunk and asleep, that is, to be narcotized so that we give up any expectation for what God will do. We live in a narcotized society in which our alertness is put to sleep by consumer satiation, by excessive confidence in the fixes of technology, and by the accumulation of money and power that lets us dream of self-sufficiency. All of that belongs to sleepiness.

Children of the light live already in response to the new rule of God. Paul's letter is not a speculation about the time or the mode of the day. Rather he has a practical, pastoral aim in mind, that those who belong to the day should "build up each other." The term "build up" means actual construction of an architectural site. Thus members of the congregation are to help each other build a life of hope that refuses the sleepiness sponsored by dominant society.

Wednesday after Easter 5

Psalm 72; Leviticus 19:1–18;
1 Thessalonians 5:12–28; Matthew 6:19–24

God of the Commandments, we pray for gospel freedom that comes in glad obedience. Deliver us from phony obedience, that our walk may more fully and faithfully mirror your walk. In his name. Amen.

These readings voice imperatives addressed to the faithful. Three dimensions of obedience are voiced in this chapter from Leviticus. First, there are ritual disciplines concerning the proper performance of peace offerings. Second, we can identify almost all of the Ten Commandments here: Honor parents, keep Sabbath, have no idols, do not steal, do not bear false witness, do not use God's name falsely; one can extrapolate the other commands that are not voiced. But third, interspersed through the chapter are explicit requirements of justice concerning the poor who must share in societal abundance, for the disabled (deaf, blind) who must be protected, and finally concerning the neighbor who must not be exploited. The culmination is "love your neighbor" that Paul says sums up the whole of the Torah (Galatians 5:14).

The notion of such radical, demanding obedience concerning material aspects of life is a blockbuster in our self-indulgent society. We prefer to think of ourselves as free and not accountable to anyone. The gospel tradition, however, recognizes that if we do not obey the Torah of the covenant God, we likely will be fully engaged in some other obedience. Thus the Gospel reading concludes with the declaration, "You cannot serve God and wealth." It is strange to think that we might serve money. In a society that reduces all value to commodity, however, we do indeed serve money. We permit it to propel our lives and define our relationships. An alternative obedience to the God of covenant who commands neighbor love requires disciplined intentionality.

Thursday after Easter 5

Psalm 70; Leviticus 19:26–37;
2 Thessalonians 1:1–12; Matthew 6:25–34

God who overflows in abundance, grant that we may trust you and depart our fear of scarcity. Curb our insatiable desire for more, that we may luxuriate in and share your good gifts. In his name. Amen.

The disciples are like the rest of us. They are preoccupied with questions of security and material well-being. Jesus has just told them in the preceding verse that worship of money is inimical to God. So they wonder, "How will we live without money?" They are anxious about it. Their anxiety is an inclination that is fed and nourished by a fear of scarcity. The ideology of scarcity among the well-off is powerful among us and propels much of our society. Jesus bids his disciples disengage from anxiety that is always desirous of more.

Jesus offers his disciples a stunning contrast. Birds and flowers trust the gifts of creation. By contrast King Solomon, the quintessential predator who thought he never had enough, always sought to have more. Solomon is a model for a life propelled by an ideology of scarcity. The alternative to Solomonic acquisitiveness is the abundance of creation and the faithful God who gives good gifts. The disciples ask what they should do instead of seeking more. Jesus answers, "Strive first for the kingdom of God and his righteousness," that is, work for the common good and the well-being of the neighborhood. The rest will follow.

Jesus is not engaged in abstract economic theory. He focuses on the simple reality of a community of neighbors who share. The mandate entails face-to-face generosity. But the term "righteousness" also concerns public policy and the proper administration of social goods, social power, and social access. Jesus summons his followers to a very different way in the world, one that resists the ordinary covetousness of much present practice and policy among us.

Friday after Easter 5

Psalm 106:1–18; Leviticus 23:1–22;
2 Thessalonians 2:1–17; Matthew 7:1–12

*Giver of life in all its material wonder, we thank you for markers of time
that attest that our lives come from you and are to be lived back to you
in gratitude. In his name. Amen.*

This chapter of Leviticus offers a festival calendar or, we might
say, a schedule for the "church year" in Judaism and derivatively in the church. Such a calendar offers specific times for
dramatic celebrations that mark remembrance, fidelity, and
gratitude.

We may notice several accent points in this calendar. The
first is the accent on Sabbath rest and doing no work. The
pressures of ordinary life require us to be endlessly connected
and busy, a way of life that yields anxiety, fatigue, and self-
preoccupation. The festival practice of Sabbath is a reminder
that our life does not depend on us.

Second, the festival calendar marks both history and nature.
The Passover is a historical memory of the exodus emancipation, an affirmation that the economy need not be predatory
and oppressive. The other festivals live very close to agricultural reality, asserting that sustenance for life comes out of the
good earth and witnesses to the blessing that the creator God
has ordained in creation.

Third, focus on the gifts of God in history and creation
evoke a regularized practice of offerings of gratitude. We are
on the receiving end of everything, receiving freedom from
the God of the exodus, receiving life from the creator God. In
order that we do not take life for granted, responsive gifts of
gratitude are much in order. A life that does not give back to
God may soon come to think it is self-made.

All these accents are countercultural: rest instead of
eternal busyness, gifts of history and creation instead of self-
securing, expressions of gratitude instead of self-sufficiency.

Saturday after Easter 5

Psalm 75; Leviticus 23:23–44;
2 Thessalonians 3:1–18; Matthew 7:13–21

We thank you for the work you sent Jesus to do that is the work of our heavenly Father. We thank you that you have invited us to share in that good work. Give us imagination to understand good work in its gospel dimension. In his name. Amen.

Few biblical texts have been so often taken out of context as verse 10 of our Epistle reading: "Anyone unwilling to work should not eat." Out of context, the verse is often taken to mean that nonproducers in our capitalist economy are owed nothing and should be left in their unproductive misery.

But we may read these verses in a much thicker way.

— The work that Paul has in mind is contribution to the common good of the community. That contrasts with laissez-faire economics of indifferent individualism.
— The next verse concerning busybodies suggests that the idle were not only the nonproductive but also those with too much time on their hands who destabilized the community. Thus it is not "work" in isolation that concerns Paul, but the upbuilding of the community.
— When the text is taken along with the Gospel reading, work may be understood as bearing good fruit. When read that way, work that counts is work marked by justice, righteousness, compassion, and mercy. Any work that does not meet that standard does not count.

Roland Boer in his analysis of ancient economy asks: "How does one feed and clothe the nonproducers? . . . How does one enable the nonproducing ruling class to maintain the life to which its members had quickly become accustomed?"* Now the nonproducing rich come within the purview of the verse. In the end we may ponder how *work* in evangelical faith is understood in relation to *rest* and *prayer*.

---

*Roland Boer, *The Sacred Economy of Ancient Israel* (Louisville, KY: Westminster John Knox Press, 2015), 203.

Sixth Sunday of Easter

Psalm 93; Leviticus 25:1–17; James 1:2–8, 16–18; Luke 12:13–21

God who forgives sins and cancels debts, give us freedom to imagine out-side our economy of indebtedness, that we may put neighborhood ahead of our private economic interest. In his name. Amen.

The man who petitions Jesus is in a conflict with his brother over family property . . . nothing unusual. In the parable Jesus sketches out a participant in an economy of greed who is busy with endless acquisition of surplus wealth. Nothing out of the ordinary there either. Quarrels over property and insatiable hunger for more are quite ordinary practices among us.

The Torah provision for jubilee, however, is a profound interruption of that ordinariness of greed, quarreling, and surplus. The premise of the Torah provision is that the stable and irenic well-being of the community is more important than endless accumulation. For that reason, the endless expansion of a competitive economy is decisively and regularly inter-rupted by the year of jubilee, a year of rest for agricultural land and a year of economic restoration for the neighborhood. It is crucial for this Torah provision that those engaged with us in the economic process are rated as neighbors, not as rivals, competitors, or threats.

Both texts understand that surplus and debt are tools of an economy that is inimical to a viable neighborhood. We might conclude that the Jesus movement is especially concerned with an alternative economy that accents neighborly well-being. This is evident in the fact that forgiveness of debts is at the center of the Lord's Prayer. The hard work for us is to translate this urgent evangelical imperative into practice and policy in an economy that locks too many people into hopeless, long-term debt. The news of Easter is that God's gift of new possibility pertains to every dimension of our life, not least the economic.

Monday after Easter 6

Psalm 80; Leviticus 25:35–55; Colossians 1:9–14; Matthew 13:1–16

Lord of rich and poor, let us keep in purview all this day those paralyzed by hopeless debt. We give thanks that they, like us, are subjects of your good Easter truth. In his name. Amen.

This Torah provision has in purview communal solidarity for all the "kin" of Israel. (This passage does not yet reach beyond the kinship group, but the Torah is on its way to a larger solidarity that runs beyond "kin" to all participants in the economy.) This passage knows that collecting interest and making a profit and exploiting others is a way ahead in conventional economy.

But the passage is saturated with the memory of the exodus. The God who speaks here is the God who emancipated Israel from the predatory economy of Pharaoh; those addressed here are children and heirs of that emancipation. For that reason they are commanded to entertain, in their present landed circumstance, the emancipatory practices of the exodus in the face of the present predatory economy of Canaan. The geography has changed from Egypt to Canaan, but nothing has changed about the risks and opportunities of social relationships. Because all belong to the Lord of the exodus, none can, by economic sharpness, be reduced to debt slaves.

Jesus teaches in parables because what he teaches is so demanding that it cannot be faced frontally. He acknowledges that dull hearts, heavy ears, and closed eyes preclude our getting his point. In our circumstance we may conclude that the unresponsiveness to his teaching of our hearts, ears, and eyes is because we have become so inured to the claims of a competitive economy that we are unable to compute his teaching that community solidarity overrides conventional practices of debt, interest, and profit. We may pray for sharper sensibility, that his teaching may penetrate our willful obtuseness.

Tuesday after Easter 6

Psalm 78:1–39; Leviticus 26:1–10; 1 Timothy 2:1–6; Matthew 13:18–23

Good God of creation who has given us commandments for our well-being, give us good perceptiveness about our systemic disobedience, and good hope for an alternative common life. In his name. Amen.

The Lord of the exodus speaks in this Torah passage. The opening verses cite two of the Ten Commandments . . . have no idols, keep Sabbath. (We may judge that the other eight commandments are tacitly operative as well.) We may consider the peculiar way these two voiced commandments are linked to each other. Worship of idols means giving reverent devotion to commodities that are lifeless and cannot give life. No doubt the endless pursuit of commodities is an ideology alive and well among us. The thing about the pursuit of commodities is that we never have enough of them. The pursuit of "more" is inexhaustible; one result is that we can never take a break to rest, that is, never keep Sabbath. Thus idols and their insatiable demand and Sabbath contradict each other; and Israel is summoned to decide.

The text promises that shunning idols and keeping Sabbath will lead to a life of blessing in which there will be agricultural abundance, peace (shalom), and an absence of military threat or the fear of military threat. Such a connection between Torah obedience and shalom is not a supernaturalism. It is rather observable evangelical common sense. Once one acknowledges that the world is morally coherent and depends on responsible conduct and policy, well-being will follow. It is verifiable. Conversely, it is observable that the endless chase after commodities with continual restlessness generates a society of competition that readily morphs into mean-spiritedness and violence. That also is verifiable. Easter is the stunning awareness that it could be different . . . beginning with alertness about idols and Sabbath.

Wednesday after Easter 6

Psalm 119:97–120; Leviticus 26:27–42;
Ephesians 1:1–10; Matthew 22:41–46

God of an ordered life, give us courageous insight into our refusal of your gift of life. Give us more courage to enact reversal in our public life, that we may yet again receive your good blessing. In his name. Amen.

This long chapter in Leviticus continues reflection on covenantal blessings and curses. Israel is indicted for disregard of the commandments of Sinai and faces the outcomes of such disobedience. Among the outcomes of disobedience, we may notice three. First is the devastation of the land by military invasion. The second, surely voiced with some irony, is that the land will be abandoned and so will have rest. Israel's refusal to keep Sabbath rest will result in a long rest for the land, because the economy will fail and there will be no one to cultivate the land. The third is deep fear over imagined threats, so that the elaborate thirst for "national security" will be without satisfaction.

As we saw yesterday with respect to blessing, these anticipated outcomes are not an act of supernatural imposition. They are rather the predictable and inescapable results of policies and conduct that go against the grain of God's will for creation.

It requires no imagination to see that this rather simple formulation illuminates our national condition of greedy, anxious disobedience that has resulted in an increasingly troubled life. We are, for all of that, surprised by the final verses. There is again a simple if-then formulation: if Israel reverses field, confesses, and makes amends, then God will remember in fidelity. The creator God is ready to renew the juices of life for Israel and for the land. The condition for renewal is reversal of policy and conduct. The Easter news is that the God who gives life leaves opportunity for new beginning. That opportunity, however, requires a deep change in social commitment.

Ascension Day

Psalm 8; Daniel 7:9–14; Hebrews 2:5–18; Matthew 28:16–20

Lord Jesus who has come, via death, to new life and power, give us fresh discernment of your authority, and freedom to see that other claims to authority do not merit our final loyalty. In your name. Amen.

The reading from Daniel provides the imagery used in the early Christian confession of the ascent of Jesus that we regularly confess in the creeds. In the Daniel text, we meet two actors, the *Ancient of Days*, who is understood in the tradition as the eternal God who is fully transcendent and who rules in a remote way, and the *son of man*, a divine figure who travels on a cloud to come into the elevated presence of the Ancient of Days. (It is likely that the imagery was appropriated from an ancient rain god who traveled by cloud to seed the earth with abundance.) In the book of Daniel the spatial imagery of "clouds of heaven" is an attempt to situate the real authority and power of God beyond and above the reach of the regime of Syria that badly exploited Jews. The imagery asserts that there is another ("higher") authority that overrides the authority of Syria.

In telling the story of Jesus, the church took over this imagery to trace the way that *Jesus* (Son of Man) came to share authority with *the Father* (Ancient of Days). The rhetoric asserts a governance beyond that of the Roman Empire. In the Gospel declaration, "All authority . . . has been given to me"; no ultimate authority is given to Rome.

In our own context, we might consider the claims of "the last superpower" and its rising rivals, China and the Arabic powers, each of whom exercise power in violent and oppressive ways. The ascent of Jesus denies ultimate authority to any such claimant. Such doxological assertion creates critical freedom for a life other than the one compelled by any worldly power.

Friday after Easter 6

Psalm 85; 1 Samuel 2:1–10; Ephesians 2:1–10; Matthew 7:22–27

God of Easter power, we thank you for the great interruption you have performed in our lives and in the life of the world. Give us zeal to live this day on the far side of your great interruption. In his name. Amen.

Paul here gives classic expression to the primary gospel claim of the church. In this Epistle reading, everything turns on the adversative "but." On both sides of that conjunction Paul piles up the rhetoric. Before the "but," we get all the negativity: "passions of our flesh," desires of body and mind, disobedience, wrath; this is a portrayal of life out of sync with the will of God.

After the "but," we get a rich vocabulary of well-being: mercy, great love, make alive, unsearchable riches, grace, kindness, gift. This cluster of terms attests that God's transformative work has made new, joyous life possible.

It will be useful with this text in front of us to ponder the adversative "but" upon which everything turns. That conjunction is occupied with the power of God enacted in the life and resurrection of Jesus. To fill in the force of his life for us we have (a) the stories of his direct impact on his immediate world: "the blind receive their sight, the lame walk, the lepers are cleansed, the deaf hear . . ." (Matt. 11:5; Luke 7:22), (b) the creedal affirmations of the church tradition, and (c) the many concrete mediations of his power that take the form of many human persons who have performed his life-giving generosity. That transformative "but" is indeed "once for all" in the Easter life of Jesus. But because we all know about the continuing force of the "passions of our flesh" and the desires of our body and mind that propel us toward self-destructiveness, the "but" of gospel truth must always again be reexperienced.

Saturday after Easter 6

Psalm 87; Numbers 11:16–17, 24–29;
Ephesians 2:11–22; Matthew 7:28–8:4

God who makes outsiders into insiders, give us clear vision to see the walls on which we rely, and the courage to accept the ways in which you dismantle our favorite distinctions. In his name. Amen.

Dominant culture is always tempted to exclude, able to identify those who are "brought near" in privilege, entitlement, and proper qualification, and those who are "far off" and who do not qualify for inclusion. In the epistle, this exclusionary temptation concerns the "brought near" Jewish Christians and the "far-off" Gentile Christians. In the Gospel reading, it concerns the leper who is considered unclean and so dangerously disqualified from social relationships.

The distinctions that encourage exclusiveness continue to be powerful among us. They pertain to gender, as women have too long been excluded from too much; to race, whereby people of color have been kept out; and now to class, with the growing gap between privileged haves and left-behind have-nots.

The entire ideology and social structure of exclusiveness is abruptly countered by the witness of Jesus Christ: "He is our peace." He is our mode of reconciliation. He has crashed the gate and broken down dividing walls of hostility. He did that by giving insider and outsider equal "access to the Father." Imagine the shock and scandal the day that leper was cleansed and rendered acceptable. It was an act that violated all conventional notions of how to manage social order and power. Given these texts, this is a good day to reflect on the force of exclusiveness among us and the way in which the gospel tells otherwise. The gospel is, to be sure, an assurance of inclusion. It is also a summons to be about the work of dismantling the walls that seem so normal but that violate the intent for the "new humanity."

Seventh Sunday of Easter

Psalm 66; Exodus 3:1–12; Hebrews 12:18–29; Luke 10:17–24

*Creator God who shakes the world and offers an unshakable alternative,
let us see, like innocent disciples, the wonder of your subversive way in
the world. In his name. Amen.*

The texts offer three contrasts that may feed our imagination concerning the strange power of the gospel that is unlike any other power. The first contrast is between Mount Sinai (fire and trumpets) and Mount Zion. The latter refers to a Jerusalem that hosts the living God. Welcome to the new Jerusalem, source of new life! It is quite unlike Mount Sinai that is marked by danger.

The second contrast is between the old world that is being shaken by profound upheaval that places all in jeopardy, and the "kingdom that cannot be shaken," that is, the new world sponsored and governed by the God of the gospel. The old world of disobedience should not be trusted; the new world of fidelity is utterly reliable and will endure amid every upheaval.

The third contrast is between the sightings of powerful people (kings and prophets) who are shortsighted and blind to seeing the truth of the gospel that comes in vulnerability, and the disciples who are permitted to sojourn with Jesus and thereby to witness to the inexplicable reality of transformation that cannot be seen or embraced by those who are stuck in illusions of self-sufficiency.

These contrasts, voiced in highly impressionistic rhetoric, present us with alternative ways of being in the world and our place in it. The first triad tempts us to trust in the transient that cannot be sustained; the second triad invites us to an existence inhabited by the vulnerable transformative power of Jesus. The poetic idiom allows us much room in which to probe the hidden places through which we may relocate ourselves in a durable zone of well-being and fidelity.

Monday after Easter 7

Psalm 89:1–18; Joshua 1:1–9; Ephesians 3:1–13; Matthew 8:5–17

God who makes and keeps promises, give us eyes to notice the great company —from east and west, north and south —who are glad recipients of your good gifts. In his name. Amen.

The narrative of faith begins in the Bible with Abraham and Sarah, to whom God makes a promise of land. Joshua's entry into the land is presented in the biblical tradition as the fulfillment of God's promise to Abraham and Sarah.

We may notice three aspects of the promise. First, God's promise in the Bible is pointedly *material*. The promise is not about an idea or any religious phenomenon but about concrete living space. That accent on the material comes to full expression, in Christian tradition, in the bodily life of Jesus.

Second, the Joshua text makes clear that the land is linked to *Torah obedience*. Since *torah* ("the law") in this text refers to the book of Deuteronomy, we may notice the accent in that Torah text on economic justice. Land given will be retained if economic justice is enacted.

Third, in a reach beyond the ancient promise, the Gospel reading has Jesus make a remarkable statement. He finds greater faith in the Roman soldier than in Israel; consequently *many people* from everywhere will participate in the company of the family of Abraham. That is, the promise is extended in the gospel beyond the family of Abraham. It follows that the land of promise will be shared beyond Israel by all those who keep the Torah of economic justice.

We may consider the *materiality* of our faith, the requirement of *Torah obedience* concerning economic justice, and the *reach to many*. In sum, the ministry of Jesus is an enactment of material well-being (healing) for all sorts of people who come to trust his strange authority.

Tuesday after Easter 7

Psalm 97; 1 Samuel 16:1–13a; Ephesians 3:14–21; Matthew 8:18–27

Lord Jesus, master of the storm, grant that we may find our only safety in your presence, without yearning for what must be left behind. In your name. Amen.

The terse command of Jesus is "follow me." There is no elaboration, no qualification, no assurance, only a simple, direct imperative. Initially a scribe in the crowd is prepared to follow. But Jesus cautions that he (and his followers?) would have no safe habitat. That caution must have given some a second thought about their initial willingness to follow in obedience.

We hear no more from the first scribe who was so eager to sign on. A second recruit is not quite as eager. He wants at least to attend to old business before following. But Jesus has no patience for such lingering loyalty to things past: he simply states his terse imperative. The disciples learn that they have to leave all that they have treasured for their new life with Jesus. This terse command now looms large among us, because we are in a time of leaving behind much that we have treasured that has given us assurance and security.

The disciples who followed learned a second thing. They learned that the world—when all is left behind—is a scary, chaotic place, as signified by a great storm. They panic and wish for a safe place. Jesus responds to their anxiety with a lordly assurance. His rebuke causes the chaos to retreat into order. He is the creator who manages chaos for good.

We keep learning what the disciples learned:

— Discipleship requires giving up much we have treasured.
— Life with Jesus takes us to scary places.
— In those scary places, his masterful management is sufficient.

The disciples must have asked, "What have we gotten into?"

Wednesday after Easter 7

Psalm 101; Isaiah 4:2–6; Ephesians 4:1–16; Matthew 8:28–34

You who are the church's one foundation, give us this day simple honesty about our own part in the church. Match that honesty with the gift of self-giving love, that we may give care and respect to other members of the church, especially the ones who differ from us. In your name. Amen.

This Epistle reading is a great advocacy for the unity of the church. In an acutely polarized society like ours, the unity of the church is under stress because of our fervent certitude that we transport into the church and transpose into claims of faith.

In the letter, the term "doctrine" is not used positively. It stands alongside "trickery," "craftiness," and "deceitful scheming," all strategies to dupe and distort the church. In our circumstance, such doctrine is likely to be liberal or conservative passion and ideology that reflect not the will of Christ but our own uncritical vested interest.

In response to such toxic divisiveness, Paul proposes that we recognize different gifts and honor them. Thus it might be affirmed that liberal progressivism and evangelical conservatism keep alive different aspects of the tradition, all of which are essential to the faithfulness of the church. Such honoring of difference is contrasted with our practical excommunication of those who think differently.

The wondrous phrase for this stance in the church is "the truth in love." The *truth* part concerns honesty about the world where God has put us, and the greater truth that the riches of the gospel outflank all our waywardness. The *love* part is that all of our truth telling is done in generative respect for the other in the church so that the whole church may be built up.

Thursday after Easter 7

Psalm 105:1–22; Zechariah 4:1–14; Ephesians 4:17–32; Matthew 9:1–8

Giver of new names, new identities, and new selves, give us freedom to move beyond the old self that has been formed in fear to a new self that is daily "lost in wonder, love, and praise." In his name. Amen.

The Epistle reading plunges us into the drama of "old self" and "new self" that constitutes both the wonder and the hard work of Christian life. The old self is a way of being in the world that participates in the fearful, destructive habits that are toxic for social well-being. In our society that may be greedy anxiety about getting ahead that is enacted in hostility toward others.

The new self is a way of life that is centered in the truth and grace of the gospel and that has no need to engage in the destructive ways of the world. Ephesians 4:25–32 details some aspects of the new life:

— Anger without sin, that is, without need or desire to hurt those with whom we are angry

— Honest work that contributes to the well-being of the community; a refusal to freeload off society in elite privilege and luxury or by lethargic dependence

— Negatively, no bitter speech or action; positively, a readiness to forgive

The move from old self to new self is marked in the sacrament of baptism wherein we receive a new self "marked as Christ's own forever," as the *Book of Common Prayer* says.

While the act of baptism is dramatic, in fact our move from old to new self is a lifelong enterprise in which we grow slowly in grace; we sometimes relapse and must begin again with our new identity. The baptismal self requires great intentionality. The tradition of Calvin has a wondrous phrase, "perfecting one's baptism." We may consider what perfecting of the new self is worth our sustained effort.

Friday after Easter 7

Psalm 102; Jeremiah 31:27–34; Ephesians 5:1–20; Matthew 9:9–17

God who gives rules, regulations, and guidelines and then violates them in amazing ways, grant that we may enter into the full joy of your glad welcome. In his name. Amen.

The God of the gospel is a giver of newness. Newness might be welcome, but it requires a serious relinquishment of what is old and treasured. Sometimes that task of relinquishment is readily embraced; sometimes it is vigorously resisted.

Jesus' case study of newness is that he ate with "tax collectors and sinners," the kind of people who are most often excluded and despised, because they do not honor the protocols of proper society. The newness of Jesus is that he breaks the old patterns of exclusion and visibly enacts acceptance of the despised. When he is challenged about his action, he quotes the old prophet Hosea, "Mercy, not sacrifice." "Sacrifice" had become a code word for a well-managed religious system of quid pro quo costs and benefits. But "mercy" refuses all such calculations.

The "new wine" is the welcome of God to all sorts and conditions of people. The "old wineskins" are patterns of social approval and social control. Obviously the generous welcome of God cannot be fit into any usual protocol of approval and control. For that reason, the old patterns must yield to the new welcome of God.

I suspect that all of us participate in this conversation of welcome and exclusion and almost all of us, at one time or another, resonate variously with both the old wineskins and the new wine. Sometimes we cherish the old protocols and are glad to exclude some. At other times we ourselves know about being excluded or left out and are glad for the welcome of God. Today is a good day to reconnoiter our habits about welcome and exclusion. It is a good day to celebrate the unfettered welcome of God that is as joyous as a wedding party.

Saturday after Easter 7

Psalm 107:33–43; Ezekiel 36:22–27;
Ephesians 6:10–24; Matthew 9:18–26

*God of surprises that we readily resist, deliver us from the ease with
which we doubt your newness. Do your newness of life, even when death-
liness seems so intransigent. In his name. Amen.*

The well-beloved daughter was dead. There is no ambiguity in
the report. But Jesus came and said, "She is not dead but sleep-
ing." Jesus contradicted the obvious fact about the girl. And
they laughed at him. Can you imagine? When he contradicted
what they knew for sure, they laughed at him in ridicule. They
laughed at him because he violated their knowledge and their
plausibility structure. They laughed at the Messiah who did
not fit their preconception. Such laughter means to discredit
the agent who proposes newness. But Jesus is undeterred by
their laughter. He raises her! I wonder if there was anyone in
the room who did not laugh, who was prepared for the reality
of Jesus that broke the accepted reality of her death.

And then I wonder: Might Jesus' subversive power evoke
our mocking laughter grounded in our incredulity? We might
laugh at his possibility that we do not need to live in a society
of violence, that we could redefine social relationships between
the rich and the poor, between police and citizen. We might
laugh at the prospect that we do not need to have a permanent
poverty class in our society, that the abundance we have might
be distributed differently. We might laugh at the hope that the
church might cease to be a disputatious matrix, that conservatives and liberals might gather together in transformative
solidarity. Stuff like that happens when Jesus enters into the
room! Any one of us could be the person in the room who does
not laugh at such outrageous evangelical possibility, being prepared for his news that overrides our assumed deathly reality.

PENTECOST

Pentecost Sunday

Psalm 118; Deuteronomy 16:9–12; Acts 4:18–21, 23–33; John 4:19–26

God who comes in spirit and in truth, we know you discredit our favorite epicenters. Help us to relinquish them and to receive you. In his name. Amen.

Jesus takes the Samaritan woman with utmost seriousness. He invites her to consider the legitimacy structure of her life, the way she has organized meaning in her life. He calls into question the legitimacy of the central shrine in Samaria where a sect of outsider Jews continued to worship in the time of Jesus. He debunks the old claim of that old epicenter.

Then in order to reassure her that he is not simply an advocate for Jerusalem, a shrine that rivaled Samaria, he adds that Jerusalem, his holy city, will not be the epicenter either in the time to come. He has delegitimated both very old claims about venues of meaning. That is what the Messiah does: he disrupts and discredits our much-treasured venues of meaning.

That delegitimation is followed in his speech by a positive alternative. The new worship appropriate to the new era will not be in our treasured fixture but in spirit and in truth. To worship in spirit appropriate to this Pentecost Sunday means to recognize that God's generative, emancipatory energy is out in front of us, leading us beyond ourselves. This new worship may take many forms, but its defining mark is freedom for transformed life. To worship in truth is to gather around the truth embodied in Jesus: new life comes by losing our lives, the last will be first, the humbled will be exalted.

The woman took Jesus seriously. But still, she did not recognize him. Even in his presence, she was still waiting. Pentecost affirms the truth that God in Christ comes among us in ways that we do not readily recognize or embrace, because he accommodates none of our old habits.

Monday after Pentecost

Psalm 106:1–18; Ezekiel 33:1–11; 1 John 1:1–10; Matthew 9:27–34

Lord Jesus, who by touch made the world new, grant that we may be touched to newness by your presence. Even more, grant that we may be holy touchers who do your work. In your name. Amen.

The ones in need, first of all the two blind men and later a mute demon-possessed man, come to Jesus. They are helpless. They chase after him, taking the initiative. Their intention is gathered in one word, "mercy." They bid for help of a generous kind beyond the quid pro quo world they inhabit. Their imperative petition is simple and direct, without decoration. They place themselves, quite literally, at the mercy of Jesus. And when they are healed, they are eager to share their good fortune.

Jesus touches them. He is unafraid of their disability. The action is terse, no explanation. It is clear in the words of Jesus that the needy have a decisive role to play in their restoration. It is "according to their faith." (Elsewhere we are told that Jesus was stymied in his transformative work among other people "because of their unbelief.") These blind men are clearly engaged in their own transformation. The touch of Jesus is everything. But it depends on and evokes their faith. In an economy of words, the narrative points to Jesus. He is the Lord of well-being. He is the master of health. It is a puzzle in the Pentecost season how it could be that the transformative touch of Jesus is alive in the world by the work of the Spirit and in the presence of the church. The church is never confused with Jesus, but his transformative touch is peculiarly entrusted to the church.

Tuesday after Pentecost

Psalm 120; Ezekiel 33:21–33; 1 John 2:1–11; Matthew 9:35–10:4

Jesus, who gives a command and the capacity to obey it, we thank you for our peculiar assignment in the world. Grant that this day we may know joy in obedience to your single commandment. In your name. Amen.

The Jesus movement is under the single mandate of the old commandment made new. That is all. It is one commandment that is quoted from the old Torah of Judaism. It is the commandment that binds the followers to the leader, the disciples to the master. Over long generations the church has picked up many other assignments and chores, many of which detract from this simple directive. That simple commandment, moreover, constitutes a total redefinition of "religion." It turns out that faith, in the Jesus movement, has nothing "religious" about it, so that the character, purpose, and presence of God are redefined by love of sister and brother, eventually neighbor. Pentecost is a good time for the church to slough off much in the church that is a distraction from that single mandate.

In the Gospel reading, the earliest disciples, representatives of the entire church, are given authority. They are not only commanded but also given energy and capacity to obey the commandment of neighbor love in concrete and transformative ways. They are to heal; they are to cast out demons and restore to sanity. That is their raison d'être.

And we are heirs! We in the church are heirs of the commandment; it is our proper business in the world. We are heirs to that authority. We have been empowered to do that work. That work is a dazzlement in the world. It is, moreover, a vexation to imperial officials who resist that authority. That work happens in a world that does not ponder the neighbor much and that does not anticipate much healing. We know better!

Wednesday after Pentecost

Psalm 119:145–176; Ezekiel 34:1–16;
1 John 2:12–17; Matthew 10:5–15

*Good shepherd God, we thank you that you authorize "shepherds" who
have important responsibilities. Give us political courage and insistence
that the shepherds we have should do their proper work of well-being for
your realm. In his name. Amen.*

The oracle of Ezekiel sounds the familiar accents of God's judgment and God's hope. It does so through the imagery of shepherd and sheep. The clue to the oracle is the awareness that in
the ancient world "shepherd" was a widely used metaphor for
"king." The king has responsibility for the care, protection, and
well-being of the realm that is cast as a flock.

The oracle begins with the prophetic judgment that the
long series of kings in the family of David have been, in sum,
a failure because the shepherd kings have not done their job
but instead have used the "flock" to their own advantage. The
sheep have suffered because the kings have been negligent and
self-indulgent.

The good news is that God ("I, I myself") will now act as the
good shepherd. The oracle is addressed to Jews who have been
"scattered" (exiled, deported) from their homeland. The good
shepherd will bring them home and do the good work of the
shepherd: God will bring back, bind up, feed, and strengthen;
the sheep will prosper.

This imagery can be carried in several important directions.
First, it is from such imagery that we get the picture of God
as the Good Shepherd. Second, the imagery is extended, in
Christian interpretation, toward Jesus as the Good Shepherd.
Third, in the Gospel reading the apostles are given the work
of being good shepherds. Fourth, the imagery of the shepherd
king invites reflection on the role of government; the king is to
guarantee the well-being and welfare of the entire realm. Bad
kings produce big trouble for all the sheep.

Thursday after Pentecost

Psalm 131; Ezekiel 34:21b–28; 1 John 2:18–29; Matthew 10:16–23

Good shepherd God, we thank you for the good shepherd Jesus who has come among us. Give us courage this day, that we may continue to act out his strange governance of transformation that yields well-being for the world. In his name. Amen.

The imagery of the good shepherd king is continued from our reading of yesterday. Here the anticipation advances: there will be a new king of the line of David who will be a good king. After the destruction of Jerusalem there was, among other expectations, a hope that the Davidic throne would be reestablished. Israel always hopes for the next good king! Unlike the line of failed kings, this new David would be a good king. That long-expected good king would be the messiah (the anointed) who would save his people.

In Christian tradition, this expectation of "my servant David" is extended to Jesus, who was affirmed in some traditions as "Son of David" and who would govern Israel well. In any case, the political imagery of "Son of David" is significantly transposed in the life of Jesus; this authority does not have to do with raw political power but with the "royal" responsibility for human welfare and well-being.

The outcome of this new rule, says Ezekiel, will be a "covenant of peace" (*shalom*) in which there will be political harmony because all will be cared for by this generous governance. Insofar as the apostles continue the work of Jesus as good shepherd, they are warned in our Gospel reading that they will be as vulnerable as sheep. The new governance will collide with the powers of fear, greed, and violence. Against all political pretense, the church tradition exercises a very different authority, a transformative capacity marked by exposed vulnerability.

Friday after Pentecost

Psalm 140; Ezekiel 39:21–29; 1 John 3:1–10; Matthew 10:24–33

God of all faithfulness, give us freedom today to imagine the way you value each of us and the hairs on our heads; we know that you value all the other heads and hairs alongside us, and we are grateful. In his name. Amen.

The oracle of Ezekiel places us in the acute pivot point of Israel's faith in the Old Testament. The point of accent is God's new resolve for Israel's future in this moment of fresh possibility. God resolves to "restore the fortunes of Jacob." In the next sentence the speech of God makes an extraordinary linkage that is elemental for biblical faith. On the one hand, there will be *mercy for Israel*. God will act graciously and rescue Israel from its most vulnerable circumstance. On the other hand, this act of God will *enhance God's holy name*, that is, God's reputation. The oracle asserts an intimate, indivisible connection between *Israel's good future* and *God's self-enhancement*.

In the Gospel reading, that attachment between *God and Israel* is transposed to the attachment of *Jesus to the apostolic church*. The enemies of God do not welcome the gospel of vulnerability. In the face of that reality, there is an assurance: "your Father" is totally attentive to this exposed faithful community.

In both cases the holy God will protect and preserve every member of the beloved community. In Ezekiel, "none of them" will be deserted among the nations. In Matthew, "the hairs of your head are all counted." In both witnesses the holy God has cast God's lot with specific historical reality. The missionary imagination of the church, moreover, has extended this linkage: God is committed to all the creatures. This creator God has no will for life apart from this much-valued creation, even its sparrows!

Saturday after Pentecost

Psalm 137; Ezekiel 47:1–12; 1 John 3:11–18; Matthew 10:34–42

*God of restorative generosity, we thank you for the many places in which
you overcome the arid quality of our life with the limitless abundance
of your life-giving gifts. Move us this day out of our fearful parsimony.
In his name. Amen.*

The clue to this passage in Ezekiel is awareness of a very arid
climate that is always in need of water. In this vision there is a
flow of fresh water out of the temple. The vision is a rearticu-
lation from the creation narrative of Genesis 2:10–14 in which
the four rivers that give life to the world flow out of God's garden of well-being. Now, in a new artistic horizon, the temple
has replaced the garden.

The prophet is acutely attentive to the specificity of the flow
of water, because he wants to accent its limitless abundance.
The repeated measure of the water exhibits its ample supply.
Thus it is ankle deep; then it is knee deep; then it is waist deep.
It is deep enough to swim in. The water flows everywhere, all
over creation, even to the dry territory of the southern des-
ert, and into the "stagnant waters," that is, the Dead Sea. At
the spring of En-gedi (a real spring!), fish are caught from the
Dead Sea that are compared to fish of the "Great Sea," the
Mediterranean. Who would have thought that the abundance
of God would make the Dead Sea like the Mediterranean?
Creation is restored! New life is possible.

A small link to the Gospel reading: after a deep summons,
the reading ends with a specific modest mission of faithfulness,
a "cup of cold water" given to a disciple, a sure sign of welcome.
Where in that hot climate is one to get a cup of cold water? No
doubt from the spring of En-gedi! We can attest the creator's
limitless abundance, even in the face of our abuse of creation.
And then we can consider how to share it as generously as the
Creator has given it to us.

Trinity Sunday

Psalm 29; Isaiah 6:1–8; Revelation 4:1–11; John 16:5–15

Holy God beyond us, Holy God present to us in Word and sacrament, Holy God well ahead of us in mission, we thank you for your otherness that resituates us. With all those who worship you this day, we expect to be relocated by your holiness. In his name. Amen.

God is three times holy. In the reading in Isaiah, the doxological affirmation is on the lips of the seraphim. In the reading from Revelation, the same doxological affirmation is on the lips of the living creatures. In neither case is the formula of the Trinity explicit. It is not yet formulated in the time of Isaiah, and in Revelation the doxology is addressed to "the Lord God the Almighty" and then to "our Lord and God." What strikes us about these doxologies is the sense of God's utter difference from us.

We are invited to join these heavenly creatures in worship; that is all we can do in such a presence. The one we worship is wholly beyond us in mystery, yet known in the human specificity of Jesus, whose continuing presence among us is given in the Spirit. It is no wonder that we worship. We have no categories of explanation and so must yield. We have no bargaining rights in the presence. We have nothing to bring that is worthy of the one we worship.

Such worship is our proper human vocation. Such worship is recognition and acknowledgment of this God given as inordinate mystery and as palpable power and as compassionate companion before whom we can only yield. Such yielding has a long definitional impact on our lives: maybe to prophetic vocation or resistance to empire, or to joy that is beyond tribulation. Trinity Sunday is not for the arithmetic of three in one. It is rather an occasion for belonging outside ourselves, engaging with and responding to God's mystery on terms other than our own. We are summoned and sent not by command but by overwhelming presence.

Monday after Trinity Sunday

Psalm 1; Proverbs 3:11–20; 1 John 3:18–4:6; Matthew 11:1–6

Lord Jesus, who let your life touch the life of the world, we thank you for your transformative presence and for the continuing bodily ministry entrusted to us. In your name. Amen.

We easily sing the hymns of faith, recite our favorite mantras of the gospel, and end our prayers "in Jesus' name," as though reference to Jesus is obvious. In fact the claim that Jesus is "sent by God" has never been easy or obvious. He did not fit with standard expectations. For that reason, in the Gospel reading they question him. Israel had long expected a messiah, and they wonder if he is that messiah. Jesus, as usual, avoids a direct answer, because such questions are often a trick. Instead of an answer, he urges them to look at the evidence presented through his actions.

The evidence is that he performed transformations for the disabled and those left behind. His answer catalogs such acts, but the Gospel narratives provide specificity about which lepers and which poor people. His evidence is that he exercised transformative power over the bodily, social life of the people. The matter is crucial in the Epistle reading; the test for true prophets and true spirits is the affirmation that "Jesus Christ has come in the flesh." Jesus has come in bodily, historical form; he is preoccupied with bodily, historical matters. This means, derivatively, that he cannot avoid political economic issues, because these are always issues of bodily well-being.

At the end of his response, Jesus recognizes that his investment in the bodily life of the world could be offensive to some. It is a rule of thumb that the more secure, prosperous, and affluent we are, the more we prefer a savior who is not implicated in bodily matters that always raise hard questions about the status quo. We are always summoned, yet again, to such bodily matters. When we are, we get the answer to our questions: Yes, he is the one expected!

Tuesday after Trinity Sunday

Psalm 5; Proverbs 4:1–27; 1 John 4:7–21; Matthew 11:7–15

Creator God who has ordered your world toward an abundant life, be our teacher this day, that we may move from the foolishness that kills to be habituated in your life-giving wisdom. In his name. Amen.

The wisdom tradition affirms that there is a generative, coherent moral assurance and requirement that lets all creation function in life-giving ways. This coherent assurance and requirement is called "wisdom." It is the force of good, life-giving order that is ordained in the fabric of creation. But it is hidden. The shape, limit, and demand of wisdom in any circumstance are not obvious beforehand. The task of our lives, for that reason, is to order our actions and our attitudes so that they are in sync with that wisdom, because living in sync with wisdom is the source of well-being, security, and joy.

Such wisdom is quite practical and concerns the texture of daily life and social relationships. In every time and circumstance we are tempted to confuse technical knowledge with the wisdom of God, because technical knowledge permits us to do almost anything we want.

The sage in our reading from Proverbs playfully suggests that such technical capacity amounts to a "sacrament" consisting of the "bread of wickedness" and the "wine of violence." Unencumbered technical knowledge produces a jungle of violence variously embodied in a predatory economy, exclusionary politics, and unchecked racism. All of that can be engineered by our smarts.

The wise sage who speaks here knows that such a way in the world leads to death via "crooked speech" and "devious talk" that skews social relationships. All of that is countered by the imperative to the contrary: "Get insight."

Wednesday after Trinity Sunday

Psalm 119:1–24; Proverbs 6:1–19; 1 John 5:1–12; Matthew 11:16–24

God who presides over the concrete realities of our life, this day we reflect, in your presence, on the way in which our daily reality exhibits your will for a viable life in an ordered world. Save us from our foolishness. In his name. Amen.

The voice of the sage in the book of Proverbs offers practical theology. It is the voice of experience that wants to forewarn the young who are easily seduced to foolishness. There are two primary accents. The first is money. The sage sounds like a senior citizen who grew up in the Depression, warning about foolish loans and the danger of debt. In context, however, it is likely a warning about high interest rates in the Persian economy of the fifth century: do not participate in such an economy, for you will end in hopeless debt. The point among us is to warn of the predatory economy with its payday loans, subprime seductions, high interest rates on college loans, and the avarice of a banking system that preys on the poor and the innocent.

Second, the young are warned against laziness. Perhaps the point pertains now to an advanced adolescence in which the ownership class allows the young excessive leisure time that is called "education" but that is without productive contribution to society. The outcome of the foolish handling of money and the avoidance of work may be "lazybones" and ne'er-do-wells that endanger the health of the community.

Only late in the reading do we get explicit reference to "the LORD." Matters that damage social relationship are said to be abhorrent ("an abomination") to the Lord. This inventory of negative behaviors implies positive counterparts. The positive point is to become a responsible, contributing member of the community. That is what the Lord loves. We may resolve today to embrace this gospel truth in concrete ways.

Thursday after Trinity Sunday

Psalm 18:1–20; Proverbs 7:1–27; 1 John 5:13–21; Matthew 11:25–30

Lord of easy burden and light yoke, we give thanks for the simple, direct truth of your life. Grant that we may accept and embrace your truth in concrete ways today. In your name. Amen.

The "yoke" of which Jesus speaks is an obligation or a burden. In his context, the burdensome yoke might have been the acute scruples of some forms of Judaism that required attentive vigilance. Or the usage may refer to the heavy tax burden imposed by Rome. Either way, the pressure to perform and meet obligations was acute. In our time, the heavy yoke for many people is an overly busy life, made so by the demands of competitive consumerism with its interminable electronic connectedness that yields fatigue.

In the ancient world or in our world, Jesus is an offer of an alternative yoke that is "easy" and "light." The demand of the gospel, in the form of discipleship, makes faithfulness a light alternative to the demands of conventional politics and conventional religion. Jesus' requirement is simply traveling light in neighbor love, without competitive aggressiveness or the pressure to keep up or measure up.

Jesus avers that his followers are "infants" in innocence who know only a little. What we "infants" know is that in seeing and knowing the Son, we see and know the Father. The stories we tell about Jesus concern his transformative power that he enacts for all sorts of undeserving people. Jesus observes that "the wise and the intelligent" do not and cannot know this, even though they know many things. Knowing how to make their way in the world, they do not, he says, know what infants know, namely, that transformative power enacted as neighbor love is readily available because it is the will of the Father. Living this truth lets us live without fatigue or exhaustion.

Friday after Trinity Sunday

Psalm 16; Proverbs 8:1–21; 2 John 1–13; Matthew 12:1–14

Lord of the Sabbath and all our rules of engagement, we thank you for your emancipatory restorative power. Give us openness to notice its working in our midst this day. In your name. Amen.

Dominant power is kept in place by uncompromising protocols. That power is sustained and kept legitimate by rules and procedures that are taken to be normative and beyond criticism. For some forms of Judaism in Jesus' time, the commands of Sinai, specifically the requirement of Sabbath, had become an uncompromising rule that was the center of religious observance. Jesus, as an emancipatory agent sent by God, collided with that dominating normalcy. He makes two startling assertions. As Lord of the Sabbath he trumps the dominant protocols.

We might reflect on what the dominant protocols are in our time that characteristically combine economic ideology and religious requirement. Social power and social privilege are kept in place by claims of normalcy and legitimacy that are beyond question.

The force of the gospel is the claim that human well-being trumps all sorts of protocols. Thus the emancipatory power of the gospel subverts dominant power arrangements of class, race, and gender in the interest of human well-being. Our contemporary equivalents of the Sabbath protocol (such as, perhaps, qualifications to vote) keep the world running in a certain way that favors some over others.

Jesus heals a man and makes him whole. The healing evokes urgent hostility: his opponents "conspired against him, how to destroy him." The beneficiaries of old protocols of class, race, and gender will go to great lengths to sustain the status quo. The narrative affirms that the emancipatory power of the gospel will not be held in place by such protocols, much as we might prize them.

Saturday after Trinity Sunday

Psalm 20; Proverbs 8:22–36; 3 John 1–15; Matthew 12:15–21

Creator God who has ordered the world toward life, give us humility to live in accordance with your ordering; give us wisdom to respect the givenness of your creation, and joy in our dwelling in it. In his name. Amen.

This reading from Proverbs is one of the loveliest and most important reflections in the Bible on the mystery of the world. Wisdom delineates its peculiar and defining relationship with the creator God. Wisdom is a "master worker" who engineered the creation of the world. And even before that, the creator God played with and found joy in the company of wisdom. This lyrical affirmation declares that wisdom, that is, generative moral coherence, is ordained into the structure of created reality. The world is not elementally a place of contestation or dispute or violence. It is rather ordered by the power of wisdom so that all its parts are united into a generative whole. That ordered world, it is asserted in earlier verses in our chapter, is the foundation of all right power in the world.

The end of our text yields important practical counsel. As wisdom is the delight of the Creator, so human creatures must come to terms with the reality of wisdom in the structure of the creation. The world is not endlessly amenable to our will and purpose. Living in sync with wisdom brings happiness, life, and blessing. Missing out on wisdom, acting foolishly without regard for the given ordering of the world, can result only in injury and death.

This remarkable claim for wisdom (a) segues in Christian imagination to a vision of Jesus as the embodiment of this wisdom, (b) invites reflection on our environmental crisis, and (c) amounts to a critique of our technical reason that knows no limits to exploitation of the world. The claim of wisdom has enormous implications for policy going forward.

Proper 4

Psalm 63:1–8; Ecclesiastes 1:1–11; Acts 8:26–40; Luke 11:1–13

Giver of gifts, give us courage to be persistent about new possibility,
persistent in your presence, persistent in the neighborhood. In his name.
Amen.

The juxtaposition of the readings in Ecclesiastes and the Gospel pose a compelling contradiction about which a decision must be made. The beginning of Ecclesiastes is reflective of faith that is exhausted, if not defeated. The speaker has tried everything and is now out of energy. This is the voice of one who has lived in the rat race of competitive consumerism and finally ends with Woody Allen's durable question, "What's the point?"

That text, however, is juxtaposed to the Gospel reading wherein Jesus instructs his disciples in the art of prayer. He imagines a scenario in which even a friend, in the night, will not be bothered to help. That vignette suggests an exercise not unlike that of Ecclesiastes; it is all futile. Jesus, however, does not quit there in resignation. He instructs his listeners to nag the friend: be persistent! In the end, the friend will help in the night not because he cares but because the persistence has worn him down; he acts so that he can return to his sleep. The prayer ends with three imperatives: ask, knock, seek!

These two texts imagine different worlds. The fatigued world of Ecclesiastes imagines no dialogic interaction and so no new possibility; there is no one to address. The world narrated by Jesus is a world of demanding dialogic engagement in which imperatives addressed to a partner can evoke new possibility. That world is one in which God can be addressed and urged (compelled?) to newness. Such newness evoked by insistence suggests a counter to the judgment that there is "nothing new under the sun." The world of Jesus summons us to be active agents in the evocation of new worldly possibility.

Monday after Proper 4

Psalm 41; Ecclesiastes 2:1–15; Galatians 1:1–17; Matthew 13:44–52

God of abundance, we are overwhelmed by your good gifts. Give us pru-
dence to sort out and courage to choose the good and to value the durable;
give us discipline to refuse the easy offer of more. In his name. Amen.

We may again juxtapose the readings from Ecclesiastes and
the Gospel. The reading in Ecclesiastes is dominated by the
first-person pronoun with which the speaker reviews his tor-
rent of great action and his mighty achievements. He was propelled, he reports, by limitless, undisciplined desire to have
everything that could possibly bring him pleasure. He succeeded in his quest! He sounds like a successful champion of
consumerism or a mighty investment banker or a zealous academic who goes over the top in ambition. But he is caught up
short by a verdict of "vanity." His great achievements are all
futile. He discerns at the end of it all that he has been a fool for
being undisciplined and indiscriminate in his wants.

Jesus, to the contrary, offers four case studies. In each case
there is discrimination so that some things are considered better than others. In the first case, the field that contains the treasure is preferred to all else. In the second case, the pearl of
great price is preferred above all else. In the third case, good
fish are sorted out from the bad. In the fourth case, the angels
judge between evil and righteous. *Sell all, sort out, separate* indicates three judgments. Wisdom knows what is better, but foolishness has no basis for judgment.

Jesus' final statement concerning "new" and "old" requires
interpretive agility that is grounded in the deep reality of wisdom. Such wisdom is urgent in a society that wants more, that
in its fear wants security at all costs, that believes that truth is
relative to the interpreter, that craves newness, and that treats
life as self-indulgent entertainment. In such a society, good
judgment grounded in wisdom is a compelling vocation.

Tuesday after Proper 4

Psalm 45; Ecclesiastes 2:16–26; Galatians 1:18–2:10; Matthew 13:53–58

Lord Jesus, great agent of wisdom and power, let us this day enact some of your God-given wisdom and God-given power, that we may refuse resignation that renders us helpless and passive. In your name. Amen.

The text of Ecclesiastes expresses world-weariness that ends in despair. The outcome of the exhaustion for the writer is that he settles for safe modesty that gives up on the big questions that admit of no obvious resolution: "There is nothing better . . . " Even so, he cannot completely dispose of the God question. He reverts to the most simple (or is it simplistic?) moral equation: please God and prosper, sin and get hard work. None of that, however, eases his sense of futility.

Such resignation is countered in the Gospel narrative by the generative ministry of Jesus. By his teaching and his transformative actions, he continues to evoke an alternative world with fresh possibility. Even those opposed to him in his hometown acknowledge his authority expressed as "wisdom" and "power."

We may contrast, in these texts, the wisdom that leads to resignation and wisdom that results in an alternative transformed world. It is easy enough now, as it was in the Persian economy, to settle for resignation and to limit expectation to modest matters mostly concerned with the well-being of the self. It is possible to feel helpless in a rapidly changing world where large amounts of money and large deposits of intelligence seemingly outflank our capacity to act as effective public agents. Awareness of such reality, of course, abates resignation.

But the Gospel is a call away from such resignation. The performance of Jesus in this narrative is an affirmation that human agency, with poignant wisdom and generative power, can make a difference. Even the "unbelief" of his contemporaries did not deter his life and ministry.

Wednesday after Proper 4

Psalm 119:49–72; Ecclesiastes 3:1–15;
Galatians 2:11–21; Matthew 14:1–12

God of all our times, guide us in casting off what is over and done, in receiving newness you give, and in treasuring your hidden constancy amid our hard choosing. In his name. Amen.

In Ecclesiastes we get the tone of world-weariness of one who has seen it all before. The writer seeks to locate the proper human place and stance in the big picture of God's inscrutable order. On the one hand, there is the awful incomprehensibility of the big picture. God withholds the mystery of the beginning and the end, all of which is in God's hidden hand.

On the other hand, the writer has an appreciative sensibility for the poignant moment of human awareness and human choice. Sib Towner nicely observes that God has "given human beings a sense of having a place in the stately unrolling of the universal."* In that modest place, there is occasion for joy and well-being while the larger matters are left to God's undoubted governance.

In that moment extended to human agency, the key issue for this biblical writer is to know what time it is and what is appropriate to the time. The familiar opening verses of this text invite us to reflect on our particular time that God has entrusted to us. Ours is indeed a time of "plucking up" and "throwing away" as we witness the loss of much that we have treasured. Thus we watch while old patterns of racial and gender entitlement disappear. We notice that the old assurances of national exceptionalism fade away before our eyes. We watch while the old packaged certitudes of orthodoxy collapse in our midst. We are left to wonder how much to cast away and how to gather new social realities that permit us to live in well-being. The text invites submission to the hiddenness of ultimate reality and responsible well-being in the midst of that hiddenness. Our role will never be confused with that of God's!

*W. Sibley Towner, "The Book of Ecclesiastes," in *New Interpreter's Bible*, vol. 5 (Nashville: Abingdon Press, 1997), 306.

Thursday after Proper 4

Psalm 50; Ecclesiastes 3:16–4:3; Galatians 3:1–14; Matthew 14:13–21

God of tears and giver of bread, give us attentiveness today to the tears of the oppressed and to the systems that produce those tears. Give us generosity with bread that consoles the tearful. In his name. Amen.

Ecclesiastes gives us yet another rendition of resignation; he anticipates that human persons and beasts share the same fate, that the oppressed and oppressors alike cannot find comfort. I want to linger over his phrase, "the tears of the oppressed." The writer is not unmoved by the suffering produced by economic exploitation. Workers who are exploited may have deep grief. Attention must be paid to their unbearable lot and the tears that it produces.

But I notice that Antonio Gramsci, an Italian Marxist, has suggested that the moment when the victims become conscious of their historical lot "is the small door through which Messiah might enter."* Gramsci could speak of "Messiah" as a wedge of newness that is evoked amid human suffering. If we ponder Gramsci's telling phrase, we might see in the Gospel reading that Jesus, the Messiah, readily walked through that small door opened by human misery. He sees a "great crowd" and has compassion on them. Who constitutes that great crowd? Well, not the well-off, not the well-employed. The crowd consists of hungry people without bread. Jesus, the Messiah, is moved with compassion and brings effective comfort to those who "had no one to comfort them." The resignation of Ecclesiastes is in a world where Messiah never comes. The cycle of misery is broken only by death. But gospel news is that the cycle is broken. Jesus is allied with the tears of the oppressed. We might take this interruption made by gospel bread as an opening of the small door for messianic action. It is action that results in twelve baskets of surplus bread, a sure sign of the Messiah.

*See Enrique Dussel, *Ethics of Liberation in the Age of Globalization and Exclusion* (Durham: Duke University Press, 2013), 243.

Friday after Proper 4

Psalm 40; Ecclesiastes 5:1–7; Galatians 3:15–22; Matthew 14:22-36

Holy God of unutterable mystery and uncompromising governance, we thank you for access to your presence. Let us this day consider what it means to stand before you, from whom we receive all our futures. In his name. Amen.

For all his impulse to resignation, the writer of Ecclesiastes can nonetheless engage in a bit of practical theology. He wants to curb self-indulgent, overly eager self-expression. His counsel is to act like an adult at worship. Perhaps he is dealing with people who are not yet "church trained" and who do not know the conventional expectations for worship. I wonder what he might have said about the use of cell phones during the Scripture reading!

The writer does not have a vibrant view of God, but he does recognize the awesome transcendence of God, before whom reverence and awe constitute proper conduct. He chides "fools" who run off at the mouth and who imagine, even in worship, that they are the center of attention. "Many cases" and "many words," that is, much self-expression, leads to the trivialization of worship. Better to listen, to pay attention, to be instructed, because no one is beyond more instruction. Those who in worship have made up their minds too completely may miss out on the gifts yet to be given in the mystery of God.

We might well consider the transcendence of God in a society that imagines ready intimacy with God who is a good friend or a real pal, or alternatively imagines God as a benign spiritual force who gently guides but who never contradicts and from whom there is never a discouraging word. The writer puts the accent on the otherness of God who is the center of worship; that otherness has the effect of decentering us, of inviting us into a world beyond our control or explanation where this writer lived.

Saturday after Proper 4

Psalm 55; Ecclesiastes 5:8–20; Galatians 3:23–4:11; Matthew 15:1–20

God of stunning emancipation, your good news of liberty takes our breath away. Forgive us for the ways we cling to old bondages that make us feel safe. In his name. Amen.

The common theme of the Epistle and Gospel readings is the freedom of the gospel. Paul writes in the midst of a dispute concerning Torah obedience and the emancipatory impact of faith. In the midst of the dispute he delivers the threefold formula that was perhaps used at baptism. The statement shows that "in Christ Jesus," that is, in the new community of the gospel, old social divisions are nullified and overcome. This nullification pertains to (a) ethnic separation of Jews and Greeks, which was a matter of immense concern in the early church that sought to include both groups in its body, (b) class distinctions between free and slave, with all the economic advantages or disadvantages linked to them, and (c) gender distinctions between male and female. Baptism into the gospel means that they no longer have compelling authority.

In Matthew, Jesus joins issue with the scruples of the "tradition" of Judaism that focused on purity and defilement. He pushes behind such scruples to focus on relational matters that have their rootage in the Ten Commandments. Thus the freedom of the gospel that he proclaims is freedom from preoccupation with ritual matters of qualification that permit stratification in the community. Our society continues to be preoccupied with such matters, for example, in the long-running dispute about same-sex relations that have been regarded all too much as matters of purity and defilement. Or the debate among us about which immigrants are qualified for our nation, which is variously about ritual purity or economic or ethnic qualification. In Pentecost the Spirit swept away many of our treasured distinctions and divisions. The freedom of the gospel is in many ways a scary free fall into God's faithfulness.

Proper 5

Psalm 24; Ecclesiastes 6:1–12; Acts 10:9–23; Luke 12:32–40

Lord of the new regime, give us openness to your new rule, give us honesty about what we have yet to unlearn, give us alertness that we do not miss your jarring gift to us. In your name. Amen.

In the Acts narrative, Peter is summoned outside the box by an inexplicable experience. Because of the intrusion of the voice of heaven, Peter has to unlearn what he most trusts. He had been well schooled in purity codes of his religious community. And now, in an abrupt moment, he is summoned away from his legacy of purity and cleanness to a new world: "What God has made clean, you must not call profane." He is able to compute that this trance is not about unclean animals but about people — Gentiles — whom he had been taught were unclean.

We have, in our society, been in the process of unlearning our purity codes. We thought (we whites) for a long time that people of color were unclean and we could not eat with them. We thought (we men) that women were unqualified and could not be ordained. We thought (we straight people) that gay people were a threat that should not be welcomed. We are now preoccupied with welcome or unwelcome for immigrants. Peter's unlearning was not the last chapter in evangelical unlearning. Now we are being called to unlearn a great deal. It turns out that what we learned was not the truth but simply a power arrangement to exclude some and maintain privilege for others.

Jesus speaks about "the kingdom" that will come stealthily. Old power arrangements and old entitlements come to an end abruptly as God's purposes come to fruition. Peter was taught to treasure old notions of purity, and now Jesus invites us to resituate our "treasure" in the presence of God. The unlearning must have been a shock and threat to Peter, but he does not resist for long. We face no lesser task.

Monday after Proper 5

Psalm 56; Ecclesiastes 7:1–14; Galatians 4:12–20; Matthew 15:21–28

Lord Jesus, we thank you for this story through we watch as you grow into greater purpose. Grant that we may grow as you have done and not settle in narrow places. In your name. Amen.

The Gospel narrative reports a stunning confrontation in the life of Jesus. He is met by a "Canaanite" woman. The term "Canaanite" is an anachronism, because there were none of them anymore. The term refers to any outsider who was culturally unwelcome and religiously rejected by Judaism of a certain ilk in his time. The woman, however, is like all mothers. She wants her sick daughter to be healed and has no interest in sectarian identity. Before Jesus can speak or act, his disciples want to dismiss her. And indeed, Jesus is not responsive to her either. Jesus rejects her appeal because he understands his mission to be to Jews.

His assumption and that of his disciples are abruptly questioned by her insistent petition: "Help me!" A second time Jesus speaks to repel her. He utilizes the imagery of "children" and "dogs": children = Jews, dogs (a quite derogatory term) = Gentiles. He suggests that the gifts of God he carries are reserved for Jews. Her second response is more demanding. She refuses his answer, appealing to his imagery and accepting the derogatory term: dogs (Gentiles) are entitled to some spillover of his gifts. In that moment of the exchange Jesus is shaken out of his tribal presupposition. By her insistence she dislocates him and receives healing for her daughter.

Jesus is interrupted, even though we do not expect him to be further educated. She will not let him alone in that narrow locus. She is an interrupter who creates a new scope for God's healing. We might consider the way in which we are interrupted in old assumptions, or we might accept our role of interrupter to summon others to new growth in their faith. It is a double task: interrupted/interrupter.

Tuesday after Proper 5

Psalm 61; Ecclesiastes 8:14–9:10; Galatians 4:21–31; Matthew 15:29–39

We confess, inscrutable God, that the working of your world is beyond our explanation. Let us practice a near-term realism —given your hiddenness —to live fully the days you give us, free from dread and fatigue. In his name. Amen.

The preacher in Ecclesiastes takes up the difficult issue of theodicy, the question of why good people suffer and evil people prosper, that is, why is there injustice in God's world? It is an assumption of much popular religion and in the bottom line of most conventional biblical faith as expressed in both the covenantal tradition of Deuteronomy and in the teaching of the book of Proverbs that good people prosper and evil people suffer. Now the preacher readily acknowledges, after Job, that such reliance on the justice of God is simply not valid. The claim is no longer contested, as in the book of Job. Beyond that, he says, thinking about this question is a futile exercise and we should not do it. And then he makes three important responses to the quandary.

First, we cannot "find out." We cannot reason through it, even though philosophers continue forever to wonder about it. Second is the recognition that everyone—righteous and wicked—comes to the same fate. All will die, so the question is a moot one that merits none of our energy.

Third, the preacher is not overwhelmed by these two conclusions and is not driven to despair. Rather he makes something out of this reading of human destiny. On the one hand, given the "same fate" for all, it is still possible to live well and joyously in the time we have. On the other hand, do some significant work, even if it has no durable significance. Live fully in the present. This realism may protect us from both pie in the sky and despair. This is an honest embrace of the limit of human life entrusted to us. More we do not ask and do not need.

Wednesday after Proper 5

Psalm 72; Ecclesiastes 9:11–18; Galatians 5:1–15; Matthew 16:1–12

God of truthfulness, we thank you for the good bread of the gospel that causes us not to hunger for false leaven. Let us this day see your world more clearly and so live in it more faithfully. In his name. Amen.

The Sadducees and Pharisees, presented in the Gospel narrative as opponents of Jesus, set a trap for Jesus by asking for a sign. They appeal away from the world that is in front of them. By contrast Jesus is preoccupied with bread, the practical concrete stuff that sustains life. From that preoccupation with bread he borrows the image of leaven to warn against the "leaven" of his opponents. It turns out, however, that he is not speaking of bread or leaven or anything related to them. He is talking about false teaching that yields a false interpretive world. The contemporary term for such false teaching that yields a false world is "ideology," a way of perceiving that is out of touch with reality.

When we are out of touch with reality (as were they), we cannot read the signs of the times. We cannot identify harbingers of the future. We cannot see what is going on in front of us in the world. Jesus warns his disciples against such a false field of perception.

This imagery invites us to consider two facets of truth telling. First, what are the signs of the times to which attention must be paid? Among them might be the rising indexes of poverty or the growing environmental crisis, each of which hints at the future. Second, we might ask, what is the false leaven (ideology) that prevents us from taking seriously the signs of the times? Such false leaven might include bad economic theory or long habits of racism or overheated patriotism. When we cannot see more clearly, we cannot follow more nearly.

Thursday after Proper 5

Psalm 70; Ecclesiastes 11:1–8; Galatians 5:16–24; Matthew 16:13–20

God of an alternative way of life, give us good resolve and honesty today, that we may choose rightly and so contribute to the peaceableness and well-being of the world. In his name. Amen.

Biblical faith repeatedly puts before us a deep either-or that has powerful theological rootage and quite practical outcomes. In Deuteronomy, it is life or death. In Proverbs, it is wisdom or foolishness. In the Sermon on the Mount, it is the narrow path or the easy way. In this Epistle reading, Paul lines out the either-or in an inventory of behaviors that exhibit excessive preoccupation with self or conduct supporting the well-being of the community. He urges his congregants to choose the latter, as they are free to do in the gospel.

The "desires of the flesh" bespeak a life that is propelled by self-advancement at the expense of others and a passionate will to have one's own way. It is fair to say that the competitive world bequeathed to us by modern individualism, reinforced by market ideology, evokes a way of life that is destructive of community. While the more blatant forms of such desires are readily rejected among the kinds of people who read this sort of literature, Paul's judgment is that even "nice" people and "pious" people have the force of self-indulgence, even when a more credible social face is put on it.

Conversely, the fruit of the Spirit is the outcome of a life that is given over to the gospel and that is empowered by the Spirit of God. A life so situated has no need for self-advancement or self-securing, because one is already secure in gospel love and truth. No doubt the reason that biblical testimony continually returns to this either-or (in a variety of forms) is that for all of our faithful resolve, we are always again seduced to a lesser way. Choosing faithfully is a lifelong project in which we are engaged. We may even today choose differently in our gospel freedom.

Friday after Proper 5

Psalm 69:1–23, 31–38; Ecclesiastes 11:9–12:14;
Galatians 5:26–6:10; Matthew 16:21–28

*Lord of the church, who has bound us to each other in the church, we
thank you for our baptized sisters and brothers, some of whom vex us
and some of whom delight us. Give us largeness of spirit appropriate to
our membership. In your name. Amen.*

Paul, the pastoral theologian, continues his mentoring of the
church. He has no doubt that life in the Spirit is life in a regis-
ter very different from the way the world practices life. Paul's
vision is that the Christian community by its internal relations
exhibits to the world another way of life. This alternative life is
empowered by God's Spirit that overrides all ordinary assumptions and protocols. Belonging to the church is a permit and a
requirement to order life differently.

At the center of Paul's pastoral counsel is a tension (con-
tradiction?). On the one hand, "Bear one another's burdens."
Membership is a big deal to Paul; we belong to each other:
"We share our mutual woes; our mutual burdens bear."*
Such membership defies the common calculus of our society.
We have both commitment and obligation to each other that
includes emotional support and economic support as well.

On the other hand, Paul insists, "All must carry their own
loads." The letter is a summons to responsibility in order to fend
off dependence. Both interdependence and personal responsibility are urged. Such trusting, committed relationality refuses
to reduce the tension to a formula or to a foolproof calculation.
It is always a work in progress, under negotiation. What lies
behind the tension for Paul is a lively, committed community
that devotes energy, time, and money to the well-being of the
community. The conclusion of "the good of all" is sharpened to
focus on those who belong to the congregation. Membership
is not incidental. As a result, the church has conversations that
occur nowhere else and takes initiatives that belong peculiarly
to its life.

*John Fawcett, "Blest Be the Tie that Binds" (1782).

Saturday after Proper 5

Psalm 75; Numbers 3:1–13; Galatians 6:11–18; Matthew 17:1–13

God who has set some in authority and some in subservience, give us this day a clear critical eye that we may see probingly what it is like to be assigned a lesser or a greater role or status. In his name. Amen.

This reading from Numbers gives us a chance to reflect on the complex, esoteric history of priesthood in ancient Israel. You, dear reader, may have no interest in this complex history but linger for a minute. An important distinction is made among the priests God authorizes. On the one hand, Aaron and his sons are made to be priests. They are peculiarly holy and invested with immense sacerdotal responsibility. On the other hand, the Levites are appointed by Moses to "assist" Aaron and to "perform duties for him." They are assigned menial, maintenance tasks and are quite subordinate to the Aaron crowd. The tension between the priestly order of Aaron and the priestly caste of Levites gives us an occasion to reflect on stratification in society and in the church. One way to perceive the "lower" status of the Levites is to recognize that menial maintenance tasks are indispensable to any social operation, and one may be glad for and accepting of such assignments. Conversely, one might see that such stratification of authority and social regard serves to enhance the sons of Aaron at the expense of the Levites. One can spot instances of great tension in the Old Testament between the groups. Some narratives expose the Aaron group as high-handed. And some texts celebrate the fidelity of the Levites.

Take time today to consider social stratification in church and in society. Consider who has power and influence and how it is exercised; consider your own social location and what access you have to the holy mystery of life.

Proper 6

Psalm 93; Numbers 6:22–27; Acts 13:1–12; Luke 12:41–48

God of blessing, grace, and peace, we give you thanks for priests, pastors, and ministers who are authorized and trusted with the power of benediction. May we trust ourselves fully to that gift, confident of your watchful parental care for us. In his name. Amen.

This blessing of Aaron in Numbers 6 is so familiar to us that we scarcely notice its remarkable anticipation. A beginning point is to take note of the recurring declaration of the name of "the LORD" (YHWH). By this repetition Israel recalls and makes present the wonder of creation by YHWH and the inventory of YHWH's saving miracles. The second thing to notice is that we have the term "bless" three times, once in the actual benediction. The word "bless" recalls God's original blessing of creation in Genesis, the infusion of life force into the processes of creation. Such an infusion of life blessing is the hidden, constant, and generative commitment of God to the world. This is the assurance that all life is under the providential care of the creator God who sees the need of all creatures and supplies what they need. That assurance of God's providing care is filled out in the blessing by a pattern of terms. At the beginning we have "keep," that is, watch over and protect, and at the end, "peace" *(shalom* or well-being). Inside those words we have the double use of the "face" or "countenance" of God; God will look and see in the way that a parent sees a child caringly. At the center is the word "gracious," the gift of God given freely without any merit on our part.

The liturgic act of blessing by a pastor is a dramatic claim that in the moment of liturgic utterance all the generative force of the creator God is gathered and mobilized and transferred (conventionally by the gesture of a lifted hand of power) to the receiving congregation. We depart the moment with life changed, trusting in the blessing, surrounded by God's goodness.

Monday after Proper 6

Psalm 80; Numbers 9:15–23; 10:29–36;
Romans 1:1–15; Matthew 17:14–21

Giver of every new gift, we thank you for the array of wonders from your hand that well up in our midst every day. Give us eyes to perceive and hands to receive the newness you would give us. In his name. Amen.

As long ago as aged Abraham and Sarah in the book of Genesis (18:14), the crucial question was asked: "Is anything impossible for God?" Or alternatively, "Is anything too hard for God?" As the story goes, that "impossibility" was enacted by God and Isaac was born. Now Jesus returns to the question in the presence of his disciples who are not able to heal the epileptic man. They lack faith enough to heal. Jesus indicts them for their "little faith." They could not do the wonders that Jesus could do because of their little faith.

The question and the affirmation concerning the impossible are tricky and seductive, because they invite speculation about wondrous deeds that defy reason. But since for some days we have been reading the book of Ecclesiastes, we can set the issue of the impossible in the midst of that text in which "there is nothing new under the sun." Little faith may conclude that nothing new can happen, that things will always be the way they are, that what has been will be. In that context, faith — as contrasted with little faith — is the conviction that the future is open as it was for the epileptic man, that newness may be given, that inexplicable gifts can come among us. A world that is reduced to technological imagination assumes that everything possible must be extrapolated from what is. In the world of relationships (as distinct from technological reasoning), however, newness happens. We often stand alongside the disciples in their little faith. But Jesus contradicts such little faith. As a result, the blind see, lepers are cleansed, the dead are raised, the poor rejoice, all in the midst of his generative presence.

Tuesday after Proper 6

Psalm 78:1–39; Numbers 11:1–23; Romans 1:16–25; Matthew 17:22–27

God of wilderness meat, we thank you for your provision and fidelity amid our precariousness. Give us courage to be present to you in honest ways that, when necessary, can be demanding. In his name. Amen.

In the Old Testament reading, being in the wilderness means to be outside the reach of Pharaoh and outside the guaranteed food supply of the dominant economy. It is a place of immense anxiety for Israel. This narrative in the wilderness exhibits three dimensions of faith. First, in the wilderness Israel is completely dependent on YHWH. It has no other resources, certainly none of its own. YHWH, moreover, is unproven among them; they do not know if YHWH will be faithful. Second, there is ample food in the wilderness when YHWH grants it. In the end, water, bread, and meat (quails) are given in abundance. YHWH is found to be reliable with sufficient resources for Israel.

But third, the intense interaction among the characters in the story holds our attention. All three characters have a role to play. Israel complains in its anxious need. Moses disputes with YHWH and reminds that Israel is YHWH's burden and not that of Moses. YHWH has responsibility for this people who have been created out of a company of slaves. YHWH is shown to be capable of a full spectrum of emotional engagement. Thus YHWH can be indignant about being doubted: "Is the LORD's hand too short?" YHWH can be accessible: YHWH will "come down and talk." YHWH is faithful and gives meat.

The narrative is a script for covenantal interaction and negotiation. In Pharaoh's domain there is no such risky interaction. We, however, are destined for life in the wilderness, a matrix of demanding engagement.

Wednesday after Proper 6

Psalm 119:97–120; Numbers 11:24–35;
Romans 1:28–2:11; Matthew 18:1–9

God of sovereign rule, your hard ways are sometimes more than we can bear and always a mystery to us. Give us openness to your will; give us stamina to stand in hard places when our faith requires it. In his name. Amen.

These readings awaken us from any soft romanticism about the God of the gospel:

In Numbers: "The anger of the LORD was kindled."
In Romans: "You are storing up wrath for yourself."
In Matthew: "Better for you if a great millstone . . ."

What to make of this recurring accent? This articulation of God, like every articulation of God in the Bible (or anywhere else), is filtered through human imagination. Perhaps the filter for this "revelation" of God consists in human authority of a stern kind that will not be mocked.

Our inclination is to explain away such hard sayings. After we have used our best strategies, we are still left with a disclosure of God that is jarring indeed. In Numbers, the divine judgment is because of excessive "craving." In Romans, it is a more generic "hard heart," that is, a refusal to allow for the generous, gracious rule of God. In Matthew, it is because of manipulative treatment of a vulnerable child. In each case there seems to be a combination of a real affront and the huffing and puffing of a God who will not be mocked.

Difficult as it is, I suggest that we may learn from these readings that God, as given in the text, is a real character and a lively agent who stands over against us in our willful desire to have life on our own terms. Such a claim is surely hard to bear in the religious culture of the United States, especially when one does not want to fall into "hellfire and damnation." At least this much is certain: God must be taken seriously as God, rather than an echo of our religious propensity.

Thursday after Proper 6

Psalm 83; Numbers 12:1–16; Romans 2:12–24; Matthew 18:10–20

Living Lord of the church, we give thanks for the specific church fellow-ship in which we are involved, for its leadership and its pastoral atten-tiveness. Give guidance to us by your Spirit that we may both reach out to others among us and maintain the disciplines that upbuild our common life. In your name. Amen.

Living in a Christian congregation is no piece of cake, and it never was. Matthew sees that such shared life requires effort and intentionality. First, the Gospel reading speaks of the "little ones," the ones who are regarded by the more "mature" members of the congregation as insignificant. Such seemingly insignificant members are to be valued and taken seriously because they are well regarded by the angels in heaven.

Second, the Gospel reading concerns those who have "gone astray," who have dropped out due to error or loss of faith or simple indifference. The reading commends pastoral care to restore such persons to active participation in the community. In a culture of "nones" and "dones" and "spiritual but not religious" inclination, such restoration to participation is an important responsibility. Attention must be paid, and effort must be made.

The remainder of the reading is concerned with the procedure in the congregation for the management and resolution of conflict. The text seeks to outline due process that may go with a willing heart for restoration.

This text invites reflection on responsible participation in the life of the congregation. Even at the outset, the life of a congregation is marked by tension, dispute, and fracture. Such characteristic markings of the church require deep investment for the sake of the well-being of the body. This is indeed no piece of cake, never as easy as a company picnic.

Friday after Proper 6

Psalm 88; Numbers 13:1–3, 21–30;
Romans 2:25–3:8; Matthew 18:21–35

*God of compassion toward us, give us the freedom to act out your com-
passion this day, to break the chain of debt, and to begin again from
your generosity. In his name. Amen.*

Of course forgiveness is the defining mark of gospel faith. We
count daily and in regular liturgic performance on the ready
forgiveness of God. But forgiveness as a practical, neighborly
act is more difficult and complex. The Gospel reading nonetheless insists that God's forgiveness to us (represented in the
parable by the king) is intimately related to the forgiveness of
our neighbor (represented in the parable by the servant). That
same defining relationship is voiced in the familiarity of the
Lord's Prayer when we petition that God's forgiveness of us
(our debts, sins, trespasses) should be "as" our forgiveness of
the debts, sins, trespasses of our neighbor.

In the parable, the king is fully ready to forgive debts. But
the king anticipates that his act of forgiveness will generate
a continuing process of forgiveness down the socioeconomic
ladder to extend to the least and most hopelessly indebted. The
parable turns on the refusal of the forgiven servant to extend
the chain of forgiveness toward his neighbor. Everything turns
in the parable on the fact that the king acted "out of pity." The
king breaks the quid pro quo dealings by an act of compassion.
The debt is interrupted by compassion!

But consider compassion or pity or empathy in our society.
The data are clear that we live in a society that is increasingly
short of compassion. Our commitment to individualism at the
expense of communal solidarity, our fatigue from the rat race,
and our eagerness to win at the competitive game of wealth
and power all tell against compassion. This is a good day to
interrupt the momentum of a compassionless society to perform an overt act of forgiveness. The God of the gospel does
it every day!

Saturday after Proper 6

Psalm 87; Numbers 13:31–14:25; Romans 3:9–20; Matthew 19:1–12

God of promises, we rely on the promises you have made. We will, as we have courage, be in your face to insist that you remain faithful to those promises. In his name. Amen.

In the Old Testament reading, Israel is at a crisis point. The future into the land of promise looks too frightening to them; they are prepared to return to the predatory economy of Pharaoh, where they had been reduced to slavery. The question of whether to go back to slavery or forward in promise is an urgent and demanding issue. God, moreover, is prepared to give up on them in their lack of trust.

The narrative pivots on the courageous action of Moses, who intervenes with God on behalf of the people. Moses must remonstrate with God. He does so by reiterating the catalog of the traditional markers of YHWH's fidelity. He does so, moreover, by quoting God back to God, "you promised." The quote back to God is from God's utterance in Exodus 34:6–7. Now Moses shames God into keeping that promise to Israel.

We might focus on three accent points here. First, the key issue is whether to walk into a fearful future or to return to old-time bondage; freedom is scary! Second, the only way into that future is by trusting in God's faithfulness. But third, and oddly, in this text God must be urged back to fidelity so that the matter turns on the very human courage of Moses, who talks God back into God's promised faithfulness. Talk about urgent prayer! For our society now, and in the church, we are acutely faced with the same issue: a fearful future accompanied by a faithful God . . . or . . . return to the good old days that were not as good as we now remember them. Israel—and we—could choose beyond those remembered times of bondage.

Proper 7

Psalm 66; Numbers 14:26–45; Acts 15:1–12; Luke 12:49–56

God of good futures, we pray for trust and courage and wisdom, that we might engage your futures well, shunning both reticence and rashness. In his name. Amen.

We may take the crisis of land entry in the Old Testament reading as a question of entering into fearful futures according to God's promises. As with us and our future, the outcomes for Israel in the wilderness were not at all clear. We can see the profound uncertainty in the narrative.

That indecision includes the following elements. First, the spies who looked at the new land brought back a "bad report." The land was too dangerous. Fear about the future overwhelmed them. Second, Caleb and Joshua—only these two—are identified as the wave of Israel's future. They are marked not only by great faith in God's future but also by wisdom, ability to discern the right time to act. Third, after the death of many of the faithless, the people who had mourned their death resolve to go immediately into the new land anyway, even though they are warned by Moses not to go. The outcome is that in their rashness they are defeated. What might have been trusting faithfulness on their part turned out to be foolish rashness. Thus the matter of faith and mistrust and faith and foolishness are central to the narrative.

The report does not hesitate at all to make a distinction in the rising generation between Caleb and Joshua on the one hand and all the others on the other hand. What distinguishes the two of them is their readiness to trust the promises and to be led by the wisdom of Moses. That great divide is perhaps an anticipation of the great divide that Jesus has come to establish. Here there is no Rodney King sentiment, "Can't we just all get along?" The gospel requires risky, dangerous living. We may ponder where we stand amid the divide.

Monday after Proper 7

Psalm 89:1–18; Numbers 16:1–19; Romans 3:21–31; Matthew 19:13–22

God of expansive acceptance and of deep expectation, grant that in the company of Jesus we may forgo the distinctions on which we count so heavily. Give us the gift of trust in you that we may rely on none of our "qualifications." In his name. Amen.

The great conviction of Paul in the Epistle reading is "No distinction!" It is the most radical claim of the gospel. From the outset the early church was vexed as it pursued its vision of one community including both Jews who obeyed Torah and Gentiles who did not. The apostolic affirmation is that all stand in need of God's love and live by God's goodness.

The impulse to make distinctions is a powerful one among us. It shows up in the church as stratified leadership. It shows up because some are more pious than others, some are more generous than others, some are more pushy than others. In civil society, the practice of distinction and stratification is evident in the economy. We determine who is better, who has better health care or better schools or better jobs. The epistle declares that we are not all equal. It rather affirms that in Christ we have been rendered first class without meeting certain criteria.

In light of such a dazzling claim, the Gospel reading may give us pause. The man who addresses Jesus had kept all the Commandments. He is devoted to Torah. Jesus, moreover, does not take Torah obedience lightly. He commends it. But then, he urges the man to go farther in complete trustful self-abandonment. That self-abandonment is specified as giving away all of one's goods.

We struggle now in our society with all kinds of distinctions, such as race, class, and gender, through which we have historically established privilege and entitlement. We order society through such stratification. In the new rule of Jesus, however, we are—all of us—included among the best qualified.

Tuesday after Proper 7

Psalm 97; Numbers 16:20–35; Romans 4:1–12; Matthew 19:23–30

Lord Jesus, who makes stringent demands of your followers, we are resolved to be among your followers. Give us freedom and readiness to embrace your path to an alternative world. In your name. Amen.

We begin by recognizing that in the Gospel reading the phrase "kingdom of God" means, among other things, a radically different economic arrangement in which the abundance of the community is shared by all. Following Jesus is following a path of divestment.

In his reflection on his encounter with the man, Jesus observes that it is hard for a *rich person* to enter into *the kingdom of God*, as the two phrases seem to be a contradiction. But notice, he says it is not easy. He later says that it is "possible" with God. But we may wonder: does he intend that the rich person should be given a pass into his kingdom? In light of his stringent teaching, that is unlikely. The alternative might be that by the transformative power of God the rich person may be moved to divest of wealth and so become an acceptable candidate for the kingdom. There is no doubt that Jesus intends divestment, as is clear in his final statement about the first and the last.

For this day, let us consider what it might mean to divest of wealth. It is not likely that many of us will abruptly give away all of our surplus. There are dramatic examples of that, but not many. More likely the divestment appropriate to his kingdom will happen slowly by growth, by maturation, and by a Spirit-transformed consciousness of the alternative. Divestment will happen by the embrace of the common good apart from which there can be no sustainable abundant life. Thus divestment might mean the development of generous public policies whereby abundance is shared among the first and the last.

Wednesday after Proper 7

Psalm 101; Numbers 16:36–50; Romans 4:13–25; Matthew 20:1–16

God, father of Abraham and Sarah, we are dazzled by your capacity for newness. Give us freedom from all old immobility, fear, and despair, that we may this day live into your wondrous newness. In his name. Amen.

In the Epistle reading, Paul goes behind the Torah of Sinai to father Abraham, who becomes the ground for his conviction that Jews and Gentiles can be in the Jesus movement on equal footing together. He makes three remarkable claims that draw our attention.

Because Abraham is prior to Torah, God is not singularly the possession of the people of Israel. His call from God is to be a blessing to "many nations," that is, to the Gentiles who share the blessing of God.

Second, Paul bears witness in doxological form to the God who has called Abraham. He asserts that this God "gives life to the dead," a reference to the resurrection of Jesus, and that this God calls into being that which does not exist, a reference to the *creatio ex nihilo* in the Genesis creation text. Not only does this God have immense authority, but God is willing and able to mobilize that authority for the sake of new life. Everything turns, in apostolic faith, on the conviction that the goodness and power of God are not hemmed in by the realities in front of us, the realities of death and chaos.

Third, Paul affirms that Abraham trusted this God completely. He trusted in his old age that God would give a son and heir in defiance of Abraham's biological limitation. And, of course, the birth of Isaac attests the truth of that claim.

Given this pre-Torah God of blessing and Abraham's trust in that God, Paul makes the judgment that the single requirement for the Jesus community is to trust one's life to this God. Such trust means emancipation from the old world of fear and threat.

Thursday after Proper 7

Psalm 105:1–22; Numbers 17:1–11; Romans 5:1–11; Matthew 20:17–28

Lord Jesus, who by vulnerable solidarity contradicted the top-down authority of lordly power, grant that we today may find ways to join in your daring, transformative contradiction. In your name. Amen.

What mother does not want her child promoted to a better future? So with the mother of two disciples. Her request indicates that she has no clue about the ministry and purpose of Jesus or the destiny of her sons. Jesus immediately turns from the mother to the sons and quizzes them about their capacity to walk with him. He asks them about "the cup," that is, the destiny of suffering that will come to his followers. They answer eagerly in the affirmative. We may suspect that they, faithful to their mother, think their affirmative embrace of the cup of suffering is simply a prerequisite for a good appointment in his coming kingdom.

But, of course, their willingness suggests that they understand no more than did their mother. Jesus accepts their affirmative answer about the cup. But he denies them any expected reward for their obedience. He focuses only on the task at hand, which is an end in itself.

And then Jesus elaborates on his vocation into which they have been inducted. In a world of "great ones," the call is to servanthood. Jesus contradicts the world of power and the expectation of his disciples. He does so because the kingdom he will bring is a contradiction to both Roman power and Jewish entitlement. Such a contradiction, of course, brings big trouble. But he sees unambiguously that restoration of those damaged by top-down great people requires a completely different enterprise. We might consider engaging in that contradiction in our own time. Contradiction of greedy commoditization is urgent among the vulnerable who are rendered helpless and hopeless by our dominant power arrangement.

Friday after Proper 7

Psalm 102; Numbers 20:1–13; Romans 5:12–21; Matthew 20:29–34

Jesus, who attends to cries for mercy, pay heed to those cries for mercy that are sounded this day. And because we have been heard in our cry, give us courage to follow you into your future. In your name. Amen.

The other day we saw Paul's testimony that the God of the gospel "calls into existence the things that do not exist." Now we have a case study concerning that remarkable claim. In the Gospel reading, by the hand of Jesus, God transforms two blind men into men who can see.

The Gospel narrative follows a familiar pattern. First there is the need and the petition of the needy. The blind men cry for "mercy," for generosity beyond what they might deserve. Second, Jesus responds with an intake interview. He asks about their hope. When they answer, he touches them in a transformative way. He does so, we are told, because he is "moved with compassion." He is available to be deeply and intimately impacted by human need. Third, the outcome is that the two men can see. Their need is resolved. Their hope is fulfilled.

There are, beyond this familiar dramatic pattern, two other matters to note. First, the crowd tries to silence the two men. We do not know why. Perhaps the crowd thought that they were undeserving and attention should not be paid to them. They are, however, insistent beyond the silencing force of the crowd. Their continuing urgency draws Jesus' attention. The other note is the closing report that they "followed him." They became his disciples. They traveled with the company of Jesus and continued the work of restoration. The drama is a bid for *mercy* that is answered with *compassion*. *Mercy* broke the silence of resignation. *Compassion* broke the quid pro quo assumptions of the crowd. We who attend to the narrative may belong to the company of those who live forward into the future-generating gospel.

Saturday after Proper 7

Psalm 107:33–43; Numbers 20:14–29;
Romans 6:1–11; Matthew 21:1–11

Lord Jesus, who was crucified and raised to new life, we thank you for our baptism whereby we are sealed as your own forever. Give us fresh imagination that we may see ways in which we may live out our baptism in boldness that matches your generosity. In your name. Amen.

From his own lived experience, Paul understood about the continuing power of the "old self." He knew that the rest of us, alongside him, walk around in our old selves. In the later Epistles to the Ephesians and Colossians we get a fuller exposition of the old self, one that inured to fear, self-indulgence, and antineighborliness. While Paul understood the power of the old self in visceral ontological terms, he was a wise pastoral educator who also understood that the old self is massively reinforced by the passions of a culture that evokes and authorizes the old self. In our case that cultural reinforcement of the old self takes, among other things, the form of commodity consumerism that trades on scarcity and fear that in turn require greed.

Paul's focus, however, is on the good news that the power of the old self has been broken in Christ's crucifixion so that the new self can emerge via his resurrection. That story of Christ is practiced and appropriated in the drama of baptism wherein the participants reiterate their death and their new life. Familiar confessional, liturgical language links together the effective narrative of Jesus and our appropriation of it in our lives.

We might spend this day pondering the new self that is marked by the fruits of the Spirit: love, joy, peace, gentleness, kindness. In another catalog, it includes kindness, tenderheartedness, and forgiveness. This is a day to remember our baptism. It is also a day to consider how we may forget our baptism and revert to the old self of fear, anxiety, and scarcity. Baptism is a gift from God; it is also a vocation that we engage with discipline and intentionality.

Proper 8

Psalm 118; Numbers 21:4–9, 21–35; Acts 17:12–34; Luke 13:10–17

God of newness we cannot contain, give us today ears to hear for the first time, that we may have our habits interrupted by your good news of new life. In his name. Amen.

The Gospel and Epistle readings offer contrasting dramas about the good news. In the narrative in Luke, Jesus confronts the rulers of the synagogue with fresh unsettling authority. Those rulers of the synagogue are habituated religious authorities who have faith packaged in manageable ways so that the truth and power of God operate by the clock. But Jesus breaks their schedule by healing on the Sabbath. Jesus reasserts the true identity of the infirm woman as a "daughter of Abraham"; he restores her to the promise.

By contrast, Paul is preaching in Athens. He names "the unknown God," the Creator, and then brings the claim of deity down to "a man whom he has appointed" and raised from the dead. The anointed, not yet named, is Jesus of Nazareth. Thus Paul enunciates the core, audacious claim of gospel faith. This is a "new teaching" delivered for the first time among these Gentiles. The narrative adds tersely, "Some of them joined him and became believers." They were hearing this for the first time, as with new ears. They resolved to "hear this again."

With new ears they were so unlike the synagogue authorities who never expected to hear anything new. These men in Athens were more like "the crowd" at the end of the Gospel reading who respond to "all the wonderful things." These readings suggest to me that we reflect on how jaded we have become about the gospel, so jaded that we do not notice. When we do not notice, we remain "on the clock" of old habitual faith. Imagine what might happen if today we heard as for the first time. Hearing "for the first time" might interrupt our old habits of control and certitude in a way that restores our primary identity in the promise of God.

Monday after Proper 8

Psalm 106:1–18; Numbers 22:1–21;
Romans 6:12–23; Matthew 21:12–22

Ruler of all nations and all peoples, you hold us, our friends, and our enemies in your hand. Give us large vision to imagine that your good purposes may be other than ours. In his name. Amen.

This remarkable tale in Numbers juxtaposes Balak, the king of Moab, with the seer, Balaam. Balak wants to impede the movement of Israel toward the land. His best strategy, in that prescientific, "pre-rational" world, is to secure a divine curse against this enemy. Balak recruits Balaam the seer to pronounce the curse. Except that God interrupts the scheme, queries Balaam, and then prohibits Balaam from undertaking the work. Balaam is permitted to accompany Balak, but he is kept on a short leash by God.

This narrative lets us see how religion can engage in useful political purposes. Even in a scientific, rational political era like ours, the power of religion to bless or curse is available. For that reason we can see religious authorities regularly sign on with various ideological enterprises.

But God is the fly in such a convenient ointment. God prohibits the cursed. When the story continues we see this odd mystery unfold. Thus far, what we know is that God has signed on with and protects vulnerable Israel on the way to the promise. It turns out that religious authority (Balaam) is not free to collude with political power but is under restraint by the purposes of God.

Consider today, the vexed world of enemies. Notice the enemies we might prefer to curse. Consider the providential governance of God who may side with one's perceived enemies. What might it mean in our circumstance to imagine that the providential governance of God may lead to futures other than the future we would choose for ourselves?

Tuesday after Proper 8

Psalm 120; Numbers 22:21–38; Romans 7:1–12; Matthew 21:23–32

God, creator of all things, seen and unseen, let us see your purposes clearly. Where we cannot see, let us walk by faith, yielding when we prefer to control. In his name. Amen.

Balaam the seer is caught, as people of faith often are. He is well paid to serve Balak the king and to produce the results that the king desires. But he is also alert to powerful divine resolve that contradicts the king's desire for a curse. The story is made more complex by other agents who work the will of God. This story makes clear that the Bible, in its imaginative articulation of the world, is not limited by our rationality. It expects in us a readiness to enter into the imaginative playfulness to receive a world other than the one we daily take for granted.

In that world of playful imagination, we encounter both an angel dispatched by God and a talking donkey. The angel is an armed agent assigned to establish a blockage. But, of course, the angel is not seen by Balaam. For much of the story, the donkey is more perceptive than is Balaam, who is slow to catch on. When Balaam belatedly sees the angel, he is penitent and ready to obey. But after the blockade, Balaam is permitted to go on toward Balak. He is, however, limited to what God will permit him.

Balaam lives in a world where he is accountable to what he cannot see. So are we. We live in an "enlightened" world that has dispelled the mystery and reduced our historical reality to manageable proportion. In such a world, we can imagine that we are in charge. That is what both Balak and Balaam presumed. The Bible and its theological claims, however, constitute an awkward outlier. The Bible insists that the world is stranger, more open, and more unmanageable than we normally imagine. It claims that unseen purposes are at work among us, often contradicting our willful or wise preferences.

Wednesday after Proper 8

Psalm 119:145–176; Numbers 22:41–23:12;
Romans 7:13–25; Matthew 21:33–46

*God who governs among us and who retains for yourself ultimate gover-
nance, move through our proximate governance with your good purposes
for justice, mercy, and peace. In his name. Amen.*

Balaam is punctilious in his preparation of the site of his prophetic utterance to come; Balak is filled with keen anticipation for the delivery of a curse against his enemy, Israel. Then
Balaam speaks. He acknowledges that his assignment is to
curse, but he must refuse the assignment. He cannot curse
those whom God has not cursed. And then he envisions a wondrous future for Israel in the land that contradicts the fervent
hope of Balak, a fulfillment of the old promise made to father
Abraham.

Balak, of course, is disappointed and indignant. He does
not understand that this is what God's faithful witnesses must
do. They often bless those whom the world would curse. In
the horizon of the Old Testament, the blessing of Israel, since
Abraham, is incontrovertible. When carried into the New Testament, the blessing of God is on those whom the world little blesses. In Jesus' Beatitudes in his Sermon on the Mount,
the blessings of happiness, well-being, and good fortune are
on the poor in spirit, those who mourn, the meek, those who
hunger and thirst after righteousness, the merciful, the pure in
heart, the peacemakers, and the persecuted. As we celebrate
Independence Day this week, we might consider the way in
which the blessing of God is carried by those who are repeatedly and often judged negatively by dominant power. Those
blessed summon our commonwealth to another vision of historical reality.

Thursday after Proper 8

Psalm 131; Numbers 23:11–26; Romans 8:1–11; Matthew 22:1–14

God of freedom, who refuses our domestications, give us commensurate freedom that we may gladly submit to your will when it is other than our own inclination. In his name. Amen.

This intense, continuing exchange between Balak and Balaam embodies a huge challenge for faith. Balak wants Israel to be cursed because he perceives Israel as a threat. He wants that which threatens him to be condemned by God. (Don't we all!) Balaam would be willing to do what Balak wants, except he is restrained by his conviction about the reality of God.

In this reading we get three statements about God over which we may linger. First, "God is not a human being." God is not simply an echo or a reiteration of our preferences. God has a will and an intention that is quite independent of our preferences, and Balaam is resolved to honor that will and intention.

Second, God is "with them," that is, with Israel. Evidence cited for his claim is the exodus. God has made a commitment and an alliance as God chooses, often other than the choices we would make. In this case, Balak cannot countenance the thought that God is with Israel. And beyond Israel, the gospel asserts that God has made other commitments other than we would choose. So the early church discerned that God would be with Gentiles. Belatedly we have seen that God can be with the poor, the disadvantaged, the excluded, the left behind.

The two claims—God has an independent will and God makes particular commitments—lead to the third claim embraced by Balaam, that God must be obeyed even if that obedience contradicts our likely propensity. Balak could not imagine such a God who stands apart from his own hope for a curse on his enemy. Balaam is a model for faithfulness that knows otherwise and does not give in to attempts at domestication.

Friday after Proper 8

Psalm 140; Numbers 24:1–13; Romans 8:12–17; Matthew 22:15–22

God of truthful seeing, faithful hearing, and reliable understanding, renew our organs of sensibility this day, that we may see clearly, hear well, and understand faithfully. In his name. Amen.

Under normal circumstances Balaam would have delivered on Balak's request for a curse on his enemy. He is a prophet for hire. He is in the employ of Balak. He would under normal circumstances fulfill his mandate. Balak would give him a "house full of silver and gold," normal payment for a job well done.

This, however, is not a normal situation. Balaam is not a normal prophet. What makes him abnormal, refusing Balak's normal, is that he is a man whose eye is opened, who hears the word of God, who sees visions of the almighty. The prophetic tradition, echoed by Jesus, notices that many (including the disciples of Jesus) have eyes but do not see, ears but do not hear, and hearts but do not understand. They are fogged over and cut off from the truth of reality.

But Balaam is not one of them! He sees and hears and knows and understands otherwise. For that reason he speaks otherwise about a good future for God's people that God will give. No wonder he leaves Balak utterly bewildered.

The transaction between the king and the prophet matches Paul's distinction between being of the flesh and of the Spirit. Balak is of the flesh and chooses curse and death. Balaam is of the Spirit and so utters blessing and will live. Balak would reduce life to quid pro quo interactions based in fear. Balaam could say, "Abba! Father!" He knows the giver of life.

We might consider the condition of our eyes, ears, and hearts. They may be open for a second seeing, a second hearing, and a second understanding, a condition that yields blessing.

Saturday after Proper 8

Psalm 137:1–6; Numbers 24:12–25;
Romans 8:18–25; Matthew 22:23–40

God of all peoples, we are grateful for your blessing to us. Give us large-ness of spirit to notice how you bless those who are beyond our particular identity. In his name. Amen.

Balaam delivers a final oracle to Balak. Now Balaam looks to return home to "my people" (Israel). He anticipates a "star" and a "scepter," images of political power with military clout. The metaphors may reflect anticipation of the dynasty of David. In any case, in the future "Jacob" will "rule." This is indeed a powerful blessing for Israel.

But then Balaam recites a roll call of other nations who were, at one time or another, enemies of Israel. He anticipates devastation for Moab, Edom, Amalek, the Kenites, Asshur (Assyria), and Eber. This is a long, bitter curse against Israel's enemies.

There is surely some suggested irony in the fact that the prophet who refused to pronounce a curse on Israel and obe-diently recited a blessing on Israel now lapses into a recital of lethal curses against Israel's enemies. It is clear that Balaam's perceived horizon of divine blessing is limited to "my people" Israel. He has no capacity for blessing beyond this single peo-ple. He has no larger vision of divine governance that might be positive and restorative for other peoples beyond his own.

His strong faith that helped him to resist the pressure of Balak has now lapsed over into ideology of a chauvinistic kind. Our temptation, as we celebrate how richly God has blessed our nation-state, is to imagine in the most provincial way that the blessing of God extends no further than this single people. Balaam's faith is very deep! It is also lamentably quite myopic. We may wonder if the God of blessing has no blessing beyond the one for us. Surely there is more!

Proper 9

Psalm 146; Numbers 27:12–23; Acts 19:11–20; Mark 1:14–20

Living Lord, we thank you for your powerful name. Give us courage to take the name of Jesus with us all through this day. In his name. Amen.

The narrative of the book of Acts reports that Paul was able to reperform the wonders of Jesus. Like Jesus, he healed and he cast out demons. The report indicates that the work of the apostolic church was (is!) to continue the transformative ministry of Jesus.

The main accent of the narrative, however, concerns those who try to replicate Paul. This included exorcists and magicians, including the sons of a high priest. They, however, had no power over the evil spirits. The end of the report is that they had tried to monetize the power of Jesus, anticipating that such a religious capacity could be a big seller. Gospel power is always being monetized, by religious hucksters, by stewardship campaigns, and by our endless calculation for "earning" the healing grace of the gospel. But such "paid for" transformations are fakes that have no sustainable significance.

Behind the issue of fake healers in the name of Jesus, we are given access to the actual testimony of the evil spirits who themselves know the name and power of Jesus and who cannot resist the life-restoring power of God. Thus after contrasting the authentic authority of Paul and the phony authority of his imitators, the narrative testifies to the power of Jesus. It is no wonder that the final word in the text is that the word of the Lord "grew mightily and prevailed." It is the singular word of the gospel that transforms the world. The summons is to recognize that good word in its unfettered force and to obey it. Temptations are all around, especially in the church, to package that word in "effective" or "attractive" ways. Truth is that the lively word of God has its own attractiveness and its own efficaciousness without any clever packaging.

Monday after Proper 9

Psalm 1; Numbers 32:1–6, 16–27; Romans 8:26–30; Matthew 23:1–12

Lord Jesus, who took upon yourself the form of a servant, grant that we may more fully join in your vocation, that by our investment in others the public good may prosper. In your name. Amen.

Jesus' teaching is a reflection on the hazards of privilege, entitlement, and excessive authority. He presents a mocking portrait of leaders in his community. The Pharisees are the most pious and attend to the Torah. The scribes, the specialists in fine print, are the most learned. Because they are the most pious and the most learned, they enjoy something like celebrity status. They are assigned the best seats at public events (like box seats at NFL games). They are honored in the synagogue. They eat first at festivals. They are well regarded at the mall. They do not, however, practice what they preach. In their privilege, they imagine stringent religious requirements on common folk. We could, by analogy, imagine the imposition of heavy interest rates and tax rates on ordinary people, imposed by leadership that bears no such burden itself.

And then Jesus comes, in his discourse, to the adversative "but": but you, you disciples, you baptized, are not to participate in such seduction or exploitation under the guise of piety or learning. He offers three titles of social authority, only to reject them:

1. Do not be called rabbi, as if you knew everything.
2. Do not be called father, as if you were a figure of patriarchal authority.
3. Do not be called master, as though you were the all-controlling leader.

Only God is true rabbi, true father, true master. Do not assume God's place! Disciples have a different life to live, one of vulnerable service.

Tuesday after Proper 9

Psalm 5; Numbers 35:1–3, 9–15, 30–34;
Romans 8:31–39; Matthew 23:13–26

*Lord of fidelity, whose will and purpose permeate the world, give us
emancipated energy to move beyond our little protocols of maintenance
to your big resolve for neighborly well-being. In his name. Amen.*

Jesus describes a society that has its priorities all screwed up.
The screwup, moreover, is not accidental; it is the deliberate
work of leaders of society. Such mistaken priorities include
punctilious requirements about proper worship that in turn
yield rules, laws, and protocols that skew socioeconomic relations. The danger of such rules, laws, and protocols is that
they distort responsibility and detract from proper social
engagement.

And then Jesus identifies three covenantal practices that
stand at the center of the Torah of Judaism:

1. *Justice* in the Torah is the insistence that everyone is
   entitled, by their presence in the community, to a viable, secure life. Injustice permits the strong to confiscate
   what the vulnerable have.
2. *Mercy* in the Torah is the capacity for active empathy and
   solidarity with those who are in need. A lack of such solidarity permits one to treat vulnerable neighbors according to one's own desire.
3. *Faithfulness* in the Torah is a practice of reliable companionship with neighbors. Faithlessness is to live as though
   one had no such obligation.

We have immense work to do to restore and recover proper
practices in church and in society. These practices, grounded
in God's will, reflect wise pragmatism, for they are essential for
a sustainable public order.

Wednesday after Proper 9

Psalm 119:1–24; Deuteronomy 1:1–18;
Romans 9:1–18; Matthew 23:27–39

*We thank you, keeper of promises, for every new beginning. Give us
clarity for newness, that we may do the hard work of faithful interpretation and the equally hard work of neighborly justice. In his name.
Amen.*

The book of Deuteronomy is presented as guidance for Israel
as it enters the land of promise. In these opening verses of
Deuteronomy, we may notice two matters. First, the work
of Moses is to expound the Torah. His work is not simply to
reiterate the commandments of Mount Sinai but to interpret
them so that they are intensely pertinent to the new situation of
Israel in the land. We can see in the book of Deuteronomy that
such interpretation requires leaps of imagination, introduction
of new themes, and intensification of imperative appeal. Such
dynamism in interpretation precludes any fundamentalism or
any originalism, for the Torah commands are lively and insist
on commentary.

Second, Moses' first concrete act of leadership in this new
beginning is to create a judicial enterprise to share the burden of maintaining justice in the community. It is of immense
importance that justice questions have priority in the land. We
are given, moreover, a hint of the kind of justice that is appropriate to the covenant. There will be no partiality; "the small
and the great" are to be treated in the same way. The laws to
follow devote great attention to the "small," to the politically
powerless and the economically vulnerable, in order that they
can be regarded as full, first-class members of the community.
We might on this day reflect on the many ways in which our
society gives priority to the "great" against the "small" in such
matters as interest rates, tax arrangements, and voter repression. Moses' vision is that matters of justice dictate neighborly
policy and practice.

Thursday after Proper 9

Psalm 18:1–20; Deuteronomy 3:18–28;
Romans 9:19–33; Matthew 24:1–14

*God from age to age, grant that in our present upheaval we may remain
unflappably faithful, not compromising the vocation to which you have
called us. In his name. Amen.*

There is an ominous notion of the "end" in Gospel testimony.
That anticipation of the end is complex; we may identify two
facets of it. On the one hand, there is the "end of the age."
Such phrasing means the end of present power arrangements
in the world, an ending that will come via great turmoil and
upheavals. That, however, is an ending that can be faced, for it
constitutes birth pangs for newness that God will bring.

On the other hand, the end voiced in Matthew 24:14 is the
fulfillment of God's will and intent for the world, when the governance of Christ will be all in all. The gospel community is not
alarmed by the end of the age, for it has no abiding investment
in present arrangements. But the end as fulfillment is much to
be hoped for and welcomed when it comes.

The practical urging that emerges from this reflection is
that the faithful "endure," that is, remain in fidelity. If we read
this text in our own time, we can observe the huge upheaval
in the world economy, in the international political order,
and not least in the institutional church. Such upheavals are
signs of birth for the new world God is evoking. The faithful
are to live through that ending and through the birth pangs
to receive the new world that is being formed. The upheaval
brings with it fear and anxiety that evoke much violence. In
such an upheaval, it is easy enough to lose sight of the gospel
mandate to love God and to love neighbor, that is, to be talked
out of the covenantal ethic that seems so vulnerable and maybe
irrelevant in such a time. To "endure" is to persist obediently in
neighborly hospitality and generosity and not yield to the fear.
Those who endure are the ones who come to joy in the end.

Friday after Proper 9

Psalm 16; Deuteronomy 31:7–13, 24–32:4;
Romans 10:1–13; Matthew 24:15–31

*God who offers us a more excellent way of life and instructs us in how to
live it, by your Spirit we will this day learn and live in response to you.
In his name. Amen.*

The law is an endless vexation for Christians because it tempts
us to imagine that our obedience to the law of God will earn us
points of merit with God. The great awareness of Paul is that
our "righteousness" grounded in adherence to the law of God
is no occasion for merit. Thus obedience to the law of Moses in
the early church was seen to be no advantage, so that Jewish
Christians who kept the law had no advantage over Gentile
Christians who did not.

Given such a conviction, however, we read Moses' instruction to Joshua that teaches that adherence to the law is important for life in the new land of promise. But everything changes
when we take the term "law" and remember that the Hebrew
term is *torah*, which means "guidance, teaching, instruction."
The Torah of Moses, eventually the Torah of Judaism, is no
simple set of commandments. Rather it is a culture of covenantal responsiveness that evokes certain attitudes, conduct,
and policy. The commandments at Sinai are shorthand for living in a culture of covenantal responsiveness to the emancipatory, transformative goodness of God.

Quite clearly covenantal responsiveness entails and imposes
specific disciplines on our common life. With equal clarity we
may see that an absence of covenantal responsiveness, that
is, indifference to Torah, eventuates in greedy, destructive,
unsustainable behavior. Thus economics without covenantal
responsiveness becomes predatory. Agriculture without covenantal responsiveness becomes destructive of the land. Our
reflection might consider how we are and may be children of
the Torah, living in covenantal responsiveness to God. Such an
identity precludes both fearful legalism and prideful, despairing autonomy.

Saturday after Proper 9

Psalm 20; Deuteronomy 34:1–12; Romans 10:14–21; Matthew 24:32–51

Giver of good gifts and giver of our US "land of promise," help us to engage critically in our habitation in the land of promise, that we may not be indifferent to your commandments or to our neighbors. In his name. Amen.

The moment in which Moses from Mount Nebo saw the land of promise is an awesome moment in the tradition of Israel. That rich moment that is elemental to biblical faith has been carried forward in two specific ways. On the one hand, contemporary Zionism in the state of Israel understands itself to be the heir to that land of promise. That same "land of promise" has been claimed by people in what is now the United States since the first Europeans came to America and continues to energize national discourse among us.

In both cases, however, there are two important blind spots operative in the claim. First, in both Zionism and US rhetoric, there is no acknowledgment of any already-present population in the land of promise. Thus there is no positive recognition of "Canaanites" in the land of promise and no genuine recognition of Palestinians in the contemporary land of Israel. In the same way, US nationalism has made no serious acknowledgment of the native population. Second, Moses instructed Joshua concerning the importance of keeping Torah in the new land. The long history of Israel in the Old Testament is a tale of disregard of the Torah. Likewise in US political rhetoric and practice, the land of promise has been treated as though there were no restraining caveats or conditions. As heirs to the good land we might consider both of these issues: What about the native population and all the "outsiders" in the land? And what are the requirements of a neighborly kind that are non-negotiable for the prosperity of the land? After that moment of seeing the land of promise, hard, critical work remains for us.

Proper 10

Psalm 148; Joshua 1:1–18; Acts 21:3–15; Mark 1:21–27

Spirit of God who stirs up witnesses to your truth, we thank you for those witnesses. Help us to think clearly about the deep risks that belong to our faith and about the courage to take those risks seriously. In his name. Amen.

It is easy enough to forget that the appearance of Jesus (and the subsequent witness of the early church) constituted an immense scandal. In the Gospel reading, Jesus has just announced the "kingdom of God," followed by his summons to his first followers, which amounted to a wholesale challenge to the established order that featured a "peace" imposed by Rome with the cooperation of Jewish elites. His listeners rightly perceive that this new "kingdom" constitutes a compelling alternative to present power arrangements.

In Acts, Paul was preaching the resurrection of Jesus, the news that God had unleashed the power of new life in the world. That reality was a threat to all status quo authority. As Paul prepares to go to Jerusalem (even as Jesus had to go to Jerusalem to confront the authorities), Paul is endangered because "the Jews" (the elite who colluded with Rome) would hand him over to "the Gentiles" (Roman authorities). It sounds like a replay of the story of Jesus! Paul is not deterred or intimidated.

These readings might lead us to two reflections. First, we may reflect on the bold contemporary witness of the church in hostile circumstance that has placed witnesses at risk. This is not just an ancient tale but a present reality. The gospel is a threat to established order.

Second, we might reflect on why the church in our society has been so domesticated and rendered innocuous that it is nowhere perceived as a threat. We might wonder what witness to the gospel would be an evocative scandal in a complacent consumer culture like ours.

Monday after Proper 10

Psalm 25; Joshua 2:1–14; Romans 11:1–12; Matthew 25:1–13

God whose deeds we celebrate, give us readiness and openness to find allies for the mission wherever they may appear. We notice in your presence that the practice of good faith may reach across many differences. In his name. Amen.

The goal in the Old Testament reading is to arrive safely in the land of promise. The dramatic focus of this narrative is a Canaanite prostitute, Rahab, who offers cooperation with the Israelites' purpose. The company of Joshua has no hesitation in recruiting this disreputable prostitute as an ally in their cause. They willingly sign her on. We are told that her motivation for cooperation is fear. She acts out of self-interest because she knows which way the wind is blowing.

We may learn that a good missional cause may seek and find allies wherever they may be, allies who may be disreputable and acting out of self-interest. The promise of durable "good faith" is sufficient ground for cooperation. We might ask about disreputable allies who may be signed on for missional enterprise.

We observe that Rahab attests that her fear of the invading Israelites is based on her awareness of the exodus tradition and the fate of the two Transjordanian kings. She decides that the power of Israel, legitimated by YHWH, is too much to resist. This suggests that the power of the tradition of faith, the story of the exodus in this case, is greater than we might allow. The tradition has appeal to outsiders to the faith, while insiders may be so jaded about the tradition that we are immune to its compelling power. In the Epistle reading, Paul alludes to the Elijah narrative and the seven thousand faithful. Focus on Rahab suggests that some of the faithful (allies in mission) might be found outside the circle of the usual suspects in places we little imagine.

Tuesday after Proper 10

Psalm 26; Joshua 2:15–24; Romans 11:13–24; Matthew 25:14–30

God who presides over the mystery of the church, deliver us from our petty management of your truth and give us willingness to welcome even as you discriminate. Grant that we should not trivialize your kindness or your severity. In his name. Amen.

Paul is preoccupied with a church that can, according to God's will, include both Jewish Christians and Gentile Christians. To make that argument, he lays out a theological *thesis* and employs a rich, suggestive *metaphor*. The theological thesis concerns "the kindness and the severity" of God. The sum of this thesis is that God is God and is not subject to our criteria of "in and out." The image he utilizes is that of a tree with many branches. The image serves the thesis by a claim that God, as master of the tree, can graft in those whom God will and can lop off those whom God will.

The grafting in concerns, in the first instance, the Gentile outsiders who become a part of the "Israel" that Paul is redefining. The lopping off is the exclusion of those who had belonged to Israel but who are now dropped out of the new Israel. This concerns Jews who have belonged to Israel but who are not included in the new Israel of God. Paul will then allow that Jews may be later grafted on again but that also means coming to terms with the identity of Jesus.

This argument has a wider contemporary pertinence because the question of "in and out" continues, even if the issue in question changes. The point is that there are no permanent guarantees that anyone is assured membership or that anyone is in principle excluded. The matter of belonging is not based on doctrinal or moral norms but concerns the good news of the gospel. Belonging is a fluid process held closely by the will of God and not by our constructs of propriety.

Wednesday after Proper 10

Psalm 38; Joshua 3:1–13; Romans 11:25–36; Matthew 25:31–46

Lord of the least, we thank you for your way to a joyous future. Give us steadfast resolve that we may, in our present tense, choose well. In his name. Amen.

This familiar Gospel reading occurs in a series of parables about the alternative kingdom of Jesus. Because it contains a scene of fierce judgment, it intends to set our imaginations to work around the insistence that matters will be assessed differently in the new rule of Jesus, and we must give answer to that very different assessment. We live in a culture that acknowledges nothing about a "counterkingdom" mode of life and that assumes we are autonomous without having to answer. Thus the parable makes sense only if it is heard amid the countercultural expectations of Jesus.

One future is chosen—we may believe, unwittingly—by those who perform neighborly acts of care and generosity for the "least." These neighborly acts have to do with bodily care and bodily need. They are, moreover, acts toward those whose bodies are most vulnerable, most in need, and least valued by ordinary society. A good future depends on caring for the bodies of the most vulnerable and most in need. Likewise a different future is chosen—also unwittingly—by those who are socially indifferent, who do not care for or even notice the vulnerable, and who invest nothing in their bodily needs. We are daily choosing our futures in such unwitting ways.

My impression is that the church is good at caring for bodily needs on a one-to-one basis. We are not so good at care of a more systemic kind. The parable invites us to probe why, in an economy of abundance, there are hungry people. Or why health care is mostly delivered only to those with resources. Or why prisons have become warehouses for poor black men. Imagine choosing a better future every day!

Thursday after Proper 10

Psalm 37:1–18; Joshua 3:14–4:7; Romans 12:1–8; Matthew 26:1–16

Lord Jesus, who calls us to alternative disciplines for the sake of an alternative world, we give thanks for our particular gifts and pray that we may use those gifts for the sake of the entire neighborhood. In your name. Amen.

Paul has been building a case for life in the world of God's free gifts. That world is a profound contrast to the dominant world in which there are no free gifts and no free lunch but only quid pro quo transactions. Now, on the basis of his doxological argument, Paul commends an ethic that is fully congruent with the new world of free gifts.

Everything in his ethical inventory that follows turns on the central contrast of *conform* and *be transformed*. To live in *conformity* is to live in a world of quid pro quo that depends on various merits, whether moral credit or economic productivity. In that world, one plays the game of merit and reward, with a dismissive contempt for those who do not behave properly, whether in terms of goodness or productivity.

The accent, however, is on a *transformed life* that relies on God's free gifts. In that alternative world in that ancient time, this may have meant a refusal to live by the requirements of the Roman Empire. In our context of market ideology, such a refusal to a world of conformity might mean not pursuing more wealth or not being propelled by eagerness for more commodities. To be transformed, in Paul's following verses, includes (a) thinking soberly, realistically about one's self, that is, not the narcissistic self evoked by market ideology and its by-product, consumerism, (b) employing one's particular gifts for the sake of the community, and (c) being willing to receive gifts from others in glad solidarity. This life resists notions of self-sufficiency and self-securing; it begins in thinking differently, with a renewed mind.

Friday after Proper 10

Psalm 31; Joshua 4:19–5:1, 10–15;
Romans 12:9–21; Matthew 26:17–25

Creator God who has blessed the earth with fruitfulness, give us restrained wisdom that we may manage the abundance you give responsibly for the sake of the entire neighborhood. In his name. Amen.

The crossing of the Jordan River in the book of Joshua is a sharp symbolic marker in the journey of faith. It signifies exit from the wilderness and entry into the land of promise. It is a move from precarious life that depends on God's gift to land possession that permits property-owning agriculture. That move is signaled by the declaration, "The manna ceased." Now Israel depends on "the produce of the land."

Such a transition signifies three things. First, it suggests economic autonomy; one need not any longer depend on God's generosity but can grow one's own. Second, it means entry into vexed economic issues of production and distribution. Thus faith is plunged decisively into hard political questions. And third, implied in the crossing is a new responsibility for the care of the earth that is now the proximate source of life.

There are those who want the church to stay out of politics. That mantra, however, tends to be on the lips of those who have so much land, produce, and capital that it feels like an abundance of manna. Entry into public questions is necessary to assure that those without land, produce, and capital also can live an abundant life. "Manna" requires no public political action, but "produce of the land" does indeed require such action. Perhaps we may understand Paul's imperatives to "contribute to the needs of the saints" and practice hospitality as an opening to a different economy in which the goods of some constitute produce that belongs to all. The Bible is relentless in its insistence that the produce of the land must be in the service of all creatures.

Saturday after Proper 10

Psalm 30; Joshua 6:1–14; Romans 13:1–7; Matthew 26:26–35

*God of side-taking active engagement, you surprise us with your soli-
darity with the marching peasants. Give us courage and resolve to situate our lives alongside yours. In his name. Amen.*

The familiar story of the "battle of Jericho" provides a socio-
logical map of ancient Israel and a strong clue about how to
read the Bible. It is most likely that ancient Israel was constituted as a company of peasant farmers who lived in a marginal
agricultural economy. That peasant economy is contrasted to
the city-state of Jericho that was presided over by a city king
and occupied by a socioeconomic elite of scribes, priests, and
bankers who enjoyed surplus wealth based on taxation of subsistence farmers. Social reality consisted in tension between
subsistence peasants and urban elites. The city of Jericho is an
emblem of surplus wealth that is legitimated by temple priests
and protected by military preponderance.

The march of Israel is a political demonstration of protest.
We notice two crucial matters about this march. First, while
it is popularly called "the battle of Jericho," there was no battle. There was only the mobilization of bodies that the citadel
could not finally resist. And second, the ark of the covenant
is at the center of the march, signifying that the God of the
exodus had signed on with the peasants against the citadel of
the elite. The trumpet constitutes a wake-up call to all parties;
perhaps it recalls the radical note of jubilee, for the Hebrew for
"trumpet" is *ybl*, that is, "jubilee." Such a signal would anticipate the redistribution of goods and the cancellation of debts.
We may no longer be sociologically innocent about the Bible.
The recurring tension in the Bible is between *surplus wealth* and
subsistence existence. The narrative attests that the God of covenant has taken sides. We linger over the question, "Which side
are we on?"

Proper 11

Psalm 63:1–8; Joshua 6:15–27; Acts 22:30–23:11; Mark 2:1–12

God of Easter newness, give us Easter imagination to entertain new possibility for our common life beyond taken-for-granted inequality. In his name. Amen.

The march of the subsistence peasants, led by Joshua and accompanied by the Lord of the covenant, succeeded. The citadel of wealth could not withstand the vigorous witness of peasants grounded in God's resolve. So the narrative attests! This narrative constitutes a singular deliverance. We have important contemporary parallels to such successful protest, as in South Africa and Eastern Europe. We have to decide how seriously to take the testimony of such a narrative. It, of course, flies in the face of conventional social reality. That, however, is the nature of such bold action that every time intends to defy the conventional.

In any case, the scene is like a wild, eager crowd of resentful peasants storming the citadel and finding within incredible opulence that is the consequence of coercive taxation. Inevitably the question arose: what to do with the loot that the surging crowd discovered? Joshua offers two imperatives. First, the loot must be totally destroyed and cannot be confiscated. Second, Joshua provides that the hard wealth of silver, gold, bronze, and iron should be offered to YHWH, to whom credit is given for the victory. These two provisions serve to assure that the destruction of the predatory system of the city-state would be permanent and irreversible; there dare be no recurrence of such a system.

We may not simply apply this text to our contemporary scene. This old narrative may nevertheless stir our imagination to look again at our own situation of immense economic inequality more clearly. We may see the God who takes sides and view this violent exchange differently.

Monday after Proper 11

Psalm 41; Joshua 7:1–13; Romans 13:8–14; Matthew 26:36–46

God of great abundance, we confess that our lack of neighborliness distorts our neighborhood, fouls your gifts, and evokes risk for us all. In his name. Amen.

Paul echoes the summary of Jesus concerning the Torah. Paul focuses on the second of the two great commandments: "Love your neighbor." The teaching is as old as Moses in Leviticus; it is as urgent as today. It is as radical as it was in the early church. No wonder we have ongoing disputes concerning who constitutes our neighbor, who is in, and who is out.

Paul offers a contrast to neighborliness. The alternative is summed up as "desires of the flesh," a phrase that for Paul concerns preoccupation with self and narcissistic self-indulgence. Such self-indulgence always means disregard of the neighbor and the selfish use of resources and energy that might properly go to the neighbor.

Our Old Testament reading takes up this same issue. Israel, in its entry into the land of promise, needs all members of the community to give themselves over to the land entry in a covenantal mode. When they experience defeat in that effort, Joshua laments and protests to God. God's response is clarifying. The reason for the defeat is selfishness that distorted the common effort: "They have stolen, . . . and they have put them among their own belongings."

The issue of neighbor and the withholding of resources and energy from the neighbor is an urgent matter in our society, with its expanding inequality. While there are dramatic examples of greedy self-indulgence, for the most part withholding from the neighbor is less dramatic. It consists in large part in unfair tax laws, low wages, exploitative interest rates, and deregulation that permit destructive greed. The either-or is clear enough. The implementation of other ways requires the slow, hard work of public action.

Tuesday after Proper 11

Psalm 45; Joshua 8:1–22; Romans 14:1–12; Matthew 26:47–56

Lord Jesus, in whom we live and move and have our being . . . and die, we thank you for the freedom you give us beyond our commitment to party spirit, ideological passion, and pet scruples. Give us courage for such freedom that contradicts many of our favorite habits. In your name. Amen.

Paul had a singular passion for the unity of the church, even while he knew a great deal about its divisiveness. He had that singular passion not only for pastoral, practical reasons but also because he understood genuine unity to be itself an articulation of faith. Such unity witnesses to the singular governance of Jesus that overrides all grounds for division.

His argument here begins with the specific issue of unclean food. The Torah of Judaism had rigorous rules about unclean food, rules taken seriously by many Jewish Christians. Paul himself, though a Jew, believes that such a specific religious scruple does not have any authority in Christ. But he takes the scruple seriously for those who practice it. The difference between the two attitudes, he insists, is no ground for division, because both ways of being church do what they do "in honor of the Lord."

Paul moves beyond the specific issue of food to a lyrical affirmation that all, in life and in death, belong to Christ. The claim is reiterated in doxological fashion in the Heidelberg Catechism: My only comfort in life and in death is that "I belong—body and soul, in life and in death—not to myself but to my faithful savior, Jesus Christ." We cannot finally belong to a tribe, an ideology, or a party, as though we belong self-sufficiently to ourselves. We may reflect on what it means concretely to set down our lives, with our particular passion, in the gospel truth.

Wednesday after Proper 11

Psalm 119:49–72; Joshua 8:30–35;
Romans 14:13–23; Matthew 26:57–68

*Living Lord of the church, we give hearty thanks for the good news of
your great love. Grant that we may not diminish that transformative
love by our small-minded need to be right or to be in control. In your
name. Amen.*

The covenant made in the reading in Joshua expresses, in dramatic liturgical fashion, the ultimate belonging of the faithful.
Paul, as a child of that covenant, is at his best as a pastoral
theologian in our reading. He understands that the covenant
is not a contract but a relationship. He sees, moreover, that
while the covenant concerns loyalty and obedience to God, it
also bespeaks intense solidarity among the participants in the
relationship. Love of God morphs into love of neighbor. If we
transpose that ancient covenant into the church's covenant-
making drama of baptism, we may ask, with Paul, how are the
members of the baptized community to practice solidarity with
each other, given acute differences?

Paul's case study is unclean food. He is unambiguous about
the matter: "Nothing is unclean in itself." He refuses the distinctions made in the Torah between unclean and clean food.
But then he makes a stunning pastoral move that allows
for subjective judgment that does not square with his absolute, objective verdict: "It is unclean for anyone who thinks
it is unclean." We could call that "liberty of conscience"; the
recurring issue in the church is how to assent to the normative and make room for those who stand apart from that norm.
His counsel is practical, relational, and humane. The issue is
not being right. It concerns, rather, righteousness, peace, joy,
"mutual upbuilding." Those who traffic in absolutes always
want to judge and exclude. Paul is an agile practitioner of situation ethics; he sticks to the main claims of the gospel and
refuses to be distracted by lesser matters.

Thursday after Proper 11

Psalm 50; Joshua 9:3–21; Romans 15:1–13; Matthew 26:69–75

God of all nations, tongues, and peoples, who shows no partiality, give us freedom from our fear that excludes and from our pride that puts us first. Grant that we may be agents of welcome for those unlike us. In his name. Amen.

The propulsion to tribalism, the desire to be with our own kind, is immense. Tribalism, however, is for the most part unsustainable and in any case is inimical to the gospel. In the Old Testament, the ideology of tribalism is operative in Israel. While Joshua made peace with the Gibeonites, the intense ideologues wanted to kill them. A weak settlement was made to accept the Gibeonites as a second-class presence in the community assigned to menial tasks, no doubt with low wages.

The same impulse was operative in the early church. Some wanted to limit the church to their own kind, that is, to Jewish Christians. Paul is the great resister to such tribalism. Paul says: Please your neighbor, not yourself; "welcome one another." And then he offers a lyrical set of Old Testament texts to welcome Gentiles. In his final benediction, Paul acknowledges that it is "the power of the Holy Spirit" that moves beyond tribalism.

The impulse toward tribalism operates in the church. We divide into denominations according to class interest. We have been racist in our exclusion for a long time. And now most acutely, we divide into conservatives and liberals. And Paul says, "Welcome one another." The same impulse operates in civil society. Thus there is a powerful impulse to nativism that wants to exclude from entry or from voting or from civic participation those unlike us, that is, nonwhites, immigrants not of European extraction, and Muslims. The huge invitation of the gospel is a welcome that defies our fearful tribalism.

Friday after Proper 11

Psalm 40; Joshua 9:22–10:15; Romans 15:14–24 Matthew 27:1–10

How great thou art, good Creator! We continually draw you down to our petty projects. We praise you and confess your glory beyond our hopes for our tribal requirements. In his name. Amen.

There are two interesting and exceedingly difficult issues in our Old Testament reading. First, Joshua and Israel enter battle to protect the Gibeonites; God is deeply involved in the violence. The question of God and violence is problematic beyond any resolution. The matter is evident by the way in which God is drawn by ideological innocence into our most passionate causes. This may all be an interpretive mistake in the ancient text. Perhaps so. But before we use too much energy in critiquing ancient testimony, we may permit the text to critique our own recruitment of God into our preferred violence. The entire project of Western privilege and white supremacy has been grounded in a sense of divine providence. We tacitly assume God's blessing on our historical success that has been violent at its core. This long history of abuse requires repentance, perhaps on God's part as well.

The second issue is the strange report that the sun paused to give more daylight hours for battle, an early form of daylight saving time, more time for killing. We cannot, in our modern scientism, imagine that God would violate natural law. But the world teems with happenstance that leads to improbable outcomes that may be no more than coincidence. The claim made in the story is recognition that the goodness of God is not contained in our best decipherment of reality. Such claims invite wonder that gladly affirms, "How great thou art." Such doxology is deeply embarrassing to our reason. We do nonetheless sing in response to such happenstance in doxologies that defy our reasoning.

Saturday after Proper 11

Psalm 55; Joshua 23:1–16; Romans 15:25–33; Matthew 27:11–23

God beyond God, who will yield to none of our safekeeping idolatries, our best selves embrace the largeness of your fidelity and compassion. Grant that today we may live out that best self. In his name. Amen.

This text from Joshua brings to voice tensions that mark faith, and we do well to face into those tensions.

1. Joshua affirms that God, who promised the land to Abraham, has kept the promise. God is faithful; no promise has failed.
2. Israel's mandate is to "love the LORD your God," an accent that is at the center of the dominant theology of Deuteronomy (see Deut. 6:5).
3. The specifics of that loyalty are expressed in the "book of the law of Moses," most likely the book of Deuteronomy. Love of God is not an amorphous inclination but entails quite specific disciplines. In Deuteronomy, the disciplines pertain exactly to care for the poor.
4. That love of God drifts off into tribalism; Israel is enjoined not to marry outside the covenant community because such intermarriage will lead to the forfeiture of the land.

Thus the text runs from the grand themes of promise and love of God to protection of the tribal community. This interface suggests to me questions with which we always struggle concerning the love of God and God's faithfulness: How large is God's love? How expansive is our love for God? How inclusive is God's promise? It is the long history of the church to embrace the expansiveness of God and to respond in kind but then also to limit love from God and love for God to more parochial zones. As a result of such limit, the church has often been a wounding operation. It has judged and excluded "unqualified" persons. The church, moreover, has often colluded with tribalism, nationalism, and racism to support ideologies of violence. It remains for us to sort this out.

Proper 12

Psalm 24; Joshua 24:1–15; Acts 28:23–31; Mark 2:23–28

Lord of the church, we give thanks for the good ministries you have entrusted to us. Give us good hearts, ready ears, and attentive eyes, that we may remain unhindered in our vocation that serves your good news. In your name. Amen.

In our reading from Acts we have a final paragraph concerning Paul's preaching in Rome. His insistent theme is the kingdom of God. Imagine, he preached that in Rome, right under the nose of Caesar, as an alternative to the kingdom of Caesar! It was surely a challenge to speak such a gospel that contradicted the normal order of the empire in Rome.

Two things strike me about this narrative. First, "others refused to believe." They were not convinced that the kingdom of God was a viable, legitimate alternative to Rome. In expositing that resistance to the gospel, the text quotes from Isaiah 6:9–10, in which the old prophet, Isaiah, was given a ministry among those who would not see or hear or accept the truth of the gospel. As a result, they could not be healed. This note warns us concerning any expectation of church growth or any easy wholesale acceptance of the gospel. While we may despair about the diminishment of the church in our culture, we might anticipate from this text that the kingdom of consumerism is more attractive than the gospel. We can also investigate the condition of our own ears, eyes, and hearts to see how we may or may not be attentive to the good news.

Second, in the face of that obduracy we notice that the last clause of the text reports that Paul preached "without hindrance." This phrase suggests that his sustained motivation for his ministry was not in the response he received. It was, rather, his own passionate conviction about the truth of the gospel that kept him at it in the face of resistance. Reason for staying at the truth of the gospel is found in the gospel itself, hard as that is in our culture.

Monday after Proper 12

Psalm 56; Joshua 24:16–33; Romans 16:1–16; Matthew 27:24–31

For the goodly fellowship of the church, we give you thanks. We name in your presence sisters, brothers, and saints by whose faith and witness we are sustained. In his name. Amen.

I once spoke with Hans Walter Wolff, a distinguished Old Testament professor at the University of Heidelberg. He had been a young pastor in the Confessing Church in Germany in the 1930s when that small community of courageous people withstood Hitler and National Socialism. I asked him what resources they had to sustain their resistance. He answered quickly: "We prayed and sang, and we wrote many letters to each other." We know that the early church sang and prayed: "Are any among you suffering? They should pray. Are any cheerful? They should sing songs of praise" (Jas. 5:13).

And Paul himself is the champion letter writer. All three actions suggest a vigorous community solidarity in which members uphold each other in difficult circumstance. Such actions assure each person that "I am not alone."

This final chapter in Romans is remarkable because it contains no theological argument or even pastoral advice. It is simply a greeting in which Paul remembers and names church companions for whom he is grateful. Many he simply names. Some of them he recalls for quite specific reasons. Paul is a connector among actual people who are living out their faith in concrete ways. This text suggests to me that concrete effort in connecting the church in its parts is urgently important. Such letters of friendship in the church constitute care packages of gratitude and hope. It is no wonder that Paul can say of his beloved church members, "You are a letter of Christ" (2 Cor. 3:1–3).

Tuesday after Proper 12

Psalm 61; Judges 2:1–5, 11–23; Romans 16:17–27; Matthew 27:32–44

Lord Jesus, who refused every false title and label, who saved others, but who had no interest in his own rescue, let us dwell in your presence, that we may refuse any false sense of self, any "pretend church," that we may be our true selves in your company. In your name. Amen.

Paul abounds in chutzpah! In this Epistle lesson he links a specific congregational body to the largest claims of the gospel. The linkage is crucial, because the local congregation, if shut off from the grand claims, is helpless and left to its own resources. If the grand claims are not linked to concrete congregational reality, they float off in abstract space. But Paul insists on the linkage.

Try this: Think about your local congregation. Name the saints specifically . . . the big generous givers, like Jerry and Linda; the missionally passionate, like Carol and Judy. Name the squeakers who stay unhappy, like Marilyn and maybe Connie. Name the healers, like William and Roger. All of them regularly gather at the table together; but in between, it is a challenge and an effort to be together. This company sounds very much like Paul's list of members . . . the wise, people with an "appetite" for self, the fair and the flatterers, the simple-minded, the deceitful and the obedient, all of them in the body together.

This company, outrageous as it seems, is indeed the "one holy, catholic, apostolic church," a fact not always easy to remember. It is this company, says Paul, that God strengthens. It is in this company that the "mystery kept secret" is revealed, the secret that the crucified is Lord, that the humble are exalted, that the last one is the first one. It turns out that this company that we know too well is the carrier and embodiment of that mystery. Talk about chutzpah!

Wednesday after Proper 12

Psalm 72; Judges 3:12–30; Acts 1:1–14; Matthew 27:45–54

Holy Spirit, we pray for your coming among us, that we may be moved in inconvenient ways beyond our business as usual. In his name. Amen.

The beginning of our reading in the book of Acts brings us to the core text of Pentecost.

Continuing from the Gospel of Luke, we move from the Jesus narrative to the church narrative. The shift from one narrative to the other is triggered by the report of Jesus being "lifted up" from the sight of the disciples. Now in a new circumstance they are to act with reference to their risen Lord, who is no longer with them. His presence is replaced by the coming of the Spirit. It is now the Spirit who authorizes and sustains the church. We might reflect, in these days with the book of Acts (given our awareness of the church as an institution), on what it means for the church to be a community occupied by the Spirit.

In this text we may identify three elements of church reality. First, the church is to be "my witness," to tell the good truth about Jesus in Jerusalem (the center of Jewish power), in Judea, in Samaria (home of those unlike the "Jews"), and to the ends of the earth, the sphere of the Roman Empire. The good truth about Jesus is pertinent in every zone of life. Second, such witness requires "power" that will be given by the Spirit who violates all conventions but who energizes and leads the witnesses. Third, the church, it is reported, spent much time in prayer, submitting to and waiting for the gift of the Spirit. These three facets of church life are deeply countercultural among us. To be witnesses to the new life of Christ is to refuse to accept the world's business as usual. To receive power means to rely on resources other than our own, either our wealth or our wisdom. To spend time in prayer is to pause in our busyness and wait for God's prompting. On all three counts, the text invites us to an alternative way of life.

Thursday after Proper 12

Psalm 70; Judges 4:4–23; Acts 1:15–26; Matthew 27:55–66

God who presides over all our efforts at self-security, free us that we may attend to the surge of new life that you give that overrides our deep thirst for old ways of security. In his name. Amen.

On the first anniversary of the terrorist attacks against the United States on 9/11, my well-beloved colleague at Columbia Theological Seminary, Charles Cousar, led us through this text from Matthew. I am glad to share his exquisite interpretation that pivoted on the governor's instruction to those who would guard the tomb. Pilate wants to be sure that the body of the executed Jesus will not be stolen in order to perpetrate a fraud against the empire. Pilate is doing the work of established order, namely security, the first work of empire.

As the story goes, they make the tomb very secure. By the third day, however, the security system of the empire is futile, because God's power for new life enacted in Jesus cannot be contained. The security system of Rome is no match for God's will for new life given in Easter.

Our penchant for security is immense. Our huge military apparatus, the screening system at our airports, and our guarding of our borders aim at security that matches our enormous anxiety. More than that, those of us who have long enjoyed social advantage work to ensure that we will retain those advantages.

Such security systems, however, do not make us safe. They render us more at risk. It turns out that the way to security is not weapons or more alarm systems. The way to security is through the development of a neighborly fabric that includes, as much as possible, those we regard as threats. The early church, with its practices of hospitality, solidarity, and compassion, is a model for an alternative security system.

Friday after Proper 12

Psalm 69:1–12; Judges 5:1–18; Acts 2:1–21; Matthew 28:1–10

Great God to whom we dance and sing, we thank you for the new life you give. Keep us engaged in your emancipatory work. In his name. Amen.

I have long been fascinated by two verses in our reading from Judges, a poem dubbed "The Song of Deborah." It is a victory song, a victory attributed to God, but there was great human heroism as well. Israel is to "tell" (bear witness) to the victory when they ride, when they sit, and when they walk, that is, all the time. This call to celebrate all the time is parallel to the instruction of Moses in Deuteronomy 6 to instruct children in faith when they sit, when they rise, when they go out, and when they come in . . . all the time! The reality of YHWH is to saturate the imagination of the community. They are to celebrate the victory "at the watering places," that is, at the village well that was the place of gossip and news. The best news, repeated over and over, is the great victory won for God's people. The news, moreover, is to be set to the sound of music. It is to be sung . . . and no doubt danced. The jubilant victory song and dance is central to the identity of the community. The repetition bestows identity, as every TV ad person knows.

The subject of repeated jubilation at the village well is the emancipation done by YHWH. Repeat often God's victory. But wait! The victory is the work of the peasants. Well, it is both. It is the good work of God and the good work of the peasants, because the peasants are in the service of God. In Christian rendition, the victory of God (and the Peasant from Galilee!) is over evil, death, and sin. The outcome of God's struggle with evil must be sung and danced often, because it is the best news we could possibly know. In the face of oppression, coercion, addiction, we can sing with Deborah, "free at last."

Saturday after Proper 12

Psalm 75; Judges 5:19–31; Acts 2:22–36; Matthew 23:11–20

Lord Jesus, who taught us to love our enemies, grant that we should not grow cynical or numb about our seemingly endless enmeshment in war. Maintain in us a deep sense of our human solidarity with those who suffer at our hands. In your name. Amen.

An amazing reversal of mood occurs in the Song of Deborah. In our verses for today, we have a description in slow, vivid detail of the death of a Canaanite general, killed by a courageous Kenite woman. It is as though the poet relishes the death of the enemy general.

But then the scene shifts dramatically. We are transported to the gathering of Canaanite women whose husbands, sons, and brothers had gone to war against Israel. The poet dares to imagine what it was like for the waiting mothers, wives, and sisters in the enemy camp. The mother of General Sisera thinks he should have returned from battle by now. She looks nervously out of the window, through the lattice. She wonders why he is so late and why she does not hear the sound of his horse and chariot. The other wives wait with her and make excuses to reassure this anxious mother. But every mother, wife, and sister in such circumstance knows better. The general is delayed because he is not coming home. He has lost and been killed, yet another war casualty.

This remarkable scene shows an Israelite poet with empathy for those left behind in the battle. The poet knows that the anxiety and grief of the enemies is as painful as that of Israelite women would feel in such loss. Empathy for the enemy is important for us, as we seem now to be committed to endless war and impersonal killing by drones. Those many deaths that we inflict concern real people who are sons, husbands, and brothers of real women. They are not statistics, but real people killed. Sadness is the proper order of the day, even amid success.

Proper 13

Psalm 93; Judges 6:1–24; 2 Corinthians 9:6–15 Mark 3:20–30

Great, good creator God, let us in your presence count our many bless-ings. Break our patterns of parsimony and our fearfulness that makes us stingy. May we answer your abundance with our generosity. In his name. Amen.

Paul is raising funds for the desolate Christian community in Jerusalem. He bids the congregation in Corinth to come to the effective aid of fellow Christians. In this paragraph of the epis-tle Paul states his assumption at the outset. How we act now determines how our future will be, so pay attention to how we act now. He lays out his appeal in four affirmations:

1. Everything is a gift from God. Nothing is an achievement or accomplishment, but all is given in God's generosity. No self-sufficiency!
2. God has given ample gifts of sustenance. There is an abundance, so much that it can be readily shared.
3. The Jesus movement is called to glad obedience. It is a mandate of the gospel to be generous. The motivation for such obedience is gratitude and thanksgiving. Once we recognize that it is all a gift from God given in limitless abundance, we can only be dazzled and grateful.
4. When we are dazzled in gratitude, we need keep nothing back in our anxiety, but we are able ourselves to be gen-erous to those in need.

It is unmistakably clear that Paul's reasoning intends to undo all parsimony. As we ponder Paul's pastoral advice, we may be aware that we live in a dominant doxology that traffics in fearful parsimony: You can keep what you have and owe no one anything! Those who are without do not merit gifts of well-being and should be left behind! Paul's appeal contradicts such self-justifying parsimony. We baptized people are called to a different life.

Monday after Proper 13

Psalm 80; Judges 6:25–40; Acts 2:37–47; John 1:1–18

*Living Lord, we thank you for our ancient mothers and fathers in faith.
Grant that we may be good heirs of their disciplines, their passions, and
their courage. In your name. Amen.*

In the book of Acts, the Jesus movement goes on to bold witness and daring transformative action. It could do so only because it was a community that practiced disciplines that rendered it powerfully faithful to the gospel:

The people had all things in common. They shared their resources and resisted the predatory greed of their culture.

They prayed, presenting themselves as glad supplicants before the goodness of God, thus refusing the imagined self-sufficiency of their culture.

They broke bread in a sacramental way, eschewing the temptation to treat bread (and all sustenance) simply as a commodity rather than as a powerful sign of life given as gift.

They devoted themselves to apostolic teaching. They understood themselves as situated in and defined by an emerging normative narrative about Jesus. The core of that teaching is given in our Gospel reading: "The Word became flesh and lived among us . . . full of grace and truth." This is the nonnegotiable normative claim of gospel faith, the affirmation that Jesus is the visible, present, palpable embodiment of the Word that is the self-giving rationality of creation. That self-giving rationality that permeates the world is full of grace and truth.

All these disciplines, taken together, are a source of energy and authority. But the last of these—apostolic teaching—is at present so crucial because it differentiates from much religious confusion in our culture. The identification of the historical Jesus with the truth of creation is indispensable for our faith. We baptized are enjoined to these practices.

Tuesday after Proper 13

Psalm 78:1–39; Judges 7:1–18; Acts 3:1–11; John 1:19–28

Lord of the church, who summons us into transformative action, empower us to go beyond our easier custodial acts, trusting that the world is open to your healing capacity. In your name. Amen.

Imagine yourself as a member of the Jesus movement alongside the lead apostles, Peter and John. You and they are on the way to worship. The Jesus movement is still Jewish; they worship in the temple in Jerusalem. On the way to worship, as often happens, they encounter a lame man begging. His begging for alms is an act of despair. He does not imagine that his condition will change. He only wants to get through the day.

It would be easy for you and Peter and John to give him alms and move on. But the apostles refuse conventional custodial care. They do not move on. They stop and take the man seriously enough to see him and to address him. Peter refuses him money, perhaps because the apostolic church does not deal in the conventional economy. Instead of custodial maintenance for which he is asking, they offer him transformative imperatives: stand up and walk! The imperatives are issued in the name of Jesus Christ of Nazareth. Peter does not doubt the authority given him.

His utterance evokes an immediate wonder. The man is touched and raised up. Immediately he is made strong. Immediately he stands, walks, leaps, and praises God. The verbs are all strung together. It is not a surprise that everyone present is filled with awe and amazement. That is what happens in the company of the apostles. Imagine yourself in that company. Consider how you participate in custodial care, as do almost all of us. Think what would happen when, instead of giving routine alms, you stopped, noticed, and spoke transformative words or took transformative action.

Wednesday after Proper 13

Psalm 119:97–120; Judges 7:19–8:12; Acts 3:12–26; John 1:29–42

God of Abraham, Isaac, and Jacob, we thank you for ancient sources of blessing. Help us to receive them with acute awareness, like blessings that you give in their contemporary life-giving immediacy. In his name. Amen.

This reading in the book of Acts narrates a critical reflection evoked by the transformative healing we considered yesterday. This reading is framed by two references to father Abraham. At the outset, the God of the ancestors in Genesis is evoked. At the end, God's promise to Abraham in Genesis 12 is reiterated. Presumably Peter's contemporaries whom he addressed knew the Abraham tradition well and treasured it as their very own. They were, however, unable to recognize that the old tradition had immediate contemporary force. And so in their failure to understand, they had acted against the contemporary shape of the tradition.

The tradition of Abraham, so Peter asserts, had led to Jesus. The God of Abraham glorified Jesus. The power of blessing to Abraham is enacted in Jesus. But they, the Jewish resisters of Jesus, had failed to interpret and extend the tradition. Nonetheless, the lame man had been healed in the name of Jesus. The "perfect health" of the lame man attests to the power of the tradition that operates in the life of Jesus and in the life of the apostolic church.

Consider the tradition of our faith and then the part of it that you especially treasure. And then consider how the tradition that you treasure has contemporary efficaciousness. The church not only remembers its memory but also witnesses to the contemporary force of that memory. It anticipates that the claims of our memory have transformative power in generating new futures that seemed impossible.

Thursday after Proper 13

Psalm 83; Judges 8:22–35; Acts 4:1–12; John 1:43–51

God of our public faith, unleash your Easter power in our world, that our politics may be recast as an arena for transformation. In his name. Amen.

Who knew that the healing of the lame man outside the temple would evoke such a confrontation? The healing of the lame man led Peter to preach the resurrection of Jesus in a way that resulted, in turn, in many new followers of Jesus. Peter makes a definitive connection between the healing of the lame man accomplished by the apostles and the resurrection of Jesus, because it is the risen Christ who does the healing. Easter is no past event. It is as immediate and contemporary as that healing.

Peter's preaching that produced an immense public response also evoked the attention of the authorities. These authorities are intensely vigilant and keep matters under close surveillance. They perceive Peter's proclamation as an inciting of disorder that is an immediate threat to their control. They are decisively anti-Easter in their stance because they do not want any disturbance of new life. The carriers of Easter power inescapably constitute a threat to established order.

This narrative is a perfect study of religion and politics. The intrusion of religion into politics is generally resisted by the privileged status quo and welcomed by those who are kept on the outside of social power. Here we are able to see that religion (the healing juice of Easter) and politics (the tight practices of control) are not distinct or separate spheres. It is inevitable that Easter faith in its concrete performance will clash with status quo politics. This inevitable clash invites reconsideration and redefinition of both religion and politics. Gospel religion is the performance of new life. Politics is the arena in which such new life may emerge beyond our status quo protocols of resistance.

Friday after Proper 13

Psalm 88; Judges 9:1–6, 19–21; Acts 4:13–31; John 2:1–12

Holy Spirit, who from time to time shakes our worlds, give us courage for faithful prayer and for faithful living. In his name. Amen.

In this extended narrative sequence in Acts, the dramatic components are by now familiar to us:

- There is the healed man standing beside the apostles who is more than forty years old. He will not go away or disappear. He remains the bodily evidence for healing that makes the Easter case unarguable.
- There are the authorities who are disturbed by this inescapable newness that stands visible in the midst of their firm control. They cannot dispute the evidence of the restored man, but they can do damage control by freighted warnings.
- There are the irrepressible apostles who cannot and will not be silent. They will not be intimidated by the authorities. They must speak about the resurrection of Jesus, whose new life shatters all other authority.

After his abrasive encounter with the authorities, Peter prays. It is remarkable that in his prayer he does not ask God for safety or protection or deliverance from his adversaries. He asks only for boldness that he may exercise courage and freedom in his testimony. His prayer is promptly answered in a dramatic way. The place is "shaken." The Spirit comes among them and the apostles receive the boldness for which they had prayed.

As we participate in this drama of witness and encounter, we might consider our prayer in the midst of the encounter. The apostles are so urgently committed to the Easter truth that they do not think of themselves. They think only of the dangerous truth entrusted to them.

Saturday after Proper 13

Psalm 87; Judges 9:22–25, 50–57; Acts 4:32–5:11; John 2:13–25

Holy Spirit who searches hearts, you know, even as we know and acknowledge before you, that we are not fully committed to your future. Move us to new places in our faithful travel with you. In his name. Amen.

The courage and boldness of the Jesus movement continues without interruption in the book of Acts. That courage and boldness, we may believe, is grounded in acute solidarity. We are reminded both that the apostles' witness to the resurrection was undeterred and that there were no needy people among them because there was intense economic solidarity. Barnabas is cited as an example of that commitment that ensured economic solidarity in the church.

In this reading, that effective solidarity is disturbed. The narrative turns on an adversative conjunction: "but." Ananias and Sapphira, two members of the community, cheated. They held back income from property they had sold . . . and they died! The narrative is terse and explains nothing. Both of them "fell down and died." There is no suggestion of divine punishment. But it was inescapable.

We tend to suspect that this is a romanticized report of the practice of the early church, one that is remote from our own church life. We seldom if ever practice such economic solidarity in the church, given our anemic notions of stewardship and pledges, a mode of economics that is modern and compromised. But still, the narrative asks questions about being "all in" on loyalty to the movement. The believers needed to give their money in order to be fully committed to the truth of Easter, for Easter truth and life in the congregation cannot be separated from each other. No wonder "great fear" came on the church.

Proper 14

Psalm 66; Judges 11:1–11, 29–40;
2 Corinthians 11:21b–31; Mark 4:35–41

*God, who hears our oaths and knows our passions, deliver us from kill-
ing ideologies that break faith with those whom you summon in love. In
his name. Amen.*

This reading in the book of Judges is one of the most disturbing
in all of Scripture; it has received great attention from feminist
interpreters and surely merits our close attention. Jephthah
had a troubled family history. That trouble notwithstanding,
the elders of the tribes recruit him to be their military leader in
a time of great distress when the community is under assault.
He accepts the assignment; he vows, seemingly gratuitously,
that if God brings him victory over the Ammonites, he will
offer as a sacrifice to God the first person he sees upon his
return home. It would seem that his oath is an attempt to win
support from YHWH in a dire circumstance.

He does prevail in the battle, a win that is construed as faithfulness from YHWH. God's faithfulness is matched by his own
faithfulness to his vow. The first person he sees on his return is
his daughter, his only child, who remains unnamed. She is cel-
ebrating his victory. He, however, does not waver in his oath,
and so he sacrifices her "according to the vow he had made."

This strange narrative surely offends us in its brutality.
Jephthah holds to his vow at the expense of his daughter. His
religious passion trumps his most precious relationship. Of
course we would never do that. Except . . . as a society we
are regularly engaged in military commitments that put our
daughters and sons at risk. The religious component of such
passionate commitment is not as explicit as it is with Jephthah.
But the religious fervor that feeds and sustains participation
in and support of military adventurism is not remote from this
narrative. We might reflect on how our ideological passions
override the human reality of our sons, our daughters, and our
enemies.

Monday after Proper 14

Psalm 89:1–18; Judges 12:1–7; Acts 5:12–26; John 3:1–21

Holy Spirit who authorized the apostles and defied conventional author-
ity, we tremble before your work. Give us good hearts to be led in new
ways for the sake of your gospel. In his name. Amen.

Everyone now knows about the crisis of the institutional church in our society. That institutional church is failing in its capacity to connect with great numbers of people (most especially millennials) and seems stuck in conventional practices that lack energy and imagination. The early Christian movement, long before it became an institution, is portrayed with two important dimensions. First, it was a popular movement that attracted ordinary people in great numbers. These great numbers of people eagerly heard the gospel news of God's power and noticed signs and wonders done by the apostles. Second, the movement exhibited evidence of a plus factor that defied normal explanation. The narrative in Acts expresses that factor as the work of the Spirit and the agency of an angel. Such talk defies reason and surely escaped the categories of the governing officials and religious authorities. Thus it was "an angel of the Lord" who opened prison doors and sent the apostles to preach. The officials resisted such a happening, but the church of popular support and holy imagination eluded the control of the authorities, who had to be rescued from the fervor of the people.

We may spend some time today pondering (a) how this movement of popular support and visiting angels was reduced to conventional institutional, bureaucratic modes and (b) how this conventional institutional, bureaucratic mode of life could be transformed to popular movement with visiting angels. The Spirit always surprises us by making available what had seemed impossible. A Spirit-led movement regularly perplexes the managers of the old order.

Tuesday after Proper 14

Psalm 97; Judges 13:1–15; Acts 5:27–42; John 3:22–36

God of Easter power, who refused the silence of execution, give us courage and freedom to be on the side of Easter talk and Easter walk, that we may be aligned with your new futures. In his name. Amen.

The book of Acts tells the story of the earliest church as an ongoing confrontation between the apostles and the conventional authority of both Rome and the Jewish leadership. The recurring confrontation pivots around the claim of the apostles that Jesus has been raised from the dead and is alive in the world. That proclamation is unsettling to established authority because it asserts that the future is open to new possibility beyond present arrangements. That the future is open means that there are possibilities for those left behind in present arrangements, just as there are possible negations to come for those who now are dominant. When we arrive at surplus well-being, we want to freeze the future the way it is now.

For that reason, the authorities try repeatedly to stop their preaching and to silence the apostles. But the apostles, led by Peter, are undeterred. They answer the authorities in terse, decisive fashion: "We must obey God rather than any human authority." Obedience to God means proclaiming an open future governed by the risen Christ. The wise rabbi Gamaliel advises caution, because silencing the apostles might be opposition to God! The authorities accept his counsel, but they nonetheless flog the apostles and then release them. But the apostles refuse to silence their bold Easter talk.

We might consider the silencing pressures in our society: intimidation, social pressure, threat of legal action, social ostracism, coercion. We might consider the bold voices that refuse to be silenced. There are, in our own time, voices of emancipation and transformation. We ourselves might be on the side of silencing. Or not!

Wednesday after Proper 14

Psalm 101; Judges 13:15–24; Acts 6:1–15; John 4:1–26

*Risen Lord Jesus, we thank you for the work of talk and of walk that
you have given us. Leave us unafraid before old resistant order, that your
new life may stare eagerly into our faces. In your name. Amen.*

The life of the church is constituted by "talk" and by "walk."
Very often the church prefers talk to walk. The apostles were
preoccupied with Easter talk. Their preaching of Easter kept
opening new futures and jeopardizing old status quos. But the
church cannot rely on talk without the walk of concrete action
that is congruent with Easter talk. For that reason the apostles
needed assistance in "waiting on tables," that is, in doing the
daily work of bodily care. The test case for them was widows,
those without male guarantors in a patriarchal society. Provision for their care was required.

The decision to appoint individuals to perform such quo-
tidian responsibilities led to seven duly ordained deacons. The
narrative pivots on the first named among the seven, Stephen.
Stephen, it is reported, did "great wonders and signs." These
"wonders and signs" are not described, but they may be astonishing acts of hospitality that paid attention to the needy.

Whatever they were, Stephen is such a threat to the establishment that he is framed on a false charge. Could he be a
threat to the leadership because his work constitutes valori-
zation of the devalued in society? Stephen asserts that Jesus
of Nazareth will destroy the temple, the citadel of certitude in
Jerusalem. The companions of Jesus are ill at ease with such
privileged certitude and therefore are perceived as a threat to
all established order. One might have anticipated that a person
so at odds with the authorities would be stressed out or fearful.
But not! Even before the authorities he is at peace, with an
angelic face. He rests his life in Easter truth.

Thursday after Proper 14

Psalm 105:1–22; Judges 14:1–19; Acts 6:15–7:16; John 4:27–42

We love to tell the story, dear God, of your transformative deeds, of your sustaining wisdom, and of your abiding faithfulness. Give us courage to trust this story more fully. In his name. Amen.

Stephen is charged, in the book of Acts, with declaring that the risen Christ will destroy the temple and change the Torah of Moses. Likely these charges are much overblown, for there is no evidence that Stephen had said this. But he does not bother to refute the charges. The authorities ask him concerning the charges, "Is this true?" That little question is all that is required for Stephen to launch into extended testimony that constitutes a review and recital of the entire history of God with God's people in the Old Testament. That is, in order for Stephen to answer about the subversive authority of the risen Christ, he must answer with the sum of the tradition. It turns out that the Easter resurrection is not an isolated event. It is rather the culmination and extreme expression of God's continuing work of transformative power.

In this segment of his testimony, Stephen summarizes the memory of the ancestors in Genesis, a memory that is a series of resurrection acts in which the power of God accomplishes a new future for Israel that overrides the reality of established order. Thus the departure of Abraham and the rise of Joseph constitute God's acts of transformative power.

The invitation of the witness of Stephen, as given in this text, is to resituate ourselves in this narrative account of the past, an account that is permeated with inexplicable transformations. Readiness to resituate ourselves in this narrative is an intentional act of relocation accomplished through prayer, liturgy, and critical reflection. It will involve a departure from other narrative accounts of reality, perhaps a narrative of despair or woundedness or self-sufficiency. Stephen would declare that these other stories are false. Easter is the plot of our true narrative.

Friday after Proper 14

Psalm 102; Judges 14:20–15:20; Acts 7:17–29; John 4:43–54

God of promise who summons human agents to enact your deliverance, we thank you for your attentiveness to our common life. We thank you as well for human agents who gladly do your will in the world. In his name. Amen.

Stephen's testimony before the authorities continues in our reading from Acts. The authorities had asked him if it is true that the risen Jesus will upset the established certitudes. He answers by a review of our narrative memory of faith. In this segment, Stephen tells of the birth and emergence of Moses. It is an easy move, in the tradition, from Genesis to Exodus.

Moses was born beautiful. He grew up in wisdom. But then he vested his life with his own folk, the Hebrew slaves. He identified with the "scum of the earth" who were powerless. He discovered that such powerless people always live in a social context of exploitative violence. Slaves are always on the receiving end of violence that propels a successful economy that prospers the ownership class, in this case, Pharaoh.

Moses understands, as his people did not, that he was sent to deliver them. Stephen does not say exactly, but surely he implies that God raised up Moses for this emancipatory act. Moses is a pre-Easter Easter guy! As a result Moses commits an aggressive act against brutal slave-controlling power. Consequently he becomes a fugitive and flees for his life.

And now, via Stephen, we are invited to locate ourselves in this story. It is an abrasive account in which the Abrahamic God of promise is deeply engaged. If we resituate in this narrative, many of us will not be directly involved in such confrontational actions as those of Moses. But we will inescapably notice things differently. We will notice that a vibrant economy often depends on exploitation of cheap labor. And we will notice that God intends otherwise.

Saturday after Proper 14

Psalm 107:33–43; Judges 16:1–14; Acts 7:30–43; John 5 1–18

God of covenantal fidelity, help us to see clearly the either-or before which we stand. Give us courage to choose faithfully for your Easter alternative. In his name. Amen.

Stephen's response to the authorities concerning Jesus' Easter power continues. In this reading Stephen compacts a good bit of the tradition of Israel. In doing so, Stephen contrasts two Gods who always compete for the loyalty of God's people. On the one hand, Stephen bears witness to the God of the burning bush, the God who made promises in Genesis. This God dispatched Moses to Pharaoh, then chair of a predatory economy. In quick order Stephen alludes to the exodus emancipation, the wilderness sojourn, and the "living oracles" at Mount Sinai that took the form of Torah commandments. The work of Moses is to create, out of the company of slaves, a new community in covenant with the emancipatory God.

Stephen lines out the refusal of Israel to trust Moses and the God of the covenant. The result is that the out-of-control priest, Aaron, offers to Israel an alternative god, the golden calf, a figure of virility and money, a commodity that can do nothing. Worship of this god, says Stephen, leads to false worship and eventually huge trouble.

The schematic fashion of Stephen's assertion bears witness to the either-or of gospel faith. He does not say so but surely implies that the authorities whom he addresses are in fact agents of idols not unlike the ancient calf, idols who cannot save. We in our own faith are always situated, as was ancient Israel and as were the authorities, before the either-or of gods, either the God of emancipatory sustenance or the idols of commodity. In the shorthand of Jesus, it is God or mammon, and we cannot have it both ways. Easter is the reperformance of the exodus God.

Proper 15

Psalm 118; Judges 16:15–31; 2 Corinthians 13:1–11; Mark 5:25–34

Rescuing Lord of the wounded, we thank you for your continuing bodily touch in the world. Let us this day be touched by your healing ways, that we may in turn touch in healing ways. In your name. Amen.

The Easter Christ occupies the Gospel reading. He is with common folk among whom is a needy woman without resources. She has a hemorrhage about which medical experts could do nothing. She, however, is not fully in despair. She still hopes that healing and restoration are possible, so she takes an improbable initiative with Jesus, her last best hope. When we scan the narrative, we notice that the accent is on bodily matters. She has a "hemorrhage." She "felt in her body." And three times, there is "touch": If I *touch* his garments. Who *touched* my garments? Who *touched* me?

It is all about the body; it is about her needy body; it is about his power-laden body. It is about bodily need meeting bodily well-being. And because it is about the body, we are propelled into political and economic questions (the body politic!), because these spheres of life are all about who has access to Easter restoration. How odd that we have learned to construe the gospel as a spiritual matter, when the story is about power going forth from his body.

The narrative moves toward healing and restoration, the transformative power for life moving from his body to her body. As we read this text, we remember that the church is "the body of Christ," the continuing bodily presence of the power of the Easter Christ in the world. The faithful work of the church is to be engaged with the needful bodies in the world, bodies made needful by political and economic decisions. Today notice needful bodies all around. Imagine transformative Easter power going from our bodies to those bodies.

Monday after Proper 15

Psalm 106:1–18; Judges 17:1–13; Acts 7:44–8:1a; John 5:19–29

Living Easter Jesus, we thank you for your grace-filled death and your continuing life among us. We are grateful to be in the company of those who have followed you in faith and obedience. In your name. Amen.

Stephen's testimony before the authorities continues and comes to its end. His speech moves through the tabernacle (tent of witness) and David. He comes to Solomon, builder of the temple. He does not, however, praise Solomon. He rather understands Solomon's temple construction as a case of stiff-necked disobedience, thereby making a connection to the temple of his own time that the Easter Christ will destroy. Thus the tradition ends, according to Stephen, in an act of disobedience by betting on the temple, a citadel of assured divine presence. That act of perfidy is trumped only by the execution of Jesus, the "Righteous One." The recital of the tradition ends in harsh contemporaneity.

It is no wonder that the authorities whom he has addressed are "enraged" at his charge. They thought that in the execution of Jesus they had removed a dangerous blasphemer. In truth they had killed the one who fulfills the old tradition. This charge is so unwelcome to the authorities that they stone Stephen and thereby silence him.

The accent is on the clash between Easter truth and the ruling authorities who resist that Easter truth. Stephen's response to their violence is a reperformance of Jesus on the cross. Stephen echoes the crucified Jesus. He relinquishes his life to God, as did Jesus: "Into your hands I commend my spirit." He forgives, as did Jesus: "Father, forgive them; for they do not know what they are doing." This dramatic moment exhibits the church's first martyr imitating the life of Jesus before the authorities. The authorities could not bear it: they "covered their ears."

Tuesday after Proper 15

Psalm 120; Judges 18:1–15; Acts 8:1–13; John 5:30–47

Lord of the church, we give thanks for brave witnesses whose heirs we are. Let your Easter power seep into our lives this day. In your name. Amen.

It is as an old and recurring story in three steps:

1. The apostles preach the word of Easter. They attest that Jesus is alive, the real Lord of the world and the guarantor of an alternative future.
2. That preaching evokes hostility from the authorities that leads, in turn, to persecution and prison so that the others are "scattered" into hiding. The authorities recognize that Easter faith is dangerous to the status quo and want to stop such proclamation.
3. The multitudes hear and see signs. Those without access to an official future are glad to welcome the alternative future of Easter. Easter truth makes compelling sense to the outsiders. But the signs of Easter are even more compelling. They see peoples' lives transformed from disability and emancipated from all kinds of demonic occupation. It is no wonder that there was "great joy in that city," a kind of folk festival, an evangelical Woodstock that made the managers of status quo even more nervous. But the apostles, even when fearful, could not stop. In this instance, it is Philip the apostle who gets his fifteen minutes of fame. It is reported that he preached the good news, he baptized, and he did wonders. His was a generative faith.

We see here, as in so many places, something of a class conflict between the ownership class and the excluded. The wonder is that over time, those (maybe like Simon) who have some authority are drawn as well toward Easter truth. To be baptized into the kingdom of God entailed departure from the old kingdoms. It was for many a very glad departure.

Wednesday after Proper 15

Psalm 119:145–176; Judges 18:16–31; Acts 8:14–25; John 6:1–15

Lord Jesus, giver of ample bread, grant that we may embrace your abundance, forgo our fear of scarcity, and live in shared abundance. In your name. Amen.

Bread goes two ways in the Gospel reading. The bread is a sign. It signifies divine presence. It makes visible the work and blessing of the creator who blessed creation so that it would produce abundance. And now, Jesus has performed that abundance; he does the work of the creator! He is recognized as a prophet; they want him to be their king, because it is the work of a king to guarantee abundant well-being.

The church has taken bread as the defining element in its primary sacrament, the Eucharist. The name of the sacrament, "Eucharist," is the Greek word for "thanks." Tagging the broken bread that is his body under the rubric of "thanks" indicates that it is all gift. It is not and cannot be a possession or an achievement. Consequently bread evokes gratitude. We do not seize the bread; it is given and we are on the glad receiving end of it.

But bread in this narrative episode is also nourishment for a hungry crowd that needs food. It is bread "for the world." It is a desirable, necessary commodity that costs money, which means it is available only to those who have resources. We who are privileged eat bread (and all kinds of food) in a world where many are hungry and do not have enough food. The bread we have and the bread we receive from Jesus remind us of hunger in a world that does not share the bread that we have in surplus. On both counts—bread as sacrament and bread as bodily nourishment—Jesus is the giver of abundance, twelve baskets left over, enough for all. The narrative is an invitation to depart our commonly shared fear of scarcity. In the regime of Jesus, there is enough for all. And it can be shared.

Thursday after Proper 15

Psalm 131; Job 1:1–22; Acts 8:26–40; John 6:16–27

Giver of good gifts, deliver us from the illusion that we deserve an abundant life and from the anxiety that we must earn it. Give us a capacity to trust in your generous goodness. In his name. Amen.

There is among us an endless temptation to reduce faith to a bargaining calculation. It is easy enough to take religion as a quid pro quo in which we expect to benefit or gain from our faithfulness or our piety or our morality. The defining question posed about Job is exactly this: "Does Job fear God for nothing," that is, without hope for gain? Or is Job a "blameless and upright man" because it works for him and causes him to be blessed by God? The story of Job is, among other things, a probe of that issue. In the Gospel reading, Jesus indicts those who seek him out for the same reason, because he gives them bread. Very much religion has such a dimension of merit to it.

But, of course, the gospel tradition intends that we should not participate in such calculation, because God is a giver of good gifts to those who have not earned them. The outcome of the book of Job is left ambiguous and unresolved. In the end Job receives back all the property he had lost. But we do not know if that is reward or if it is gift. We are not told. The matter is unambiguous in the Gospel narrative. An alternative to "calculated bread" is Jesus' offer of "food that endures." His rhetoric suggests that "food" is a figure or image that stands in for eternal life, that is, an abiding relationship that is an alternative source of well-being. It is that relationship that finally will sustain as will nothing else. These two texts pose an either-or about *calculation* or *trust*. We are invited to life in trust that begins in *God's generosity* and that ends in *our gratitude* that is expressed as *glad obedience*. Such trust knows that it is all gift!

Friday after Proper 15

Psalm 140; Job 2:1–13; Acts 9:1–9; John 6:27–40

*God of sustaining regularity and God of awesome new disclosure, give
us openness to receive your interruptions and readiness to live in terms
of your unsettling newness. In his name. Amen.*

A life of faith is an interrupted life, even when we think we
have it all worked out.

The reading in Job concerns a man "blameless and upright"
who is pious and prosperous. The story imagines an aggressive
interruption by Satan, who tests and probes Job's intention
and motive.

The reading from Acts features Saul, who is portrayed as
a vigorous persecutor of those who "belonged to the Way"
of Jesus. He is well credentialed and is determined to stop
the Jesus movement. His life is interrupted by a "light from
heaven" and a voice. He is bewildered but witnesses to the
interruption that includes the astonishing assertion, "I am
Jesus." He is met by the one he will serve. He is left without
sight; he must for now walk by faith.

In the Gospel narrative, we may presume that even poor
peasants in Galilee had regular sources of bread. But this new
bread from Jesus is very different. It is bread given by God. In
the end, it is Jesus himself who is the bread of life, unlike any
bread they had before. His faithful generosity supplies what is
needed for well-being.

We tend to organize our lives so that they are not interrupted. As much as possible, we prefer an environment without
surprises. The dominant modes of life in our society, moreover,
teach us that if we are smart and rich enough we can reduce
our lives to manageable regularity. These texts witness mightily against such an illusion. These narratives of interruption
require extreme imagery that defies the ordinary—Satan, a
disembodied voice, alternative bread in the form of Jesus. The
holiness of God is beyond our safe management!

Saturday after Proper 15

Psalm 137:1–6; Job 3:1–26; Acts 9:10–19a; John 6:41–51

You, Lord Jesus, give bread and are bread in order that we may live. You, Lord Jesus, designate "chosen instruments." Give us grace and courage to be recruited as you intend. In your name. Amen.

The reality of gospel faith defies our ordinary reasoning. Such defiance of our ordinary is very difficult to accept, given the force of modern rationality. The inexplicable, extraordinary claims of faith make us so nervous that we want, as we are able, to minimize the danger of reality that does not fit our categories. As a result, various forms of fundamentalism and literalism serve to reduce the intense mystery to a rational articulation. Or conversely, various forms of liberal and progressive thought evaporate into an amorphous spirituality that is not cognitively embarrassing.

These texts, however, attest otherwise. In the reading from Acts, Ananias is dispatched to mobilize Saul, who is designated as a "chosen instrument." It is Jesus who speaks. It is the missional work of Jesus to which Saul is to be summoned, and that missional work, we know, is the giving of self in ways that evoke suffering. In the Gospel reading, it is Jesus who uses the first-person pronoun of self-announcement: "I am the living bread." It is all beyond our reasoning.

In the epistle and in the Gospel reading, it is the Lord Jesus upon whom the new life turns. It is the Lord Jesus who is to be "believed," that is, trusted. It is the Lord Jesus who is to be obeyed. The living reality of the Lord Jesus makes our future into a sustaining and demanding, lively relationship. This relationship cannot be hardened into a formula; nor can it be dissolved into an amorphous sensibility. This is a real Lord who summons, about whom we must, in each new interruption, decide again.

Proper 16

Psalm 146; Job 4:1–6, 12–21; Revelation 4:1–11; Mark 6:1–6a

Lord Jesus, before whom all our knees bend, before whom all our tongues confess, we praise you and give thanks for your gracious rule in our world. In your name. Amen.

A great deal of attention is given to the end time. This is evident in many end-time films. We get such articulations when society is anxious about the present and profoundly anxious about the future that seems out of control. How does this all end? Might it all be a tale told by an idiot, signifying nothing? Such a tale evokes Woody Allen's poignant question, "What's the point?" Nihilism is alive and well among us! Or credible science judges that we will, in the end, either freeze over or burn up. Our reading in Revelation refuses such scenarios. Instead it proposes that it will end in doxology. Such a vision is perhaps prescientific. More likely, it is the other way around: Enlightenment rationality seeks to domesticate God. If God be cast simply as a private player in the present-world arrangement, and no more, then despair is in order.

That, however, is to misunderstand and underestimate the gospel world of God, the creator before and the Lord after, for which we have only the language of doxology and poetry. The rule of God is not defined by our small take on reality, because God is other. The vision of a God in doxological dialect concerns all the tribes of God's people singing gladly together in a reconciled community. They sing to the holiness of the Lord God . . . three times holy. In the doxology that runs on into chapter 5, these ultimate singers praise the Lamb along with the Holy God. The Lamb is the crucified one who is raised in power and now is worthy. The title "our Lord and God" concerns the Lamb raised and worthy. It will all end with his life of generosity, compassion, and forgiveness ultimately enthroned. We are invited to sing that doxology now along with all the elders.

Monday after Proper 16

Psalm 1; Job 4:1; 5:1–11, 17–21, 26–27; Acts 9:19b–31; John 6:52–59

*Lord Jesus raised in glory to power, for your very different rule in
our world we are grateful. We are glad for your transformative power
whereby we may become our true selves. In your name. Amen.*

The good news of the gospel concerns the inexplicable power
of transformation. The tradition is filled with many examples
of transformed life. None is more dramatic than that of Saul/
Paul. He was a fervent persecutor of the Jesus movement, and
now he is a most convinced advocate for the gospel. While we
have narratives about his transforming vision, what happened
or how is kept hidden from us. All we know is the outcome of
that experience and the difficult time his contemporaries had
in trusting that his experience was genuine.

Paul, now renewed, is caught in a very tight place. On the
one hand, followers of Jesus are highly suspicious and fearful of him because they know of his previous reputation. On
the other hand, "Jews plotted to kill him" and "Hellenists . . .
were attempting to kill him." He does not flinch. We learn two
things about him. First, he is forthright in his new conviction.
He attests in the synagogue: Jesus "is the Son of God." He
says that as a trusting Jew. He understands the good news in
Jewish tradition and in Jewish context. "Son of God," in that
usage, means "king," now Lord and sovereign. But second,
for all his boldness, Paul fully relies on support from his new
friends, notably Barnabas, who worked with him and for him.
Quite in contrast to Job, Paul had real friends who sustained
him. For most of us, new life is not as dramatic as it was for
Paul. For many of us, new life is not an abrupt change but slow
maturation. It is clear, whether it happens abruptly or in slow
process, that the gospel truth of our life is that we are, by the
mercy of God, being transformed, becoming who we were not.
It is like being lost and now found.

Tuesday after Proper 16

Psalm 5; Job 6:1–4, 8–15, 21; Acts 9:32–43; John 6:50–71

You, dear Jesus, have the words of eternal life. They are words of mercy, compassion, truthfulness, and grace. We do not doubt your good word. In your name. Amen.

Peter looms very large in the memory and imagination of the early church. He is cast in historical tradition as the first pope. However that may be, he is surely cast as a bold apostle and as a representative of profound faith. Thus in our Gospel reading, he is bold in his confession of faith: "You are the Holy One of God." He has no hesitation in affirming Jesus.

In a different New Testament tradition, he is presented as one who was able and ready to act out his bold confession in concrete ways. In the Acts narrative, he is credited with two wonders. He raised Aeneas, a paralyzed man, to new life. It happened "immediately." He revived the deceased Tabitha and "showed her to be alive." The narrative explains nothing; it does not even display any curiosity. It seems to assume that such a capacity for resurrection rightly belongs to the apostles or at least to this lead apostle.

To be sure, the Gospel narrative and the account in Acts reflect two different interpretive traditions with different intentions. If for this day we hold these two texts in juxtaposition, they suggest this affirmation: bold unqualified confession of faith (trust) in Jesus is linked to a practical capacity to override the power of death and generate new life. Apostolic succession in the church is not magic and is not, in my judgment, monopolized by bishops. Rather "apostolic succession" might refer to all those believers over the generations who have made a bold confession and who have been trusted with transformative power. We ourselves might indeed be a part of that succession of those who have no intention of forsaking Jesus.

Wednesday after Proper 16

Psalm 119:1–24; Job 6:1; 7:1–21; Acts 10:1–16; John 7:1–13

God of freedom, we bring before you our many enslavements. We pray for your freedom, that we may live faithfully in response to the abundance of your grace-filled fidelity. In his name. Amen.

The complaint of Job is that he is worn out with too much divine surveillance by the God of quid pro quo requirements. He complains that he is unable to escape the supervisor who is never satisfied. Job wants only to be left alone long enough to swallow! Very many people have been nurtured in that tradition of divine supervision as a mode of social control.

In this reading from Acts, Cornelius, a Gentile, is dispatched to Peter. His contact with Peter comes just after Peter's encounter in a vision. Peter had responded to the heavenly voice with an assurance that he himself was punctilious in observance of religious scruple. He never ate unclean food! Peter does not chafe at such religious requirements, but he is quite aware of them.

The voice from heaven in response to his religious scruple about unclean food declares that God has cleansed the food and made it acceptable, even for a Jew who observes Torah. In that heavenly utterance, the purity laws are swept away, and Peter moves into a new freedom, the very freedom for which Job yearns.

Today we may ponder the "religious scruples" to which we practice loyalty. They may be details of piety and morality. They may be, alternatively, requirements of the market, like much hard work or much lavish shopping. Or they may be the compulsions for health: much exercise and dieting, or the rules for beauty and youthfulness requiring elaborate self-care. Any of these disciplines, when overly compelling, may be a parallel to the scruples from which Peter was emancipated. The news, which Job learned only belatedly, is that God is not overly invested in such compulsions.

Thursday after Proper 16

Psalm 18:1–20; Job 8:1–10, 20–22; Acts 10:17–33; John 7:14–36

*Lively God who moves into our settled lives and makes all things new,
give us vigilance this day to spot your interruptive work in our lives. In
his name. Amen.*

Clearly the writer of our Acts reading (Luke!) understood
that Peter's vision of the unclean being made clean was of piv-
otal importance for the force of the gospel in the church. It is
important enough that our writer has Peter reiterate his learning. That learning represented a critical turn in the history of
the Jesus movement, making way for Gentiles to belong to the
movement.

Peter's summary report to Cornelius is terse; it turns on the
disruptive conjunction "but" that connects the two parts of his
testimony. The first part is what Peter had always known: "It
is unlawful [against the Torah] for a Jew to associate with or
to visit a Gentile [anyone of another nation]." Peter had always
known that, learning it from the ancient purity laws, surely
learning it as a child from his mother.

Then comes "but." And Peter reports on what he had just
learned that required a great unlearning of what he had always
known: "I should not call anyone profane or unclean."

His learning is adjusted from "anything," a snake or a bird,
to "anyone," as he transposes his awareness from the unclean
in the Torah to the people who are in front of him, namely,
Gentiles.

This is a good day to watch for the interruptive "but" in our
lives that disrupts what we had always known with what we
have just learned from the gospel. The gospel does not readily
fit with what we always thought we knew. It requires a huge
unlearning. God has now put us in a season of great unlearning. It is hard to overstate the challenge this was to Peter . . .
and is to us!

Friday after Proper 16

Psalm 16; Job 9:1–15, 32–35; Acts 10:34–48; John 7:37–52

Holy Spirit, who crashes the gates of our secure tribalism, give us eyes to see your work today, whereby our world is broken open for the sake of other neighbors alongside us. In his name. Amen.

Peter's sermon summarizes the church's faith concerning Jesus: Jesus was connected with the work of the Spirit. He went about doing good, healing and emancipating. He was a threat to established power that finally executed him. God raised him up. He is ordained by God to judge the living and the dead, all peoples in all times.

Peter's sermon is the primal script of all Christian proclamation. The narrative in Acts goes on to report that an outcome of Peter's preaching was that the Holy Spirit "fell" on them when they heard Peter. While it is not said that his preaching caused the coming of the Spirit, it is clear that that is how it was experienced by his hearers. The preaching offered them a narrative concerning an alternative world in which the power of God for life is stronger than the power for death enacted by the frightened establishment. Being drawn to an alternative world, they are available for the "strange-making" arrival of the Spirit.

It is reported that "circumcised believers," that is, Jewish Christians, were astonished that the Holy Spirit was poured out on Gentiles. Who knew? Who knew that the Spirit could fall on those unlike us, after we thought we had a monopoly on the Spirit? Who among liberals knew that about conservatives? Who among whites knew that about blacks? The Spirit is not contained in our preferred tribalism that seems normal and normative to us. The Spirit violates borders, transgresses our limits, and makes outsiders to be insiders. The only viable response is to admit the Spirit-occupied other to the community.

Saturday after Proper 16

Psalm 20; Job 9:1; 10:1–9, 16–22; Acts 11:1–18; John 8:12–20

Giver of good gifts, grant that we may be grateful to you and that we may be glad for others who share your good gifts. In his name. Amen.

Now a third time Pater's jarring transformative encounter with the risen Christ through a trance is relayed to us. First, the trance happened to Peter. Second, the trance was reported to Cornelius and the visiting Gentiles. Now the trance is reported to the "circumcision party," Jewish Christians. One step at a time, the narrative works at the education and transformation of every part of the Jesus movement. The new phrase is that "the same gift" is given to "them" as to "us," to Gentiles as to Jews. It is all gift! It is not the same virtue or the same merit or the same accomplishment. It is the gift, new life that need only be received.

We in the church have a long past of grudgingly recognizing the "same gift" in "them" as in "us." We have learned that women had the same gift as men. More recently, we have been learning, often reluctantly, that gays have the same gift as straights. And after all of that, we still have intransigent racist conviction in our society, still the hard work of recognizing the same gift among racial and ethnic minorities as among whites of European extraction. The "same gift" is the capacity to live responsively according to the generous will and reconciling hope of the risen Christ. When we seek to live apart from gift on our own through possession, achievement, or entitlement, we readily drift toward practices of fear, greed, and violence. We see those practices everywhere, in society, in the nation-state, and in the church. Resurrection to new life is to forgo those old patterns of fear, old practices of greed, and all assumptions about being in control. It dawned on Peter and on other Jewish Christians that they had no advantage. It keeps dawning on us, and we are summoned to respond. It is all gift for all of us.

Proper 17

Psalm 148; Job 11:1–9, 13–20; Revelation 5:1–14; Matthew 5:1–12

Lamb/Lion Jesus, we are glad for your transformative power and for our capacity to walk into your empowering vulnerability. Deliver us from lionlike life that knows nothing of lamblike living. In your name. Amen.

The writer of Revelation works with the imagery of a scroll that contains the disclosure of the mystery of all reality, the revelation of how the world actually works. That scroll, however, is closed and not accessible. Its content is hidden from us. The question then is: Who will open the scroll? Who can disclose the deep mystery of all reality?

The claim of the text, indeed the claim of the gospel, is that Jesus knows how to open the scroll. The text luxuriates in its doxological presentation of Jesus who is "the Lion of the tribe of Judah" and "the Lamb that was slaughtered." He is both *lion and lamb*, the embodiment of both fierce authority and extreme vulnerability. That double imagery is like the riddle of wave and particle in physics. Jesus as lion of Judah trades on an old phrasing of the throne of David. The imagery of lamb posits Jesus as the lamb slaughtered at Passover, the crucified. The church confesses that the one crucified in vulnerability is risen to a new mode of transformative power.

The church confesses that it is the presence of this *lamb/lion* himself who is the embodiment of the scroll of life. Not only does he open the scroll, but he himself is the content of the scroll. He himself is the mystery of all life. He has shown us by his self-giving love (and by his teaching, as in the Beatitudes) that the blessed are those who practice transformative vulnerability. He himself embodies the poor (in spirit), the meek, the peacemaker, and the merciful. He and those who accompany him are the wave of God's future. Living lionlike without "lambness" is well short of the mystery.

Monday after Proper 17

Psalm 25; Job 12:1–6, 13–25; Acts 11:19–30 John 8:21–32

Living Lord of the church, we give you thanks for the church community most immediately local to us, for its fellowship and its missional initiatives. We give you thanks as well for other congregations toward which we have responsibility. Give us large, great passion for all our sisters and brothers in faith. In your name. Amen.

The interaction between the congregations in Jerusalem and the congregation in Antioch invites reflection on evangelical geography. The congregation in Jerusalem was the first and oldest Christian congregation. It was a Jewish congregation that was in sore straits and needed aid. The congregation in Antioch was more recent and had in it both Jewish and Gentile members, and its numbers were growing. These two congregations, different as they were, were deeply engaged with each other. Barnabas, a trustworthy leader in Jerusalem, is dispatched to the community in Antioch. Along with Saul, Barnabas taught them in matters of faith. The more prosperous church in Antioch sent relief to Jerusalem.

These interactions between a church old and needy and a church younger and prosperous suggest two analogues. First, in our society many inner-city churches serve needy populations without adequate resources. Very often in the same communities there are newer, prosperous suburban churches. The analogue suggests that the inner-city churches have something to teach the younger churches, even if they require help. More broadly, the old churches of Europe and the United States are weakened, while younger churches in South America and Africa flourish. It behooves us in the West to recognize the changed situation and our displacement as the center of the church's future. Churches have different gifts to give each other. We are pushed outward by the Spirit toward all those who are finally called "Christian."

Tuesday after Proper 17

Psalm 26; Job 12; 13:3–17, 21–27; Acts 12:1–17; John 8:33–47

God of deep, faithful resolve and hidden ways, deliver us from confor-
mity to the world around us. Liberate our imagination to hope for and
recognize your governance that eludes our tamed expectations. In his
name. Amen.

When the church is faithful, as were the apostles, it is always at risk before "principalities and powers." In this narrative in Acts, the force of principalities and powers is enacted by King Herod, agent of Rome. The apostolic church is perceived by imperial authorities as a danger and threat because it proclaimed that the future is open to God's power for life. As a result, Peter is imprisoned in an effort to silence and dispose of him.

Then follows a church narrative that would never appear in the annals of the royal court. Everything now turns on "an angel of the Lord," an inexplicable wild card that eludes the explanatory capacity of the empire. This inexplicable agent takes charge of the narrative and issues a series of imperatives to Peter. Peter thinks it is all his imagination, but he finds himself free from the prison of Herod. He concludes that it was the angel of the Lord who had defeated Herod's internment.

When Peter arrives back with his people, they think he is crazy. They think that because their expectation, like ours, is completely contained in the reasoning of Herod. They did not anticipate that anything could happen outside of Herod's control. We may reflect on how our imagination is largely contained within dominant reason. But in fact the church has always lived by the odd transformative turns of affairs that defy explanatory powers. When we limit our explanations to what the world allows, we end in defeat and despair. The apostolic church has always lived by inexplicable turns in our lives; and every pastor sees them all the time.

Wednesday after Proper 17

Psalm 38; Job 12:1; 14:1–22; Acts 12:18–25; John 8:47–59

God of faithful, resolute governance, forgive our collusion with the violent ideologies of this world. Let us be joyous participants in your alternative story of reality. In his name. Amen.

This reading from Acts sketches out, in hyperbolic rhetoric, the defining conflict between the empire, with its immense brutal power, and the fragile apostolic community, with its bold alternative witness. The escape of Peter from prison by the agency of an angel has unnerved Herod's regime. The failure of security embarrasses the regime, and somebody has to pay! Beyond that, the diplomatic exchange between Herod and the leaders of "Tyre and Sidon" (a cliché for an extended territory) concerns a royal supply of food. The narrative does not report that Herod provided any food. Instead he delivers a speech that is designed to enhance royal prestige. His ploy works; he is saluted as a god, not a man. Thus the story is all about strident, visible imperial authority.

The narrative, however, turns abruptly on "immediately." Something beyond the reach of Herod is operative. The newly introduced agent is the angel of the Lord who had freed Peter from prison. Now that same angel, the same inexplicable operator, acts summarily to eliminate Herod. He is no god; he is unceremoniously deconstructed and dismissed from the narrative. His assumed autonomy from God is a measure of arrogance that could not be sustained.

After the disposal of the king, we get a disjunctive "but" that contrasts the well-being of the church with the defeat of Herod. Now for the church, all is serene and successful. The gospel word prospers and grows. This is indeed a counternarrative; and we who read it seriously participate in a counternarrative that tells a very different story of the world, one permeated with gospel goodness.

Thursday after Proper 17

Psalm 37:1–18; Job 16:16–22; 17:1, 13–16, Acts 13:1–12; John 9:1–17

*God, giver of commandments whose will is for the well-being of all cre-
ation, forgive our "magic" illusive ways of thinking, that we may commit to your straight path of justice and neighborly well-being for all
your creatures. In his name. Amen.*

The apostolic community in the book of Acts is destined for
many confrontations, because the gospel is itself in conflict
with the dominant reasoning of the culture in which it exists.
We begin with recognition of the remarkable pluralism of the
congregation in Antioch. In addition to Barnabas and Saul
(Paul) as teachers, it includes Gentiles and Jews, as well as a
member of Herod's court. The gospel was infiltrating the offi-
cialdom of Roman power!

The story, however, turns on a confrontation with a "magician." We are not told of his "magic," but we may imagine that
it was a sleight of hand that claimed to escape the real world
that was in front of him. Such "magical" thinking in our time
includes pretense about the realities of the social, economic,
and biological world.

With his newly found advocacy for the gospel, Paul is filled
with the Holy Spirit, a fact that causes him to be in conflict with
the magician. He indicts the magician for "making crooked the
straight paths," a phrase that suggests that the dispute was
not over theological matters but concerned ethical norms. The
phrasing calls to mind the ancient imagery of Isaiah 40:3, when
the straight paths will make possible a gospel journey, a phrase
appropriated for John in his announcement of Jesus (Luke
3:4). The exchange suggests that Paul (and the early church)
cared a great deal about ethical probity. The matter is important in our society where anything goes amid large patches of
narcissism. The magician is struck down, and the court official
is amazed at the rigor of teaching in the church.

Friday after Proper 17

Psalm 31; Job 19:1–7, 14–27; Acts 13:13–25; John 9:18–41

Lord Jesus, whom we confess as the Messiah of God, give us readiness to accept your surprising way in the world, and the courage and stamina to imitate your way in our own lives. In your name. Amen.

The earliest Christian movement was a movement inside Judaism. As early as this text in Acts, there is no thought of departure from Judaism as a separate movement. For that reason, it is not a surprise that the narrative is thoroughly Jewish in every regard:

> The place is the synagogue, where the Scripture of the Hebrew Bible is regularly exposited.
>
> The time is the Sabbath day, the day when the primary synagogue meeting was held.
>
> The invitation to Paul is issued by the elders of the synagogue, who perceive him as a trusted teacher among them.

The genre of Paul's speech is characteristic for a Jewish homily. Paul is at pains to demonstrate that the Jesus movement and its claim for Jesus as Messiah is deeply and unmistakably grounded in Jewish faith and tradition. He then makes the interpretive move that is characteristic in apostolic preaching. As God has made a promise to David that from his "posterity" will come one who will save Israel, so now Jesus is that savior from the line of David. The debate to come concerns the power of God and Jesus' identity as the Messiah. Because the Messiah is linked to Davidic promises, we think in terms of political success and power and military triumph over against the power of Rome. It is clear that Jesus as Messiah does not square with those expectations. For many of us who are not Jews, the surprise of Jesus is as acute as it is for Jews. For that reason, the cross looms as a defining symbol of gospel faith; it attests to the self-giving vulnerability to which he lived and to which he calls his followers.

Saturday after Proper 17

Psalm 30; Job 22:1–4, 21–23:7; Acts 13:26–43; John 10:1–18

We give you thanks, holy God, for the lively tradition of Judaism that has provided us with categories through which to embrace Jesus as Messiah. Grant that we, like those earliest adherents, may continue in your good grace. In his name. Amen.

Paul's sermon in this text from Acts continues to be addressed to Jews in the synagogue. He is irenic toward Jews who had failed to recognize the Messiah, who had misread their own Scripture concerning him, and who cared enough to lay him in a tomb. This rhetoric strikes me as a wise way to make a strong connection with his Jewish listeners.

Paul then turns to the good news he has to tell Jews in the synagogue. God raised Jesus from the dead! Paul makes the case for the claim by appeal to a series of texts from the Old Testament in order to show that the resurrection of Jesus makes sense in terms of the categories and exposition of Israel's Scripture.

Paul then makes a second interpretive move: Forgiveness of sin is given through Jesus, notably sins that have not been forgiven by way of the Torah. The link between resurrection and forgiveness is asserted and not spelled out. Clearly Paul had found in the news of resurrection profound experience of personal emancipation. Paul understands that the ordinary provisions and rules of society and of religion allow for no such forgiveness. The resurrection breaks and violates all claims that keep us unforgiven.

The narrative concludes with the report that many Jews who had heard him wanted to hear more such good news the next Sabbath day in the synagogue. Paul's preaching persuaded many Jews that Jesus is the real thing. The final word of Paul and Barnabas is a continuation in the grace of God. These Jews who heard the apostolic preaching knew much of this; but they heard it as if for the first time.

Proper 18

Psalm 63:1–8; Job 25:1–6; 27:1–6;
Revelation 14:1–7, 13; Matthew 5:13–20

Lord Jesus, who came among us so that lepers could be cleansed, the deaf
could hear, and the lame could walk, give us energy this day to connect
our lives to the work of shalom as our proper work. In your name. Amen.

The Old Testament and Gospel readings invite reflection on a
life of righteousness. On the one hand, Job makes a vigorous
defense of his own righteousness. He asserts to his friends that
he has fulfilled all righteousness, kept the Torah, and refused
any compromise in his obedience. On the other hand, Jesus,
who insists on every iota and dot of the Torah, declares that
the righteousness of scribes and Pharisees isn't enough. It is
not necessary or persuasive to equate the early righteousness
of Job and the later righteousness of the Pharisees to see that
they tilt in the same direction. Both of them are vigilant about
the requirements of Torah.

But we must ask about a greater righteousness, one that
exceeds conventional rigorous righteousness. The term "righteous" in ancient Israel refers to generative acts of transformation that make the community "right," that is, that let it
function in the ways of shalom. We can see that "right wising"
in the life of Jesus. For example, conventional righteousness
would avoid lepers, because they were ritually unclean and
dangerous. But Jesus touched lepers, letting the force of his
life-giving capacity heal them. His right wising overpowered
the disease with which they suffered and because of which
they were unwelcome.

In our context or in any context, the greater righteousness
of the gospel is to bring life energy into circumstances of suffering and by generative action to override the dysfunction.
The gospel is a summons to be proactive agents of life-giving
shalom in a world where shalom is scarce.

Monday after Proper 18

Psalm 41; Job 32:1–10, 19–33:1, 19–28; Acts 13:44–52; John 10:19–30

Jesus who is the light of the world, help us to be carriers of that light that reflects not our tribalism but your expansive governance. In your name. Amen.

The earliest Jesus movement was Jewish in its constituency. The earliest conflicts in the Jesus movement were with other versions and other visions of Judaism. The clash in this reading from Acts is between the preaching of Paul and Barnabas that presented the risen Christ as the Jewish Messiah and other interpreters of Judaism who resisted and refused their central claim about Jesus. In this text it appears that it was that rejection of the gospel of Jesus that caused Paul and Barnabas to preach to the Gentiles. They did so with a claim to be authentic Jewish interpreters. In the service of legitimacy for their gospel, they quote Isaiah, that Israel (their version of Israel!) should be "a light to the Gentiles." They invite Gentiles into the gospel community.

This narrative exposes the deep tension and problematic of the earliest church in its effort to be faithfully Jewish in its adherence to Judaism and at the same time to reach to Gentiles who gladly signed on. Inescapably the question arose: how to *sustain communal identity* while *reaching out to others* who seem to challenge that identity, for the Gentiles did not propose to keep Jewish Torah. It is the strange truth of communal identity in the Jesus movement that *communal identity* means *a reach to and embrace of the other*. The work of the apostles is to help responsive Gentiles to situate their lives in the reality of Jesus as Messiah. From that it follows that we as members of the Jesus movement are to be about the work of embrace of the other who is unlike us. The work is not to convert the other to be like us but to permit and evoke a transformed other in the company of Jesus. Such work contradicts the temptation to view the gospel community as a tribe consisting of our kind of people.

Tuesday after Proper 18

Psalm 45; Job 29:1–20; Acts 14:1–18; John 10:31–42

Lord of great demands and great promises, we acknowledge today that
our world seems to be in free fall. We remember better days, and in your
presence we voice our disappointment in our loss. In his name. Amen.

We now consider a four-day sequence of texts from the book
of Job that are the culmination of Job's argument about his
integrity before God. In today's reading, Job affirms the wonder of the good old days that are now gone. He recalls that
he was intimate with God (who is now remote from him). He
remembers how he was honored in the village square because
he cared for orphans, the blind, the lame, and the poor. He was
generous, and for his generous living, he was much praised
and blessed by his contemporaries. He actively resisted the
"fangs of the unrighteous," that is, he intervened (likely in
court) against exploitation. His efforts made his social community work well, for every community depends on people like
him to function properly. In light of his virtuous, generous life,
he rightly anticipated a secure future where he could prosper
in the land.

This long statement of self-affirmation is evoked by the present reality that he has lost it all! His speech is an engagement
in nostalgia for the world that is now gone. There is implicit
in his nostalgia an argument that the world is no longer morally coherent, that is, that God is not a reliable guarantor of
good order and does not watch over those who are effectively
responsible. His loss is inexplicable to him.

It is perhaps ironic that this text comes up around Septem-
ber 11, because 9/11, date of a searing terrorist attack against
the United States, signifies in our society the loss of a well-
ordered world in which doing good leads to well-being. The
facts of 9/11 lead us to nostalgia for the good old days that are
over and must be relinquished.

Wednesday after Proper 18

Psalm 119:49–72; Job 29:1; 30:1–2, 16–31;
Acts 14:19–28; John 11:1–16

*God who has abandoned old good ways, we stand today alongside those
who know themselves displaced, stripped of certitude and security, and
robbed of good fortune. Hear our shared prayer of anguish. In his name.
Amen.*

Job's reflective scenario continues. After his happy remembrance of the good old days in chapter 29, in chapter 30 Job
now considers his present circumstance that is sharply contrasted with his glorious celebrated past. The "But now" of
verse 1 (echoed in the "and now" of verses 9 and 16) asserts
that his new days of the present are not good. In fact they are
for him unbearable. Job suffers many afflictions, and he does
not understand why. His exchanges with his three friends have
helped him not at all.

Because he is a genuinely pious man, he knows that his
unbearable troubles must be brought to God. Indeed, he trusts
in a well-ordered creation governed by a faithful creator. As
a result, the sum of his affliction and loss requires address to
God. He names and addresses God: "He has cast me into the
mire." And then we get a series of statements addressed to God
with a direct "You": You have been cruel to me; you persecute
me; you "toss me about." Job sees that his own great faithfulness contrasts to God's shameless fickleness, and so he must
give honest voice to his deep anguish at his great loss. He is
indeed reduced to nonhuman status: "a brother of jackals, and
a companion of ostriches," a real lowlife!

This uncompromising complaint and lament are appropriate for many people in our world, given the forfeiture of our
good old "managed" security, well-being, and certitude. The
contrast between then and now must be voiced in anguish
before God. It must be voiced seriously; it cannot be answered
glibly.

Thursday after Proper 18

Psalm 52; Job 29:1; 31:1–23; Acts 15:1–11; John 11:17–29

Lord of Torah commandments, grant that in our readiness for respon-
sible living we should not be blind to the deep enigma of your absence.
We ponder today how to trust you when we do not see you in our world.
In his name. Amen.

Job's mighty challenge to God continues in our third day of
reading his speech. Having yearned for the good old days of
then and faced the bad days of now, Job pushes his challenge
to God further. He has cast his life in a vigorous calculus of
covenantal symmetry in which covenantal responsibility guarantees prosperity. In the verses we read today, Job issues a
defense of his life of great responsibility in adherence to God's
expectations.

His statement of innocence and virtue is likely the best
catalog of covenantal expectations that we have in the Bible.
Because of his defiant insistence on his own integrity, the matter is curiously stated in an if-then mode of insistence. The "if"
of responsibility should lead to the "then" of positive blessing,
and the negative "if" to a negative "then." His "if I have" should
be interpreted as "I have not" and therefore I deserve no negative treatment from God. We can usefully scan the speech for
the social exploitation that Job has shunned and social welfare that Job has enacted. Job has cared for the vulnerable,
the hired help, the poor, the orphan, the blind, the hungry.
In his estimate (that is nowhere refuted), he has operated a
private welfare agency; he deserves better than he has received
from God.

It is clear that Job still believes passionately that the world
is morally coherent. He still trusts that a responsible life should
yield good outcomes. The poem of Job holds this deep faith to
the hard circumstance of lived reality. The poem asks us: How
shall we puzzle out a world in free fall when God is absent? No
easy answer will suffice. Does Job live an illusion?

Friday after Proper 18

Psalm 40; Job 29:1; 31:24–40; Acts 15:12–21; John 11:30–44

We pray to you, Lord God, in your absence. We continue to trust in your sovereign rule and the reliability of your world. We are, however, impatient for your attentiveness to us. In his name. Amen.

Job concludes his if-then statement of innocence and virtue. He has not trusted gold; he has not celebrated the ruin of his adversaries. He has not engaged in surreptitious evil. His last statement of innocence is especially interesting. He has not abused the land. If he has, then let thorns take over his arable land. But, of course, he has not and so deserves no such outcome on his farm.

But before his final if-then appeal, we come to Job's most poignant challenge to God. What Job wants from God is a hearing. He thinks in judicial terms and wants to go to court with God. He is prepared to give evidence in court; he is sure he will be acquitted and God will be found negligent concerning God's obligations toward him.

The scene he describes is one of immense chutzpah. He imagines himself summoned into court to give an account of his obedience to God. When he goes to court, he imagines, he will be no humble suppliant. He will take the bill of particulars charged against him and wrap it as a turban of status. He will walk into court with royal splendor, confident of his case against God. While much Christian piety has urged humility and submissiveness before God, Job appeals to a strand of Jewish spirituality that is grounded in covenantal chutzpah. We may imagine ourselves before God in the dock. When we believe God is fully the creator, we have no option. We must raise the question. Finding ourselves in such contestation with God, we are free, alongside the poet, to imagine the next step.

Saturday after Proper 18

Psalm 40; Job 38:1–17; Acts 15:22–35; John 11:45–54

*In your majestic presence we are mindful of your generous rule disclosed
to us in the regularities of creation, in the reliability of sun and moon,
in the generativity of sunshine and rain. We are grateful for our good
place in your well-loved world. In his name. Amen.*

God's response to Job's challenge is quite extended. It is also a
grand, majestic mismatch to Job's statement. Given our culture
of excessive pastoral attentiveness, we might have expected
that God would exhibit compassionate attentiveness to Job in
his suffering and affliction. But God displays not a cubit of
interest in Job's condition; the Almighty abruptly changes the
subject on Job. As Job had approached God with chutzpah,
so God's own presentation overmatches Job's nerviness. We
might take this long poetic speech as self-praise in which God
asserts, "How great I am!" From God's doxological perspective, Job is a not very significant creature who has no claim to
make on the creator God. The huge contrast between God and
Job is established by the series of sweeping questions to which
Job can muster no answer.

Western culture already in the eighteenth century had taken
a "turn toward the subject," that is, we have come to think that
the human "I" is the center of creation and the most proper
subject for reflection. That turn to the human "I" has reached
exaggerated fruition in our culture of selfies in which we imagine that the human self is endlessly interesting to everyone.

The divine speech addressed to Job directs him to make a
turn back to God and away from the narcissistic human self
that Job had become. Job had wrongly imagined that his theological moral dilemma was interesting to God. It is not! We
are invited back to the sovereign wonder of God who has no
need to conform to our modest categories of explanation and
meaning.

Proper 19

Psalm 19; Job 38:1, 18–41; Revelation 18:1–8; Matthew 5:21–26

Our doxologies to you, Creator God, resituate our little systems of money and power in the midst of your splendor. We see them, in your presence, as less compelling and important than we had thought. In his name. Amen.

The subject of the vision in Revelation is mighty Babylon, an ancient empire of dominating power and greedy wealth. That empire, in this vision, has fallen. In context, however, we know that the text is not concerned with ancient Babylon. Rather "Babylon" here is a code word for the Roman Empire, the single superpower at the time of the early church. Rome acted like all empires, obsessed with its own power, wealth, and domination. In its imagined autonomy with answer to none, the empire would take no notice of the God of Job's whirlwind and could recognize nothing of the splendor of God beyond its own splendor.

When we read such a vision, we ourselves are no more concerned with ancient Rome than was the writer concerned with ancient Babylon. Our proper concern in such a text surely must be the empire in our own time, the superpower that proceeds, like every empire, with dominating power and greedy wealth. A likely candidate for such an empire among us is the out-of-control force of free market theory that in our time has established itself as the single norm that has reduced everything to a commodity.

The vision in Revelation knows that the power of Babylon/Rome/free market theory is immense. And so the writer says to the fragile, exposed church: "Come out of there, lest you get caught in its sin." The church is summoned to live a life that is very different from the commoditization of the empire. It is only the grand doxologies that let us recognize that the empire is penultimate and so does not merit our life commitment.

Monday after Proper 19

Psalm 56; Job 40:1–24; Acts 15:36–16:5 John 11:55–12:8

*In your presence, Creator God, we cannot live by a tight moral calculus,
nor need we grovel in self-abasement. By your will we are dispatched in
great freedom to be your faithful partners. In his name. Amen.*

After the long self-celebration of God in the speech from the
whirlwind, Job is summoned to answer. He finally gets his
day in court that he so much wanted. But Job answers with
the cadences of divine splendor ringing in his ears. Now he
has no majesty wrapped in an august turban. His chutzpah
has evaporated. He acknowledges in God's presence, "I am of
small account." He is reduced to silence and will say no more.

God, however, will not leave it there. I have learned to
read what follows from my dear friend Sam Balentine. Sam
has noticed that God says he made the mighty Behemoth 'as I
made you" (Job). The great creature is a model for Job: like
Behemoth, Job in strength and power is endowed for generating life. Like Behemoth, Job has regal qualities and is a primal
creature who is nearly equal to God. Like Behemoth, Job is
made so that he can respond to violence without fear or loss
of nerve.*

The emotional edginess of this passage is worth pondering.
In his brief speech, Job is modest and reduced to silence. But
the creator God will not let Job remain so. God reminds Job,
by way of Behemoth, that Job is meant for more than that.
This does not mean that Job now may be satisfied in the tight
moral calculus that he had previously embraced. It means,
rather, that Job is mandated to freedom, self-assertion, and
self-confidence. Job transcends the old pattern of quid pro
quo. In doing so he becomes a worthy partner and counterpoint to the majestic creator God.

---

*Samuel E. Balentine, "What Are Human Beings, That You Make So Much of
Them?" Divine Disclosure from the Whirlwind: "Look at Behemoth," in *God in the
Fray: A Tribute to Walter Brueggemann*, ed. Tod Linafelt and Timothy Beal (Minneapo-
lis: Fortress Press, 1998), 259–78.

Tuesday after Proper 19

Psalm 61; Job 40:1; 41:1–11; Acts 16:6–15; John 12:9–19

Lord of life, we thank you for every sign that your will for life is stronger than the power of death. Grant that we may trust your power for life today. In his name. Amen.

The triumphal entry of Jesus (narrated here in the Gospel of John) is so well known to us that we may miss its dramatic force. What is distinctive in this version of the story is the presence of Lazarus, whom Jesus, in the Gospel of John, has raised from the dead. The mention of Lazarus in the story permits the evangelist to trace out opposition to Jesus more graphically. That Jesus is saluted by a "great crowd" as "King of Israel" constitutes a threat to the rule of Rome. It makes Jewish authorities nervous, for they had reached a viable modus operandi with Rome and did not want it disturbed. But Jesus is precisely such an unwelcome disturbance, because Lazarus is alive, palpable testimony to the capacity of Jesus to govern even death. The authorities hoped to eliminate Lazarus and so to preclude the mandate of the crowd. But the popular response to Jesus, in the presence of Lazarus, is too great and too passionate, and the authorities dare not intervene. They are helpless before the magnetic power of Jesus. Once again we see that Jesus connected to the throng of needy people at the expense of the power elite.

So who is this Jesus? He is the Messiah sent by God. He is the king in Israel, clearly a political threat. He is, moreover, more than that, for he presides over issues of life and death. He does the work of the creator God, and Lazarus is offered as primary evidence of that. This narrative witnesses against our readiness to accept the world as it is, to contain our hopes in dominant status quo arrangements, and so to end in despair and conformity. The gospel for which the living Lazarus is a sign tells otherwise. It declares that God's power for life is on the loose in the world in a way that flummoxes ruling authorities.

Wednesday after Proper 19

Psalm 72; Job 42:1–17; Acts 16:16–24; John 12:20–26

We thank you, God of truthfulness, that we may be your faithful part-
ners in the intellectual work that informs honest life in the world. In his
name. Amen.

The end of the book of Job is enigmatic. We may trace it out in three unequal parts.

Job's final speech is an acknowledgment of the wonder of God. Our usual translation of his final verse suggests that he is, at the end, docilely submissive to God and repentant. That translation, however, is far from clear; it is not the only possible rendering. It is possible to translate: "I retract my words and have changed my mind about dust and ashes." The ending is deliberately ambiguous, and we must not press it into comfortable theology. It is open-ended because the life questions that occupy Job remain unsettled.

Unlike his orthodox, reassuring friends, Job is commended by God for speaking "what is right." This divine verdict suggests that what God most relishes from human partners is vigorous contestation that shuns conformity and submissiveness. "Right speech" is recognition that God is a restless, savage mystery who cannot be contained in our packaged formulations.

God "restored the fortunes" of Job, giving back to him all that he had lost . . . except his beloved children. This prose conclusion to the book is not anticlimactic. It is a provisional settlement between two lively partners. We can imagine that in another page or two, they might go at it again, because matters between honest friends about deep issues require continued critical engagement. We ourselves are also participants in that ongoing contestation. We live in a technological society that thinks that ultimate answers are easy and obvious, or unimportant. Such an assumption invites oversimplification, or dumbing down, and intellectual conformity. Serious faith requires chutzpah to probe issues to which answers are not readily clear.

Thursday after Proper 19

Psalm 70; Job 28:1–28; Acts 16:25–40; John 12:27–36a

God of foolish wisdom who surprises us in your vulnerability, grant that our lives may bow before your hidden resolute governance and that in yielding honesty we may find the smarts to live effectively in your world. In his name. Amen.

Since the first couple ate of "the tree of knowledge," we have been on the path to knowledge, because we have known that knowledge is power. Eventually we hope for a grand theory so that we can sing, "Ah, sweet mystery of life, at last I've found you."* This text in Job is a meditation on knowledge with the compulsive hope that by scientific investigation or exploration or precise reasoning we might acquire mastery. The writer of this text came to recognize that all the knowledge in the world does not finally lead to wisdom. And indeed, we live in a technological society that has grossly confused knowledge and wisdom.

Wisdom is the mystery, held by God, about how and why life works, how creation holds together, and how human reason has it limits. In the end, wisdom is God's secret and even our bold Enlightenment expectations do not touch that secret. This chapter in Job ends in a stunning modesty when we might have expected a deeper disclosure. Wisdom consists in recognizing limit before the mystery of God. Human wisdom, it turns out, is "the fear of the Lord," awe and reverence and a bit of trembling before God, who cannot be caught in our categories. Understanding is to depart evil! Depart violation of neighbor! Depart violation of the earth! Knowledge is about control; wisdom is otherwise. It smacks of modesty and humility before impenetrable mystery. It undermines every attempt to control and culminates in yielding gladness.

---

*From an operetta, "Naughty Marietta," by Victor Herbert (1910).

Friday after Proper 19

Psalm 69:1–23; Esther 1:1–4, 10–19; Acts 17:1–15; John 12:36b–43

Living Lord of the church, we give thanks for courageous witnesses who tell the truth and stir the pot. Give us readiness to be in the company of those for whom the world is turned upside down. In your name. Amen.

A great deal has happened in the book of Acts during our long detour into the book of Job. Mainly, Gentiles have been accepted as legitimate first-class members of the Christian community. The reading in Acts narrates the core contestation in which the church is always engaged, namely, a dispute about the claims of Christ. We can identify five players in this ongoing contestation. First are the apostolic witnesses who bore the testimony to Jesus that evoked the dispute. Second are responsive Jews who found the apostolic witness to Jesus a compelling version of Jewish faith. Thus "some of them were persuaded. . . . They welcomed the message very eagerly." Third are the responsive Gentiles, many devout Greeks, "not a few" Greek women. But fourth are "the Jews." It is unfortunate that the Jews who resisted Christian preaching were labeled "the Jews," because in fact they were just some of the Jews, that is, Jews were divided and in disagreement about Jesus. And fifth are the Roman authorities who wanted to stop the disturbance and maintain civic order.

The dispute about Christ went public and clearly required the early church community to be involved in politics. But the dispute is about more than politics. The issue, as it always is for us, is Jesus as Messiah. Jesus contradicts and unsettles the world, the world of Roman authority, the world of Jewish certitude, and the world of Greek sophistication. Jesus is too dangerous because he evokes actions that "turn the world upside down." Jesus refuses to be toned down by our strategies to make him more palatable to the authorities.

Saturday after Proper 19

Psalm 75; Esther 2:5–8, 15–23; Acts 17:16–34; John 12:44–50

Lord God, who governs in inscrutable ways and yet exhibits particular wonders, grant that we may draw these grand doxological claims into the specificity of our lives, that we may be surprised by your transformative authority. In his name. Amen.

Paul's public proclamation in Athens addresses the intellectual elite in Greek culture. The argument concerns Greek philosophy and reasoned discourse. Paul's proclamation dares to give a name to the "unknown" God of the Greek philosophers. The "unknown" quality of God does not mean they could not find a name for God. It means rather that the mystery of God refused their explanations. But Paul knows the identity and character of this God. This is the creator God known in Judaism. It is the God who created heaven and earth.

We may notice two things about this articulation of Paul. First, he does not mention Jesus until the end, after he has made the case from Jewish faith. But second, his declaration is framed by Jesus. At the outset, listeners recall that he preached "Jesus and the resurrection." At the end, "they heard of the resurrection." In this remarkable rhetoric the awesome mystery of God is framed by the particularity of Jesus and his resurrection. The large doxological affirmation he makes is grounded in the specificity of Jesus. It is the resurrection of Jesus that vouches for the majesty of creation. The capacity to hold these two claims together is an intellectual embarrassment to us, because the linkage contradicts all conventional reasoning. It takes one's breath away to entertain Paul's witness that the unknown God is the one known in the Easter wonder, that the creator who brought the world into being is the one who brings life out of death. It is no wonder that some "scoffed" at this intellectual embarrassment. It is also no wonder that some "joined him and became believers."

Proper 20

Psalm 93; Esther 3:1–4:3; James 1:19–27; Matthew 6:1–6, 16–18

In response to your call, Lord Jesus, we accept that we are called to be different in the world. Give us the freedom of good discipline and the energy for our proper purpose in the world. In your name. Amen.

The apostle James is a practical theologian. Given the gospel claim for God's generous grace, he affirms that serious faith consists in concrete bodily engagement that is visible in the human community. His premise is that faith is not a parlor game of intellectual or liturgical practice. It is active participation in the affairs of the world.

His argument is in two parts. He warns his fellow followers of Jesus not to be caught in (stained by) the assumptions and practices of "the world," that is, the conventional world ordered by Rome. This includes anger and unbridled speech, available enough in the world. James knows that words matter. And if one practices the uncritical speech of the world by strategies for constructing a phony world, one is hindered in access to God. We cannot compartmentalize.

"Pure" religion is "to care for widows and orphans." Paul cites two recurring groups of vulnerable people in a patriarchal society, those without a male advocate. We may take "widows and orphans" as a metaphor for all those who are left behind and devalued in a predatory economy. Thus attentiveness to widows and orphans consists in a valuing of the forgotten that amounts to a critique and a resistance to a political economy that specializes in wealth, power, and success. In our time "widows and orphans" surely takes the form of gays, racial and ethnic minorities, immigrants, people with disabilities, and now Muslims in our society. Remaining "unstained" is an insistence that the Jesus movement has a vision and a practice that is distinctive from the ground up.

Monday after Proper 20

Psalm 80; Esther 4:4–17; Acts 18:1–11; Luke 3:1–14

Lord Jesus, who came in the night to Paul and then came in the night to Martin, give us attentiveness to your promptings that provide us ways and means for faithfulness and courage. In your name. Amen.

Paul is relentless in his vocation. He continues his bold witness for the risen Christ. He works among Jews, some of whom are persuaded. He works among Gentiles, some of whom are also persuaded. The work is deeply disputatious. He does not, however, yield or give up, so resolved is he about the truth of Jesus.

At the end of our reading, we are given the ground upon which Paul stood and the reason he stayed at his bold risky venture. The report is terse. He is abruptly visited in a night vision by "the Lord." From this report we know the words of assurance that came to him: "Do not be afraid; . . . I am with you." These words are the recurring formula of a "salvation oracle" in the long tradition of Judaism. It is the assurance of the Lord Jesus that allows Paul to proceed fearlessly. It is the same word that was spoken to Moses at the cusp of the exodus and the same word that was spoken via Isaiah to Israel in exile. This pattern of speech entertains no doubt that the assured presence of God (here Jesus) outweighs all the risks and dangers.

The closest cognate I know to this report is the "kitchen experience" of Martin Luther King. At a very low point in his courageous ministry, just after his home was bombed, King was alone in his kitchen at night. In the quiet of the night, a voice came to him, the voice of Jesus quelling his fear and assuring King of God's presence with him. King reports that from that night forward, he was never afraid or intimidated by police or dogs or other ominous threats. Such secret assurances in the face of great danger have propelled the greatest courage in the church.

Tuesday after Proper 20

Psalm 78:1–38; Esther 5:1–14; Acts 18:12–28; Luke 3:15–22

We give you thanks for the apostolic tradition of faith and the long procession of faithful teachers and witnesses who have kept it enlivened for us. Deliver us from intellectual laziness about our faith. In his name. Amen.

This narrative in the book of Acts introduces us to two briefly appearing characters in the story of Paul. First is Gallio, a Roman magistrate before whom Paul is brought by hostile Jews. Their charge against Paul is that he teaches "contrary to the [Roman] law." But Gallio will have none of it and throws out their case. He sees that their dispute with Paul does not concern Roman law but "your own law," that is, the Torah of Judaism. The dispute concerns the relationship of Judaism to the claims made for Jesus, and that does not concern Rome.

The second character introduced to us is Apollos from the church in Alexandria. I am particularly intrigued by a twofold use of the term "accurate." Apollos taught the gospel "accurately" and knew "the Way of the Lord." His adequacy as a teacher of faith was qualified, however, by the fact that he knew only the baptism of John. He is instructed by Paul's allies, Aquila and Priscilla, who explain to him "more accurately" the "Way of God." The distinction between "accurately" and "more accurately" suggests that there was a normative teaching that had to be learned and properly transmitted to new Christians. The account of the "things concerning Jesus" is especially important, it seems to me, in a church culture that is careless about the claims of faith and is tempted to reduce the claims of faith to comforting emotive dimension or to a vague ethical passion. The tradition attested here insists on a normative narrative that must be learned. That normative narrative appears to be the teaching given and authorized by Paul. The early church understood that it was required to love God with its mind.

Wednesday after Proper 20

Psalm 119:97–120; Esther 6:1–14; Acts 19:1–10; Luke 4:1–13

Lord Jesus, who freshly enacted the kingdom of God and who leads us on the new way of obedience, deliver us from indifference or feebleness of spirit, that we may be faithful to our baptism. In your name. Amen.

Apollos is inducted into the Pauline community, moving beyond the baptism of repentance to baptism with the Holy Spirit. The latter constitutes a dramatic transformation. Karl Barth writes of it: Baptism of the Spirit leads to "a new garment which is Jesus Christ Himself, his endowment with a new heart controlled by Jesus Christ, his new generation and birth in brotherhood with Jesus Christ, his saving death in the presence of the death which Jesus Christ suffered for him."*

It is impossible to overstate the new beginning made in this dramatic act!

With this act concerning Apollos, Paul continues his disputatious engagement with the Jewish synagogue. Two phrases reflect the substance of his argument. First, he contends about the "kingdom of God" that he understood to be the rule of Christ. This is a new arrangement of power and life in the midst of the Roman authority.

Second, he engages with Jews concerning "the Way." The term in Judaism refers to the Torah; for Paul, it is discipleship to Jesus and readiness to follow his dangerous path of life. To be on "the Way" with Jesus is not an escape but always to be on the way to a face-off with the way the world is presently organized. His way of vulnerability is always in confrontation with the rulers of the present order, as Paul's life attests. This sequence of baptism–kingdom of God–the Way is crucial for Paul's declaration of the gospel. It might be for us as well.

---

*Karl Barth, *Church Dogmatics*, IV/4, *The Doctrine of Reconciliation* (Edinburgh: T&T Clark, 1956), 34.

Thursday after Proper 20

Psalm 83; Esther 7:1–10; Acts 19:11–20; Luke 4:14–30

Giver of commandments and Lord of the covenant, we thank you for
your requirements that keep us alert to our relationship with you. Give
us courage to see how your requirements pertain to us in our society. In
his name. Amen.

Jesus' presence in the synagogue at Nazareth permits Luke
to provide an interpretive clue for his Gospel. It is found in
his quotation from Isaiah: "the year of the Lord's favor." This
phrase from the prophet alludes to the jubilee year in Leviticus 25, a time when debts are canceled and economic via-
bility is restored to those who have been left behind. Jesus'
hometown hearers loved what he quoted; that is, until he commented that the anticipated jubilee was now to be implemented
beyond the safety of the in-group. His intent, as the Gospel of
Luke shows, is that Jesus' ministry will be preoccupied with
bringing well-being to those left behind, a restoration that will
require a radical revision of the political economy. His hearers
erupt in a near riot to think that leveraged indebtedness would
be canceled and, therefore, economic advantage would be lost.

It is telling that Jesus cites the prophets Elijah and Elisha
(see 1 Kgs. 17; 2 Kgs. 8), the gadflies in the ancient economy
who were champions of the left behind and the destitute in the
old power arrangement. Clearly Jesus understands his own
life and vocation to belong in the same unsettling tradition.

The proclamation of Jesus concerning his enactment of the
jubilee pertains to our own time and place, in which the economy is rigged to favor the haves at the expense of the have-
nots, who are kept in hopeless debt. We are likely to treasure
economic stability. But Jesus insists otherwise. He invites
fresh thinking and bold action that will permit the economically vulnerable to share in the well-being of our society.

Friday after Proper 20

Psalm 88; Esther 8:1–8, 15–17; Acts 19:21–41; Luke 4:31–37

Jesus, whose authority dazzles us, give us freedom to trust ourselves to your emancipatory power. In your name. Amen.

Jesus casts out demons and empowers his disciples to do the same. The notion of demon possession is not easy for modern readers. Our inclination is to reduce the notion to a clinical disorder. But entertain for a moment an alternative. Consider that our society is indeed demon possessed, by the demons of greed, anxiety, and violence that disorder social relationships, that make our institutions toxic, and that deny us freedom for a life of shalom. Consider further that our society gathers these systemic demons and locates them among the vulnerable left behind who then must bear the cost of our shared addictions to greed, anxiety, and violence.

Into such a debilitating situation comes Jesus with his full authority. He does not have the authority of a pedigree; rather he has the authority of his empowered personhood that is able to overpower the demons. As a result the demons obey him and depart before great damage has been done.

It is no wonder that observers were amazed. They could not have imagined demon-free people. They could not have imagined a demon-free community. They could not have imagined a society that was free from the claims of greed, anxiety, and violence. In the presence of Jesus, all of that changes. The demons lose their power and their capacity to do damage. But the authority to master the demons comes from below, not from worldly wisdom but from foolishness, not from worldly power but from vulnerability, and not from worldly wealth but from poverty of spirit. He has that kind of authority and would give it to us.

Saturday after Proper 20

Psalm 87; Hosea 1:1–2:1; Acts 20:1–16; Luke 4:38–44

God of great promises and exasperated alienation, we are grateful for your readiness to forgive and to call us by new names. Give us confidence today in your readiness to forgive us. In his name. Amen.

This narrative of Hosea is partly biography and partly divine disclosure; it is impossible to tell where one stops and the other begins. The substance of the divine oracle is in two parts. The first part is dominated by "whoredom." This label refers to the woman Hosea married; it refers as well to Israel, who refused loyalty to YHWH and shacked up with other gods. The response of YHWH, the offended husband in the relationship, to Israel is expressed with three negative names for children: Jezreel, "the place of the undoing of Israel"; Lo-ruhamah, "not pitied"; and Lo-ammi, "not my people.' The children exhibit alienation and rejection.

But second, the narrative anticipates an abrupt reversal of fortunes. The children will be given new names: "my people,'' "pitied," and "Jezreel" (sown). The new names reflect God's new commitment to Israel. Out of abandonment will come a new future for God's people, even as Hosea anticipates a new future with his wife.

Everything turns on the "yet" wherein God reverses field and reloves Israel. The "yet" in Israel's experience is return from exile after a seemingly complete abandonment. The "yet" is the capacity and readiness of God to reverse field precisely because God's readiness to love overpowers God's inclination to abandon. For good reason the psalmist can declare, "He will not always accuse, nor will he keep his anger forever" (Ps. 103:9).

The ultimate reality of the God of covenant is to keep promises and remain faithful. Short-term alienation is in the context of long-term fidelity.

Proper 21

Psalm 66; Hosea 2:2–14; James 3:1–13; Matthew 13:44–52

We have, good lover God, misunderstood our relationship to you. We discover now that you are a passionate lover capable of deep anger and deeper love. Help us to move beyond conventional faith to meet you in your deep passion that concerns our future. In his name. Amen.

Our reading in the poetry of Hosea is one half of a longer poem. This half is an imagined courtroom scene of divorce in which husband YHWH addresses wife Israel because she has been unfaithful through her trust in other gods. YHWH is presented as a jealous husband who cannot tolerate such fickleness.

The text is organized around three uses of "therefore" that bespeak the outcome of Israel's infidelity. The first divine "therefore" is in response to Israel's infidelity. The consequence is that YHWH, the giver of all good gifts, will now block agricultural production upon which she counts. The second "therefore," in response to Israel's reliance on other gods, is that YHWH will stop Israel's many crops . . . grain, wine, and olive oil. The extended tirade of YHWH, the offended husband, bespeaks the complete socioeconomic undoing of Israel and an end to its religious confidence.

At the end of the reading, we arrive at a third "therefore," from which we anticipate more devastation from this wounded husband. This third usage, however, is a rhetorical trick. It does not carry more threat. Instead, YHWH now resolves, in an inexplicable reversal, to woo Israel in order that she will return to her husband YHWH and live a faithful life. This angry husband has become the gentle, courting lover. It happens that way in honest marital relations, but we did not expect that from God. But the use of the marital metaphor permits the poet to imagine God in turn capable of anger but finally capable of deep, compelling love.

Monday after Proper 21

Psalm 89:1–18; Hosea 2:14–23; Acts 20:17–38; Luke 5:1–11

God of deep commitment and emotive freedom, give us honesty and pas-
sion for our life with you, toward whom we make great promises and
from whom we have great expectations. In his name. Amen.

Our reading in Hosea begins with the third "therefore" from
yesterday's reading. This final "therefore" anticipates God's
new initiative in restoring a viable covenant of trust with God's
people. At the very center of today's prophetic oracle, YHWH
anticipates a different future of fidelity with Israel, nothing
less than a restored relationship of marital fidelity. To that end
YHWH makes a series of promises to the restored marital
relationship, three of which take the form of a wedding vow.
(Hosea is compelled by his own marital experience to cast his
imagination of God in these categories.) At weddings we regularly promise, I take you to be my spouse. Now YHWH says
three times:

"I will take you for my wife forever;
"I will take you for my wife in righteousness and in jus-
     tice. . . .
"I will take you for my wife in faithfulness."

This wedding vow utilizes five words that in the Old Testament together express complete covenantal solidarity: justice, righteousness, steadfast love, mercy, faithfulness. In sum
they declare utter fidelity without reservation and amount to a
divine oath of fidelity by the creator God. The prophetic tradition relentlessly imagines the God-people relationship in a rich
variety of images, the most poignant being marital. This imagery means that the relationship has a deep emotional dimension and consists in profound expectations from the partner. It
concerns issues of fidelity, God's fidelity to God's partner, our
fidelity to God. It concerns willing, mutual trust.

Tuesday after Proper 21

Psalm 97; Hosea 4:1–10; Acts 21:1–14; Luke 5:12–26

Creator God who in wonder wills creation to flourish, in your presence we are aware that our way of living is a huge impediment to your will for creation. In his name. Amen.

The early verses of Hosea's prophetic poem permit a most succinct model of prophetic imagination. It begins with an "indictment" indicating that Israel in its waywardness has singularly violated the Ten Commandments of Sinai: swearing, lying, killing, stealing, adultery . . . with the other commandments implied. Given the dramatic, prophetic "therefore," the poem traces out the consequences of such singular disobedience. Creation is undone! Beasts, birds, and fish are dying.

Connections can be made in poetic imagination that do not need to be factored in scientifically. Thus the poet can declare that *violation of the Ten Commandments* leads to *the undoing of creation*. The implication is that the Ten Commandments are not singularly religious rules; they are rather the nonnegotiable structural requirements of creation.

Who knew? Who knew that the violation of the commandments would place creation in jeopardy? We can, however, fill in the details to see that this is a compelling reminder that our indifferent exploitation of the environment will lead to global warming that eventually will make the earth unlivable. All we need to do is translate the substance of the Ten Commandments into more contemporary practical terms, and then the connection is clear. Violation of the Ten Commandments leads to disregard of human life, to the collapse of a viable social infrastructure, to a disregard and a collapse that are energized by insatiable greed and narcotized unawareness that the creaturely infrastructure requires attentive care and protection. There is indeed a will at work in creation that will not be flouted or outflanked by us.

Wednesday after Proper 21

Psalm 101; Hosea 4:11–19; Acts 21:15–26; Luke 5:27–39

*God of old legacies treasured and new possibilities to be received, give us
freedom to participate in your futuring that is not fully to our liking.
In his name. Amen.*

In the book of Acts the defining issue of church unity continues. It remains a question of how to accommodate Jewish
Christians who continue to honor and practice their Jewish
legacy and how to welcome Gentile Christians who have no
interest in or commitment to that Jewish legacy. Paul is something of a volatile, certainly agile figure as he accepts a central
role in this urgent dramatic issue. It is he who has most vigorously championed Gentile participation in the community of
the gospel. But here he is eager to confirm his credentials as a
practicing Jew by participation in purification rites.

The juxtaposition of the Epistle and Gospel readings is suggestive. It will not do, of course, to equate Jewish practice in
the Acts reading with the Pharisees and scribes in the Gospel;
nor can we equate in any way the Gentiles in the epistle with
the tax collectors and their companions in the Gospel reading.
But something of the same issue persists in the two readings.
The Pharisees are among the serious Jews who want to honor
religious discipline and scruple, most especially concerning
table purity. The tax collectors are Jews who have colluded
with Rome and have taken their Jewish identity very lightly
indeed. Thus the same issue is on the table in the two texts:
traditional loyalty and identity and freedom for such restraint.
Jesus is presented in the Gospel as one who is prepared to
enjoy table fellowship with the "impure." His response to the
probes of the Pharisees is that he himself speaks and embodies radical newness that cannot be contained in old patterns of
regulation or discipline. Clearly respect for the "old garment"
and "old wine" and openness to the new requires both discipline and imagination.

Thursday after Proper 21

Psalm 105:1–22; Hosea 5:8–6:6; Acts 21:27–36; Luke 6:1–11

Good Lord of the Sabbath, give us energy and stamina for a life of restoring withered hands. Deliver us from illusions of rest that are excessively preoccupied with ourselves. In his name. Amen.

The Sabbath, among the Sinai commandments, was simply work stoppage. It was work stoppage that honored the rhythm of work and rest ordained in creation that contrasted with the endless production quotas of Pharaoh. Over time, however, Sabbath had been drawn into punctilious performance of religious duty.

Questions about Sabbath are triggered in our Gospel narrative by the conduct of Jesus' disciples. Jesus preempts the questions by his assertion that Sabbath belongs to the Son of Man, that is, to the future that Jesus is creating. He wrests Sabbath away from the calculations of the religious bean counters. He recovers Sabbath for his purpose, which is the restoration of creaturely flourishing. He does so by his terse action in restoring the withered hand of the man. He shows the true intent of Sabbath that is remote from his opponents, who have imposed requirements on Sabbath that he negates.

This text invites us to reflect on Sabbath in our society. Sabbath is a hot topic among us because of our endless busyness that we suspect is pointless. As a result, Sabbath is drawn into all kinds of "spirituality" or it is treated as a retreat from 24/7 connectedness in order to reengage that endless connectedness with fresh energy but without any critical awareness. What is lost in our skewed understanding is that Sabbath is an awareness, that it is for serious investment in neighborly well-being. Jesus insists on the social, communal neighborly restorative work that is proper to Sabbath. His opponents who want none of that are filled with fury!

Friday after Proper 21

Psalm 102; Hosea 10:1–15; Acts 21:37–22:16; Luke 6:12–26

*Our times are all in your hands, our present time and your time to come.
Let us this day attend to the ways in which our "now" is ending and your
newness is arriving. In his name. Amen.*

The Beatitudes of Jesus from Matthew's Sermon on the Mount
are well known. But the version of Beatitudes in Luke is perhaps more interesting, compelling, and demanding because
the four statements of "blessed" are matched by four "woe"
statements that are not present in Matthew's version. The juxtaposition of blessing and woe is shaped by the double use of
"now" in the blessings and the parallel double use of "now" in
the woes. In both cases the "now" might properly be extended
to all four statements. In this way Luke has Jesus contrast the
now with the coming time that will be very different from our
present.

The blessings are for those who are poor, hungry, and weeping now, because in time to come they will be well-off, full,
and joyful. Conversely the woes are pronounced on those who
enjoy today by being rich now, being full now, and laughing
now. That picture portrays an excessively self-indulgent community that lacks any self-awareness and that has no sense that
the present that is so good can be jeopardized or limited. Jesus
brings a realistic critique of the extravagant now and anticipates a great reversal in time to come. This great reversal was
already signaled by Luke when he located Mary's Magnificat
at the beginning of his story with the anticipation that the hungry will be filled and the rich sent away empty.

We may read this as an awareness that an overindulgent
now is unsustainable. There is an expectation that the rule of
God will prevail against an unjust now for some at the expense
of others that clearly are not congruent with God's will.
We might, in reading this text, assess our own investment in
now and our passion for God's alternative future that is sure
to come.

Saturday after Proper 21

Psalm 107:33–43; Hosea 11:1–9; Acts 22:17–29; Luke 6:27–38

God of sovereign severity and holy resolve, we thank you for the access you give us to the costly interiority of your own life. Grant us the same measure of honesty with which you engage us. In his name. Amen.

This poem in Hosea is the most poignant in all prophetic poetry. YHWH is cast as a father and Israel as a son. The poem begins with YHWH's reflection on his life as Israel's faithful father who has cared for and protected and sustained Israel in every way. But then the imagery suggests that YHWH's well-beloved son has become a recalcitrant teenager. The poem cites Israel's long history of refusing to deal faithfully with father YHWH; as a result this loving father turns into a ranting, angry voice who can no longer tolerate such a wayward son. The father is now ready to abandon the son to the poor choices he has made.

But then, abruptly, the father interrupts his own tirade with a moment of acute self-awareness. The father reflects on his deep anger and his readiness to abandon son Israel. And in a sweep of profound anguish the father recognizes that he is unable and unwilling to treat his son in this way. He acknowledges his compassion for his son and resolves to be his better self, truly a holy God and not a ranting, angry parent. The poem discloses to us the deep internal struggle of God to act well toward a son who merits nothing good.

The poem is so poignant because every parent of a teenager can relate to it. The poem, moreover, reflects on the long history of Israel's life with God, a life of recalcitrance that has turned to alienation. Beyond that it discloses God's own life; we recognize that forgiving compassion is not easy or cheap for God. We are drawn away from detached or cool theology to a dialogic relationship that is demanding and astonishing.

Proper 22

Psalm 118; Hosea 13:4–14; 1 Corinthians 2:6–16; Matthew 14:1–12

In our honesty we stand exposed before your holiness. As we are able, we submit ourselves to your holiness, bidding that it be marked toward us by great generosity that we do not doubt. In his name. Amen.

Warning to readers: What follows contains offensive ideas. This poem voices Hosea's harshest version of YHWH's judgment against Israel, suggesting that:

Israel has no alternative to YHWH, who has been gracious and sustaining.
Israel has been grossly unresponsive to YHWH.
YHWH will now be savage toward Israel.
Israel will find no help in its political or religious institutions.
Israel could be given a new future, but it is too stupid to receive it.
God will mobilize the cosmic powers of death against Israel.

What a mouthful! Offensive indeed! Of course there is among us a desire to articulate a God of love with whom there is no negation or judgment. I get that, and no doubt Hosea got that.

Except that in prophetic rhetoric the God of Sinai is the God of holiness who takes sovereignty seriously and who will not be mocked. The poem invites us to entertain a God of moral seriousness and covenantal insistence who is not reduced to our preferred calculation.

It is no doubt a saving recognition that this is poetry. It is not a syllogistic argument or creedal certitude. It offers a range of metaphors that invite us to explore and probe dangerous dimensions of divinity that lie beyond our comfort zone. Israel learns, in ways that are not loving, that it cannot have life on its own terms. Something cruel awaits us when we live out of sync with the mystery that takes the form of holiness.

Monday after Proper 22

Psalm 106:1–18; Hosea 14:1–9; Acts 22:30–23:11; Luke 6:39–49

God of future possibilities, we thank you for the ways in which you create newness for our lives. You are indeed the father and mother of all orphans; we sometimes feel like a motherless child! In his name. Amen.

In this final poem Hosea gives us a glimpse into a new possibility with God that is on offer to Israel. That new possibility of reconciled life with God is voiced in two modes. First there is a series of imperatives voiced in divine oracle that affirm that new possibility depends on a change of heart by God's people. The imperatives include two times the verb "return," two times "take," and a remarkable "say" through which Israel is instructed on what to say to God by way of repentance. Israel is to acknowledge that it cannot be saved by arms (horses) and that it will stop its idolatry. Remarkably, Israel is to assert that God is a God of mercy for orphans. It is as though God needs to be prompted in order to accept orphaned Israel, that is, to be reminded of that role in the world. On the other hand, we are given a divine declaration that God will heal and love freely and will cause agricultural prosperity. It is not clear how these two segments of text are related to each other. Is the second dependent on the first? Or is God's own resolve a unilateral act? We are not told.

Mostly we do not speak or think about getting right with God. But we do think and hope often that our lives might be fuller, more whole, more joyous, more coherent. In gospel perspective, all those yearnings depend on being right with God. In the contemporaneity of this text, we are invited to changed attitude, conduct, and policy: no more idols, no more self-securing, but acknowledgment of our status as orphans bound for home as we are addressed by YHWH. More and better are possible in our lives than we are likely to imagine.

Tuesday after Proper 22

Psalm 120; Micah 1:1–9; Acts 23:12–24; Luke 7:1–17

Giver of life, we thank you for the wonder of our life and the ways in which you endlessly surprise with new gifts of life. Deliver us from the illusion that we are the source of our life; give us trust and confidence that we may be able to receive your great gift of life when and where it is given among us. In his name. Amen.

In this Gospel narrative, Jesus is twice confronted with the reality of death. In the first instance, a slave is sick. In the second case, a widow has lost her only son to death. In both cases, vulnerable human persons have been assaulted by the negating power of death. We can make sense of this narrative, I judge, only if we credit the assumption of that ancient world that human existence is an ongoing contest with the mighty power of death that shows up in many forms: disability, weakness, hunger, poverty, despair . . . anything that diminishes life. That power of death victimizes lives and drives to despair. The only hope is that God's power for life—in the form of health, well-being, food, prosperity—can be mobilized, evidencing that God's power for life is stronger than the power of death.

The narrative exhibits Jesus' response to the two episodes where death has been at work. In both cases, Jesus is the carrier of God's power for life. It is no wonder that the spectators were fearful and glorified God, because they could sense that something awesome, extraordinary, and inexplicable had just happened before their very eyes. The narrative does not want to report a miracle. It wants rather to attest that Jesus is a carrier of God's power for life that is stronger than the negating power of death. Within the Gospel narrative, these stories are prep work for the culmination in Easter. Easter is the news that God's power for life is at work in this Jesus. The church bears witness, through its life, to that Easter truth that is operative among us every day.

Wednesday after Proper 22

Psalm 119:145–176; Micah 2:1–13; Acts 23:23–35; Luke 7:18–35

God of the vulnerable, who intends that none should lack viable, secure living space, help us to see more clearly what is at stake in our time and place and to act faithfully for the sake of all our neighbors. In his name. Amen.

The opening lines of Micah's poem voice a reprimand and rebuke to big-city (Jerusalem), moneyed interests that prey on vulnerable small-acreage peasants. Micah indicts them for "coveting" the land of the peasants, utilizing the term of the Tenth Commandment, "You shall not covet." The moneyed interests are propelled by their greed to seize property that is not rightly theirs. This destabilization of village economy will evoke severe judgment, says the prophet, on the greedy class.

Daniel Smith Christopher, in his recent commentary on Micah, notices notorious contemporary land grabs from Native Americans, Aboriginal Australians, and the Maori in New Zealand. More immediate for us is the wealth grab of the "1 percent" that preys on the vulnerable in our society. That wealth grab is accomplished in legal ways through high interest rates on loans, low wages, regressive tax policy, and exploitative credit arrangements.

Jesus' answer to John about his identity and work of restoration is to the point. In his catalog of restoration wrought by his inexplicable authority ("the blind receive their sight, the lame walk, . . . the deaf hear"), the final element is that "the poor have good news brought to them." The "good news" that is characteristic of the Gospel according to Luke is that Jesus has the will and authority to restore what has been lost by the poor. Micah's oracle lets us see that what has been lost is a viable, secure living space, which has placed a large population at profound risk. The Gospel narrative affirms that this unbearable state need not be perpetuated.

Thursday after Proper 22

Psalm 131; Micah 3:1–8; Acts 24:1–23; Luke 7:36–50

God of truth, who stands against predatory systems of greed, we thank
you for prophetic voices that tell your truth. Give us ears to hear and
freedom to walk in the light of your truthfulness. In his name. Amen.

Micah's poem is in two parts. The first part concerns the managers of the urban economy who prey on vulnerable village
peasants with a practice of economic cannibalism. In a quick
change of scenes, "then" (very soon) in an emergency, those
same predators, when attacked by Assyrian armies, will cry
out to YHWH for help. YHWH, however, will not listen to
their prayers because their predatory practices have alienated
YHWH. As a result, they will be left exposed and helpless
before the ruthless Assyrians. Imagine . . . our predatory class
left helpless before ISIS because of our predation!! (Just a
thought!)

But now, Micah rebukes the religious legitimators of the
system, popular prophetic types who advocate "peace through
strength," that is, control through military domination ("Praise
the Lord and pass the ammunition!"). God will cut off from
them any useful insight, because they have signed on with the
system of predation in an uncritical use of religion.

Thus far we have diagnosis concerning the future of the
predatory class and the religious community that serves the
predatory class. All of that, however, is countered at the end
of the poem by Micah's exclamation: "But as for me!" As for
Micah! As for prophetic truth! As for prophetic utterance
that has not caved. Micah's singular vocation, over against the
predatory system, is to be fourfold "filled"—filled with power,
filled with God's spirit, filled with justice, filled with authority—filled enough to tell the truth. A prophetic scenario of history is stunningly different. The oracle poses the hard lingering
question: which side are we on?

Friday after Proper 22

Psalm 140; Micah 3:9–4:5; Acts 24:24–25:12; Luke 8:1–15

God of present failures and God of possible futures, give us trust to place all our times in your trustworthy hands. In his name. Amen.

Poets are capable of surprising disjunctive thought. So it is with this poetry from Micah. In the first part of the oracle, Micah issues one of the most devastating judgments of Jerusalem, namely, its anticipated demise and destruction. The poet identifies the exploitative practices of the urban economy against the village peasants. The astonishing part of the conduct of the predators whom he addresses is that after their exploitative practices they come to the temple and imagine that they are safely kept by the God of the covenant because they belong to the covenant. To the contrary, says the poet! Jerusalem will be depopulated and left in ruins as a result of their predation. The Lord of the covenant will not protect those who violate neighborly commandments.

But then, there is a pause in the poetry, perhaps a very long pause. The poem turns from threat to possibility. Micah can imagine a great procession of all nations, streaming together to Jerusalem. Now the temple in Jerusalem is not the citadel of the predatory class (king, priests, scribes). Now it is the locus of God's Torah ("instruction") that is offered to all peoples. According to prophetic imagination, all nations will come and learn Torah together. When they learn Torah, moreover, they will not learn war but will engage in glad disarmament so that all nations can live together in peace and security, because there will be no aggressive acquisitiveness. In the final verse Micah adds a coda. He anticipates that all nations will join the parade of peace and justice. They will do so, moreover, in the name of their own gods . . . all peoples, all gods on the road to well-being together! It is a remarkable journey undertaken in prophetic cadences.

Saturday after Proper 22

Psalm 137:1–6; Micah 5:1–4, 10–15; Acts 25:13–27; Luke 8:16–25

God of alternative futures, lead our society away from our false notion of self-security. Give us freedom to hope again, this time in a different mode. In his name. Amen.

Micah's poem is in two parts. The first part exposes God's intention to start over from the ground up with a community that has ended in hopeless displacement. That displacement has come about, in prophetic imagination, because the Davidic dynasty and the Jerusalem establishment trusted in military might. Now God will go back to Bethlehem, David's home village, and will start over with a new trajectory of governance from a new Davidic family line in Bethlehem. That new line of governance, unlike the failed line of David, will be committed to well-being and security by way of peace.

The second part of our reading is dominated by the verb "cut off." The poem may be addressed to the Assyrians who threatened Jerusalem with military assault, or it may be addressed to the Jerusalem regime under threat. Whether it is addressed to Assyrians who threaten or to Israel that is threatened, it is addressed to a political entity that relies on military strength. Thus "horses" and "chariots" bespeak weapons. "Strongholds" are military fortresses, and "sorceries," "images," and "pillars" are vehicles for religious imagination that undergird military ideology. God will terminate all of that.

The two segments of poetry together articulate a powerful alternative to business as usual. The first part articulates an idyllic scene of well-being. The shepherd king is a political figure not unlike the Good Shepherd of Psalm 23. But in order to have such rule, false reliance on military power must be ended. This poetry is a massive critique of present practice and a vigorous alternative to which the nations are summoned.

Proper 23

Psalm 146; Micah 6:1–8; 1 Corinthians 4:9–16; Matthew 15:21–28

Forgive us, good God, for imagining that we might be kept safe by our possessions. By your Spirit, give us freedom to trust our life with you and with our neighbors. In his name. Amen.

Micah 6:8 must be the most familiar of all prophetic texts, the most succinct voicing of prophetic alternative. In a series of questions, Israel asks what it will take to make and keep God happy. The questions are likely not requests for information; Israel asks in exasperation each time, Is that enough? Will the sacrifice of thousands of rams be sufficient? Or lots of valuable olive oil? Or what about my firstborn son? The questions all concern valuable commodities. It is widely observed, moreover, that this series of questions keeps escalating the value of the proposed commodity all the way to the most valuable, the firstborn son. The questions, all the way up, assume that more commodities of value, if they are valuable enough, will please God.

The final, familiar verse interrupts all commodity thinking. God will not be pleased by any commodity, no matter how valuable, because God has no need of or desire for our commodities. What God does ask (the verb is better read as "ask" than "require") is a trustworthy relationship. The thick quality of a covenantal relationship of mutual faithfulness is lined out in three parts. While each term has a distinct nuance, the point is much the same in all the terms. The doing of justice means including the vulnerable in shared life. The enactment of fidelity means risking loyalty in every circumstance. And the final point concerns modesty appropriate to a life lived in the goodness of God where no arrogance is useful. Each of these flies in the face of a society that orders life according to the accumulation of commodities. Micah presents a deep either-or of commodity or companionship, and that in a society where we find companionship with the vulnerable inconvenient, to say the least.

Monday after Proper 23

Psalm 1; Micah 7:1–7; Acts 26:1–23; Luke 8:26–39

God whom we trust, in your absence in our contexts of desperation, we
wait and hope for you in active and transforming ways, just the ways in
which you have been among us. In his name. Amen.

This poem of Micah describes a situation of social failure
voiced as acute personal distress. The social failure is characterized as a collapse of a viable neighborly infrastructure in
which everyone looks only to his own interests. Life is indeed
short and brutish! No one can be trusted. This circumstance
may be the result of war or drought, or simply exasperation
at the destabilization caused by the urban predatory economy
that so dominates the horizon of Micah. In any case, the circumstance leaves one in despair, perhaps the kind of displacement many feel in our failed social infrastructure.

All of that, however, is only context. What interests us is the
distinctive voice of Micah himself. At the outset, "Woe is me!"
At the end, again as in 3:8, this self-assertion of the prophet, "As
for me." Micah differentiates himself from his context of desperation and despair. He has a different perspective that is fully
counter to "woe is me." He identifies himself over against his
circumstance on the basis of three groundings. First, he looks
to YHWH. This is in contrast to the situation just described in
which there is no mention of YHWH. Second, he "waits." The
term means "hopes." He is confident, even now, that the God
of the saving tradition will act. In the meantime he will endure
what he must, because he knows God will, in due course, give
a better future. Third, he is certain that God will hear his cry
and will answer. He is not undone by social failure because he
is deeply based in a better tradition that gives hope, energy,
and confidence to act rather than to yield in defeat.

Tuesday after Proper 23

Psalm 5; Jonah 1:1–17a; Acts 26:24–27:8; Luke 8:40–56

God known to us in the particularity of Jesus, we thank you for the bold initiatives that you undertake. We want today only to be "insane" for the sake of your truth. In his name. Amen.

Paul has just borne extensive witness to his experience of the risen Christ and to his faith in Christ crucified and risen. He is then caught in a three-way conversation with the Jewish king Agrippa and the Roman governor Festus.

Festus, the voice of the Roman Empire, rejects Paul's personal testimony and declares him to be "insane." What makes Paul "insane" is his reliance on the resurrection of Jesus, who was executed by the Roman state. Festus could not entertain the prospect that God's power could open futures beyond imperial control.

The interaction with King Agrippa is different. These two Jews, Agrippa and Paul, have much in common. Agrippa recognizes Paul's dialect as a Jew, but he is not mad enough to risk his current identity and office for such a crazy claim. So it is with evangelical testimony; the truth of Jesus is cast in a way that contradicts both established Jewish tradition and Roman rationality.

Paul's situation before Roman authorities is ambiguous. On the one hand, he is respected and well treated in light of his citizenship. On the other hand, he remains a prisoner because he has violated the protocols of the empire. In the face of such risky ambiguity, however, Paul is undaunted in his witness. In the face of the empire, he boldly asserts the rule of Christ. The narrative may remind us that God often puts God's witnesses in demanding, ambiguous situations where the truth must be told.

Wednesday after Proper 23

Psalm 119:1–24; Jonah 1:17–2:10; Acts 27:9–26; Luke 9:1–17

Creator God of trustworthy regularities, give us alertness enough to notice the world beyond our explanatory powers. When we notice, give us courage to embrace and risk. In his name. Amen.

In these readings we have a big fish, an angel, and twelve baskets of surplus bread. It is quite a cast of characters. The fish appears to be a mighty threat of chaos but turns out to be God's strategy for the rescue of Jonah. Jonah had hoped to plunge himself into nonbeing, but God had a different intention.

Paul, like Jonah, is caught in a great storm at sea. The crew of his cargo ship is in a panic, and all hope is lost. Paul offers them a magisterial assurance: "Take heart!" The ground of his assurance is "an angel of the God to whom I belong" who uttered a world-changing "fear not."

Jesus is in a world of need, surrounded by demons, diseases, and hunger, with few visible resources. He enacts abundance for the crowd, a performance of the kingdom of God he has just proclaimed.

The three characters—big fish, angel, and surplus bread—have nothing in common, except this: They are all *inexplicable vehicles for transformation*. The big fish transforms the life of Jonah. The angel transforms the circumstance of the sailing crew. The surplus bread transforms a landscape of hunger. And they are all inexplicable. They are given in a world where God governs. These narratives, taken together, are a reminder that we cannot domesticate biblical faith to our reasonableness. Nor can we explicate the world in which we live according to our conventional explanations. The world as God's creation is occupied by transformative mystery that lies beyond our explanatory capacity. Faith notices and ponders the emergence of the extraordinary amid the ordinary that occurs before our very eyes.

Thursday after Proper 23

Psalm 18:1–20; Jonah 3:1–4:11; Acts 27:27–44; Luke 9:18–27

God of bottomless generosity and limitless graciousness, we are always again made mindful that your ways are not our ways. Give us freedom to abandon our ways in order to embrace your ways. In his name. Amen.

Jonah is a stubborn resister. He refuses his vocation from God. And when he finally reluctantly performs that vocation, it produces outcomes that he deeply resents. Nineveh, the hated enemy, repents; in turn God retracts anger and judgment against Nineveh. God acts according to God's self-declaration. And then Jonah faults God.

Jonah can recite back to God the truth about God's self: "You are a gracious God and merciful, slow to anger, and abounding in steadfast love." Jonah quotes an old formula already given to Moses in the episode of the golden calf. These qualities of God—gracious, merciful, ample steadfast love—mean that God is able to move beyond quid pro quo calculation to enormous, gracious forgiveness. That is what God does for Nineveh. And Jonah is furious, because he wanted to see Israel's classic enemy punished by God.

Jonah discovered the immense generosity of God. He also discovered that God's way contradicted his own expectation that had fearful tribal limitations. We are able to see that already here an expansive capacity for graciousness marks God, an expansiveness that we have seen as well in the story of Jesus. This is a time of urgency for such theological awareness in our society, which is now beset by deep anxiety. In my church a woman recently said in all seriousness, "I wish Jesus had never said, 'Blessed are the peacemakers.'" She wanted so much to go to war. Often, moreover, we wish he had not commanded that we love our enemies. We might embrace this reality of God. Or we might, like Jonah, pout in disappointment.

Friday after Proper 23

Psalm 16; Ecclesiasticus 1:1–10, 18–27; Acts 28:1–16; Luke 9:28–36

Creator God who orders the world for its flourishing, grant that we may grow wisdom, that our lives should be in sync with your nonnegotiable will for our world. In his name. Amen.

In the Bible, wisdom is an elusive, multifaceted notion. Ecclesiasticus* is a late voice of wisdom in the Jewish tradition when the old buoyancy of covenantal faith had morphed into prudence and world-weariness. In this first chapter, Ben Sira (the author) asserts the elemental conviction that "fear of the Lord" is both the "crown" and the "root" of wisdom. One cannot begin with human reasoning or technological control or scientific logic. A viable life begins with "fear of the Lord." The term "fear," of course, is tricky; it certainly entails awe and reverence. But it includes a kind of edginess, a recognition that engagement with God is not on our terms but on God's unaccommodating terms. Thus the ability to live well means living with the reality of God who is creator and guarantor of the life processes of the world.

Wisdom is an acknowledgment that the stuff of life consists in gifts from God that cannot be earned, and not in possessions, achievements, or accomplishments. Wisdom is the recognition that the reality of God imposes limits on human possibility. The limits of ethical freedom and acceptability must be faced, as in the contemporary issue of the practice of torture. Wisdom is the acceptance that the ultimate meaning of life is hidden from us, and we have only proximate access to that hiddenness. The acknowledgment of *gift*, *limit*, and *hiddenness* deeply contradicts our pornographic age in which nothing is kept hidden or left to the imagination. We are tempted to think that our technological capacity can master all life processes. Against such an illusion, wisdom is an honest theological awareness concerning our true locus in the world before God. Such awareness evokes not arrogance but gratitude.

*Readings from the book of Ecclesiasticus, also known as Sirach, can be found in appendix A. It is not included in many Protestant Bibles.

Saturday after Proper 23

Psalm 20; Ecclesiasticus 3:17–31; Acts 28:17–31; Luke 9:37–50

God who holds and hides the sense and meaning of our creaturely life in your inscrutability, give us modesty about our shared life in the neighborhood, that we may be about the generous business of giving and receiving. In his name. Amen.

In this text from Ecclesiasticus, Ben Sira pursues the theme of wisdom in its hiddenness from human access. Israel had vouched for the hiddenness of wisdom in its initial narrative when the tree of knowledge was already off-limits to the first earthlings in the garden of paradise. Ben Sira reflects on those who seek to know beyond that limit; such knowledge is power through which we may secure our own future. In our text, those who operate with such a refusal to accept limits are characterized in several polemical ways. They are twice said to have a "stubborn mind," to be hasty in judgment (shunning the slowness of wisdom) and proud in their capacity for control. Such aggressiveness, moreover, is given a moral connotation as stubbornness is linked to "sin" and wickedness. The effort to know what is beyond human availability is not only a cognitive matter. It is a moral concern because those who seek such knowledge do not let the elemental difference between God and humankind stand in the way of their autonomous ambition.

We are scarcely prepared for the abrupt and simple response to such pride at the end of our paragraph. As water is to fire (extinguishes it and so nullifies!), so alms may extinguish and nullify sin. There is a strong tradition among both Jews and Christians that almsgiving has saving impact, because it exhibits solidarity in the human community between haves and have-nots, exactly the opposite of stubborn mind and pride. Almsgiving bespeaks generosity and modesty in the face of the hiddenness of wisdom. It is enough to do that as an antidote to seeking to know too much.

Proper 24

Psalm 148; Ecclesiasticus 4:1–10;
1 Corinthians 10:1–13; Matthew 16:13–20

God of abundance, who has provided enough for all your creatures, give us ears to hear and eyes to see our neighbors who are the most vulnerable. In his name. Amen.

In the ancient world, before any legislation that protected the vulnerable, orphans were the most at risk of all people. They lacked a male protector in a patriarchal society and so fell through the crack of care. Long since the psalmist had declared that God is the "father of orphans and protector of widows" (Ps. 68:5). It belongs to the God of the gospel to protect the most vulnerable. Now Ben Sira, a most practical theologian, issues an imperative: "Be a father to orphans." He addresses the men of substance and authority about how to use their power.

But his imperative is not literally only about orphans. It is "be *like* a father," so that the sphere of responsibility in his horizon extends beyond orphans to include the poor, the needy, the hungry, those in want, the beggar, and the afflicted suppliant, that is, all those who are left behind and devalued by dominant society. Those whom we may regard as an inconvenience become the focus of sustained attentiveness.

Ben Sira sees, moreover, that such attentiveness is a matter of theological urgency. On the one hand, the Creator will hear the prayers of those who care for the orphan. On the other hand, those who do so will be loved by God because God cares acutely for the poor, needy, and vulnerable. Such attentiveness is urgent in any case, both in terms of face-to-face conduct and in policy formation, because we live in a predatory world that is largely indifferent to such fellow creatures. His final word is, do not act like an indifferent stepfather! Be a real father! These are not stepchildren of God; they deserve being treated with respect as valued sons and daughters.

Monday after Proper 24

Psalm 25; Ecclesiasticus 4:20–5:7; Revelation 7:1–8; Luke 9:51–62

God of truth, who recruits us to live in the zone of your truth, forgive our ready conformity to this age. Let us this day be transformed to be more fully in your company all the day long. In his name. Amen.

This reading from Ecclesiasticus (Sirach) is a series of terse exhortations. They are given with great authority, as though they are no more than obvious common sense for mature people. It would be useful indeed to select three of these imperatives for today's reflection.

First, Ben Sira urges a passion for truthfulness. This includes courage to speak up at critical times, respect for truth that resists conventional accepted mendacity, and commitment to the truth even to death. This mandate matters in our society, in which truth is treated fast and loose, so that we tend to live in a fantasyland.

Second, Ben Sira warns against greed and urges generosity. Don't brag about wealth; don't engage in self-indulgence; do not fail to pick up the tab for the costs of social well-being.

Third, don't count on cheap grace from God, sinning with certitude of God's mercy, as though God's norms for conduct do not matter.

The world that Ben Sira advocates is a well-ordered one in which human conduct matters decisively. In some ways such a world seems excessively innocent to us. In other ways it is excessively rigorous in our society of narcissistic indulgence and easy moral relativity. Ben Sira has in mind a quite alternative life that refuses to be defined by the passions, seductions, or opportunities of ordinary discourse and commerce. It is a life lived with acute intentionality before God.

Tuesday after Proper 24

Psalm 26; Ecclesiasticus 6:5–17; Revelation 7:9–17; Luke 10:1–16

What a friend we have in Jesus, all our sins and griefs to bear!
What a privilege to carry everything to God in prayer!
O what peace we often forfeit; O what needless pain we bear,
All because we do not carry everything to God in prayer!

Have we trials and temptations? Is there trouble anywhere?
We should never be discouraged; take it to the Lord in prayer!
Can we find a friend so faithful who will all our sorrows share?
Jesus knows our every weakness; take it to the Lord in prayer![*]

There is no doubt that loneliness is a mark of our society in which there are an infinite number of electronic connections and a plethora of hookups that may satisfy a momentary desire. Such connections and hookups, however, do not satisfy our deep longing. Ben Sira offers a reflection on friendship: a faithful friend is "life-saving medicine," a substance that cures all ills, a force that sustains life indefinitely, that has transmutative powers, a presence that makes life good.

Consider the loneliness you sense today. Consider friends you have, friends you have had and lost, friends you hope to acquire. Consider today ways in which you have been a friend . . . or not. In a society that seeks to reduce everyone and everything to a commodity, consider what is on offer in the world of advertising as substitutes for friendship that promise well-being that cannot satisfy: cars, computers, beer, prescription drugs, cosmetic surgery; and then imagine what is lacking after we have accumulated all the commodities for which we could hope. Imagine alternatively finding a "sturdy shelter" in the face of every anxiety and every elation.

---

* Joseph Medlicott Scriven, "What a Friend We Have in Jesus"(1855).

Wednesday after Proper 24

Psalm 38; Ecclesiasticus 7:4–14; Revelation 8:1–13; Luke 10:17–24

Creator God who has called your creation good, help us to accept that good creation on your terms and to live in it in peaceable joy and thanks and with care for its restoration. In his name. Amen.

We get more pastoral commonsense advice from Ecclesiasticus (Sirach). It all depends on how we read it. This might be nothing more than calculating prudence about how to get along in the world. Or alternatively, as I think, it is a commendation of modesty befitting what is required for the full and proper functioning of a viable human community. In a monetized culture that depends on self-promotion and that casts so much of life in adversarial terms, this counsel is like a breath of fresh air. We might take it as a specific case of the affirmation:

> 'Tis the gift to be simple, 'tis the gift to be free;
> 'Tis the gift to come down where we ought to be.*

And where we "ought to be" is as fully present, self-knowing, quite intentional, contributing members of the community.

Among the many prohibitions of destructive or self-serving behavior, also in this passage positive forms of conduct are commended: prayer, the giving of alms, and the telling of truth. Prayer refers the ultimate questions of our life to the God of the gospel. Giving alms acknowledges human solidarity between haves and have-nots. Telling truth attests that there is a larger reality to which we must yield that is not finally accommodating to our wishes or whims. Ben Sira is not much given to explicit theological reference. But he implies a great deal. He offers an unflappable awareness that we live in a world that is given to us by God and that will be lived on God's terms.

---

*Joseph Brackett, "'Tis the Gift to Be Simple" (1848).

Thursday after Proper 24

Psalm 37:1–18; Ecclesiasticus 10:1–18;
Revelation 9:1–12; Luke 10:25–37

God of all nations, we give you thanks for our nation-state. We acknowledge its penultimate status before you. Save us from illusionary security and lead us to greater trust in your good governance. In his name. Amen.

In his long poem *In Memoriam*, Alfred, Lord Tennyson wrote these lines:

> Our little systems have their day;
> They have their day and cease to be;
> They are but broken lights of thee,
> And thou, O Lord, art more than they.

Ben Sira knew that long before Tennyson. The reading for today is a reflection on the transitoriness of human arrangements of power, most especially the power of nation-states. Ben Sira observes that "sovereignty passes from nation to nation on account of injustice and insolence and wealth." He judges, "The government of the earth is in the hand of the Lord." In recent time we have watched the rise and fall of nation-states, notably the fall of the apartheid regime in South Africa and the abrupt disappearance of the Soviet Union, along with the emergence of new states in the wake of the retreat of colonialism. It is not too hard to see how these several rises and falls might be read in light of "injustice and insolence and wealth"! In the midst of such rise and fall, our beloved United States waxes and wanes, a cause for celebration as a practice of freedom, but in recent time fallen to ignoble acts of brutalizing war and torture. Our nation-state, like every other, is "our little system." We know, in the long view of faith, that "our little system" will have its day and cease to be. And when we forget that status, we engage in idolatry and illusion that serve us ill.

Friday after Proper 24

Psalm 31; Ecclesiasticus 11:2–20; Revelation 9:13–21; Luke 10:38–42

God of good disclosure, we recognize that much of your will and rule are kept hidden from us. Forgive us for wanting to know too much of your hiddenness. Let us trust that hiddenness and live faithfully without being in control. In his name. Amen.

The wisdom teachers, Ben Sira included, urge that we be as wise as we can be. There are, however, two features of wisdom that tell against knowing too much. The first such feature is unexpected, inexplicable reversals of fortune for which we cannot prepare. Powerful people are reduced to powerlessness, unnoticed people come to power. The lesson is: do not count on the permanence of present arrangements. The second feature is wild cards of happenings for which there are no explanation, because the work of God is a mystery. God's works are concealed from human discernment.

These two mysterious realities—reversals and wild cards—tell against our passion for knowledge and control, certitude and security. It follows that all our best arrangements for our life are provisional. In the midst of trust beyond control, wisdom tilts toward modesty:

No faultfinding before investigation;
No commenting before you have listened;
No messing in other people's business.

Modesty permits us to be agile, to follow the flow of life that we cannot master, and to host ambiguity and live with it. These guidelines work anytime. They are particularly appropriate in our own season of acute anxiety when we quest for certitude. The so-called wisdom of our technological era is to control as much of life as we can. Ben Sira understands that in a world shot through with God's mystery, we are not in control and cannot be.

Saturday after Proper 24

Psalm 30; Ecclesiasticus 15:9–20; Revelation 10:1–11; Luke 11:1–13

Deliver us, good God, from the anxiety of self-securing, that we may give ourselves over to your good gifts, that we may yield ourselves back to you in glad praise and ready obedience. In his name. Amen.

Ecclesiasticus (Sirach) attests that God is no patsy. It is affirmed that God is wise, God is mighty in power, God keeps the world of God's creation under surveillance and is attentive to those who "fear him," that is, those who trust and obey. From this it follows that

God will be praised, but only by those who live in sync with God's purposes;

God will be obeyed, because God's intent for the world is clear and uncompromising and is known in the tradition of Torah.

The proper human response to this reality of God is first to praise God rightly, to acknowledge God as the center of all reality. And then to obey God. With no inordinate sense of human sinfulness, Ben Sira affirms, in the wake of the Moses tradition, that "you can keep the commandments."

This obedience, however, is no punctilious rule keeping, nor is it a legalism that is worried about keeping score. It is rather a process of choosing wisely and intentionally. Both the covenantal and wisdom traditions of ancient Israel recognize that choosing is a daily enterprise. Those daily choices, limited and small to be sure, are in fact choices for life or for death. Choosing life is not only commanded; it is entirely possible. Against any imagined autonomy, the Gospel reading, with its instruction to ask, seek, and knock, refers one's life to the goodness and generosity of God in expectation of bread, not stones.

Proper 25

Psalm 63:1–8; Ecclesiasticus 18:19–33;
1 Corinthians 10:15–24; Matthew 18:15–20

*Our most elemental desire is for communion with you. We find our-
selves, however, beset by many lesser desires that lead us away from you
and away from our true selves. Give us innocent hearts for a joyous life
with you. In his name. Amen.*

Ben Sira urges a life of intentionality and self-critical awareness. He warns against a life of self-indulgence lived on auto-
pilot. It is as if he mounts a critique of the kind of life modeled
and urged by consumerist advertising on TV and legitimated
by the authority of market ideology. That model of life invites
a narcotized indifference to the world around and commends
satiation of desire and appetites that for good reason remain
undisciplined. Perhaps his opener, "Before you speak, learn,"
will connect with the immediate communication of Twitter
and the lack of grace or thought encouraged by such practice.
Beyond the stupefying numbing of consumer satiation, we
might from this text ponder how our deep ideological commitments, liberal and conservative, preclude fresh and open
thinking about the future.

The instruction offered by Sirach, a mix of common sense
and modesty before the mystery of God, is to avoid rashness,
to think, plan, and reason with discipline. The big accent is
"prepare yourself." Prepare for what may come next with the
constant awareness that life is provisional and open to sharp
reversal. Thus sane reasoning will recognize that present
plenty and current wealth and prosperity are not guaranteed.
(This accent in wisdom is quite in contrast to the admonition
"Do not worry about tomorrow" in Matt. 6:34.) Wisdom does
worry about tomorrow, because wisdom is in it for the long
haul. It knows that tomorrow is not an assured continuation of
today. For that reason, one must learn, reflect, and take care.

Monday after Proper 25

Psalm 41; Ecclesiasticus 19:4–17; Revelation 11:1–14; Luke 11:14–26

We affirm that the world has come fresh from your Word and that your Word has become flesh among us, full of grace and truth. Grant that our listening and speaking may be congruent with the grace and truth of our own speech. In his name. Amen.

Would you believe that the familiar saying "Do not believe everything you hear" is this old? Ben Sira is aware of the dangerous import of careless speech and is alert to the damage done by gossip and slander.

In a positivistic culture like ours, we think that speech is incidental and unimportant, and therefore we can be glib and careless, as in so much electronic communication. But the wise know better. They understand that communities are essentially language-processing enterprises and that the work of speech is world construction. What we say is what we get! As usual, Ben Sira does not avoid the question. "Be brave," he says, and let rumors die with you. And then four times an imperative: "Question!" Find out the facts. The practice of honest, careful truth telling matters to the quality of human community we get. It is not a long leap from gossip to false advertising to ideological speech to name calling to bullying to saber rattling. All these speech practices have in common the generation of false reality that evokes false conduct. We are invited to be vigilant not only to tell the truth but to monitor and check "false truth," even if it comes from high places.

The early church, of course, knew the same. The Epistle of James (3:1–12) likens the undisciplined tongue to a flamethrower or brackish water from a spring. In our own time, the same urgency pertains to racial and ethnic profiling and gender discrimination. We are summoned to watch our mouths and the mouths of others!

Tuesday after Proper 25

Psalm 45; Ecclesiasticus 24:1–12; Revelation 11:14–19; Luke 11:27–36

Creator God, who has ordered your world for well-being, grant that this day our lives may more fully attest your intention for that well-being in our corner of your world. In his name. Amen.

In this reading from Ecclesiasticus (Sirach), wisdom speaks in the first person. "Wisdom" here refers to the force and reality of divine reason that permeates the structure and processes of the world. In the New Testament this wisdom as a sense of cosmic order (a) is presented as "the Word of God" (see John 1:1–5) through which all things were made and are sustained and (b) is embodied in the flesh of Jesus of Nazareth. That wisdom—which the Torah commandments of Judaism echo—affirms the possibilities and limits through which creation can flourish. Resistance to the rule of wisdom will surely bring death. No amount of money, power, or know-how gives immunity from the requirements of this rule.

Wisdom makes two claims in this text. First, wisdom has priority among all things in creation and was an agent in creation that assured that creation is well ordered, generative, and flourishing. And second, wisdom has taken up its dwelling in "Jacob," in "Zion," that is, in Israel. As a result, the commandments from Sinai pertain not only to Israel but to all creation. Israel is the peculiar carrier and witness to the divine reason that assures order for shalom in the world.

Christian tradition claims that this divine reason came to dwell peculiarly in Jesus of Nazareth. He is the one who knows about the right ordering of the world and the work of restoring that right order. Thus his various acts of healing and feeding are acts that restore creation to its proper flourishing. The church, as one heir to ancient Israel, is the continuation of Christ's work. When the church is faithful and not skewed by ideology or self-protection, it knows how the world is ordered and is entrusted with restorative capacity.

Wednesday after Proper 25

Psalm 119:49–72; Ecclesiasticus 28:14–26;
Revelation 12:1–6; Luke 11:37–52

*God of truthfulness, we thank you for the gift of speech, through which
we form relationships of trust, mark our suffering, and render our
praise to you. Forgive our careless practice of speech that serves neither
you nor our neighbor. In his name. Amen.*

Ecclesiasticus (Sirach) is powerfully aware of false speech
and its destructive power. Ben Sira makes two proposals for
resisting the practice and damage of false speech. His second
antidote is a series of imperatives that encourage watchful,
attentive discipline: "fence," "lock up," "make balances and
scales," "make a door and a bolt for your mouth." It is his first
antidote, however, that seems more interesting and surely
more important. One falls into the power of such speech if one
forsakes God. Thus he draws the practicality of speech into the
orbit of God's rule. I suggest that intentional adherence to the
Lord may assist us in three ways:

1. Attentiveness to God nurtures covenantal desire for good
trusting relationships and discourages desires that are propelled by commodities. Thus I hazard that false speech is given
force by the practice of false desires that require acquisitiveness that is often violent.

2. Attentiveness to God defines the company we keep and
avoids the company of those who readily traffic in false speech.
Thus the psalmist urges the avoidance of "the path that sinners
tread" and "the seat of scoffers" (Ps. 1:1). False speech has its
habitat among those who refuse to respect the neighbor and
are free to prattle on in the absence of God.

3. Attentiveness to God situates us in a context of abundance that invites gratitude. Conversely, false speech gives us
a context of scarcity that breeds resentment. Ben Sira makes
clear that speech is different because of the reality of God.

Thursday after Proper 25

Psalm 50; Ecclesiasticus 31:12–18, 25–32:2;
Revelation 12:7–17; Luke 11:53–12:12

*Lord Jesus, who fed the crowd and created baskets of surplus, who invites
us regularly to the table of gratitude, teach us this day about the surplus
of bread, that we may relinquish our fear of scarcity. In your name.
Amen.*

Table manners matter. We learned that during the sit-ins at
lunch counters in the 1960s. It matters how we eat, where we
eat, and with whom we eat. The counsel of Ecclesiasticus (Sirach) is to practice discipline and moderation. Do not act as if
you are the only one at the table. We live in a culture of enormous appetites, evidenced variously by huge portions of food
served at many restaurants and by an epidemic of obesity that
results from bad food and too much food. That appetite, moreover, is at work where there is widespread hunger and only
grudging food stamps. The endless effort at soup kitchens and
food pantries represents a feeble counterpoint to policies and
practices of greed that exclude from the table.

But, of course, Ben Sira is a poet. For that reason his com-
ments on the table concern bigger public greed and his reflection on appetites refers to our cultural appetites on larger
scale. Consequently, the subject is greed that serves the undisciplined appetites of the entitled who in turn enact legislation
and develop policies of greed that include payday loans, low
wages, and unbearable debt for the have-nots. The advice on
drunkenness is, of course, concrete and practical, but it speaks
to out-of-control self-indulgence that occupies too much space
and that brutalizes too many vulnerable people.

We may take some time today to reflect on food, how it is
produced, how it is distributed, and how it is consumed. We
could end with a reflection about our true hunger, our phony
appetites, and why it is that we participate in "Hunger Games."

Friday after Proper 25

Psalm 40; Ecclesiasticus 34:1–8, 18–22;
Revelation 13:1–10; Luke 12:13–31

God who visits us in the night with disturbance and with solace, deliver us from illusions and draw us close to our vision of the future of your world. In his name. Amen.

Ben Sira sees that living in fantasyland is profoundly destructive. He sees, against Freud, that dreams not only process unresolved pasts but also conjure illusionary futures. Ta-Nehisi Coates, in *Between the World and Me*, his harsh but perceptive commentary on race, has critiqued "the Dream" that is uncritically entertained by white people.* The Dream is a vision that whites have of being "masters of the galaxy" who are endlessly entitled and privileged to own, possess, use, and enjoy everything without labor or inconvenience. The Dream, of course, requires inexpensive support from the labor of nonwhites.

Ben Sira, like Coates after him, saw that the Dream is life in fantasyland and has profound socioeconomic implications He provides an inventory of destructive behaviors that are rooted in the Dream:

— offering sacrifices from the property of the poor
— withholding bread from the poor
— taking away a neighbor's living
— depriving an employee of wages

In sum, this sounds like a reiteration of a slave economy of the kind upon which much white wealth is based in the United States. And, of course, we are not finished with such practices yet. Our economy still largely depends on cheap labor; that cheap labor, however, remains largely unrecognized because the Dream narcotizes us against the reality. No wonder Ben Sira declares, "The Most High is not pleased!"

---

*Ta-Nehisi Coates, *Between the World and Me* (New York: Spiegel & Grau, 2015).

Saturday after Proper 25

Psalm 55; Ecclesiasticus 35:1–17; Revelation 13:11–18; Luke 12:32–48

You, Holy God, have the whole world in your hands, including those who live in deadly situations of tears. Grant that we should play our responsible part in the world, that those tears may turn to joy. In his name. Amen.

Ben Sira gets it: God loves a cheerful giver! So here is counsel to be generous at worship with glad acts of pious generosity: offerings of peace, fine flour, and thank offerings. It turns out, however, that Ben Sira is not really writing about acts of liturgical piety. Rather, his focus is on the Commandments and acts of faithfulness. Thus the offerings and sacrifices are those of a "righteous" person. And a righteous person does more than good pious acts. A righteous person obeys the Commandments and practices Torah, but such obedience is generative involvement in the well-being of the community that goes beyond charitable acts to restorative persistence. It is restorative justice that brings one into sync with the God who "executes judgment."

Ben Sira's reflection takes place in the real world where economic cards are stacked against the vulnerable. That world is saturated with "the tears of the widow" or, as my colleague Kathleen O'Connor has it in her book on Lamentations, "the tears of the world." That world is occupied by the poor, by many who are wronged, economically exploited; it is occupied by many orphans; it is occupied by many widows, those who lack adequate advocacy in a world dominated (still!) by men. It is in this world that the righteous do justice and that the obedient practice generativity.

The guarantor of justice, righteousness, and generosity is the Most High. God knows about the tears of the world. God intends effective, transformative solace to be the proper work of piety. Piety without such work is an illusion.

Proper 26

Psalm 24; Ecclesiasticus 36:1–17;
1 Corinthians 12:27–13:13; Matthew 18:21–35

God of all nations, we are grateful for the singular heritage of our nation-state. We are nonetheless mindful that you are Lord and Savior of many peoples alongside us. Give us honest modesty to go along with our gratitude for our nation-state. In his name. Amen.

The prayer offered by Ben Sira articulates the profound ambiguity that occurs among us when we claim for ourselves special status as God's chosen people. On the one hand, the prayer is a doxology of exuberant praise for the God of the covenantal tradition. The prayer affirms that "there is no God but you," the God who is "the God of the ages." Interwoven with that doxology, however, is the affirmation of Israel's singular status as the people in whom and through whom God sanctifies. For that reason the prayer dares to ask for mercy, compassion, and blessing for this particular people. That claim is reinforced by a bold contrast between "them" and "us." This same ambiguity is articulated in Psalm 24. YHWH is "the King of glory," Lord of all. But the psalm serves for a liturgical procession in the Jerusalem temple when the victorious God returns in triumph from war, the king who has defeated Israel's enemies who are seen to be the enemies of God.

In no lesser way the same ambiguity is present in US claims for exceptionalism, claims that are old and deep in US religious tradition. For good reason Abraham Lincoln termed the United States God's "almost chosen nation" in which theological claims are made for the country as God's treasured people, as the carrier of God's will for freedom and peace. Such a claim of exceptionalism, moreover, is intensified in times of anxiety and insecurity. Such claims are at best awkward, both when we consider the doxological claims made for the God of creation and when we ponder the presence of other nations who make similar claims.

Monday after Proper 26

Psalm 56; Ecclesiasticus 38:24–34; Revelation 14:1–13; Luke 12:49–59

We give thanks for the possibility of a viable economy. Guide us to correct the dysfunctions in our political economy. In his name. Amen.

Ben Sira reflects on both the indispensability and the limitation of the workforce on which society depends. He enumerates a variety of vocations that are clearly callings and not mere jobs: farmers who plow and manage farm animals, craftsmen who work in technical ways to create beauty, painters who produce lifelike images, blacksmiths who preside over hammer and anvil, potters who turn clay on the wheel.

These workers are indispensable for society because of their uncommon skills and hard work; "without them no city can be inhabited." They "maintain the fabric of the world." They make the world work! More than that, the practice of their craft is an act of piety. Their work is itself the practice of prayer. Or in the words of Washington Gladden, they do "work that keeps faith sweet and strong."*

Such an affirmation of labor, however, is qualified by the big "yet" in the text. Such craftsmen are not skilled in public action. From this perspective, the wisdom teachers (like Ben Sira) have a special role in acts of governance. Such governance requires leisure time for critical reflection, whereas craftsmen are kept busy day and night with their labor.

We may learn from such a division of labor in our disordered society, where work is not valued and governance lacks critical reflection: skilled and unskilled labor is not valued; labor is increasingly demeaned, as with the destruction of unions; we have not valued the skill and wisdom that are essential to wise governance; we have not recognized that the fabric of social stability requires a network of mutually respected gifts, skills, and contributions.

*Washington Gladden, "O Master, Let Me Walk with Thee" (1879).

Tuesday after Proper 26

Psalm 61; Ecclesiasticus 43:1–22; Revelation 14:14–15:8; Luke 13:1–9

The wonder of your world, Creator God, draws us to praise and awe. In
our practice of power and economic greed, we too often violate your will
for creation. Forgive us for counting on our own capacity in ways that
disregard and deny your generosity toward us. In your name. Amen.

Ecclesiasticus (Sirach) offers a characteristic biblical doxology
to the creator God by presenting an inventory of the wonders
of creation. That inventory follows in the wake of the doxology of Genesis 1 and the questions from God in the whirlwind
to Job. Two things happen in that doxological tradition that
are worth our notice when we are wearied by a fruitless conversation about creation and evolution and when scientists are
finding that the mysteries of creation are deeper and more vast
than any of our categories can contain or explain. In current
scientific thought, we are increasingly confronted by a mystery
that both compels our best research and exhibits the awesome
limit of that research.

On the one hand, the doxology invites us to marvel at the
enormity of creation through patient enumeration. For start-
ers—the firmament, the sun (two times named), the moon, and
the stars. And then snow, rain, hail, wind, thunder, ice, water,
mist, and dew. All regular, all reliable, all indispensable, all
beyond our explaining or controlling. One can respond only
in awe: "Wow!" We are urged not to pass by without notice of
this massive creatureliness.

But more than "wow" is in order, because the wonder of
creation is referred to the Creator: "The work of the Most
High. . . . Great is the Lord who made it. . . . On the orders of
the Holy One. . . . The hands of the Most High have stretched
it out."

We might reflect on the wonder of this reality and how we
violate that wonder by our exploitative use of the gifts of creation. We are called away from being self-sufficient users to
being grateful creatures alongside other creatures.

Wednesday after Proper 26

Psalm 72; Ecclesiasticus 43:23–33; Revelation 16:1–11; Luke 13:10–17

How great thou art: we can scarcely take it in. Forgive our explanatory pettiness. Give us imaginative freedom this day to sing unfettered before your awesome presence: How great thou art! In your name. Amen.

In doxological cadence, Ben Sira narrates the power, majesty, mystery, and elusive hiddenness of God. He affirms that God is indeed wholly other, beyond our categories of understanding or explanation. The only appropriate response is wonder and praise; indeed, "you cannot praise him enough."

The great South African novelist Alan Paton, in a letter to his son at his confirmation, attested:

> Do not address your mind to criticism of the Creator, do not pretend to know His categories.
> . . . .
> Do not think it absurd that He should know every sparrow, or the number of the hairs of your head.
> Do not compare Him with yourself, nor suppose your human love to be an example to shame Him.
> He is not greater than Plato or Lincoln, nor superior to Shakespeare and Beethoven,
> He is their God, their powers and their gifts proceed from Him.*

The huge temptation in modern time is to draw God down to our size and to our categories, to domesticate God into our explanations, and so to resist the mystery and expose the hiddenness of holiness. We do this by making God user friendly. All such drawdowns of God, however, are wee acts of idolatry that seek to conform God to our horizon of ourselves and our world.

---

*Alan Paton, "Meditation for a Young Boy Confirmed," *The Christian Century* (October 13, 1954):1238.

Thursday after Proper 26

Psalm 70; Ecclesiasticus 44:1–15; Revelation 16:12–21; Luke 13:18–30

God of good futures, deliver us from false valuing and illusionary cele-bration. Give us attentiveness this day to notice the deservedly famous and to emulate them in our lives. In your name. Amen.

Ecclesiasticus (Sirach) in these lines introduces a very long view of the history of Israel; he names and celebrates the characters who occupy the plotline of Israel's historical faith. At the outset, Ben Sira notes those whom the world celebrates: the rich, powerful, and famous and, among them, artists and writers. He has, however, no real interest in these persons. His interest is in an alternative list of persons of mercy, or persons of loyalty, those who have invested in the maintenance and well-being of the community.

This text, in its large vision, invites us to become familiar with Israel's roster of such folk. Beyond that, it invites us to formulate a further list of persons of mercy who have not sought wealth or power or fame but who have invested their lives for the good of others. Such a list would include, surely, Frederick Douglass, Eugene Debs, Susan B. Anthony, Martin Luther King, Daniel Berrigan, Nelson Mandela, and many others whom each reader will identify. Beyond those with wide public recognition, each local congregation surely maintains a roster of those who have given themselves tirelessly for community well-being. They are the ones who show up for every social emergency, for every issue of human justice, and for every act of grief, generosity, and hope. This roster is to be contrasted with the list of the rich and famous. Ben Sira bids that we should teach our children and grandchildren those who are most importantly remembered. We are to turn away from the ordinary list of persons of note to this alternative list of those who have not sought notice for themselves.

Friday after Proper 26

Psalm 69:1–23; Ecclesiasticus 50:1, 11–24;
Revelation 17:1–18; Luke 13:31–35

*You are a God who dwells with unease in our arrangements of piety,
doctrine, and liturgy. Give us courage to see the ways in which your will
and purpose stand over against much of our religious comfort zone. In
your name. Amen.*

This reading from Ecclesiasticus (Sirach) is atypical for the
book because it is so concretely historical concerning the
revivification of the temple in Jerusalem. The text reads like
a memorial booklet concerning a well-remembered liturgical
occasion. The priests, the singers, and the people play their
proper roles in the liturgy with the offer of sacrifices, the singing of praises, and the appropriate abasement before God.
The report offers a panoply of honorific titles assigned to God:
Most High, Almighty, God Most High, Lord Most High, Merciful One. Israel is awed in the presence of the ruler of all reality. Amazingly, this divine majesty is for an instant contained in
the Jerusalem temple so that the temple becomes a venue from
which to expect the peace, mercy, and deliverance of God.

When we read this report in juxtaposition to the Gospel
reading, however, we are jarred by Jesus' words that recognize that Jerusalem is a place of acute hostility to his ministry
of restoration. It is a place that kills prophets, because prophets speak a word that cannot be contained in the domesticated
liturgies of the political regime. Jerusalem, after all, is the seat
of government for King Herod. As a result, Jesus voices an
intense lament over the holy city, seeing that the city, its temple, and its government have rejected the caring offer of God.
Implied is the termination of the old regime as Jesus brings
a new life order. We are invited into this tense juxtaposition
between reassuring liturgical practice and the pathos-filled
lament of Jesus that anticipates God's rejection of our liturgical niceties.

Saturday after Proper 26

Psalm 75; Ecclesiasticus 51:1–12; Revelation 18:1–14; Luke 14:1–11

God who hears and answers, forgive us when we have not told the truth about ourselves when we thought we could get along alone, when we thought you did not notice. Give us courage to voice both our need and our thanks. In his name. Amen.

As he nears the end of his teaching, Ben Sira offers to God a characteristic song of thanksgiving, a form with which we are familiar from the book of Psalms. This song of thanksgiving voices thanks to God and then narrates the reasons for such gratitude. The reasons for thanks entail a report on the big trouble of the speaker and the way in which God has rescued from the trouble.

The big troubles here are "adversaries"; the imagery is vivid: life threatened, "choking fire," flames, deep recesses, foul tongue, and lies. The issue seems to be simply slander; but in a tight social network, slander can destroy a life, thus driving one to the brink of the grave. The hyperbolic language of trouble is matched by testimony about God. The poet remembers ancient mercies from God and, on the basis of them, makes urgent petition to God.

The divine response is prompt and effective: "You saved me from destruction and rescued me." The speaker, a person of faith, is in a dialogic transaction with God that has transformative power. The structure of all such testimonies is very simple: "I cried out. . . . You delivered." This doxological tradition characterizes God as the one who listens and answers; it characterizes the human person as the one who asks and receives. We are always tempted to step out of that dialogue either in self-sufficiency, as though we needed no listening partner, or in despair, as though there were no listening partner. The truth of our faith is that this dialogue is real and the ground of well-being into the future.

Proper 27

Psalm 93; Ecclesiasticus 51:13–22;
1 Corinthians 14:1–12; Matthew 20:1–16

*God of all truth, we thank you for the good teachers we have had along
the way. Give us energy to continue to reflect on the mystery of your way
in the world. In his name. Amen.*

In this final reading from Ecclesiasticus (Sirach), Ben Sira
delivers his valedictory that provides ground for his claim to
be a wisdom teacher. His attestation is in three parts. First, he
asserts that he has been, through his life, single-minded in his
disciplined effort to gain wisdom and be wise. From beginning
to end, from first blossom to ripe grape, all he cherished was
wisdom. His learning has a moral dimension and is not merely
a cognitive enterprise. He pursued goodness and kept himself
pure.

Second, he succeeded in becoming wise. On that basis,
third, he has been given the tongue of a teacher. He is qualified and ready. The final verses of his valedictory (beyond our
verses) are an effort to recruit those who seek wisdom to take
him as their teacher.

This claim for wisdom is not mere cognitive learning or an
elitist accumulation of erudition. It is rather a deep theological
discernment that has profound implications for social life in
the world. But that, of course, is what good teachers do. They
move beyond good and interesting subject matter to reflect
more deeply on the mystery and responsibility for good living.
Such teaching is an urgent vocation in a culture that excessively prizes instrumental reason and technological know-how,
that wants to reduce all life to problem solving and mastery.
The practice of wisdom is not mastery but humility before the
mystery of God, whose way cannot be fully decoded by us. We
might well remember the good teachers who have taught and
shaped us, and resolve to support such teaching enterprise in a
world that too much prizes thin technological reasoning.

Monday after Proper 27

Psalm 80; Joel 1:1–13; Revelation 18:15–24; Luke 14:12–24

Lord Jesus, who enjoyed the company of the vulnerable and those left behind, give us joy in such companions, that we may be your faithful companion. In your name. Amen.

The juxtaposition of the readings from Revelation and the Gospel of Luke articulates the core tension between the promise of Jesus and ordinary economic arrangements. The book of Revelation, in verses just prior to ours, has voiced an immense prophetic critique of the ancient city of Babylon for its greedy, self-indulgent wealth. In context, Babylon stands in for the city and empire of Rome. It also stands in for every social arrangement that features excessive accumulation of wealth by the few and the reduction of all life to the accumulation of commodities. Such a socioeconomic arrangement is, of course, profoundly inhospitable to those who cannot compete in the race for commodities, who are left behind and without a viable place in society.

On exhibit in the Gospel narrative is the way in which Jesus contradicts the pursuit of commodity wealth in Babylon, Rome, and the present global economy. His parable features a lavish banquet, the kind in which Babylon and Rome specialized. The surprise is that Jesus proposes that the guest list for this lavish extravagance be exactly those excluded from and left behind in a monetized society. He enumerates them: the poor, disabled, lame, and blind, those who cannot compete effectively in a predatory economy. He notices that the well-off are so sated that they refuse the invitation, and he also notices that those who welcome the disadvantaged to the table are blessed, precisely because they have stepped outside the quid pro quo calculation of wealth. Clearly Jesus intends that the noncompetitive have a full plate guaranteed by generous protocols.

Tuesday after Proper 27

Psalm 78:1–39; Joel 1:15–2:2; Revelation 19:1–10; Luke 14:25–35

Your way in the world, Lord Jesus, is one of traveling light toward an alternative future under your rule. Give us freedom to walk your walk and to resist an easier way. In your name. Amen.

Jesus' call to discipleship is impossible: "Give up all your possessions." It would be more than enough to give up the objects we treasure. It is even more demanding to give up our various social locations of status, privilege, and entitlement, such as assumptions about gender, race, or nationality. His call is total and uncompromising.

That call, however, takes on a different tone when it is placed in juxtaposition to the reading from Revelation. The text of Revelation has mounted a massive critique of self-indulgent commodity power in Rome, the very commodity power we do not want to renounce. But then the text asserts that the "great whore" (Babylon, Rome) is a smoldering ruin with smoke that goes up forever. It is a poetic way to assert that such arrangements of power and wealth cannot be sustained. They are bound to fail because they are inimical to God.

The visionary text in Revelation celebrates those who have made a decision to depart the "rich" (!) promise of wealth and power for the sake of the gospel. They did so at great cost for what they forfeited. The focus, however, is on their wondrous gain of access to the throne room of mercy. The future does not consist in more Rome, more money, or more power. It consists in glad doxologies. The joy of the doxological community is as a wedding party to which are invited the saints who have opted for the alternative of Jesus.

These texts characteristically articulate an uncompromising either-or: our lives are cast either as players in the empire of money and power or as participants in the future of the vulnerable Lamb. Most of us want it both ways.

Wednesday after Proper 27

Psalm 119:97–120; Joel 2:12–19; Revelation 19:11–21; Luke 15:1–10

Lord Jesus, who in suffering and death has overcome the great power of greedy violence, help us to notice where your alternative rule is operative among us today. In your name. Amen.

The wild imagery of the reading from Revelation is not science fiction, nor is it a depiction of a cosmic battle at the end of the world. It is, rather, poetry that invites us to imagine our life in the world differently. This act of outrageous imagination is voiced in extreme imagery, but that imagery needs to be connected to lived reality. The great contest is between the rider on the white horse and the beast. The rider on the white horse, "The Word of God" who is "King of kings and Lord of lords," is the crucified Christ; thus his robes are marked in blood. He is, however, no lone ranger, for he is followed by a vast company of the faithful. The beast is the predatory empire of Rome with its insatiable appetite to devour all it can reach.

The issue is joined between the rider and the beast, between Christ and the rapacious empire. It is, however, no contest. The rider prevails. The beast tries to kill the rider, but Easter defeats the beast! And so the Easter God presides over the hopeless remains of the empire, the kings, the captains, the mighty men, and their armaments; all are now defeated.

The drama features an intense moment of victory and defeat. It is not as though the issue is deferred; it is current reality. The truth of Christ—the truth of vulnerability and steadfastness—is always and now in deep conflict with the beast of greedy violence. The rule of Christ invites to vulnerability, to neighborly solidarity, and to generous human community, all of which contradict the predatory economy that is propelled by fear and greed. The imagery cannot be read as though there were nothing at stake today.

Thursday after Proper 27

Psalm 83; Joel 2:21–27; James 1:1–15; Luke 15:1–2, 11–32

We are aware, Lord God, in your presence that our insistent greed contradicts your will for your creation. Give us strong hearts to face reality, and bring our practice into sync with your good purpose. In his name. Amen.

The oracle of Joel is a good one to read as we ponder global warming and the coming disaster for our environment. The presenting problem in Joel is that there has been an immense agricultural crisis of drought and locust that has seriously disrupted the economy. Our verses concern restoration, but they must be read in light of the crisis and the summons of the prophet to prayer and fasting.

The news is that God, the Creator, is a faithful, powerful restorer who will recover the agricultural community of Israel. Rains will come, food will be plentiful, and God will be praised. God is a restorer of creation. Israel will get past the crisis in the goodness of God.

Israel and its land, in this act of imagination, is an inescapable partner in a dialogic transaction with God. Israel is not autonomous, nor is its land. Everything depends on covenantal steadfastness. For that reason, Israel must engage in deep acts of repentance and return to covenantal obedience.

Self-deception among us causes us to refuse a covenantal response to our environmental crisis. Or we imagine that some new technological fix will resolve our crisis of global warming. However, the prophet insists, now as then, that the precondition of a fruitful, life-sustaining creation is the practice of covenantal solidarity that curbs economic exploitation and that subordinates commodities (like fossil fuels) to the well-being of the neighborhood.

Denial is not a path to a viable future.

Friday after Proper 27

Psalm 88; Joel 2:28–3:8; James 1:16–27; Luke 16:1–9

Good Spirit of God who opens futures and creates newness, give us grace this day to imagine a fresh iota of our life outside our past tense. In his name. Amen.

The contemporaries of Joel are mostly prisoners of the present tense who cannot imagine life other than the way it is now. There are two ways to be trapped in such a present-tense prison. One is by the illusion that things are so good that they will stay this way to perpetuity. The other is the way of despair that imagines we will never get out of this. There is ample evidence of such imprisonments to which many of us subscribe:

We imagine that the economy must always feature a class war in which haves prey on have-nots in exploitative ways.

We imagine that our nation-state will always have the ability to impose its policies and goals on others because of its unrivaled military and economic power.

We imagine that the church, in its liturgical practice, its doctrinal formulation, and its polity, will always remain just as it is.

Joel's poem tells otherwise! He anticipates a coming time when all sorts of people break out of such weary imprisonment. There will be prophecy, dreams, and visions, acts of imagination opening to otherwise. Such imagination will be practiced by everyone . . . sons, daughters, old men, young men, male servants, maidservants, people of every gender, age group, and social class. All will depart the prison of present tense. As God "restores the fortunes," there will be enough freedom to forgo old habits and old biases, old certitudes and old comfort zones. Perhaps among us the sons and daughters, the young men and women, will be millennials who will lead the way. The news is that God's intent has not succumbed to our precious status quo.

Saturday after Proper 27

Psalm 87; Joel 3:9–17; James 2:1–13; Luke 16:10–17

God of neighborly solidarity who intends mercy, justice, and generosity for the entire neighborhood, break the grip of money on us. In your freedom, may we walk in obedience to your insistent vision. In his name. Amen.

Jesus knew we could not have it both ways, God and capital. His adversaries, the Pharisees, are said in Luke to be "lovers of money." James, in the Epistle reading, recognizes that money stratifies society into rich and poor, honored and dishonored. We, of course, live in a monetized society in which money defines almost everything: we stratify education, we stratify health care; we stratify housing and job opportunities. And the higher up we are in social stratification, the less we are able to notice, or want to notice, the process of stratification in which we participate.

In that kind of political economy, James writes of "the royal law": "You shall love your neighbor as yourself." By terming it the "royal law," James suggests it is the law of the new king, the new regime, that is, the kingdom of God. The good news is the overcoming of social stratification for the sake of neighborly solidarity in an economy of justice. It is important to recognize the depth of Jesus' contradiction of conventional monetary arrangements. Terry Eagleton, in noticing Jesus' solidarity with "the scum of the earth," observes: "The morality Jesus preaches is reckless, extravagant, improvident, over-the-top, a scandal to actuaries and a stumbling block to real estate agents: forgive your enemies, give away your cloak as well as your coat, turn the other cheek, love those who insult you, walk the extra mile, take no thought for tomorrow."*

The contradiction is complete. We, his would-be followers, are left to take up his imperative in concrete, bodily ways.

---

*Terry Eagleton, *Reason, Faith, and Revolution: Reflections on the God Debate* (New Haven, CT: Yale University Press, 2009), 14.

Proper 28

Psalm 66; Habakkuk 1:1–4 (5–11), 12–2:1;
Philippians 3:13–4:1; Matthew 23:13–24

Holy God, whose will is operative among us, we bow before your hidden sovereignty. We do so in hope and confidence, willing to wait for your time among us. In his name. Amen.

This poem of Habakkuk is situated a few years before Jerusalem is destroyed by the Babylonians. The poem begins with a complaint addressed to God in an urban context where "justice never prevails"; it is a bid that God should notice and respond to the exploitation by ruthless people in the city.

The divine response to the complaint is not relief or assurance. It is rather God's resolve to bring a massive brutalizing nation against Jerusalem, which turns out to be mighty Babylon. Thus the prophetic calculation is that internal disobedience to Torah evokes external threat dispatched by God.

Habakkuk responds to the divine declaration in a great doxology of trust. Habakkuk affirms that God is from everlasting, utterly reliable, and fully sovereign. He is confident that God is indeed the "Rock." He attests God's rule through the image of God as a successful fisherman who manages human history like a mess of fish.

At the end of our reading, Habakkuk wonders whether divine brutality against Israel will last forever. He does not know. He will watch and wait. Such a prophetic characterization of God is not an easy one. It includes three claims to which we might object: God's capacity to manage the nations, God's readiness for violence, and God's judgment on God's own people. We might want something more benign; but even Jesus, in this Gospel reading, can pronounce "woes" of big trouble. When we begin with confidence in God, we can watch and wait, assured that what we now see and experience is not the end. There is more from the everlasting Rock.

Monday after Proper 28

Psalm 89:1–18; Habakkuk 2:1–4, 9–20; James 2:14–26; Luke 16:19–31

Holy God before whom we bow in awed silence, we cannot keep silent about the social mess that is produced by our anxiety, greed, and violence. Accept both our silence and our honest testimony about our life in the world. In his name. Amen.

This extended poem of Habakkuk is framed with two sweeping affirmations. At the outset is a divine vision of the outcome of all things. The history of the world will come to an end that God intends. The passage ends with an affirmation of the holiness of God, before whom all the earth should be in silent awe. These two affirmations at the beginning and end are confident about the rule of God. But they also bracket a different kind of prophetic assertion. In between are a series of woes, announcements of big trouble that is to come upon those who live destructive lives. Our text has four such woes. The woe speeches anticipate inescapable outcomes from unacceptable morality, in these cases greed, bloodshed, exploitative drink, and idolatry.

The interplay of the two theological statements at beginning and end and the moral castigations between them suggest that we may discern our life in the world with a bifocal attentiveness. On the one hand, the two theological statements make a very long-term assurance in which we may trust that God is holy and will fulfill God's vision. On the other hand, the woe oracles between require of us the due diligence of moral discernment about the political economy in which we live. If we read only the woe oracles, we may end in despair. If we read only the grand theological affirmations, we may end in denial that does not notice the real world, and the woe oracles guard us from the denial of not noticing. Faith is a readiness to see with both eyes both the world as it is and the God who governs it.

Tuesday after Proper 28

Psalm 97; Habakkuk 3:1–10 (11–15), 16–18;
James 3:1–12; Luke 17:1–10

God whom we imagine in massive strength and awesome intrusiveness,
we resolve not to let our faith or our life be undermined by circumstance.
We trust in your wise rule and will wait with eager and confident long-
ing for your newness to come among us. In his name. Amen.

Like a rap singer who presents cultural disaster in hyperbolic imagery or science fiction that has catastrophe as its agenda, Habakkuk invites awe before the disruptive coming of God. In this poetic scenario designed to summon to seriousness about the state of current reality, God will sweep down from the ancient dwelling in the Sinai Peninsula to exhibit God's massive glory to the nations. Dread God that YHWH is, the divine presence will come with cosmic pestilence of disorder for the sake of YHWH's kingship. No present-world arrangement can withstand the divine intrusion. It is no wonder that Habakkuk reports that his lips quiver and his bones tremble as he anticipates that "thy kingdom come on earth as it is in heaven."

The poet's response to this scene of massive upheaval is: "I wait quietly." This is an invitation to trust confidently in God and God's rule. The poet will defy all circumstance in certitude that God's purpose will be for good. Such faith is surely a survival tactic in a world of upheaval. This confident "wait" is articulated in three parallel uses of a defiant "though," that is, "even if." Even if fig trees fail to produce, even if olive trees produce no olives, even if flocks of sheep fail to bear young . . . even if the fruitfulness of creation is terminated, even in the face of such disaster, the poet voices a resounding "yet" of resilient trust: Yet . . . nevertheless! . . . rejoice in YHWH. Yet . . . exult in the God of salvation. Faith that defies circumstance will be required in our next season of life as our old world is dismantled. Habakkuk anticipates Paul: "Be steadfast, immovable" in faith (1 Cor. 15:58) . . . no matter what!

Wednesday after Proper 28

Psalm 101; Malachi 1:1, 6–14; James 3:13–4:12; Luke 17:11–19

God who gives unreservedly, beyond our parsimony, let your generosity awaken in us a corresponding gratitude that yields its best to you in gladness. In his name. Amen.

Give of your best to the Master,
Give of the strength of your youth.[*]

We used to sing these words in all innocence at church camp; we meant them seriously in a way that resulted in many church vocations and life commitments. Such an innocent resolve recognized a great truth of faith: God must receive from us offerings that are not cheap, shoddy, or tawdry. The reason, though we did not suspect it then, is that the God of biblical faith has high self-regard, cares about the divine reputation, and will not be mocked by cheapness. Thus in this oracle of Malachi, God declares, "I am a great King." A great king requires gladly obedient subjects. God might add under the divine breath, "And don't you forget it."

Malachi presents God as being profoundly vexed by priestly offerings of inadequate gifts and sacrifices. The prophet lived in a time when the priests were lax and the people were indifferent; they offered blemished animals or those they had seized by violence. God is not, to be sure, preoccupied with commodities and has elsewhere (Ps. 50) indicated that God neither needs nor wants sacrifices. The matter is urgent, however, because what is offered liturgically is commensurate with what is offered by way of life practice. Cheap sacrifices bespeak faith that is marginal or indifferent. Sacrifices taken in violence indicate participation in a predatory economy that is excessively acquisitive. Parsimony in church matches carelessness in a life of faith. God suggests, by way of mockery: try offering such cheap stuff to the government; see how that works! The prophetic urging is to get serious and to show that seriousness in concrete ways.

[*]Howard B. Grose, "Give of Your Best to the Master," 1902.

Thursday after Proper 28

Psalm 147; Deuteronomy 26:1–11; John 6:26–35*

God of all nations, we give thanks for the abundant ways in which you have blessed America. Give us wisdom to recognize that there are many chosen peoples alongside us. In his name. Amen.

Since the master narrative created by the great Puritan pastor Cotton Mather, we have been privileged to read American history as a reperformed version of the normative narrative of ancient Israel. Like ancient Israel, America was emancipated (from European bondage), and its settlers crossed the dangerous wilderness (of the ocean) and were brought by God to a rich land flowing with milk and honey. This familiar text in Deuteronomy voices a highly stylized recital of the memory of Israel through which God has been deeply involved in the destiny of America.

This, inevitably, has been a narrative of America told from the perspective of European immigrants who have identified themselves as "the real Americans." We now must, perforce, learn to read this normative narrative of America and God beyond a European reference. That is required because the US population is now greatly pluralistic and can no longer be exclusively dominated by a Euro-American narrative. The worldwide, desperate movement of displaced refugees, moreover, requires an alternative telling. The biblical memory permits many retellings with an awareness that the plotline for many peoples consists in a story of emancipation and blessing. Such a plotline does not permit self-congratulations by Euro-Americans. Rather it invites awareness that many peoples share this story (as is declared in Amos 9:7). Beyond that, the story of such emancipation and blessing must be told with an acute awareness that many peoples have even now been denied access to the story, are still held in bondage, and are still excluded from the blessing.

*These are the assigned texts for Thanksgiving Day in the United States, which falls on Thursday after Proper 28 in 2018, but on Thursday after Proper 29 in any year when Thanksgiving is November 24 or later.

Friday after Proper 28

Psalm 102; Malachi 3:1–12; James 5:7–12; Luke 18:1–8

We give you thanks, God of justice, that we belong to a community of urgent and courageous hope. We give thanks as well that you engage with us in the deep hope we have for new possibility. In his name. Amen.

This parable of Jesus strikes me as especially important and helpful for us now, because we live in a time and circumstance that tempt us to "lose heart." We may lose heart over an economy that seems fated to massive permanent unemployment, or we may lose heart in old-line established churches as we notice free fall of the diminished numbers of people and dollars. Jesus offers prayer as an antidote to losing heart. Karl Barth says of this antidote:

> *There is no such thing as a Christian resignation in which we have either to submit to a fate of this kind or to come to terms with it. Resignation . . . is always the disconsolate consolation of unbelief. There is, of course, a Christian patience and submission, as there is also a Christian waiting upon God. But it shows itself to be genuine by the fact that it is always accompanied by the haste and restlessness of the prayer which runs to God and beseeches Him.* *

In the parable God is not unlike the obdurate judge. And those who pray rather than lose heart are like the widow. She is restless and in haste to cry out for justice; she cries out relentlessly and incessantly. The judge is indifferent and unresponsive. But she wears him down; finally out of desperation (not out of conviction), the judge yields and gives justice to the widow. In the Israelite tradition of lament complaint, circumstances of injustice are too urgent for modern prayer. The alternative is to be down and dirty toward the God who can be reached and who, at the end of such incessant imperative, may answer.

---

*Karl Barth, *Church Dogmatics*, II/1, *The Doctrine of God* (London: T&T Clark, 2004), 511.

Saturday after Proper 28

Psalm 107:33–43; Malachi 3:13–4:6; James 5:13–20; Luke 18:9–14

You've got the whole future in your hands! We do not doubt that your future will be entrusted to the peacemakers, the creation protectors, and advocates of justice. By the end of the day, we pray that you may count us in that company. In his name. Amen.

In an anticipation of the Big Sort of sheep and goats narrated by Jesus, Malachi imagines God ultimately distinguishing between the "righteous" and the "wicked." The "righteous" are those who serve and fear God and obey Torah. The final verses of Malachi (the final verses of the Old Testament) focus on those who adhere to God's purposes and their wondrous future.

For you "the sun of righteousness shall rise"; *you* will leap like newborn calves.

And finally, "I will send *you* . . . " Unlike the Hebrew Bible that ends in 2 Chronicles 36:22–23, the Christian Old Testament commonly used in the traditions of Western Christianity ends in anticipation of the return of Elijah, the wonder-worker and mighty witness to God, who had been taken up into heaven.

The Old Testament ends with an open-ended expectation for a new future that will belong to the Godfearers. When Elijah returns, he will be the great reconciler. In Christian tradition, that anticipated Elijah is embodied in John the Baptist, who opens the way for the coming of the Messiah and the new messianic age. Thus in Luke 1:17, John the Baptist will "turn the hearts of parents to their children, and the disobedient to the wisdom of the righteous, to make ready a people prepared for the Lord." This Malachi text asks: to whom does the future belong? It is easy enough to conclude that the future will be more of the same wherein the rich, powerful, and ruthless are in control. This text, however, affirms that the Godfearers will prevail in God's new future. This text provides a basis for remaining steadfast in the pursuit of peace and justice. That new future, by the mercy of God, comes soon.

Proper 29

Psalm 118; Zechariah 9:9–16, 1 Peter 3:13–22; Matthew 21:1–13

You are the God who makes and keeps very large promises. Grant that we may in bold ways trust your promises, with the freedom to act on them and the courage to refuse their domestication into trivia. In his name. Amen.

This latter part of the Old Testament was shaped in the Persian period when vulnerable Israel was held in thrall by the empire, seemingly to perpetuity. In resistance against such imperial bondage, prophetic anticipation urged, against all odds and in the face of despairing circumstance, that God's promises would bring well-being for Israel by way of the Davidic dynasty that would be restored.

It was, in retrospect, easy enough to transpose the text from a Persian imperial situation to that of Rome, for the Roman Empire seemed, in the same way, to be perpetual in its power. Jesus is seen by the early church to be the carrier of God's promise so that he is cast as the new David who will enact new historical possibility outside of Roman control. His dramatic action when he "overturned the tables of the money changers" signified the undoing of power arrangements that featured a combination of Roman power allied with Jewish piety.

While we love the dramatic memory of Jesus' triumphal entry, the deep question for us is whether and in what way the promises of God persist among us. Mutatis mutandis, we live under the aegis of a military, economic, imperial system of greed, violence, and exploitation that seems to be to perpetuity. It is difficult for us to imagine life outside that domain that co-opts everything that might challenge it. This text from Zechariah and its appropriation for the narrative of Jesus invite us to take the promises of God as ground for resistance and for alternative imagination that does not succumb to despairing domestication.

Monday after Proper 29

Psalm 106:1–18; Zechariah 10:1–12; Galatians 6:1–10; Luke 18:15–30

God who legitimates and delegitimates human power; give us honesty
to see our failed governance in political economy, and courage to be at
hope-filled work for otherwise. In his name. Amen.

Prophetic imagination characteristically concerns critique of what has failed and anticipation of alternative. In this oracle of Zechariah, that twofold articulation concerns the leaders of Judah who are dubbed, according to a common image, "shepherds" who have not cared for the sheep. They have caused the sheep of Israel to be "scattered," that is, deported into exile. The accent, however, is on the new leader, the good shepherd who will care effectively for the sheep. Reference to "the house of Joseph" and "Ephraim" means the restoration of the "lost tribes" of northern Israel so that all of Israel will be restored together.

When we read this text in Christian parlance, we get to the Good Shepherd, Jesus. The Good Shepherd will gather all the scattered sheep of the house of Israel (and of humanity). We may read this text in two ways in our context of faith. First, the Eucharist is the great gathering of the lost, so we anticipate, "[They] come from the east and the west, from the north and the south, and gather about Christ's table."* Alan Streett in his book *Subversive Meals* has shown how the Eucharist is a table that deliberately subverts the exclusionary table of the empire. But the Eucharist is also a sign of a new political economy in which we may anticipate and work for new leaders of political economy. Greedy leaders of the political economy have not tended to the flock but only to their own interest. We have witnessed the exclusion (scattering) of vulnerable sheep, the poor, disabled, minorities. The prophetic insistence for us, through the prism of Jesus, is that it does not need to stay that way. We are invited to God's new "impossibility."

---

*Based on Luke 13:29 from the eucharistic order of the United Church of Christ in *The New Century Hymnal* (Cleveland: Pilgrim Press, 1995), 5.

Tuesday after Proper 29

Psalm 120; Zechariah 11:4–17; 1 Corinthians 3:10–23; Luke 18:31–43

Son of Man who faced death and did not yield, we give thanks for the continuing newness that comes from your life in the world. In your name. Amen.

The Gospel reading is in two parts that have a somewhat tricky relationship to each other. In the second narrative part, Jesus performs a healing miracle. The interaction between Jesus and the blind beggar is initiated by the blind man. He cries out in need, seeking mercy, recognizing Jesus as the Messiah. Those closest to Jesus try to silence him, but he refuses. He asks a second time for mercy. Jesus overrules the silencers, interviews the man, finds out his need, and grants him restored sight. It all happens tersely in a way that exhibits Jesus' majestic power.

Prior to that, Jesus declares to his disciples that the Gentile authorities will execute him. It is likely that the intent of the authorities to eliminate him is evoked by his awesome restorative power that energizes the crowds. The authorities, characteristically, do not welcome innovative restoration; they prefer to keep things as they are, safely locked into a sure hierarchal order of top-down management. Jesus' intervention disrupts that pattern of power and releases new social possibility into the world. Such an innovation must be resisted in order to maintain old modes of power.

We are left with two astonishing outcomes. On the one hand, the blind man can see, thus evoking doxology. On the other hand, Jesus' last word to his disciples is, "On the third day he will rise." The fearful authorities who resort to violence will not win! It turns out that the restoration of sight is a harbinger of the restoration of Jesus and his kingdom that will, on the third day, make mercy available in the world. We may notice, in our own time, the resistant power of the old order and the wonder of Jesus' restorative capacity.

Wednesday after Proper 29

Psalm 119:145–176; Zechariah 12:1–10;
Ephesians 1:3–14; Luke 19:1–10

Good Lord who came to save the lost, we stand before you as Zacchaeus-like folk. This day give us energy and authority to reclaim our true identity as the people defined by your news. In your name. Amen.

In the Gospel reading, Jesus confronts Zacchaeus. Tax collectors were Jews who had signed on with the Roman Empire to collect taxes from other Jews for the imperial budget of Rome. The tax collector was expected to send a certain sum of tax revenue to Rome. Whatever he could collect beyond that sum was for his own keeping. The system was a ready recipe for exploitative tax officials. Evidently the system had worked well for Zacchaeus. His collusion with Rome against his own people had made him rich.

Jesus, violating the social protocols that shunned tax collectors, overlooks Zacchaeus's scandalous conduct and is ready to have table fellowship with him. At Jesus' invitation, Zacchaeus promptly promises restoration of funds to those whom he has taken advantage of. When he says this, Jesus declares to him that "salvation" has come to Zacchaeus and his household, "salvation" being full restoration to well-being.

And then Jesus delivers his final zinger, declaring that even Zacchaeus, the despised, compromised tax collector, is a "son of Abraham." He had been "lost." He had forgotten who he was. He had given up his true identity for the sake of gain. A predatory economy not only exploits people but also talks people out of their true identity as genuine human persons, reducing them to monetized entities. We live in a culture in which baptized followers of Jesus are readily talked out of our baptismal identity, accepting identities that are imposed by a humanity-destroying system. We may consider our true identity in the company of Jesus.

Thursday after Proper 29

Psalm 131; Zechariah 13:1–9; Ephesians 1:15–23; Luke 19:11–27

Holy Sovereign God, whose will for peace and justice in the world is undeterred and undiminished, we thank you for your steadfast resolve. Give us alertness and courage to be faithful to your resolve for our world. In his name. Amen.

The hard oracle in Zechariah imagines a scene of acute social chaos. There are bad shepherds (rulers; people in power). There are phony prophets who claim to speak God's truth. The outcome will be scattered sheep, that is, deportation and displacement. It takes no great imagination to see our own society through the prism of this poetry . . . bad leaders, phony prophets, failed infrastructure.

In the midst of that, however, the poem has a word that flat-out contradicts this disastrous scene: God has not quit and God will not quit! God's way of working, moreover, is to preserve a faithful remnant (one-third!); that remnant of the faithful will be refined by fire, that is, persecuted, because the power of chaos resists their way of life. The prophet evokes the old covenant formula: this God and this people will remain in fidelity to each other and consequently will come to well-being. Because Jesus quotes this text (Mark 14:27), it is easy enough to conclude that the saved faithful remnant will be faithful followers of Jesus.

Your reading of this text depends on how dismayed you, dear reader, are about our social circumstance. If you are acutely pessimistic, this text is for you. It sounds the evangelical "nevertheless": God is undeterred in resolve and in fidelity. The text invites us to recognize that we are in a time of testing. The test likely will not come dramatically but so little at a time that we do notice . . . until it is very late. The one-third are alert and notice the reality of chaos; they also notice the chance for fidelity of a generative kind.

Friday after Proper 29

Psalm 140; Zechariah 14:1–11; Romans 15:7–13; Luke 19:28–40

Holy Spirit of God, who blows beyond our fearful barriers and our pro-tective protocols, give us openness for the new future you intend. Grant that we may receive it along with many new sisters and brothers. In his name. Amen.

From the outset, Paul has been the apostle to the Gentiles. His grasp of the gospel of Jesus Christ is that it reaches beyond Jews even while Jews are welcome in the community. In this lyric text, we get four times an invitation to the "Gentiles" based on four quotes from the Old Testament in its Greek version: Psalm 18:49; Deuteronomy 32:43; Psalm 117:1; Isaiah 11:1. Paul mobilizes these texts to make his doxological point that the gospel has a big, embracive reach.

Such a text and such a gospel are urgent in a time of intense tribalism and in our political economy now tempted by a crude nativism that wants to exclude all except those like us. Such tribalism and nativism, in theological categories, reduce the gospel to the claim to be God's special people. Thus variously we have excessively celebrated the entitlement of males, the privilege of whites, and the exceptionalism of Americans. And now the frightened mantra "Take back our country" easily morphs into "take back our church" and "take back our gospel" in the old modes of entitlement. We are here invited to a very large ecumenism that recognizes that those unlike us have legitimacy in the purview of God. For good reason Paul ends his lyric with two accents. He appeals to the Holy Spirit, the presence and power of God who overrides all tribalisms. Paul bids us to "abound in hope," to expect that God's good purpose will prevail in the world. Indeed tribalism wants nothing new and nativism is a backward look. Hope refuses such resistance to God's wondrous newness.

Saturday after Proper 29

Psalm 137:1–6; Zechariah 14:12–21; Philippians 2:1–11; Luke 19:41–48

Living Christ, whose self-giving marks the truth of your good news,
help us to dwell in the midst of your crucifixion and your resurrection,
that our common life may evidence your transformative presence in the
world. In your name. Amen.

I am delighted that for the final day of this yearlong study I can comment on the Epistle reading in which Paul quotes what is likely a hymn from the earliest church. I delight because in my rigorous confirmation instruction, question 72 in our little blue *Evangelical Catechism* (under the "Second Article" of the creed) asks, "In what passage of Holy Scripture do we find the humiliation and the exaltation of Christ briefly expressed?" We scoffed at the modifier "briefly" because the answer, the longest in the catechism, was a recitation of this passage. In my tradition of German pietism, the wise ones had recognized that this text articulates in simplest form the core claim of catholic Christian faith.

That core claim, echoing the ancient formulation of Irenaeus and voiced in lyrical fashion, attests that the preexistent Christ emptied himself in obedience before the majesty of the Father. The intent of Paul and of my church fathers was to make an assertion about Christ that at the same time made an assertion about the church. Paul's lyric moves from the Christ who "emptied himself" to the Christian community that is to have "the same mind . . . in Christ." Paul characterizes having the mind of Christ: "Look . . . to the interests of others." That is what Jesus did in his ministry. And that is what the church community may do: not self-promotion, not being right, not having one's way, but attending to what is best for the other. It is no wonder that the Christ who summons and empowers is eagerly awaited as we go into the Advent season of expectation for his transformative coming.

Notes for Liturgical Years
2017–18 through 2021–22

The reflections in this resource are primarily based on the assigned readings of the Year 2 Daily Office in the Episcopal *Book of Common Prayer*, ordered and titled for the 2017–18 liturgical year, so you will find readings for every day from the start of Advent on December 3, 2017, to the Saturday after Proper 29 (Reign of Christ Sunday) on December 1, 2018. In subsequent years, flexibility will be required to accommodate the days surrounding fixed feasts like Christmas and Epiphany and to account for the varying lengths of the season after Epiphany and the season after Pentecost. For example:

— Christmas Day is on a Monday in 2017, so there are no reflections for the Monday through Saturday after the Fourth Sunday of Advent.
— Epiphany is on a Saturday, with the First Sunday of Epiphany immediately following, so there are no reflections for any days that should fall between January 6 and the following Sunday.
— Easter is fairly early in 2018, so the season after Epiphany is short (only six Sundays) and the season after Pentecost is long (starting with Proper 4). With Ash Wednesday during the week after Epiphany 6, there are no reflections for the remainder of that week or the weeks of Epiphany 7 and 8.
— Note that while the 2017–18 liturgical year happens to be Year B of the Revised Common Lectionary, the Daily Office is a two-year cycle that does not correspond to particular Lectionary years.

The notes below suggest additional and alternative readings to help you adapt this resource for use in subsequent years.

2018–19 (Daily Office Year 1, Lectionary Year C)

Christmas Day is on a Tuesday, so there is no reflection for Christmas Eve. Read Isaiah 59:15b–21 and Philippians 2:5–11.

Epiphany is on a Sunday, so there is a full week without reflections prior to the First Sunday after Epiphany. Read Psalms 1–7 and 10–18; Genesis 2:4–6:8; Hebrews 1–3; and John 1:1–2:12.

Easter is fairly late, so there is a gap with no reflections for the weeks around Epiphany 7 and 8 (Wednesday, February 20, to Tuesday, March 5). Use reflections from the weeks of Proper 4–6. The season after Pentecost begins with Proper 7.

2019–20 (Daily Office Year 2, Lectionary Year A)

Christmas Day is on a Wednesday, so there are no reflections for Dec. 23 and 24. Read Isaiah 59:15b–21; Philippians 2:5–11; and Luke 1.

Epiphany is on a Monday, so there are five days without reflections prior to the First Sunday after Epiphany. Read Psalms 1–7 and 10–18; Genesis 2:4–6:8; Hebrews 1–3; and John 1:1–2:12.

Easter falls such that there is a gap with no reflections for the week around Epiphany 7 (Wednesday, February 19, to Tuesday, February 25). Use reflections from weeks after Proper 4 and 5. The season after Pentecost begins with Proper 6.

2020–21 (Daily Office Year 1, Lectionary Year B)

Christmas Day is on a Friday, so there are no reflections for December 21–24. Read Psalms 146–150; Isaiah 59:15b–21; Philippians 2:5–11; Galatians 3:1–4:7; and Luke 1.

Epiphany is on a Wednesday, so there are three days without reflections prior to the First Sunday after Epiphany. Read Psalms 1–7; Genesis 2:4–6:8; and John 1:1–2:12.

Easter 2021 is on a comparable date to Easter 2018, so no modifications are needed to use this resource for Lent through the remainder of the liturgical year.

2021–22 (Daily Office Year 2, Lectionary Year C)

Christmas Day is on a Saturday, so there are no reflections for December 20–24. Read Psalms 146–150; Isaiah 59:15b–21; Philippians 2:5–11; Galatians 3:1–4:7; and Luke 1.

Epiphany is on a Thursday, so there are two days without reflections prior to the First Sunday after Epiphany. Read Psalms 1–7; Hebrews 1–3; and John 1:1–2:12.

Easter is fairly late, so there is a gap with no reflections for the weeks around Epiphany 7 and 8 (Wednesday, February 16, to Tuesday, March 1). Use reflections from weeks after Proper 4–6. The season after Pentecost begins with Proper 7.

Assigned Readings from Ecclesiasticus (Wisdom of Ben Sirach, or Sirach)

Friday after Proper 23 | Ecclesiasticus 1:1–10, 18–27

1 All wisdom is from the Lord,
   and with him it remains forever.
2 The sand of the sea, the drops of rain,
   and the days of eternity—who can count them?
3 The height of heaven, the breadth of the earth,
   the abyss, and wisdom—who can search them out?
4 Wisdom was created before all other things,
   and prudent understanding from eternity.
6 The root of wisdom—to whom has it been revealed?
   Her subtleties—who knows them?
8 There is but one who is wise, greatly to be feared,
   seated upon his throne—the Lord.
9 It is he who created her;
   he saw her and took her measure;
   he poured her out upon all his works,
10 upon all the living according to his gift;
   he lavished her upon those who love him.

18 The fear of the Lord is the crown of wisdom,
   making peace and perfect health to flourish.
19 She rained down knowledge and discerning comprehension,
   and she heightened the glory of those who held her fast.
20 To fear the Lord is the root of wisdom,
   and her branches are long life.

22 Unjust anger cannot be justified,
   for anger tips the scale to one's ruin.
23 Those who are patient stay calm until the right moment,
   and then cheerfulness comes back to them.
24 They hold back their words until the right moment;
   then the lips of many tell of their good sense.
25 In the treasuries of wisdom are wise sayings,
   but godliness is an abomination to a sinner.
26 If you desire wisdom, keep the commandments,
   and the Lord will lavish her upon you.
27 For the fear of the Lord is wisdom and discipline,
   fidelity and humility are his delight.

Saturday after Proper 23 | Ecclesiasticus 3:17–31

17 My child, perform your tasks with humility;
   then you will be loved by those whom God accepts.
18 The greater you are, the more you must humble yourself;
   so you will find favor in the sight of the Lord.
20 For great is the might of the Lord;
   but by the humble he is glorified.
21 Neither seek what is too difficult for you,
   nor investigate what is beyond your power.
22 Reflect upon what you have been commanded,
   for what is hidden is not your concern.
23 Do not meddle in matters that are beyond you,
   for more than you can understand has been shown you.
24 For their conceit has led many astray,
   and wrong opinion has impaired their judgment.

25 Without eyes there is no light;
   without knowledge there is no wisdom.
26 A stubborn mind will fare badly at the end,
   and whoever loves danger will perish in it.
27 A stubborn mind will be burdened by troubles,
   and the sinner adds sin to sins.
28 When calamity befalls the proud, there is no healing,
   for an evil plant has taken root in him.
29 The mind of the intelligent appreciates proverbs,
   and an attentive ear is the desire of the wise.

30 As water extinguishes a blazing fire,
   so almsgiving atones for sin.
31 Those who repay favors give thought to the future;
   when they fall they will find support.

Proper 24 | Ecclesiasticus 4:1–10

1 My child, do not cheat the poor of their living,
   and do not keep needy eyes waiting.
2 Do not grieve the hungry,
   or anger one in need.
3 Do not add to the troubles of the desperate,
   or delay giving to the needy.
4 Do not reject a suppliant in distress,
   or turn your face away from the poor.
5 Do not avert your eye from the needy,
   and give no one reason to curse you;
6 for if in bitterness of soul some should curse you,
   their Creator will hear their prayer.

⁷ Endear yourself to the congregation;
   bow your head low to the great.
⁸ Give a hearing to the poor,
   and return their greeting politely.
⁹ Rescue the oppressed from the oppressor;
   and do not be hesitant in giving a verdict.
¹⁰ Be a father to orphans,
   and be like a husband to their mother;
   you will then be like a son of the Most High,
   and he will love you more than does your mother.

Monday after Proper 24 | Ecclesiasticus 4:20–5:7

²⁰ Watch for the opportune time, and beware of evil,
   and do not be ashamed to be yourself.
²¹ For there is a shame that leads to sin,
   and there is a shame that is glory and favor.
²² Do not show partiality, to your own harm,
   or deference, to your downfall.
²³ Do not refrain from speaking at the proper moment,
   and do not hide your wisdom.
²⁴ For wisdom becomes known through speech,
   and education through the words of the tongue.
²⁵ Never speak against the truth,
   but be ashamed of your ignorance.
²⁶ Do not be ashamed to confess your sins,
   and do not try to stop the current of a river.
²⁷ Do not subject yourself to a fool,
   or show partiality to a ruler.
²⁸ Fight to the death for truth,
   and the Lord God will fight for you.

²⁹ Do not be reckless in your speech,
   or sluggish and remiss in your deeds.
³⁰ Do not be like a lion in your home,
   or suspicious of your servants.
³¹ Do not let your hand be stretched out to receive
   and closed when it is time to give.

^{5:1} Do not rely on your wealth,
   or say, "I have enough."
² Do not follow your inclination and strength
   in pursuing the desires of your heart.
³ Do not say, "Who can have power over me?"
   for the Lord will surely punish you.

⁴ Do not say, "I sinned, yet what has happened to me?"
   for the Lord is slow to anger.

5 Do not be so confident of forgiveness
    that you add sin to sin.
6 Do not say, "His mercy is great,
    he will forgive the multitude of my sins,"
    for both mercy and wrath are with him,
    and his anger will rest on sinners.
7 Do not delay to turn back to the Lord,
    and do not postpone it from day to day;
    for suddenly the wrath of the Lord will come upon you,
    and at the time of punishment you will perish.

Tuesday after Proper 24 | Ecclesiasticus 6:5–17

5 Pleasant speech multiplies friends,
    and a gracious tongue multiplies courtesies.
6 Let those who are friendly with you be many,
    but let your advisers be one in a thousand.
7 When you gain friends, gain them through testing,
    and do not trust them hastily.
8 For there are friends who are such when it suits them,
    but they will not stand by you in time of trouble.
9 And there are friends who change into enemies,
    and tell of the quarrel to your disgrace.
10 And there are friends who sit at your table,
    but they will not stand by you in time of trouble.
11 When you are prosperous, they become your second self,
    and lord it over your servants;
12 but if you are brought low, they turn against you,
    and hide themselves from you.
13 Keep away from your enemies,
    and be on guard with your friends.

14 Faithful friends are a sturdy shelter:
    whoever finds one has found a treasure.
15 Faithful friends are beyond price;
    no amount can balance their worth.
16 Faithful friends are life-saving medicine;
    and those who fear the Lord will find them.
17 Those who fear the Lord direct their friendship aright,
    for as they are, so are their neighbors also.

Wednesday after Proper 24 | Ecclesiasticus 7:4–14

4 Do not seek from the Lord high office,
    or the seat of honor from the king.
5 Do not assert your righteousness before the Lord,
    or display your wisdom before the king.
6 Do not seek to become a judge,
    or you may be unable to root out injustice;

you may be partial to the powerful,
   and so mar your integrity.
7 Commit no offense against the public,
   and do not disgrace yourself among the people.

8 Do not commit a sin twice;
   not even for one will you go unpunished.
9 Do not say, "He will consider the great number of my gifts,
   and when I make an offering to the Most High God, he will accept it."
10 Do not grow weary when you pray;
   do not neglect to give alms.
11 Do not ridicule a person who is embittered in spirit,
   for there is One who humbles and exalts.
12 Do not devise a lie against your brother,
   or do the same to a friend.
13 Refuse to utter any lie,
   for it is a habit that results in no good.
14 Do not babble in the assembly of the elders,
   and do not repeat yourself when you pray.

Thursday after Proper 24 | Ecclesiasticus 10:1–18

1 A wise magistrate educates his people,
   and the rule of an intelligent person is well ordered.
2 As the people's judge is, so are his officials;
   as the ruler of the city is, so are all its inhabitants.
3 An undisciplined king ruins his people,
   but a city becomes fit to live in through the understanding of its rulers.
4 The government of the earth is in the hand of the Lord,
   and over it he will raise up the right leader for the time.
5 Human success is in the hand of the Lord,
   and it is he who confers honor upon the lawgiver.

6 Do not get angry with your neighbor for every injury,
   and do not resort to acts of insolence.
7 Arrogance is hateful to the Lord and to mortals,
   and injustice is outrageous to both.
8 Sovereignty passes from nation to nation
   on account of injustice and insolence and wealth.
9 How can dust and ashes be proud?
   Even in life the human body decays.
10 A long illness baffles the physician;
   the king of today will die tomorrow.
11 For when one is dead
   he inherits maggots and vermin and worms.
12 The beginning of human pride is to forsake the Lord;
   the heart has withdrawn from its Maker.
13 For the beginning of pride is sin,
   and the one who clings to it pours out abominations.

Therefore the Lord brings upon them unheard-of calamities,
and destroys them completely.
14 The Lord overthrows the thrones of rulers,
and enthrones the lowly in their place.
15 The Lord plucks up the roots of the nations,
and plants the humble in their place.
16 The Lord lays waste the lands of the nations,
and destroys them to the foundations of the earth.
17 He removes some of them and destroys them,
and erases the memory of them from the earth.
18 Pride was not created for human beings,
or violent anger for those born of women.

Friday after Proper 24 | Ecclesiasticus 11:2–20

2 Do not praise individuals for their good looks,
or loathe anyone because of appearance alone.
3 The bee is small among flying creatures,
but what it produces is the best of sweet things.
4 Do not boast about wearing fine clothes,
and do not exalt yourself when you are honored;
for the works of the Lord are wonderful,
and his works are concealed from humankind.
5 Many kings have had to sit on the ground,
but one who was never thought of has worn a crown.
6 Many rulers have been utterly disgraced,
and the honored have been handed over to others.

7 Do not find fault before you investigate;
examine first, and then criticize.
8 Do not answer before you listen,
and do not interrupt when another is speaking.
9 Do not argue about a matter that does not concern you,
and do not sit with sinners when they judge a case.

10 My child, do not busy yourself with many matters;
if you multiply activities, you will not be held blameless.
If you pursue, you will not overtake,
and by fleeing you will not escape.
11 There are those who work and struggle and hurry,
but are so much the more in want.
12 There are others who are slow and need help,
who lack strength and abound in poverty;
but the eyes of the Lord look kindly upon them;
he lifts them out of their lowly condition
13 and raises up their heads
to the amazement of the many.

14 Good things and bad, life and death,
   poverty and wealth, come from the Lord.
17 The Lord's gift remains with the devout,
   and his favor brings lasting success.
18 One becomes rich through diligence and self-denial,
   and the reward allotted to him is this:
19 when he says, "I have found rest,
   and now I shall feast on my goods!"
   he does not know how long it will be
   until he leaves them to others and dies.

20 Stand by your agreement and attend to it,
   and grow old in your work.

Saturday after Proper 24 | Ecclesiasticus 15:9–20

9 Praise is unseemly on the lips of a sinner,
   for it has not been sent from the Lord.
10 For in wisdom must praise be uttered,
   and the Lord will make it prosper.

11 Do not say, "It was the Lord's doing that I fell away";
   for he does not do what he hates.
12 Do not say, "It was he who led me astray";
   for he has no need of the sinful.
13 The Lord hates all abominations;
   such things are not loved by those who fear him.
14 It was he who created humankind in the beginning,
   and he left them in the power of their own free choice.
15 If you choose, you can keep the commandments,
   and to act faithfully is a matter of your own choice.
16 He has placed before you fire and water;
   stretch out your hand for whichever you choose.
17 Before each person are life and death,
   and whichever one chooses will be given.
18 For great is the wisdom of the Lord;
   he is mighty in power and sees everything;
19 his eyes are on those who fear him,
   and he knows every human action.
20 He has not commanded anyone to be wicked,
   and he has not given anyone permission to sin.

Proper 25 | Ecclesiasticus 18:19–33

19 Before you speak, learn;
   and before you fall ill, take care of your health.
20 Before judgment comes, examine yourself;
   and at the time of scrutiny you will find forgiveness.

21 Before falling ill, humble yourself;
  and when you have sinned, repent.
22 Let nothing hinder you from paying a vow promptly,
  and do not wait until death to be released from it.
23 Before making a vow, prepare yourself;
  do not be like one who puts the Lord to the test.
24 Think of his wrath on the day of death,
  and of the moment of vengeance when he turns away his face.
25 In the time of plenty think of the time of hunger;
  in days of wealth think of poverty and need.
26 From morning to evening conditions change;
  all things move swiftly before the Lord.

27 One who is wise is cautious in everything;
  when sin is all around, one guards against wrongdoing.
28 Every intelligent person knows wisdom,
  and praises the one who finds her.
29 Those who are skilled in words become wise themselves,
  and pour forth apt proverbs.

30 Do not follow your base desires,
  but restrain your appetites.
31 If you allow your soul to take pleasure in base desire,
  it will make you the laughingstock of your enemies.
32 Do not revel in great luxury,
  or you may become impoverished by its expense.
33 Do not become a beggar by feasting with borrowed money,
  when you have nothing in your purse.

Monday after Proper 25 | Ecclesiasticus 19:4–17

4 One who trusts others too quickly has a shallow mind,
  and one who sins does wrong to himself.
5 One who rejoices in wickedness will be condemned,
6 but one who hates gossip has less evil.
7 Never repeat a conversation,
  and you will lose nothing at all.
8 With friend or foe do not report it,
  and unless it would be a sin for you, do not reveal it;
9 for someone may have heard you and watched you,
  and in time will hate you.
10 Have you heard something? Let it die with you.
  Be brave, it will not make you burst!
11 Having heard something, the fool suffers birth pangs
  like a woman in labor with a child.
12 Like an arrow stuck in a person's thigh,
  so is gossip inside a fool.

¹³ Question a friend; perhaps he did not do it;
  or if he did, so that he may not do it again.
¹⁴ Question a neighbor; perhaps he did not say it;
  or if he said it, so that he may not repeat it.
¹⁵ Question a friend, for often it is slander;
  so do not believe everything you hear.
¹⁶ A person may make a slip without intending it.
  Who has not sinned with his tongue?
¹⁷ Question your neighbor before you threaten him;
  and let the law of the Most High take its course.

Tuesday after Proper 25 | Ecclesiasticus 24:1–12

¹ Wisdom praises herself,
  and tells of her glory in the midst of her people.
² In the assembly of the Most High she opens her mouth,
  and in the presence of his hosts she tells of her glory:
³ "I came forth from the mouth of the Most High,
  and covered the earth like a mist.
⁴ I dwelt in the highest heavens,
  and my throne was in a pillar of cloud.
⁵ Alone I compassed the vault of heaven
  and traversed the depths of the abyss.
⁶ Over waves of the sea, over all the earth,
  and over every people and nation I have held sway.
⁷ Among all these I sought a resting place;
  in whose territory should I abide?

⁸ "Then the Creator of all things gave me a command,
  and my Creator chose the place for my tent.
He said, 'Make your dwelling in Jacob,
  and in Israel receive your inheritance.'
⁹ Before the ages, in the beginning, he created me,
  and for all the ages I shall not cease to be.
¹⁰ In the holy tent I ministered before him,
  and so I was established in Zion.
¹¹ Thus in the beloved city he gave me a resting place,
  and in Jerusalem was my domain.
¹² I took root in an honored people,
  in the portion of the Lord, his heritage."

Wednesday after Proper 25 | Ecclesiasticus 28:14–26

¹⁴ Slander has shaken many,
  and scattered them from nation to nation;
it has destroyed strong cities,
  and overturned the houses of the great.
¹⁵ Slander has driven virtuous women from their homes,
  and deprived them of the fruit of their toil.

16 Those who pay heed to slander will not find rest,
   nor will they settle down in peace.
17 The blow of a whip raises a welt,
   but a blow of the tongue crushes the bones.
18 Many have fallen by the edge of the sword,
   but not as many as have fallen because of the tongue.
19 Happy is the one who is protected from it,
   who has not been exposed to its anger,
   who has not borne its yoke,
   and has not been bound with its fetters.
20 For its yoke is a yoke of iron,
   and its fetters are fetters of bronze;
21 its death is an evil death,
   and Hades is preferable to it.
22 It has no power over the godly;
   they will not be burned in its flame.
23 Those who forsake the Lord will fall into its power;
   it will burn among them and will not be put out.
   It will be sent out against them like a lion;
   like a leopard it will mangle them.
24a As you fence in your property with thorns,
25b   so make a door and a bolt for your mouth.
24b As you lock up your silver and gold,
25a   so make balances and scales for your words.
26 Take care not to err with your tongue,
   and fall victim to one lying in wait.

Thursday after Proper 25 | Ecclesiasticus 31:12–18, 25–32:2

12 Are you seated at the table of the great?
   Do not be greedy at it,
   and do not say, "How much food there is here!"
13 Remember that a greedy eye is a bad thing.
   What has been created more greedy than the eye?
   Therefore it sheds tears for any reason.
14 Do not reach out your hand for everything you see,
   and do not crowd your neighbor at the dish.
15 Judge your neighbor's feelings by your own
   and in every matter be thoughtful.
16 Eat what is set before you like a well brought-up person,
   and do not chew greedily, or you will give offense.
17 Be the first to stop, as befits good manners,
   and do not be insatiable, or you will give offense.
18 If you are seated among many persons,
   do not help yourself before they do.

25 Do not try to prove your strength by wine-drinking,
   for wine has destroyed many.

²⁶ As the furnace tests the work of the smith,
   so wine tests hearts when the insolent quarrel.
²⁷ Wine is very life to human beings
   if taken in moderation.
   What is life to one who is without wine?
   It has been created to make people happy.
²⁸ Wine drunk at the proper time and in moderation
   is rejoicing of heart and gladness of soul.
²⁹ Wine drunk to excess leads to bitterness of spirit,
   to quarrels and stumbling.
³⁰ Drunkenness increases the anger of a fool to his own hurt,
   reducing his strength and adding wounds.
³¹ Do not reprove your neighbor at a banquet of wine,
   and do not despise him in his merrymaking;
   speak no word of reproach to him,
   and do not distress him by making demands of him.

^{32:1} If they make you master of the feast, do not exalt yourself;
   be among them as one of their number.
   Take care of them first and then sit down;
²   when you have fulfilled all your duties, take your place,
   so that you may be merry along with them
   and receive a wreath for your excellent leadership.

Friday after Proper 25 | Ecclesiasticus 34:1–8, 18–22

¹ The senseless have vain and false hopes,
   and dreams give wings to fools.
² As one who catches at a shadow and pursues the wind,
   so is anyone who believes in dreams.
³ What is seen in dreams is but a reflection,
   the likeness of a face looking at itself.
⁴ From an unclean thing what can be clean?
   And from something false what can be true?
⁵ Divinations and omens and dreams are unreal,
   and like a woman in labor, the mind has fantasies.
⁶ Unless they are sent by intervention from the Most High,
   pay no attention to them.
⁷ For dreams have deceived many,
   and those who put their hope in them have perished.
⁸ Without such deceptions the law will be fulfilled,
   and wisdom is complete in the mouth of the faithful.

¹⁸   To whom does he look? And who is his support?
¹⁹ The eyes of the Lord are on those who love him,
   a mighty shield and strong support,
   a shelter from scorching wind and a shade from noonday sun,
   a guard against stumbling and a help against falling.

²⁰ He lifts up the soul and makes the eyes sparkle;
   he gives health and life and blessing.

²¹ If one sacrifices ill-gotten goods, the offering is blemished;
²² the gifts of the lawless are not acceptable.

Saturday after Proper 25 | Ecclesiasticus 35:1–17

¹ The one who keeps the law makes many offerings;
² one who heeds the commandments makes an offering of well-being.
³ The one who returns a kindness offers choice flour,
⁴   and one who gives alms sacrifices a thank offering.
⁵ To keep from wickedness is pleasing to the Lord,
   and to forsake unrighteousness is an atonement.
⁶ Do not appear before the Lord empty-handed,
⁷ for all that you offer is in fulfillment of the commandment.
⁸ The offering of the righteous enriches the altar,
   and its pleasing odor rises before the Most High.
⁹ The sacrifice of the righteous is acceptable,
   and it will never be forgotten.
¹⁰ Be generous when you worship the Lord,
   and do not stint the first fruits of your hands.
¹¹ With every gift show a cheerful face,
   and dedicate your tithe with gladness.
¹² Give to the Most High as he has given to you,
   and as generously as you can afford.
¹³ For the Lord is the one who repays,
   and he will repay you sevenfold.

¹⁴ Do not offer him a bribe, for he will not accept it;
¹⁵   and do not rely on a dishonest sacrifice;
   for the Lord is the judge,
   and with him there is no partiality.
¹⁶ He will not show partiality to the poor;
   but he will listen to the prayer of one who is wronged.
¹⁷ He will not ignore the supplication of the orphan
   or the widow when she pours out her complaint.

Proper 26 | Ecclesiasticus 36:1–17

¹ Have mercy upon us, O God of all,
² and put all the nations in fear of you.
³ Lift up your hand against foreign nations
   and let them see your might.
⁴ As you have used us to show your holiness to them,
   so use them to show your glory to us.
⁵ Then they will know, as we have known,
   that there is no God but you, O Lord.

⁶ Give new signs, and work other wonders;
⁷   make your hand and right arm glorious.
⁸ Rouse your anger and pour out your wrath;
⁹   destroy the adversary and wipe out the enemy.
¹⁰ Hasten the day, and remember the appointed time,
    and let people recount your mighty deeds.
¹¹ Let survivors be consumed in the fiery wrath,
    and may those who harm your people meet destruction.
¹² Crush the heads of hostile rulers
    who say, "There is no one but ourselves."
¹³ Gather all the tribes of Jacob,
¹⁶   and give them their inheritance, as at the beginning.
¹⁷ Have mercy, O Lord, on the people called by your name,
    on Israel, whom you have named your firstborn.

Monday after Proper 26 | Ecclesiasticus 38:24–34

²⁴ The wisdom of the scribe depends on the opportunity of leisure;
    only the one who has little business can become wise.
²⁵ How can one become wise who handles the plow,
    and who glories in the shaft of a goad,
  who drives oxen and is occupied with their work,
    and whose talk is about bulls?
²⁶ He sets his heart on plowing furrows,
    and he is careful about fodder for the heifers.
²⁷ So it is with every artisan and master artisan
    who labors by night as well as by day;
  those who cut the signets of seals,
    each is diligent in making a great variety;
  they set their heart on painting a lifelike image,
    and they are careful to finish their work.
²⁸ So it is with the smith, sitting by the anvil,
    intent on his iron-work;
  the breath of the fire melts his flesh,
    and he struggles with the heat of the furnace;
  the sound of the hammer deafens his ears,
    and his eyes are on the pattern of the object.
  He sets his heart on finishing his handiwork,
    and he is careful to complete its decoration.
² So it is with the potter sitting at his work
    and turning the wheel with his feet;
  he is always deeply concerned over his products
    and he produces them in quantity.
³⁰ He molds the clay with his arm
    and makes it pliable with his feet;
  he sets his heart to finish the glazing,
    and he takes care in firing the kiln.

31 All these rely on their hands,
     and all are skillful in their own work.
32 Without them no city can be inhabited,
     and wherever they live, they will not go hungry.
   Yet they are not sought out for the council of the people,
33   nor do they attain eminence in the public assembly.
   They do not sit in the judge's seat,
     nor do they understand the decisions of the courts;
   they cannot expound discipline or judgment,
     and they are not found among the rulers.
34 But they maintain the fabric of the world,
     and their concern is for the exercise of their trade.

   How different the one who devotes himself
   to the study of the law of the Most High!

Tuesday after Proper 26 | Ecclesiasticus 43:1–22

1 The pride of the higher realms is the clear vault of the sky,
     as glorious to behold as the sight of the heavens.
2 The sun, when it appears, proclaims as it rises
     what a marvelous instrument it is, the work of the Most High.
3 At noon it parches the land,
     and who can withstand its burning heat?
4 A man tending a furnace works in burning heat,
     but three times as hot is the sun scorching the mountains;
   it breathes out fiery vapors,
     and its bright rays blind the eyes.
5 Great is the Lord who made it;
     at his orders it hurries on its course.

6 It is the moon that marks the changing seasons,
     governing the times, their everlasting sign.
7 From the moon comes the sign for festal days,
     a light that wanes when it completes its course.
8 The new moon, as its name suggests, renews itself;
     how marvelous it is in this change,
   a beacon to the hosts on high,
     shining in the vault of the heavens!

9 The glory of the stars is the beauty of heaven,
     a glittering array in the heights of the Lord.
10 On the orders of the Holy One they stand in their appointed places;
     they never relax in their watches.
11 Look at the rainbow, and praise him who made it;
     it is exceedingly beautiful in its brightness.
12 It encircles the sky with its glorious arc;
     the hands of the Most High have stretched it out.

¹³ By his command he sends the driving snow
    and speeds the lightnings of his judgment.
¹⁴ Therefore the storehouses are opened,
    and the clouds fly out like birds.
¹⁵ In his majesty he gives the clouds their strength,
    and the hailstones are broken in pieces.
¹⁷ᵃ The voice of his thunder rebukes the earth;
¹⁶   when he appears, the mountains shake.
    At his will the south wind blows;
¹⁷ᵇ   so do the storm from the north and the whirlwind.
    He scatters the snow like birds flying down,
    and its descent is like locusts alighting.
¹⁸ The eye is dazzled by the beauty of its whiteness,
    and the mind is amazed as it falls.
¹⁹ He pours frost over the earth like salt,
    and icicles form like pointed thorns.
²⁰ The cold north wind blows,
    and ice freezes on the water;
    it settles on every pool of water,
    and the water puts it on like a breastplate.
²¹ He consumes the mountains and burns up the wilderness,
    and withers the tender grass like fire.
²² A mist quickly heals all things;
    the falling dew gives refreshment from the heat.

Wednesday after Proper 26 | Ecclesiasticus 43:23–33

²³ By his plan he stilled the deep
    and planted islands in it.
²⁴ Those who sail the sea tell of its dangers,
    and we marvel at what we hear.
²⁵ In it are strange and marvelous creatures,
    all kinds of living things, and huge sea-monsters.
²⁶ Because of him each of his messengers succeeds,
    and by his word all things hold together.

²⁷ We could say more but could never say enough;
    let the final word be: "He is the all."
²⁸ Where can we find the strength to praise him?
    For he is greater than all his works.
²⁹ Awesome is the Lord and very great,
    and marvelous is his power.
³⁰ Glorify the Lord and exalt him as much as you can,
    for he surpasses even that.
    When you exalt him, summon all your strength,
    and do not grow weary, for you cannot praise him enough.
³¹ Who has seen him and can describe him?
    Or who can extol him as he is?

³² Many things greater than these lie hidden,
  for I have seen but few of his works.
³³ For the Lord has made all things,
  and to the godly he has given wisdom.

Thursday after Proper 26 | Ecclesiasticus 44:1–15

¹ Let us now sing the praises of famous men,
  our ancestors in their generations.
² The Lord apportioned to them great glory,
  his majesty from the beginning.
³ There were those who ruled in their kingdoms,
  and made a name for themselves by their valor;
  those who gave counsel because they were intelligent;
  those who spoke in prophetic oracles;
⁴ those who led the people by their counsels
  and by their knowledge of the people's lore;
  they were wise in their words of instruction;
⁵ those who composed musical tunes,
  or put verses in writing;
⁶ rich men endowed with resources,
  living peacefully in their homes —
⁷ all these were honored in their generations,
  and were the pride of their times.
⁸ Some of them have left behind a name,
  so that others declare their praise.
⁹ But of others there is no memory;
  they have perished as though they had never existed;
  they have become as though they had never been born,
  they and their children after them.
¹⁰ But these also were godly men,
  whose righteous deeds have not been forgotten;
¹¹ their wealth will remain with their descendants,
  and their inheritance with their children's children.
¹² Their descendants stand by the covenants;
  their children also, for their sake.
¹³ Their offspring will continue forever,
  and their glory will never be blotted out.
¹⁴ Their bodies are buried in peace,
  but their name lives on generation after generation.
¹⁵ The assembly declares their wisdom,
  and the congregation proclaims their praise.

Friday after Proper 26 | Ecclesiasticus 50:1, 11–24

¹ The leader of his brothers and the pride of his people
  was the high priest, Simon son of Onias,

who in his life repaired the house,
and in his time fortified the temple.

11 When he put on his glorious robe
and clothed himself in perfect splendor,
when he went up to the holy altar,
he made the court of the sanctuary glorious.

12 When he received the portions from the hands of the priests,
as he stood by the hearth of the altar
with a garland of brothers around him,
he was like a young cedar on Lebanon
surrounded by the trunks of palm trees.
13 All the sons of Aaron in their splendor
held the Lord's offering in their hands
before the whole congregation of Israel.
14 Finishing the service at the altars,
and arranging the offering to the Most High, the Almighty,
15 he held out his hand for the cup
and poured a drink offering of the blood of the grape;
he poured it out at the foot of the altar,
a pleasing odor to the Most High, the king of all.
16 Then the sons of Aaron shouted;
they blew their trumpets of hammered metal;
they sounded a mighty fanfare
as a reminder before the Most High.
17 Then all the people together quickly
fell to the ground on their faces
to worship their Lord,
the Almighty, God Most High.

18 Then the singers praised him with their voices
in sweet and full-toned melody.
19 And the people of the Lord Most High offered
their prayers before the Merciful One,
until the order of worship of the Lord was ended,
and they completed his ritual.
20 Then Simon came down and raised his hands
over the whole congregation of Israelites,
to pronounce the blessing of the Lord with his lips,
and to glory in his name;
21 and they bowed down in worship a second time,
to receive the blessing from the Most High.

22 And now bless the God of all,
who everywhere works great wonders,
who fosters our growth from birth,
and deals with us according to his mercy.

²³ May he give us gladness of heart,
and may there be peace in our days
in Israel, as in the days of old.
²⁴ May he entrust to us his mercy,
and may he deliver us in our days!

Saturday after Proper 26 | Ecclesiasticus 51:1–12

¹ I give you thanks, O Lord and King,
and praise you, O God my Savior.
I give thanks to your name,
²   for you have been my protector and helper
and have delivered me from destruction
and from the trap laid by a slanderous tongue,
from lips that fabricate lies.
In the face of my adversaries
you have been my helper ³ and delivered me,
in the greatness of your mercy and of your name,
from grinding teeth about to devour me,
from the hand of those seeking my life,
from the many troubles I endured,
⁴ from choking fire on every side,
and from the midst of fire that I had not kindled,
⁵ from the deep belly of Hades,
from an unclean tongue and lying words —
⁶   the slander of an unrighteous tongue to the king
My soul drew near to death,
and my life was on the brink of Hades below.
⁷ They surrounded me on every side,
and there was no one to help me;
I looked for human assistance,
and there was none.
⁸ Then I remembered your mercy, O Lord,
and your kindness from of old,
for you rescue those who wait for you
and save them from the hand of their enemies.
⁹ And I sent up my prayer from the earth,
and begged for rescue from death.
¹⁰ I cried out, "Lord, you are my Father;
do not forsake me in the days of trouble,
when there is no help against the proud.
¹¹ I will praise your name continually,
and will sing hymns of thanksgiving."
My prayer was heard,
¹²   for you saved me from destruction
and rescued me in time of trouble.
For this reason I thank you and praise you,
and I bless the name of the Lord.

Proper 27 | Ecclesiasticus 51:13–22

¹³ While I was still young, before I went on my travels,
   I sought wisdom openly in my prayer.
¹⁴ Before the temple I asked for her,
   and I will search for her until the end.

¹⁵ From the first blossom to the ripening grape
   my heart delighted in her;
   my foot walked on the straight path;
   from my youth I followed her steps.

¹⁶ I inclined my ear a little and received her,
   and I found for myself much instruction.
¹⁷ I made progress in her;
   to him who gives wisdom I will give glory.

¹⁸ For I resolved to live according to wisdom,
   and I was zealous for the good,
   and I shall never be disappointed.
¹⁹ My soul grappled with wisdom,
   and in my conduct I was strict;

   I spread out my hands to the heavens,
   and lamented my ignorance of her.
²⁰ I directed my soul to her,
   and in purity I found her.

   With her I gained understanding from the first;
   therefore I will never be forsaken.
²¹ My heart was stirred to seek her;
   therefore I have gained a prize possession.
²² The Lord gave me my tongue as a reward,
   and I will praise him with it.